T0138636

Web Data Mining
and Applications in
Business Intelligence
and
Counter-Terrorism

Web Data Mining
and Applications in
Business Intelligence
and
Counter-Terrorism

Bhavani Thuraisingham

CRC PRESS

Boca Raton   London   New York   Washington, D.C.

Library of Congress Cataloging-in-Publication Data

Thuraisingham, Bhavani M.
    Web data mining and applications in business intelligence and counter-terrorism /
Bhavani Thuraisingham.
        p.   cm.
    Includes bibliographical references and index.
    ISBN 0-8493-1460-7 (alk. paper)
    1. Data mining. 2. Web databases. 3. Business intelligence—Databases. 4.
Terrorism—Prevention—Databases. I. Title.

QA76.9.D343T48 2003
006.3—dc21   2003043967

Visit the CRC Press Web site at www.crcpress.com

© 2003 by CRC Press LLC

No claim to original U.S. Government works
International Standard Book Number 0-8493-1460-7
Library of Congress Card Number 2003043967
Printed in the United States of America 1 2 3 4 5 6 7 8 9 0
Printed on acid-free paper

Dedication

*To my sponsor,
the late Mr. David Bernard,
1944–2001
Internal Revenue Service, United States Department
of the Treasury*

*And to everyone who lost their lives due to the extremely tragic
events of September 11, 2001.
We must strive our best to develop technologies to put an end to
terrorism and make this world a safer place to live.*

Contents

Preface

BACKGROUND

Recent developments in information systems technologies have resulted in computerizing many applications in various business areas. Data has become a critical resource in many organizations, and therefore, accessing data efficiently, sharing the data, extracting information from the data, and making use of the information have become urgent needs. As a result, not only have there been many efforts toward integrating the various data sources scattered across several sites, but extracting information from these databases in the form of patterns and trends has also become important. These data sources may be databases managed by database management systems or they could be data warehoused in a repository from multiple data sources. The advent of the World Wide Web (WWW) in the mid-1990s has resulted in even greater demand for managing data, information, and knowledge effectively. There is now so much data on the Web that managing it with conventional tools is becoming almost an impossibility. New tools and techniques are needed to effectively manage this data. Therefore, to provide interoperability as well as warehousing between the multiple data sources and systems, and to extract information from the databases and warehouses on the Web, various tools are being developed.

We have written a series of books for CRC Press on data management:

- Book #1 (*Data Management Systems Evolution and Interoperation*) focused on general aspects of data management and also addressed interoperability and migration.
- Book #2 (*Data Mining: Technologies, Techniques, Tools, and Trends*) discussed data mining. Essentially, it elaborated on Chapter 9 of Book #1.
- Book #3 (*Web Data Management and E-Commerce*) discussed Web database technologies and discussed E-commerce as an application area. Essentially, it elaborated on Chapter 10 of Book #1.
- Book #4 (*Managing and Mining Multimedia Databases*) addressed both multimedia database management and multimedia data mining. It elaborated on both Chapter 6 of Book #1 (for multimedia

database management) and Chapter 11 of Book #2 (for multimedia data mining).

- Book #5 (*XML, Databases, and the Semantic Web*) described XML technologies related to data management. It expanded on Chapter 11 of Book #3.

This book (Book #6) elaborates on Chapter 12 of Book #5. It describes Web data mining technologies and discusses some critical applications in business intelligence and counter-terrorism. In particular, we discuss techniques and technologies for mining data on the Web, and then describe applications for Web mining, such as customer relationship management, and the increasingly important area of counter-terrorism.

WEB DATA MINING AND APPLICATIONS

With information overload on the Web, it is highly desirable to mine the data and extract patterns and relevant information. This will make the task of browsing on the Web much easier for the user. Therefore, there has been much interest in what is now called Web mining, which is essentially mining the databases on the Web or mining the usage patterns and structure so that helpful information can be provided to the user.

Data mining and the Web developed as independent technology areas in the mid-1990s. While it was thought that mining the data on the Web would be useful to help the information-overload problem, the extent to which Web mining would help key areas such as E-commerce was not well understood until recently. It was only a few years ago that researchers and practitioners seriously started to think about Web mining. There was a panel on Web mining at the IEEE ICTAI Conference in 1997, which is believed to be one of the first panels on the topic. The Web mining workshop held during the Knowledge Discovery in Databases Conference in 1999 was one of the first of its kind. In this book, we discuss developments in Web mining, including an overview of the tools and technologies, and then provide some directions. We describe a taxonomy for Web mining that is more or less standard. We divide Web mining into three categories:

1. Web content mining: Getting patterns from Web data
2. Web structure mining: Mining URLs and other Web links to help the user with various activities on the Web as well as determining the structure of the Web
3. Web usage mining: Analyzing Web logs

Closely related to Web usage mining is mining to support E-commerce. There are two aspects here: (1) mining information about competitors, and (2) mining usage patterns, getting customer profiles, and carrying out targeted marketing. This is essentially about applying Web mining for business intelligence.

Mining the data on the Web is one of the major challenges faced by the data management and data mining communities, as well as those working on Web information management and machine learning. There is so much data and information on the Web that extracting useful and relevant information for the user becomes the real challenge. Scanning the Web becomes quite daunting, and soon we are overloaded with data. The question is, how do you convert this data into information and, subsequently, knowledge, so that the user gets only what he wants? Furthermore, what are the ways of extracting previously unknown information from the data on the Web? In this book, we discuss various aspects of Web mining.

One simple solution is to integrate the data mining tools with the data on the Web. This approach works well, especially if the data is in relational databases. Therefore, one needs to mine the data in the relational databases with the data mining tools that are available. These data mining tools have to develop interfaces to the Web. For example, if a relational interface is provided, then SQL-based mining tools could be applied to the virtual relational database. Unfortunately, the Web world is not so straightforward. Much of the data is unstructured or semistructured. There is a lot of imagery data and video data; providing a relational interface to all such databases may be complicated. The question is, how do you mine such data? In one of our previous books, we discussed various aspects of mining multimedia data. In particular, we focused on mining text, images, video, and audio data. One needs to develop tools first, and then we can focus on mining multimedia data on the Web.

Much of the previous discussion has focused on integrating data mining tools with the databases on the Web. In many cases, the data on the Web is not in databases. It is on various servers. Therefore, the challenge is to organize the data on these servers. Some form of data warehousing technology may be needed to organize the data to be mined. There is little work in developing data warehousing technology for the Web to facilitate mining. Another area that needs attention is visualization of the data on the Web. Much of the data is unorganized and difficult for the user to understand. Furthermore, mining is greatly facilitated by visualization. Therefore, developing appropriate visualization tools for the Web will greatly facilitate mining the data. These visualization tools could aid in the mining process.

Recently, various standards have been developed by organizations such as ISO (International Standards Organization), W3C (World Wide Web Consortium), and OMG (Object Management Group) for Web data access and management. These include models, specification languages, and architectures. One of the developments is XML (Extensible Markup Language) for writing what is called a Document Type Definition that allows the document to be interpreted by the person receiving the document. Relationships between data mining and standards such as XML are largely unexplored. However, one could expect data mining languages to be developed for the Web. In our book on XML, we briefly explored this topic.

Another aspect to mining on the Web is to collect various statistics and determine which Web pages are likely to be accessed, based on various usage patterns. Research and development in this direction is being conducted by various groups. Here, based on usage patterns of various users, trends and predictions are made as to the Web pages a user may likely want to scan. Therefore, based on this information, a user can have guidance as to the Web pages he may want to browse. This will facilitate the work a user has to do with respect to scanning various Web pages. Note that while the previous paragraphs in this section focused on developing data mining tools to mine the data on the Web, here we are focusing on using mining to help with the Web browsing process. We can expect to see many results in this area.

Mining can also be used to give only selective information to the user. For example, many of us are flooded with e-mail messages daily. Some of these messages are not relevant for our work. One can develop tools to discard the messages that are not relevant. These could be simple filtering tools or sophisticated data mining tools. Similarly, these data mining tools could also be used to display only the Web pages in which a user is interested.

One of the major applications of Web mining is gathering business intelligence for E-commerce and related activities. Corporations want to have the competitive edge and are exploring numerous ways to market effectively. Major corporations, including retail stores, have E-commerce sites now. Customers can order products from books to clothing to toys through these sites. The goal is to provide customized marketing. For example, user group A may prefer literature novels whereas user group B may prefer mystery novels. Therefore, new literature novels have to be marketed to group A and new mystery novels have to be marketed to group B. How does an E-commerce site know about these preferences? The solution is in mining usage patterns. One needs to determine the structure of the Web pages and links. In addition, the site owner may mine various public and private databases to get additional information about these users, i.e., all three types of data mining described in the taxonomy have to be performed. Web mining can also be used to provide entertainment on the Web. This is also a variation of E-commerce. Web access and Web data may be mined for user preferences on movies and record albums, and the corporations can carry out targeted marketing. Not only can data mining help E-commerce sites, it can also help the users to find information. For example, one E-commerce site manager mentioned to me that the major problem he has: users finding his site. He has advertised in various magazines, but this is available only to those who have access to the magazines. One solution here is to have a third party make the connection between the site and the user. Another solution is to make the search engines more intelligent. Data mining could help here. The data miner could match the requirements of the user to what is being offered by E-commerce sites, and connect the user to the right site. While there is much work reported in this area, we still have much to do in applying Web data mining for business-intelligence analysis. There are numerous other applications for Web data mining in various disciplines, including medical, biotechnology, financial, manufacturing, and resource management applications. Furthermore, there are books emerging in these applications, especially on data mining for E-commerce. That is, data mining for business intelligence is an important area.

We cannot discuss Web data mining without discussing perhaps one of the most critical applications of this technology for our national security. This application is counter-terrorism. We have heard it over and over again since September 11, 2001: if only we had the big picture, and all of the data and the relationships, then we could perhaps have prevented the most devastating event in the history of the United States. We believe that effective Web data mining tools may be critical to help detect and prevent such terrorist attacks. We are not saying that data mining alone will solve all of our problems. But certainly the ability to link events and entities, and make connections and associations, would help toward finding unusual behavior and patterns. In fact, various technologies and effective policies and procedures are needed to combat terrorism. This has been receiving more attention and we can expect much research to be carried out in this area. It is also a very new area, and this book will focus on counter-terrorism applications for data mining. Essentially, we use business intelligence to solve problems in counter-terrorism. To our knowledge, this is the first book that examines the use of data mining technologies for counter-terrorism. We would like to stress that we are not claiming that data mining and Web data mining will give us even partial solutions for combating terrorism. Our goal is to raise awareness of the potential applications of data mining to prevent and detect various terrorist attacks. We believe that technology alone will not solve the problem. Data miners will have to work with counter-terrorism experts to combat terrorism. We are not counter-terrorism experts. Nevertheless, we have provided some information about threats and solutions obtained from various unclassified news sources such as television documentaries and newspapers. Our goal is to show how the various data mining and Web mining technologies could possibly help to handle the various threats that we have identified.

In summary, several technologies have to work together to effectively mine the data on the Web. These include data mining on multimedia data, mining tools to predict trends and activities on the Web, as well as technologies for data management on the Web, data warehousing, and visualization. There is active research in Web mining and we can expect to see much progress being made here. There are already a number of commercial tools. We are also beginning to see text mining tools emerge. As more developments are made on data mining and the Web, we can expect better tools to emerge on Web mining both to mine the data on the Web as well as to mine the structure and usage patterns. We can expect to hear a lot about Web mining in coming years.

ORGANIZATION OF THIS BOOK

This book is divided into three parts. Part I discusses supporting technologies for Web mining, including data mining, Web databases, information retrieval, the semantic Web, collaboration, knowledge management, and many more. We discuss many of these technologies as part of the five supporting technologies in Part I. All these technologies have to work together to make Web mining a reality. Each chapter in Part I ends with a discussion of the relationship of the technology to Web mining.

Part II discusses the key concepts in Web mining. We start with a discussion of both Web data mining and Web usage mining. Then we discuss mining the databases on the Web. Search engines on the Web and how they mine the information will be discussed next. We provide an overview of engines such as Google that use a form of Web data mining in searching for information and detecting links and connections. Next, we address information management and Web mining as well as semantic Web mining. We end Part II with a discussion of some applications of Web mining such as E-commerce, business intelligence, and medical and financial applications. We also discuss Web data mining products.

Part III focuses on one critical application of Web data mining: counter-terrorism. As we have stated, developing good counter-terrorism measures is critical for our nation and the world. We hope that this book will set the initial direction of applying data mining to counter-terrorism. We provide an overview of malicious attacks, insider threats, cyber-terrorism, and bio-terrorism. Then we discuss how each technology discussed in Part II can be applied to combat terrorism. Note that we do not have all the solutions; we provide some initial directions only. Nevertheless it is critical that we start thinking about this subject and that is the purpose of this book. It should be noted, however, that there are conflicts between data mining techniques for counter-terrorism and privacy. Therefore, we will also address trade-offs between security and privacy in Part III. We essentially exploit business intelligence to solve problems in counter-terrorism.

FINAL THOUGHTS

In general, data management includes managing the databases, interoperability, migration, warehousing, and mining. For example, the data on the Web has to be managed and mined to extract information, patterns, and trends. Data could be in files or in databases. Data may be structured or unstructured. We repeatedly use the terms data, data management, database systems, and database management systems in this book. We elaborate on these terms in Appendix B. We define data management systems as systems that manage the data, extract meaningful information from the data, and make use of the information extracted. Therefore, data management systems include database systems, data warehouses, and data mining systems. Data could be structured, such as that found in relational databases, or it could be unstructured, such as text, voice, imagery, and video.

There have been numerous discussions in the past to distinguish between data, information, and knowledge. In our previous books on data management and mining, we did not attempt to clarify these terms. We simply stated that data could be just bits and bytes, or it could convey some meaningful information to the user. However, with the Web and also with increasing interest in data, information, and knowledge management as separate areas, in this book we take a different approach by differentiating between these terms as much as possible. For us, data is usually some value represented by numbers, integers, and strings. Information is obtained when some meaning or semantics is associated with the data, such as John's salary is 20K. Knowledge is something that you acquire through reading and learning. That is, data and information can be transferred into knowledge when uncertainty about the data and information is removed from someone's mind. It should be noted that it is rather difficult to give strict definitions of data, information, and knowledge. Sometimes we will use these terms interchangeably. Our framework for data management discussed in Appendix A helps clarify some of the differences. It should also be noted that although we have chosen to call this book *Web Data Mining* instead of *Web Information Mining* or *Web Knowledge Mining*, we do discuss information and knowledge management and mining technologies for the Web. To be consistent with the terminology in our previous books, we will also distinguish between database systems and database management systems. A database management system is that component which manages the database containing persistent data. A database system consists of both the database and the database management system.

This book provides a fairly comprehensive overview of Web data mining with an emphasis on counter-terrorism applications. It is written for technical managers and executives as well as for technologists interested in learning about the subject at a high level. Various people have asked questions about Web data mining. Because of the complex way Web mining is presented in books, it is difficult to explain the concepts in a less complex way. Therefore, we decided to write this book so that the complicated ideas can be expressed in a simplified manner and yet provide much of the information needed. This was also the reason for writing the previous books on data management, data mining, Web data management, multimedia data management, and XML. It should be noted that, as with many areas in data management and data mining, unless someone has practical experience in carrying out experiments and working with the various tools, it is difficult to appreciate what is out there and how to go about developing Web sites and mining Web databases. Therefore, we encourage the reader not only to read the information in this book and take advantage of the references mentioned here, but we also urge the reader, especially one who is interested in developing counter-terrorism solutions, to work with the various data mining tools on Web databases.

As we have stressed, this book does not aim to solve the terrorism problem. Instead it discusses only how data mining could possibly be applied to form links and patterns so that terrorist activities could perhaps be detected and prevented. Our goal is to raise awareness with the reader. Because of recent events, it is critical that we protect our nation and the world. Data mining may offer some solutions to the problem. It should be noted that many technologies have to work together to combat terrorism. For example, one could form all the best links from incorrect or bad data. But these links will probably be of little use. Therefore, we need good data and we must have access to the data to form links, associations, and patterns. This is the reason we have stressed data management for Web data mining. That is, we need effective data management and data sharing. We must work with counter-terrorism experts. For example, if we are to carry out data mining for medical applications such as detecting genes, we must work with domain specialists such as molecular biologists and perhaps physicians. In the same way, to apply data mining to counter-terrorism, we must work with the domain specialists who are counter-terrorism experts. Note also that in this book we do not distinguish between counter-terrorism and homeland security. That is, the data mining technologies discussed in this book are aimed at combating terrorism as well as providing homeland security. Furthermore, we believe that business intelligence will be a major aspect as one has to learn the strategies of the adversaries and plan counter-strategies to combat terrorism.

While counter-terrorism is a major focus, we cannot forget about privacy and civil liberties. Therefore, we discuss trade-offs between security and privacy. Much of the information in Part III is based on numerous talks given on data mining for counter-terrorism, including keynote addresses at the White House, the United Nations, major conferences, and various universities. The input we have received from the audience has helped a great deal in developing the ideas for this book.

It is very likely that much of the operational work on applying data mining for counter-terrorism will be done in a classified setting using real-world data. However, it may be less expensive and more effective to first have some idea of applying the various data mining technologies in an unclassified setting with unclassified data before migrating to a classified setting. All of the information provided in this book is unclassified and represents either ideas presented at public forums or information obtained from the public literature. There are several references at the end of this book. No claims are made that a certain technique will or will not work in a real-world environment. One of the major motivations to address data mining for counter-terrorism is to encourage the data mining technologists and researchers to team with experts in counter-terrorism and develop viable solutions. It should be noted that we also need to work with sociologists and cultural experts. Terrorism has no boundaries. It is not committed to just one country. Terrorists come from different parts of the world and speak different languages. Therefore, cultural experts who may understand the motives of terrorists are also needed to form an interdisciplinary team to combat terrorism. It is critical that we start work in this area immediately in light of the tragic events of September 11, 2001.

In this book, we have often used Web data mining and data mining interchangeably. We believe that Web data mining in a way encompasses data mining. This is because with Web data mining, not only do we mine the content on the Web, which is essentially data mining on both structured and unstructured data, we also mine the structure of the Web through Web links as well as Web usage such as clickstream analysis. That is, Web mining is much broader than data mining. That is why we have focused on Web mining. We believe that eventually much of the data will be on the Web, through intranets or the Internet; or on private or public, and classified or unclassified networks.

Web data mining is still a relatively new technology that includes many other technologies. Therefore, as the various technologies and integration of these technologies mature, we can expect to see progress in Web data mining and, consequently, E-business and other applications. That is, not only can we expect to access relational databases on the Web, we can also manage multimedia databases and warehouses, as well as discover patterns and trends from Web data. We can expect rapid developments with respect to many of the ideas, concepts, and techniques discussed in this book. We urge the reader to keep up with all the developments in this emerging and useful technology area. It should be noted that this book is intended to provide a fairly comprehensive view of the critical emerging technologies for Web data mining in general and focus on some important applications such as counter-terrorism. It is important to master these technologies to carry out effective Web data mining and, more importantly, apply the various techniques to ensure national as well as international security.

ACKNOWLEDGMENTS

I would like to thank the management at the MITRE Corporation and at the National Science Foundation for giving me numerous opportunities to continue working in data management, information security, data mining, and real-time systems. My interest in applying data mining for counter-terrorism began around December 1997 when I, together with Dr. Rick Steinheiser of the CIA, began discussions with the Defense Advanced Research Projects Agency on applying data mining for counter-terrorism. Our ideas resulted from a joint work on a six-year Intelligence Community initiative on Massive Digital Data Systems. These discussions eventually developed into the current EELD (Evidence Extraction and Link Detection) program at DARPA. However, my interest in applying data mining for counter-terrorism grew exponentially after September 11, 2001. I was deeply affected by this tragedy and lost my sponsor and colleague at the Department of Treasury due to the World Trade Center attacks. I have dedicated this book to him. Since then, I have given several presentations on applying data mining for counter-terrorism, including an invited talk at the White House (February 8, 2002), Stanford University (March 19, 2002), the SIAM Data Mining Conference (April 14, 2002), the National Academy of Sciences (June 11, 2002), Cambridge University (July 29, 2002), Oxford University (August 27, 2002), the United Nations (September 6, 2002), the Next Generation Data Mining Workshop (November 1, 2002), and the ICTAI Conference (November 6, 2002).

I would like to thank my husband, Thevendra, for his continued support of my work and for sharing his excellent and insightful ideas with me while writing this book. I thank my son, Breman, for having several intellectual discussions with me, as well as motivating me. I thank Steve Funk of the IRS for his encouragement to write this book. I especially thank Dr. Rick Steinheiser of the CIA for his critique of various chapters and for the discussions on data mining for counter-terrorism. I hope that we can continue to make progress in data mining and Web technologies to address the security of our nation and the world.

I would like to point out that the views and conclusions presented in this book are those of the author and do not reflect the policies and procedures of the MITRE Corporation, the National Science Foundation, or the United States government. Unless otherwise stated, all of the examples considered in this book are hypothetical. They are used mainly to illustrate various concepts.

BHAVANI THURAISINGHAM

Chapter 1
Introduction

INTRODUCTION

Recent developments in information systems technologies have resulted in computerizing many applications in various business areas. Data has become a critical resource in many organizations and, therefore, efficient access to data, sharing the data, extracting information from the data, and making use of the information has become an urgent need. As a result, there have been many efforts to not only integrate the various data sources scattered across several sites, but it has also become important to extract information from these databases in the form of patterns and trends. These data sources may be managed by database management systems or they may be warehoused in a repository. The advent of the World Wide Web (WWW) in the mid-1990s has resulted in even greater demand for managing data, information, and knowledge effectively. There is now so much data on the Web that managing it with conventional tools is becoming almost an impossibility. New tools and techniques are needed to effectively manage this data. Therefore, to provide interoperability and warehousing for multiple data sources and systems, and to extract information from the databases and data warehouses, various tools are being developed.

With information overload on the Web, it is highly desirable to mine data and extract patterns and information relevant to the user, making the task of browsing the Internet much easier. Therefore, there has been much interest in Web mining, which is essentially mining databases on the Web, mining usage patterns by analyzing Web logs, or mining Web links to extract structure.

Data mining and the Web developed as independent technology areas in the mid-1990s. While it was felt that mining data on the Web would be useful to help the information overload problem, the extent to which Web mining would help key areas such as E-commerce was not well understood until recently. It was only a few years ago that researchers and practitioners seriously started to think about Web mining. The Web mining panel at the IEEE ICTAI Conference was one of the first panels on this topic and the Web mining workshop held during the Knowledge Discovery in Databases Conference in 1999 was one of the first workshops.

In this book, developments in Web mining are discussed, including an overview of the tools and technologies, and some directions are provided. The book also describes a taxonomy for Web mining that is now more or less standard. Web mining is divided into three categories: (1) mining usage patterns from Web data, known as Web content mining; (2) mining URLs and other Web links to help users with various Web activities, and to determine the structure of Web pages, known as Web structure mining; and (3) analyzing Web logs, known as Web usage mining. That is, business intelligence is a major application of Web mining.

Closely related to Web usage mining is mining to support E-commerce. There are two aspects here: (1) mining information about competitors and (2) mining usage patterns and customer profiles in order to carry out targeted marketing.

Mining data on the Web is one of the major challenges faced by the data management and mining community as well as those working on Web information management and machine learning. There is so much data and information on the Web that extracting what is useful and relevant for the user is the real challenge. Scanning through the Web can be quite daunting, and users soon are overloaded with data. The question is, how do you convert this data into information and knowledge so that you get only what you want? What are the ways of extracting previously unknown information from data on the Web? In this book, various aspects of Web mining are discussed. Web mining has many applications in several areas, including business intelligence analysis, insider threat analysis, and counter-terrorism.

This book provides an overview of Web data mining and discusses some applications in general, such as supporting technologies for Web mining, Web mining concepts and tools, as well as business intelligence analysis and medial applications. Then the focus turns to counter-terrorism, which is becoming one of the most important applications of data mining and Web mining. Essentially, one uses business intelligence strategies to solve problems in counter-terrorism.

This chapter discusses supporting technologies, key points, and applications for Web mining; these discussions will be elaborated on in Parts I, II, and III of the book. The organization of this book is also discussed in this chapter. To put this all together, we describe a framework for Web mining and applications. This framework helps us to give some context to the various Web mining-related technologies. Parts I, II, and III deal with Layers 1, 2, and 3 of the framework, respectively. Finally, the chapter summary includes a discussion of directions. Exhibit 1 describes the topics addressed in this book.

We believe that eventually much of the data available will be on the Web, either through intranets and private networks within corporations and

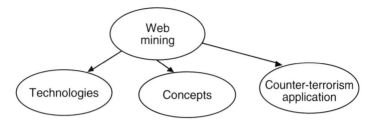

Exhibit 1.   Web Mining Technologies, Concepts, and Applications

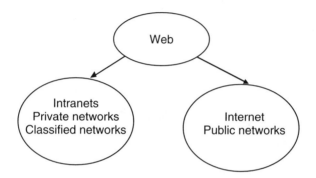

Exhibit 2.   Types of Networks for the Web

agencies or through the Internet and public networks. We illustrate our notion of the Web in Exhibit 2.

In this book, we often use the terms *Web data mining* and *data mining* interchangeably. We believe that, in a way, Web data mining encompasses data mining. This is because in Web data mining, not only do we mine content on the Web (essentially, data mining on both structured and unstructured data), we also mine the structure of the Web (mining Web links) and Web usage such as clickstream analysis. Thus, Web mining is much broader than data mining, and that is why we have focused on Web mining. The taxonomy for Web mining is illustrated in Exhibit 3.

SUPPORTING TECHNOLOGIES FOR WEB DATA MINING

We discuss some of the various supporting technologies for Web data mining. First of all, one needs an understanding of the Web. Without the Web, we would not have Web mining. Therefore, Web technologies in general are supporting technologies for Web mining. Therefore, we will start with a discussion of the World Wide Web and E-commerce. Note that we discuss E-commerce because many of the E-commerce concepts, such as business intelligence, will be of use to counter-terrorism. That is, we need to understand the strategies of the adversary to solve problems in counter-terrorism.

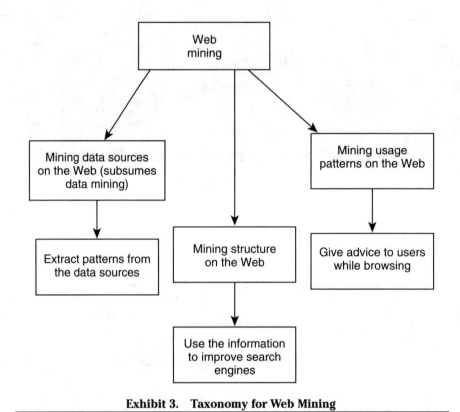

Exhibit 3.   Taxonomy for Web Mining

The other supporting technologies we will focus on are data mining, Web databases, information management, information retrieval, and the semantic Web. The Web has become the main infrastructure for various information technologies as well as the foundation upon which commercial and governmental organizations are building their businesses. Therefore, we will start the discussion of supporting technologies with a discussion of the World Wide Web and some key related technologies. Then we will focus on the remaining supporting technologies.

We start the discussion of the remaining supporting technologies with the subject of data mining. Data mining is the process of posing queries and extracting information previously unknown from large quantities of data. Another key supporting technology is Web database management. There is a tremendous amount of data on the Web; some of it is stored in files and some in databases. This data must be managed effectively. Therefore, query processing, transaction management, storage management, and metadata management all play a key role in Web data management. Note that database management is a supporting technology both for Web database management and data mining. We discuss database management in

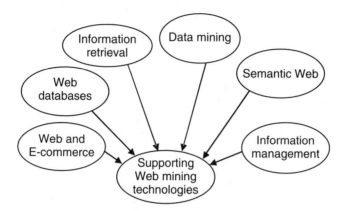

Exhibit 4. Supporting Web Mining Technologies

Appendix B because it is not possible to discuss all supporting technologies in Part I. In Part I, we focus mainly on the immediate supporting technologies for Web mining.

Closely related to Web data management is information management. Information management technologies include multimedia information management, collaborative computing systems, knowledge management, training, visualization, and agents. We provide an overview of information management.

Another technology that is becoming critical for Web mining is information retrieval. Information retrieval systems are essentially document management systems. In addition to text retrieval, we also need to provide support for managing image, audio, and video databases.

Finally, an area that is becoming increasingly important is the semantic Web. Not only will the semantic Web provide support for Web mining, Web mining can also be used to improve Web ethnologies. Therefore, we have included the semantic Web as a supporting technology for Web mining.

Exhibit 4 illustrates some of the key supporting Web mining technologies. We have called them the basic technologies. One can build on them to develop Web mining technologies. Note that Part I discusses the supporting technologies in more detail. Web mining concepts are given more detailed consideration in Part II, although we introduce them in this chapter. Applications of Web mining and counter-terrorism are introduced in this chapter and are elaborated in Part III.

Some of the supporting technologies for the technologies discussed in Part I are discussed in the Appendix. These include concepts in database management and information security. For example, database management is a supporting technology for Web database management; Web database management is a supporting technology for Web mining. Information security is one of the counter-measures for terrorism. That is, we need to protect our information from cyber terrorist attacks.

In summary, several technologies have to work together to effectively mine data on the Web: data mining on multimedia data, mining tools to predict trends and activities on the Web, as well as technologies for data management, data warehousing, and visualization on the Web. There is active research in Web mining and we can expect to see much progress to be made in this area. There are already a number of commercial tools and text mining tools are also beginning to emerge. As more developments are made on data mining and the Web, we can expect better tools to emerge to mine the data, usage patterns, and structure on the Web. We can expect to hear a lot about Web mining in coming years.

WEB DATA MINING CONCEPTS

There are various ways to carry out Web mining. One way is to integrate mining tools with data on the Web. This approach works well, especially when the data is in relational databases. Therefore, one needs to mine the data in relational databases with the data mining tools that are available. These data mining tools have to develop interfaces to the Web. For example, if a relational interface is provided, then SQL-based mining tools could be applied to the virtual relational database. Unfortunately, the Web is not so straightforward. Much of the data is unstructured or semistructured. There is much imagery data and video data. Providing a relational interface to all such databases may be complicated. The question is, how do you mine such data? One needs to develop tools first to mine multimedia data and then focus on developing tools to mine such data on the Web.

Much of the previous discussion has focused on integrating data mining tools with the databases on the Web. In many cases, the data on the Web is on various servers, not in databases. Therefore, the challenge is to organize the data on these servers. Some form of data warehousing technology may be needed to organize the data to be mined. There is little work on developing some sort of data warehousing technology for the Web to facilitate mining. Another area that needs attention is visualization of the data on the Web. Much of the data is unorganized and difficult for the user to understand. Furthermore, mining is greatly facilitated by visualization. Therefore, developing appropriate visualization tools for the Web will greatly facilitate mining the data. These visualization tools could aid in the mining process.

Another aspect to mining on the Web is to collect various statistics and determine which Web pages are likely to be accessed, based on various usage patterns. Research and development in this direction is being conducted by various groups. Here, based on usage patterns of various users,

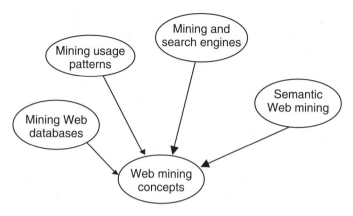

Exhibit 5. Web Mining Concepts

predictions are made about the Web pages a user may likely want to scan. Based on this information, a user can have guidance as to the Web pages he may want to browse. This will facilitate the work a user has to do with respect to scanning various Web pages. Note that while the previous paragraphs in this section focused on developing data mining tools to mine the data on the Web, here we are focusing on using mining to help with the Web browsing process. We can expect to see many results in this area.

Mining can also be used to provide only selective information to the user. For example, many of us are flooded with e-mail messages daily. Some of these messages are not relevant for our work. One can develop tools to discard the messages that are not relevant. These tools could be simple filtering tools or sophisticated data mining tools. Similarly, these data mining tools could also be used to display only the Web pages in which a user is interested. Various search engines such as Google are using some data mining techniques.

E-commerce and Web mining are closely related. E-commerce technologies are essential for Web mining. On the other hand, Web mining can be applied to improve E-commerce. Essentially, Web mining can be used to improve business intelligence. The emergence of the semantic Web also gives us new opportunities for Web mining. Part II discusses Web mining concepts and tools. Subjects include mining Web databases, search engines and Web mining, Web mining and information management, and mining the semantic Web. Exhibit 5 illustrates some of the Web mining concepts.

WEB DATA MINING, E-COMMERCE, AND BUSINESS INTELLIGENCE

E-commerce was and still is considered to be the major application of Web mining. We will examine how Web mining is used for E-commerce as we can learn much from the concepts for other applications.

Corporations want to have the competitive edge and are exploring numerous ways to market effectively. Major corporations including retail stores have E-commerce sites now. Customers can order products from books to clothing to toys through these sites. The goal is to provide customized marketing. For example, user group A may prefer literature novels, whereas user group B may prefer mystery novels. Therefore, new literature novels have to be marketed to group A, and new mystery novels have to be marketed to group B. How does an E-commerce site know about these preferences? The solution is in data mining. Usage patterns and structure have to be mined. In addition, the company may mine various public and private databases to get additional information about these users. Thus, all three types of data mining described in the taxonomy have to be performed.

Web mining can also be used to provide entertainment on the Web. This is a variation of E-commerce. Web access and Web data may be mined for user preferences on movies and record albums, and the companies can carry out targeted marketing.

Not only can data mining help E-commerce sites, data mining can also help the users find information. For example, one E-commerce site manager mentioned to me that the major problem his site faces is that of being found by users. He has advertised in various magazines, but those who do not have access to the magazines do not see the ads. One solution is to have a third-party agent make the connection between the site and the user. Another solution is to make the search engines more intelligent. Data mining could help here. The data miner could match the requirements of the user to what is being offered by the E-commerce sites to connect the user to the right site. While there is much work reported in this area, we still have a lot to do in applying Web data mining for business intelligence analysis. The challenge is to obtain accurate and useful results from Web mining and apply them to business intelligence.

There are numerous other applications for Web data mining in various disciplines including medical, biotechnology, financial, manufacturing, and resource management applications. Furthermore, there are books beginning to emerge in the these applications.

WEB DATA MINING AND COUNTER-TERRORISM

We cannot discuss Web data mining without discussing perhaps one of the most critical applications of this technology for our national security: counter-terrorism. We have heard it repeatedly since September 11, 2001: if only we had the big picture and all of the data and the relationships, then we could perhaps have prevented the most devastating event in the history of the United States. We believe that effective Web data mining tools may be critical to detect and prevent such terrorist attacks. We are not saying that data mining alone will solve all our problems. But certainly, the ability to link events and entities and to make connections and associations would help find unusual behavior and patterns. In fact, various technologies, as well as effective policies and procedures, are needed to combat terrorism. This is a very new area that is receiving more attention, recently and we see the need for research to be conducted.

This book will focus on data mining applications for counter-terrorism. To our knowledge, this is the first book that examines the use of data mining technologies for counter-terrorism. We would like to stress that we are not claiming that data mining and Web data mining will give us even partial solutions for combating terrorism. Our goal is to raise awareness of the potential applications of data mining to preventing and detecting various terrorist attacks. We believe that technology alone will not solve the problem. Data miners will have to work with counter-terrorism experts to combat terrorism. We are not counter-terrorism experts. Nevertheless, we have provided some information about threats and solutions obtained from various unclassified news sources such as television documentaries and newspapers. Our goal is to show how various data mining and Web mining technologies could possibly help to handle the threats that we have identified. Essentially, we use business intelligence to learn the strategies of one adversary and use the strategies to solve problems in counter-terrorism.

It should also be noted that we need to work with sociologists and cultural experts. Terrorism has no boundaries. It is not committed to just one country. Terrorists could come from different parts of the world and speak different languages. Therefore, cultural experts who may understand the motives of the terrorists are also needed to form an interdisciplinary team to combat terrorism. It is critical that we start work in this area immediately, considering the tragic events of September 11, 2001. Exhibit 6 discusses the various Web mining applications. The specific application we are focusing on in this book is illustrated in Exhibit 7.

ORGANIZATION OF THIS BOOK

This book covers the major topics in Web mining and applications focusing mainly on counter-terrorism in three parts: supporting technologies, such as the World Wide Web and E-commerce; Web data management and information retrieval; key Web mining concepts such as content mining, usage mining, and structure mining; and Web mining applications in areas such as E-commerce and counter-terrorism. To explain our ideas more clearly, we illustrate a three-layered Web-mining framework in Exhibit 8. Layer 1 is the Supporting Web Mining Technologies Layer. It describes the various supporting technologies that contribute to Web mining. These include data mining, Web data management, information retrieval, and the semantic Web. Layer 2 is the Web Mining Concepts Layer. This layer describes the various concepts in Web mining such as mining Web data-

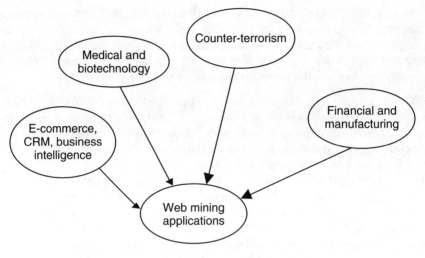

Exhibit 6.   Web Mining Applications

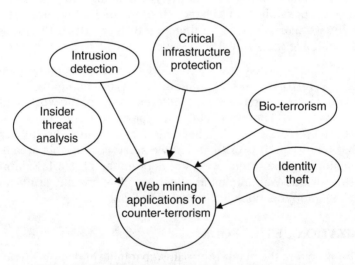

Exhibit 7.   Web Mining for Counter-Terrorism

base search engines and mining the semantic Web. Layer 3 is the Web Mining Applications for Counter-Terrorism Layer. This layer describes applications such as insider threat analysis and counter-terrorism.

Part I describes the various supporting technologies. Chapter 2 provides an overview of the World Wide Web. In particular, the evolution of the Web, E-commerce, and some related technologies are discussed. Note that toward the end of this book (e.g., Chapter 27) we will see that many of the technologies for E-commerce, such as business intelligence, will also be

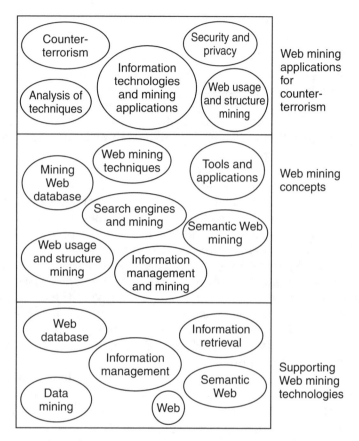

Exhibit 8. Framework for Web Mining Technologies and Applications

important for counter-terrorism. We will also see that Web data mining is useful for business intelligence. Chapter 3 describes data mining. Chapter 4 discusses some of the core data mining technologies, such as machine learning and statistical reasoning. Chapter 5 describes Web data management. Chapter 6 discusses information retrieval technologies. Chapter 7 focuses on information management. Finally, Chapter 8 discusses the semantic Web. Each of these chapters ends with the relevant relationship to Web mining, as Web mining is our main focus.

Part II addresses Web mining concepts. Chapter 9 provides an introduction to Web mining. Web mining techniques are discussed in Chapter 10. Mining Web databases is the subject of Chapter 11. Chapter 12 describes search engines and Web mining. Chapter 13 describes information management and Web mining. Semantic Web mining is the subject of Chapter 14. Mining usage patterns and Web structure is the subject of Chapter 15. Web mining products are the subject of Chapter 16. We briefly discuss Web mining applications in Chapter 17. Note that because counter-terrorism is the application we focus on in Part III, a general overview of the various applications will be discussed in Part II.

While Parts I and II address supporting technologies and concepts for Web data mining, Part III addresses counter-terrorism, a critical application of Web mining. An overview of counter-terrorism is provided in Chapter 18. Then, for each key supporting technology discussed in Part II, we discuss its application to counter-terrorism. For example, the application of Web mining techniques is the subject of Chapter 19. The application of Web database mining is discussed in Chapter 20. An overview of information retrieval, mining, and counter-terrorism is discussed in Chapter 21. Information management, mining, and counter-terrorism are discussed in Chapter 22. Application of semantic Web mining is discussed in Chapter 23. Web usage and structure mining are discussed in Chapter 24. The role of privacy and civil liberties with respect to national security is discussed in Chapter 25. In Chapter 26, we revisit the discussion of threats in Chapter 18 and discuss the applicability of the various solutions discussed in Chapters 19 through 24. Finally, in Chapter 27, we revisit the discussions in Chapter 2 of E-commerce and business intelligence, and show how various commercial developments in E-commerce can possibly be used for counter-terrorism. Essentially, we show that many of the same business intelligence concepts apply, whether they are gathered for commercial business, intelligence business, or military business, and that data mining is important to business intelligence. Essentially, we will draw some parallels between E-commerce and counter-terrorism in Chapter 27. This is one of the main reasons E-commerce, as a supporting technology, was discussed in Chapter 2.

Exhibit 9 illustrates the chapters in which the components of the framework in Exhibit 5 are addressed in this book. We summarize the book and provide a discussion of challenges and directions in Chapter 28. Each of the chapters in Parts I, II, and III starts with an overview of the chapter and ends with a summary. Each part also begins with an introduction and ends with a conclusion.

Finally, we have three appendixes that provide useful background information. Appendix A provides an overview of trends in data management technology. We essentially give some background on the evolution of data management systems technology and provide a summary of our books and how they relate to one another. In Appendix B, we provide an overview of the developments and trends in database systems. As we have stated, database management is essential for data mining and Web database management. We discuss information security in Appendix C. Information security is one of the important considerations in this book. In Part III, we will see that data mining helps various problems in information security.

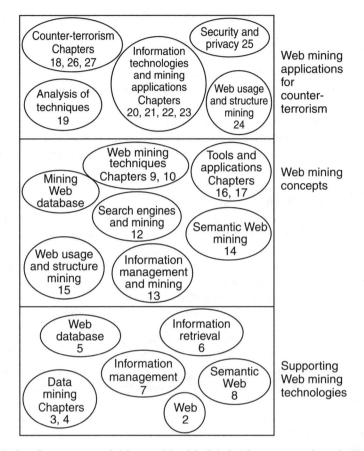

Exhibit 9.   Components Addressed in this Book (chapter numbers indicated)

However, data mining is also a threat to privacy. Part III will also address privacy.

We also provide a fairly comprehensive list of references. We have obtained these references from various journals, conference and workshop proceedings, and magazines. In addition, each appendix also has its own set of references.

HOW DO WE PROCEED?

This book provides the information for a reader to become familiar with Web mining and some relevant applications. Our purpose is not to give a tutorial on Web mining or discuss some of the theoretical concepts. For an in-depth understanding of the various topics covered in this book, we recommend the reader to the various references provided. Various papers and articles have appeared on Web data management and related areas, and are referenced throughout this book. Our main goal is to get the data mining community started on developing good data mining and Web mining solutions and apply them for counter-terrorism.

While we have tried to provide as much information as possible in this book about data mining and Web mining, there is so much more to write about. Daily, we hear about Web mining and data mining in various magazines and on the Web. It should be noted, however, that it is not our intention to educate the reader of all the details about Web mining. Instead we provide the big picture and explain where Web mining stands in the larger scheme of things. To be consistent with our previous books, our purpose is to explain, especially to technical managers, what Web mining is all about. The technologies will also benefit technologists, as this is one of the few books that puts everything into context and provides a broad picture. One of the main contributions of this book is raising awareness of the importance of data mining and Web mining for counter-terrorism. Homeland security and combating terrorism is one of the critical missions of our nation. This book will also be of use to counter-terrorism experts who want to learn about data mining. Note that to effectively combat terrorism, we need data mining specialists to work with counter-terrorism experts.

We do provide several references that can help the reader in understanding the details of Web mining. Our advice to the reader is to keep up with the developments on Web mining and data mining. Various Web mining-related conferences and workshops are being held. For further details, see [AFCE], [ICDE], [ICDM], [KDD], [PAKDD], [SIGM], [VLDB], and [WWW]. For background information, we refer to our previous books (see, for example, [THUR97], [THUR98], [THUR00], [THUR01], and [THUR02]). Some other useful books on data mining include [ADRI96], [BERR97], and [HAN01].

Part I
Supporting Technologies for Web Data Mining

INTRODUCTION TO PART I

Part I, consisting of seven chapters, describes supporting technologies for Web data mining. We start with an overview of the Web and E-commerce in Chapter 2. We discuss E-commerce to show how some of the ideas in business intelligence and related areas may be applied for counter-terrorism, discussed in Part III. Chapter 3 discusses data mining, in particular, data mining technologies and techniques. Chapter 4 goes into more detail on core data mining technologies, such as machine learning, as these technologies are also required for Web data mining.

Chapter 5 provides an overview of Web database system technology and discusses the impact of mining on this technology. In particular, data modeling and architectures database system functions, such as query processing, transaction management, and metadata management are discussed. In Part II we will elaborate on Web mining and Web databases.

Other supporting technologies include information retrieval, information management, and the semantic Web. Chapter 6 describes information retrieval systems including text retrieval, image retrieval, and video retrieval. Chapter 7 provides an overview of information management technologies such as collaboration, multimedia, and training. Chapter 8 provides an overview of the semantic Web including concepts, agents, RDF, and XML.

Each chapter begins with an overview and ends with a summary. Each chapter includes a brief discussion of the relationship to Web mining. The concepts in Web mining will be elaborated in Part II.

Chapter 2
The World Wide Web, E-Commerce, and Business Intelligence

INTRODUCTION

In this chapter, we start the discussion of the supporting technologies for Web data mining. Essentially, without the Web we will not have Web data mining. Similarly, the Web has been the main infrastructure and foundation upon which several organizations have built their businesses. These organizations include not only commercial businesses but also military and intelligence businesses. We now hear about corporate intranets as well as private and classified intranets. These intranets are based essentially on Web technologies.

The developments around the Internet have been key to the development of the World Wide Web. The Internet started out as a research project funded by the U.S. Department of Defense. Much of the work was carried out in the 1970s. It was at this time that there were numerous developments in networking. We began to see various networking protocols and products emerge. In addition, standards groups such as the International Standards Organization proposed a layered stack of protocols for networking. Internet research resulted in TCP/IP (Transmission Control Protocol/Internet Protocol) for communication transport.

While networking concepts were advancing rapidly, data management technology emerged in the 1970s. Then in the 1980s, the early ideas of Bush (in the 1940s) to organize and structure information started getting computerized. These ideas led to the development of hypermedia technologies. In the 1980s, researchers thought that these hypermedia technologies would result in efficient access to large quantities of information, for example, in library information systems. It was not until the early 1990s that researchers at CERN in Switzerland combined Internet and hypermedia technologies, which resulted in the World Wide Web. The idea is for various Web servers scattered within and across corporations to be connected through intranets and the Internet so that people from around the world can have access to the right information at the right time. The advancement of various data and information management technologies contributed to the rapid growth of the Web.

One of the killer applications for the Web is E-commerce. This chapter will discuss the evolution of the Web and then provide an introduction to E-commerce. For more details on this topic, we refer to our previous book *Web Data Management and Electronic Commerce* [THUR00]. We have discussed the Web as Web data mining is essentially based on data mining as well as the Web. We address E-commerce as Web data mining technology plays a key role in E-commerce. Business intelligence analysis is key to successful E-commerce. We will see in Part III that E-commerce, the Web, Web mining, and business intelligence have applications in counter-terrorism. That is, commercial technologies contribute much to the running of military and intelligence organizations. Furthermore, we can draw some parallels between E-commerce carried out in commercial ventures and interactions and collaborations between governmental organizations. For example, business intelligence, which is a critical component for E-commerce, is also important for counter-terrorism. That is, one needs to gather intelligence information on the Web or otherwise about various terrorist activities.

EVOLUTION OF THE WEB

The inception of the Web took place at CERN in Switzerland. Although different people have been credited as the father of the Web, one of the early conceivers of the Web was Timothy Berners-Lee, who was at CERN at that time. He now heads the World Wide Web Consortium (W3C). The consortium specifies standards for the Web, including data models, query languages, and security.

As soon as the Web emerged in the early 1990s, a group of graduate students at the University of Illinois developed a browser, which was called MOSAIC. Netscape Communications then marketed MOSAIC, and since then various browsers and search engines have emerged. The search engines, the browsers, and the servers all constitute what is now the World Wide Web. The Internet became the transport medium for communication.

Various protocols for communication such as HTTP (Hypertext Transfer Protocol) and languages for creating Web pages such as HTML (Hypertext Markup Language) also emerged. Perhaps one of the most significant developments is the Java programming language by Sun Microsystems. Java is very much like C++ without certain disadvantages, such as pointers. It was developed as a platform-independent programming language and was soon found to be an ideal language for the Web. So now there are various Java applications and Java applets, programs residing in a machine that can be called by a Web page running on a separate machine. Therefore, applets can be embedded into Web pages to perform all kinds of tasks. Of course, there are additional security restrictions, as applets could come from untrusted machines. Another concept is a servlet. Servlets run on Web servers and perform specific functions such as delivering Web pages for a user request. Applets and servlets will be discussed later in this chapter.

Middleware for the Web is continuing to evolve. If the entire environment is Java, connecting Java clients to Java servers, then one could use RMI (Remote Method Invocation) by Javasoft, a subsidiary of Sun. If the platform consists of heterogeneous clients and servers, then one could use Object Management Group (OMG)'s CORBA (Common Object Request Broker Architecture) for interoperability. Some argue that client/server technology will become obsolete because of the Web because one may need different computing paradigms such as the federated computing model. These aspects, as well as various architectural aspects, will be addressed in Parts II and III of this book.

Another development for the Web is components and frameworks. We discussed some of them in the chapter on objects (see [THUR00]). Component technology, such as Enterprise Java Beans (EJB), is becoming very popular for componentizing various Web applications. These applications are managed by application servers. These application servers (such as BEA's Web Logic) communicate with database management systems through data servers (these data servers may be developed by database vendors such as Excelon Corporation (formerly, Object Design Inc.). Finally, one of the latest technologies for integrating various, possibly heterogeneous applications and systems through the Web is Sun's Jini (see [ACM99]). It essentially encompasses Java and RMI as its basic elements. We discuss some aspects in Part II when we address Web database management.

The Web is continuing to expand and explode. There is so much data, information, and knowledge on the Web that managing all this is becoming a challenge. Web information management is all about developing technologies for managing this information. One type of information system is a database system. In Chapter 5 of this book, we provide some details on Web database management. Then we discuss technologies for Web information management in the remaining chapters of Part I. Finally, in Part III we provide an overview of counter-terrorism, and discuss how various technologies in general and Web mining in particular may be applied for counter-terrorism.

Exhibit 1 illustrates some of the Web concepts we have discussed here. Note that our assumption of the Web (corporate intranets, private networks, the Internet, and public networks) was illustrated in Chapter 1, Exhibit 2.

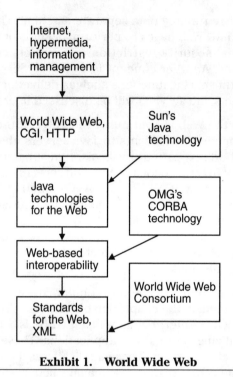

Exhibit 1.   World Wide Web

One of the major problems with the Web is information overload. Because humans can now access large amounts of information very rapidly, they can quickly become overloaded with information, and in some cases the information may not be useful to them. Furthermore, in certain other cases, the information may even be harmful to humans. The current search engines, although improving steadily, still give users too much information. When a user types in an index word, many irrelevant Web pages are also retrieved. What we need is intelligent search engines. The technologies that we have discussed in this book, if implemented successfully, would prevent this information overload. For example, agents may filter out information so that users get only what is relevant. Data mining technology could extract meaningful information from data sources. Security technology could prevent users from getting information that they are not authorized to have. In addition to computer scientists, researchers in psychology, sociology, and other disciplines are also involved in examining various aspects of Web database management. We need people in multiple disciplines to collaborate together to make the Web a useful tool to humans. One of the emerging goals of Web technology is to provide appropriate support for data dissemination. This deals with getting the right data to the user (directly to the desktop if possible) at the right time to assist in carrying out various functions. Many of these

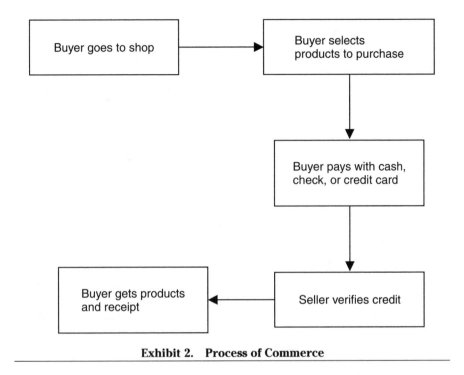

Exhibit 2.   Process of Commerce

technologies, such as agents and data mining for the Web, will be addressed in Part II.

INTRODUCTION TO E-COMMERCE

Overview

In this section we discuss what is now referred to as the killer application for the Web, E-commerce. The question is, what is E-commerce? Simply stated, E-commerce is all about carrying out commerce on the Web. It is about carrying out transactions, essentially buying and selling products on the Web. Earlier in this book, we mentioned that E-commerce could be as simple as putting up a Web page or as complicated as merging two corporations on the Web. More recently, we have heard the term *E-business*, which is much broader than E-commerce and that is doing any business on the Web. Therefore, E-commerce has come to be known as carrying out transactions on the Web, and tasks such as putting up Web pages and other activities are part of E-business. Exhibit 2 illustrates how one conducts a normal transaction (i.e., a non-Web transaction) and Exhibit 3 illustrates how one carries out a business transaction on the Web.

The next section provides a broad overview of E-commerce. We discuss some models for E-commerce. In particular, business-to-business E-com-

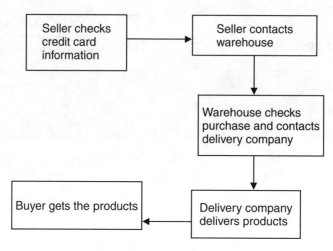

Exhibit 3.   Process of E-Commerce

merce as well as business-to-consumer E-commerce models are discussed.* It should be noted that models for E-commerce are rather immature, and as we learn more about E-commerce, various models will emerge. Next, we briefly discuss information technologies for E-commerce.

Models For E-Commerce

There are no well-defined models for E-commerce. However, two paradigms, which we can consider to be models, are emerging: business-to-business E-commerce and business-to-consumer E-commerce. In this section, we will discuss both these models with examples.

As its name implies, business-to-business E-commerce (see Exhibit 4) is all about two businesses conducting transactions on the Web. For example, suppose corporation A is an automobile manufacturer and needs microprocessors installed in its automobiles. It will then purchase the microprocessors from corporation B, which manufactures them. Another example is when an individual purchases goods such as toys from a toy manufacturer. The manufacturer then contacts a packaging company via the Web to deliver the toys to the individual. The transaction between the manufacturer and the packaging company is a business-to-business transaction. Business-to-business E-commerce also involves one business purchasing a unit of another business or two businesses merging. The main point is that such transactions have to be carried out on the Web.

Business-to-consumer E-commerce (Exhibit 5) is when an individual consumer makes purchases on the Web. In the example of the toy manufacturer,

* Note that business-to-business E-commerce is popularly called B2B and business-to-consumer E-commerce is called B2C.

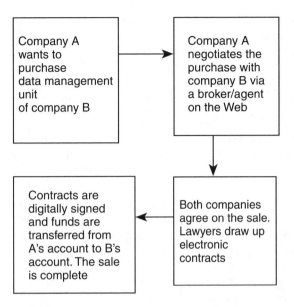

Exhibit 4.   Business-to-Business E-Commerce

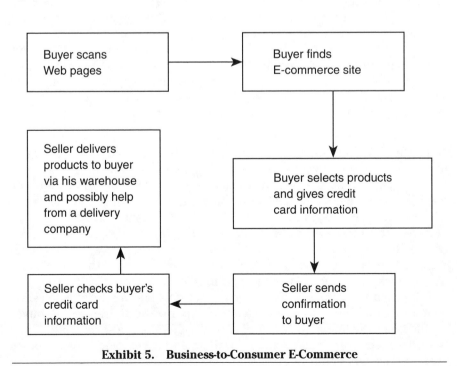

Exhibit 5.   Business-to-Consumer E-Commerce

the interchange between the individual and the toy manufacturer is a business-to-consumer transaction. It is reported in [INFO1] and [INFO2] that business-to-consumer E-commerce has grown tremendously in recent years. While computer hardware purchases are still the leading E-commerce transactions, the purchase of toys, apparel, software, and books via the Web has also increased. But many feel that the real future of E-commerce will be in business-to-business transactions, as this will involve millions of dollars.

The major difference between the two models is how a business transaction is carried out. This is similar to the real world. In a business-to-consumer transaction, people can use credit cards, cash, or checks to make a purchase. In the Web world, credit cards are used most often. However, the use of E-cash and checks is also being investigated. In business-to-business transactions, corporations have company accounts that are maintained and the corporations are billed at certain times. This is the approach being taken in the E-commerce world also. That is, corporations have accounts with one another and these accounts are billed when purchases are made. Exhibits 4 and Exhibit 5 illustrate business-to-business and business-to-consumer transactions, respectively.

Regardless of the type of model, one of the major goals of E-commerce is to complete the transaction on time. For example, in the case of business-to-consumer E-commerce, the seller has to minimize the time between the time of purchase and the time of delivery. The seller may have to depend on third parties such as packaging and trucking companies to achieve this goal. It should also be noted that with E-commerce, the consumer has numerous choices for products. In a typical shop, it is very laborious for one consumer to look at all the products displayed at the shop. However, in E-commerce the consumer has access to all the products that are available from the seller by browsing the Web pages.

Another key point to note is the issue of trust. How can the consumer trust the seller and how can the seller trust the consumer? For example, the consumer may give his credit card number to a seller who is a fraud. The consumer may not send a check when the goods are delivered. The best-known model is the business–consumer relationship. But this is not always the case in E-commerce. Some of the challenges here are not very different from the world of mail order and catalogs. If the goods do not arrive, the consumer could write to his credit card company. But this could be a lengthy process. Another solution is for the seller to establish an account with a credit card company and to establish credibility. That is, a vendor from some unknown company called XXX may not be able to establish a relationship with a credit card company and therefore the buyer would be protected. In the E-commerce world, there are several additional security measures such as secure wallets and cards, and these aspects were discussed in [THUR00].

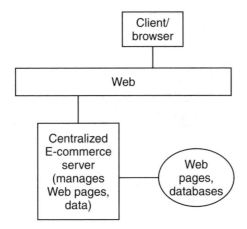

Exhibit 6.   Centralized Architecture for E-Commerce

Architectures For E-Commerce

In the centralized architecture illustrated in Exhibit 6, we assume that all of the information at the E-commerce site is centralized. Many of the issues discussed for centralized data management would apply here. The challenges include maintaining all of the data, which could be in databases, Web pages, and files. Data mining component may also be part of the central E-commerce server. The functions of a central E-commerce manager are illustrated in Exhibit 7. Note that in this case, we assume that the E-commerce business functions and the data management functions are carried out by the E-commerce server. We will illustrate an alternative in the three-tier computing architecture later.

In a distributed architecture, the information managed by the E-commerce server is distributed. This could be because the corporation's assets may be distributed across multiple sites. For example, major corporations have sites all over the world and each site may host components of the E-commerce server. The servers may be connected by a distributed processor, which we call EDP (electronic distributed processor). Exhibit 8 illustrates a distributed architecture.

Currently, E-commerce is carried out mainly in a client/server environment. Typically, browsers run in the client environment. We use browsers to access the commerce sites and specify the items we want to purchase. This is typically a client/server environment as illustrated in Exhibit 9. Note that this is a two-tier client/server system, where the server is responsible for data and Web page management. As we have mentioned previously, a current trend is to move toward a three-tier environment. Here the client is responsible for presentation, the database server is responsible for managing databases, and the middle tier (the E-commerce server) is

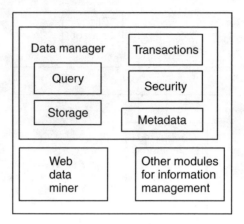

Exhibit 7.   Modules of an E-Commerce Server

responsible for managing business objects that will implement the business functions of E-commerce such as brokering and mediation. This is illustrated in Exhibit 10.

While client/server is the current trend, in a business-to-business E-commerce environment, many corporations may have to collaborate with each other, i.e., a federated environment may be needed. This is illustrated in Exhibit 11, where the E-commerce sites are connected through EFDP (E-federated distributed processor). The various E-commerce servers form a federation and cooperate with one another. They also have to maintain some kind of autonomy. The issues, problems, and solutions for federated architectures are still unknown. As we conduct more research on E-commerce and gain practical experience, some of the architectural issues will be clearer.

Next, let us look at interoperability aspects for E-commerce. OMG has a SIG (special interest group) focusing on services for E-commerce. The idea is for any E-commerce client to talk to any E-commerce server, i.e., heterogeneous applications and systems interoperate on the Web for carrying out E-commerce. Exhibit 12 illustrates an example where ORB (object request broker) services, such as mediation and brokering, help clients to communicate with servers.

E-Commerce Functions

There are three aspects to discussing E-commerce functions, as illustrated in Exhibit 13: (1) E-commerce client/server functions, which are essentially the information management functions; (2) business functions for commerce; and (3) distribution functions. We will look at all aspects.

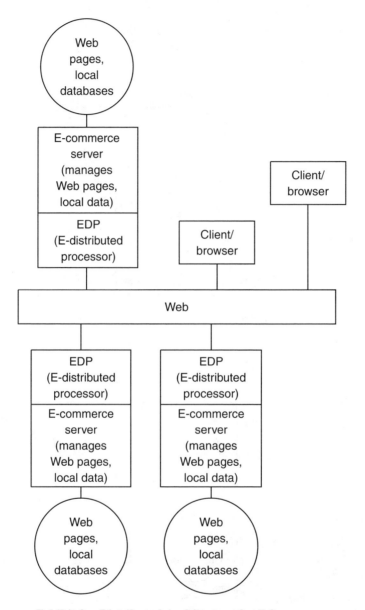

Exhibit 8. Distributed Architecture for E-Commerce

E-commerce server functions are illustrated in Exhibit 11. The modules of the E-commerce server may include modules for managing data and Web pages, mining customer information, security enforcement, as well as transaction management.

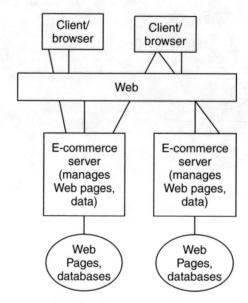

Exhibit 9. Client/Server Architecture for E-Commerce

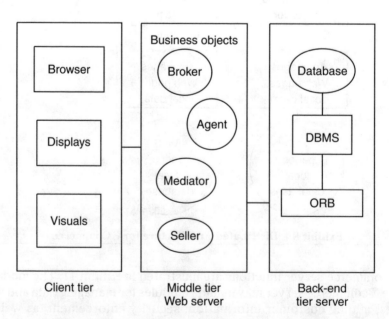

Exhibit 10. Three-Tier Computing for E-Commerce

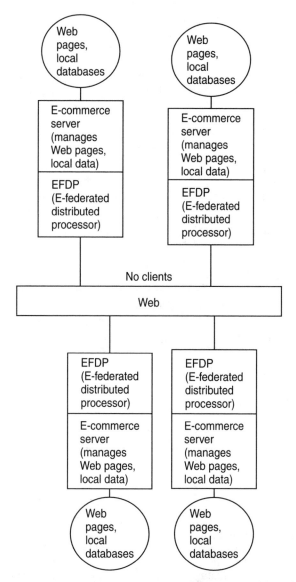

Exhibit 11. Client/Server Architecture for E-Commerce

E-commerce client functions may include presentation management, user interface, and caching data and hosting browsers. There could also be a middle tier, which may implement the business objects to carry out the business functions of E-commerce. These business functions may include brokering, mediation, negotiations, purchasing, sales, marketing, and others. The business functions are essentially the functions that are carried

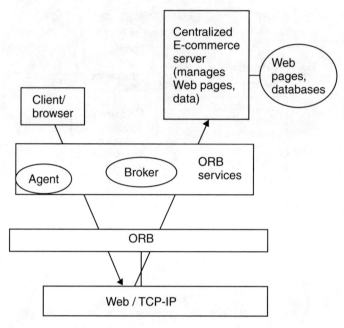

Exhibit 12.   ORB Services for E-Commerce

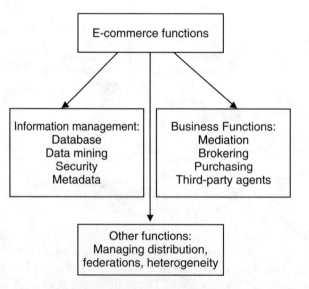

Exhibit 13.   E-Commerce Functions

out in business transactions. Additional issues for E-commerce include the legal, ethical, and political considerations to be discussed later in this chapter. The E-commerce server functions are impacted by the information management technologies for the Web. These technologies are discussed in detail in the next chapter. In addition to the data management functions and the business functions, the E-commerce functions also include those for managing distribution, heterogeneity, and federations.

Information Technologies for E-Commerce

Without the various data and information management technologies, E-commerce cannot be a reality. That is, the technologies discussed in this book are essentially technologies for E-commerce. E-commerce also includes nontechnological aspects such as policies, laws, and social and psychological impacts. We are now doing business in an entirely different way and therefore we need a paradigm shift. We cannot conduct successful E-commerce if we still want the traditional way of buying and selling products. We have to be more efficient and rely on the technologies much more to gain a competitive edge.

Exhibit 14 illustrates the overall picture of the technologies that may be applied to E-commerce. These include database systems, data mining, security, multimedia, interoperability, collaboration, knowledge management, and visualization. Details of how these technologies help E-commerce are given in [THUR00].

RELATIONSHIP TO WEB DATA MINING

This chapter has discussed the evolution of the Web and E-commerce. As we have stated, the Web is essential for Web mining. We will see that there are three aspects to Web mining: content mining (mining Web content and data), Web usage mining (mining Web logs), and Web structure mining (mining Web links). We need to mine the content, structure, and usage to carry out E-commerce. Later, we will discuss the relationship between E-commerce and Web mining in more detail.

Exhibit 15 illustrates the basic concept of Web mining. It shows how Web data miners mine various data sources on the Web. Web data miners may also mine Web logs and Web structure. As we have stated, more and more data will be on the Web, whether on intranets or public networks. We need to mine the data to extract useful patterns and trends. We also need to mine Web logs for business intelligence and building customer profiles. Web structure mining will give useful information to the user when browsing the Web. The rest of the book will discuss the other supporting technologies for Web mining as well as concepts and applications for Web mining.

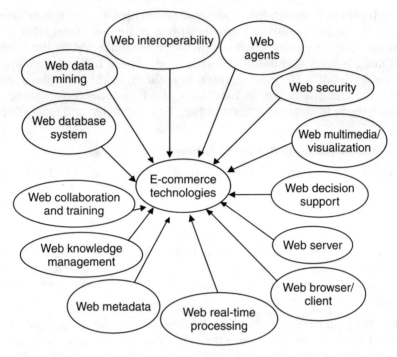

Exhibit 14.   Information Technologies for E-Commerce

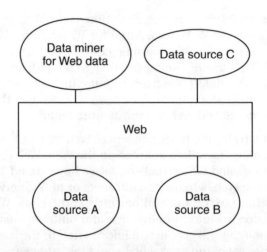

Exhibit 15.   Web, E-Commerce, and Data Mining

SUMMARY

This chapter has given a broad overview of the Web, E-commerce, and business intelligence. We started with a discussion of the evolution of the Web and then discussed the E-commerce process, which was followed by a discussion of the differences between E-business and E-commerce. Then we described models, architectures, and functions for E-commerce as well as information technologies for E-commerce.

As we have stated, the Web is a key technology for Web mining. Web mining has many applications in E-commerce, and E-commerce technologies such as Web database management, information management, and knowledge management support Web mining. One of the main purposes of discussing E-commerce is to show the similarities between E-commerce technologies and counter-terrorism technologies. In Chapter 27, we will revisit this topic. In particular, we will discuss models, architectures, and functions of counter-terrorism. That is, to combat terrorism, organizations essentially have to operate collaborative businesses. They have to be connected through private networks. We need to examine the use of federated architectures for interagency collaborations. We need to develop counter-terrorism services. Business objects for counter-terrorism have to be developed. We will see that to carry out all of the counter-terrorism tasks, Web mining and data mining will be critical in the same way Web mining and data mining are needed for E-commerce. Business intelligence will be central, both for E-commerce and counter-terrorism. We will elaborate on this in Chapter 27.

Chapter 3
Data Mining

INTRODUCTION

In this chapter, we continue with the discussion of the supporting technologies for Web mining. In particular, we discuss data mining, one of the key supporting technologies for Web mining. The increasing number of databases on the Web must be mined to extract useful information. Data mining is the process of posing various queries and extracting useful information, patterns, and trends (oftentimes previously unknown) from large quantities of data possibly stored in databases. Essentially, for many organizations, the goals of data mining include improving marketing capabilities, detecting abnormal patterns, and predicting the future based on past experiences and current trends. There is clearly a need for this technology. There are large amounts of current and historical data being stored. Therefore, as databases become larger, it becomes increasingly difficult to support decision making. In addition, the data could be from multiple sources and multiple domains. There is a clear need to analyze the data to support planning and other functions of an enterprise.

Various terms have been used to refer to data mining, as shown in Exhibit 1. These include knowledge/data/information/pattern discovery and knowledge/data/information/pattern extraction. Note that some define data mining as the process of extracting previously unknown information, while knowledge discovery is defined as the process of making sense out of the extracted information. In this book, we do not differentiate between data mining and knowledge discovery. It is difficult to determine whether a particular technique is a data mining technique. For example, some argue that statistical analysis techniques are data mining techniques. Others argue they are not, and that data mining techniques should uncover relationships that are not straightforward. For example, with data mining, a medical supplies company could increase sales by targeting certain physicians in its advertising who are likely to buy its products, or a credit bureau may limit its losses by selecting candidates who are not likely to default on their payments. Such real-world experiences have been reported in various papers (see, for example, [GRUP98]). In addition, data mining could also be used to detect abnormal behavior. For example, an intelligence agency could determine abnormal behavior of its employees using this technology.

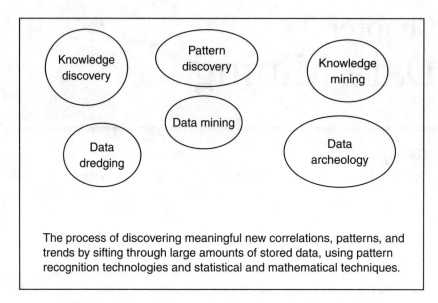

The process of discovering meaningful new correlations, patterns, and trends by sifting through large amounts of stored data, using pattern recognition technologies and statistical and mathematical techniques.

Exhibit 1.   Different Definitions of Data Mining

Some of the data mining techniques include those based on rough sets, inductive logic programming, machine learning, and neural networks, among others. The data mining problems include classification (finding rules to partition data into groups), association (finding rules to make associations between data), and sequencing (finding rules to order data). Essentially, one arrives at some hypothesis, which is the information extracted, from examples and patterns observed. These patterns are observed from posing a series of queries; each query may depend on the responses obtained to the previous queries posed.

There have been several developments in data mining. These include tools by corporations such as Lockheed Martin (for example, see [SIMO95]).

DATA MINING TECHNOLOGIES

Data mining is an integration of multiple technologies, as illustrated in Exhibit 2. These include database management, data warehousing, statistics, machine learning, decision support, visualization, and parallel computing.* We briefly discuss the role of each of these technologies. It should be noted, however, that while technologies such as statistical packages and machine learning algorithms have existed for many decades, the abil-

*We have distinguished between data management and database management and also between data, information, and knowledge. Our definitions are given in Appendix A as well as in [THUR97].

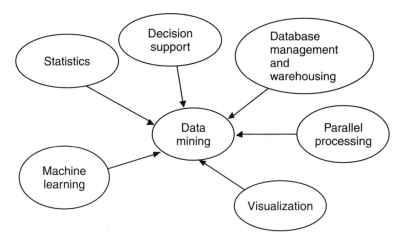

Exhibit 2. Data Mining Technologies

ity to manage and organize the data has played a major role in making data mining a reality.

Data mining research is being carried out in various disciplines. Database management researchers are taking advantage of the work on deductive and intelligent query processing for data mining. One of the areas of interest is to extend query processing techniques to facilitate data mining. Data warehousing is also another key data management technology for integrating various data sources and organizing the data so that it can be effectively mined.

Researchers in statistical analysis are integrating their techniques with machine learning techniques to develop more sophisticated statistical techniques for data mining. Various statistical analysis packages are now being marketed as data mining tools. There is some dispute over this. Nevertheless, statistics is a major area contributing to data mining.

Machine learning has been around for a while. The idea here is for the machine to learn various rules from the patterns observed and then apply these rules to solve the problems. While the principles used in machine learning and data mining are similar, with data mining one usually considers large quantities of data to mine. Therefore, integration of database management and machine learning techniques are needed for data mining.

Researchers from the computer visualization field are approaching data mining from another perspective. One of their areas of focus is to use visualization techniques to aid the data mining process. In other words, interactive data mining is a goal of the visualization community.

Decision support systems are a collection of tools and processes to help managers make decisions and guide them in management. For example, tools for scheduling meetings, organizing events, spreadsheets, view graph tools, and performance evaluation tools are examples of decision support systems. Decision support has theoretical underpinnings in decision theory.

Finally, researchers in the high performance computing area are also working on developing appropriate techniques so that the data mining algorithms are scalable. There is also interaction with hardware researchers so that appropriate hardware can be developed for high performance data mining.

It should be noted that several other technologies are beginning to have an impact on data mining, including collaboration, agents, and distributed object management. A discussion of all of these technologies is beyond the scope of this book. We have focused on some of the key technologies here. Furthermore, we emphasize that having good data is key to good mining.

CONCEPTS AND TECHNIQUES IN DATA MINING

There are a series of steps involved in data mining: getting the data organized for mining, determining the desired outcomes to mining, selecting tools for mining, carrying out the mining, pruning the results so that only the useful ones are considered further, taking actions from the mining, and evaluating the actions to determine benefits. These steps will be discussed in detail in this book. We briefly review some of the outcomes and techniques.

There are various types of data mining. By this we do not mean the actual techniques used to mine the data, but what the outcomes will be. Some of these outcomes are discussed in [AGRA93], and we will discuss them in detail. They have also been referred to as data mining tasks. We describe a few here.

In one outcome of data mining, called *classification,* records are grouped into some meaningful subclasses. For example, suppose an automobile sales company has some information that all the people on its list who live in city X own cars worth more than $20K. They can then assume that even those who are not on their list, but live in city X, can afford to own cars costing more than $20K. This way the company classifies the people living in city X.

A second outcome of data mining is sequence detection, i.e., by observing patterns in the data, sequences are determined. An example of sequence detection: after John goes to the bank, he generally goes to the grocery store.

A third outcome of mining is deviation analysis. For example, John went to the bank on Saturday, but he did not go to the grocery store after that.

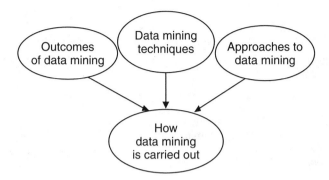

Exhibit 3. Aspects of Data Mining

Instead, he went to a football game. With this type of mining, anomalous instances and discrepancies are found.

A fourth outcome of data mining is data dependency analysis. Here, potentially interesting dependencies, relationships, or associations between the data items are detected. For example, if John, James, and William have a meeting, then Robert will also be at that meeting. It appears it is this type of mining that is of much interest.

As mentioned earlier, various techniques are used to obtain the outcomes of data mining. These techniques could be based on rough sets, fuzzy logic, inductive logic programming, or neural networks, or they could simply be some statistical technique. We discuss these techniques later. Furthermore, different approaches have also been proposed to carry out data mining, including top-down mining as well as bottom-up mining. Data mining outcomes, techniques, and approaches are illustrated in Exhibit 3 and will be discussed in detail later.

Numerous developments have been made in data mining over the past few years. Many of these focus on relational databases, i.e., the data is stored in relational databases and mined to extract useful information and patterns. We have several research prototypes and commercial products. The early research prototypes include those developed at IBM's Almaden Research Center and at Simon Fraser University. The prototypes and products employ various data mining techniques, including neural networks, rule-based reasoning, and statistical analysis. The various data mining tools in the form of prototypes and products will also be discussed in this book.

DIRECTIONS AND TRENDS IN DATA MINING

While several developments have been made, there are also many challenges. For example, due to the large volumes of data, how can the algorithms determine which technique to select and what type of data mining

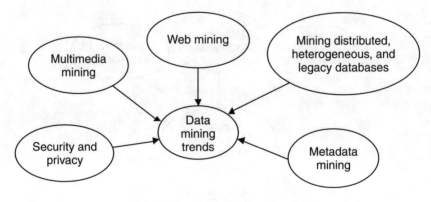

Exhibit 4.   Data Mining Trends

to do? Furthermore, the data may be incomplete or inaccurate. At times, there may be redundant information, and there may not be sufficient information. It is also desirable to have data mining tools that can switch to multiple techniques and support multiple outcomes. Some of the current trends in data mining include the following, as illustrated in Exhibit 4:

- Mining distributed, heterogeneous, and legacy databases
- Mining multimedia data
- Mining data on the World Wide Web
- Security and privacy issues in data mining
- Metadata aspects of mining

In many cases, the databases are distributed and heterogeneous in nature. Furthermore, much of the data is in legacy databases. Mining techniques are needed to handle these distributed, heterogeneous, and legacy databases.

Next, current data mining tools operate on structured data. However, there are still large quantities of unstructured data. Data in the multimedia databases are often semistructured or unstructured. Data mining tools have to be developed for multimedia databases.

The explosion of data and information on the World Wide Web necessitates the development of tools to manage and mine the data so that only useful information is extracted. Therefore, developing mining tools for the Web will be an important area. Privacy issues are becoming critical for data mining [THUR96a]. Users now have sophisticated tools to make inferences and deduce information to which they are not authorized to access. Therefore, while data mining tools help solve many problems in the real world, they could also invade the privacy of individuals. We will discuss privacy in more detail in Part III. National security efforts have resulted in an increased awareness of privacy. Throughout our previous book [THUR97], we repeatedly stressed the importance of metadata for data management. Metadata also plays a key role in data mining [THUR98].

In addition to the trends in these areas, there are also several challenges, including handling dynamic data, sparse data, incomplete and uncertain data, as well as determining which data mining algorithm to use and on what data to operate. In addition, mining multiple languages is also a challenge. Researchers are addressing these challenges.

RELATIONSHIP TO WEB MINING

Mining the data on the Web is one of the major challenges faced by the data management and mining community as well as those working on Web information management and machine learning. This is the main topic of this book. There is so much data and information on the Web that extracting information that is useful and relevant for the user is the real challenge here. Scanning through the Web becomes quite daunting, and users are soon overloaded with data. The question is, how do you convert this data into information, and subsequently into knowledge, so that the user only gets what he wants? Furthermore, what are the ways of extracting previously unknown information from the data on the Web? More importantly, how can mining the usage patterns on the Web improve the capability of an organization? In other words, electronic commerce is one of the major beneficiaries of Web mining. Exhibit 5 illustrates how data mining tools may be applied to Web databases.

SUMMARY

This chapter has provided an introduction to data mining. We first discussed various technologies for data mining, and then we provided an overview of the concepts in data mining. These concepts include the outcomes of mining, the techniques employed, and the approaches used. The directions and trends, such as mining heterogeneous data sources, mining multimedia data, mining Web data, metadata aspects, and privacy issues, were also addressed. Finally, we discussed the relationship to Web data mining.

In this chapter, we have given just enough information for the reader to understand some data mining topics related to the Web. For more details, we refer to [THUR98] and [THUR01]. Many important topics were covered in [THUR98] so that the reader has some idea of what data mining is all about. Chapter 3 discusses some of the core data mining technologies in more detail. For an in-depth understanding of the various topics in data mining, we also recommend the reader to the numerous papers and articles that have appeared on data mining and related areas. We reference many of these throughout this book. Some of the interesting discussions on data mining have appeared in [ACM96], [FAYY96], [KDD95]–[KDD98],

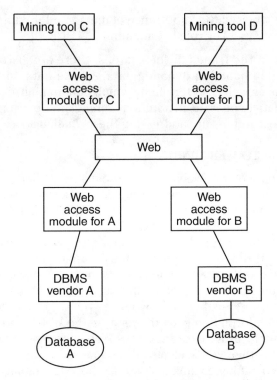

Exhibit 5.   Data Mining through the Web

[PAKD97], [PAKD98], [SIGM96], [TKDE93], and [TKDE96]. In addition, data mining papers have also appeared at various data management conferences (for example, see [DE98], [SIGM98], and [VLDB98]). Recently, a federal data mining symposium series has been established [AFCE97]. In addition to [THUR98], books in data mining include [ADRI96], [BERR97] and [HAN01].

Chapter 4
Core Data Mining Technologies

INTRODUCTION

Chapter 3 provided a brief introduction to data mining and discussed its relationship to Web data mining. This chapter provides a brief introduction to the core technologies for data mining. These core technologies contribute to data mining as well as to Web data mining. Toward the end of this chapter, we will discuss the relationship of the core technologies to Web data mining. As we have stated, we assume that eventually much of the data will be on the Web, either intranet or the Internet. Therefore, Web data mining will, in a way, encompass data mining.

The remaining chapters of Part I discuss some other supporting technologies for Web data mining, including Web database management, information retrieval, information management, and the semantic Web. That is, while the technologies discussed in this chapter contribute to data mining, data mining together with these other supporting technologies contribute to Web data mining. Exhibit 1 illustrates the relationship between the contents of the chapters in Part I to Web data mining.

One of the key technologies for data mining is database management and data warehousing. There are also several other core technologies for data mining. Notable among these technologies are statistical methods and machine learning. Statistical methods have resulted in various statistical packages to compute sums, averages, and distributions. These packages are now being integrated with databases for mining. Machine learning is all about learning rules and patterns from the data. One needs some amount of statistics to carry out machine learning. While statistical methods and machine learning are the two key components to data mining apart from data management, there are also some other technologies. These include visualization, parallel processing, and decision support. Visualization techniques help visualize the data so that data mining is facilitated. Parallel processing techniques help improve the performance of data mining. Decision support systems help prune the results to carry out management functions.

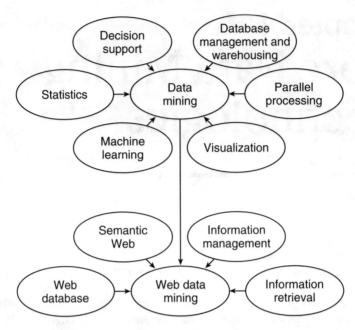

Exhibit 1.   Web Data Mining Technologies

DATA MANAGEMENT AND DATA WAREHOUSING

As we have stressed repeatedly in [THUR98], good data management is critical for data mining. In the same way, good Web data management is critical for Web data mining. Therefore, we need Web database systems to effectively manage data on the Web so that this data can be mined. These Web database systems could be data warehousing systems or the database management systems discussed in Appendix B. We will discuss Web database management in more detail in Chapter 5. In this section, we will focus on data management and data warehousing for data mining. More details on data management and data warehousing are given in Appendix B.

We focus on architecture, data modeling, database design, administration, and data warehousing issues for data mining. For example, should a data mining tool* be tightly integrated with a database system or should it be loosely integrated? What is the impact of data modeling on data mining? Can one design a database to facilitate mining? What is the impact on administration functions? Essentially, we discuss the impact of data mining on the various database functions discussed in Appendix B. These include query processing, transaction management, storage management, metadata management, data quality and integrity, security, and fault tolerance.

---

*We will also call such data mining tools data miners.

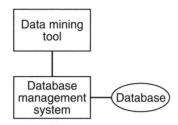

Exhibit 2. Loose Integration between DBMS and Data Miner

Data mining techniques have been around for a while. That is, various statistical reasoning techniques, neural network-based techniques, and various other artificial intelligence techniques have been around for decades. So why, then, is data mining becoming so popular now? The main reason is that we now have the data to mine. Data is now being collected, organized, and structured, and database systems have played a major role in this. That is, with database systems we can now represent the data, store and retrieve the data, and enforce features such as integrity and security.

Now that we have the data stored in databases, how can we mine the data? One approach is to augment a database management system (DBMS) with a mining tool, as illustrated in Exhibit 2. One can buy a commercial DBMS and a commercial mining tool that has interfaces built to the DBMS, and apply the tool to the data managed by the DBMS. This way the tool does not have to be burdened with getting the data to be mined. While this approach has advantages and promotes open architectures, there are some drawbacks. There could be some performance problems when you use a general purpose DBMS for mining.

The other approach is a tight integration with mining tools, as shown in Exhibit 3. The database engine has mining tools incorporated within it. One can call such a DBMS a mining DBMS. This way the various DBMS functions, such as query processing and storage management, are impacted by the mining techniques. For example, the optimization algorithms can be impacted by the mining techniques. There is much research to integrate mining into the DBMS engine (for example, see [TSUR98]). We need extensions for mining the data on the Web.

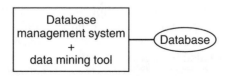

Exhibit 3. Tight Integration between DBMS and Data Miner

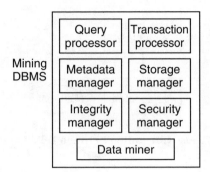

Exhibit 4.   Functions of a Mining DBMS

Mining DBMS also would mean eliminating unnecessary functions of a DBMS and focusing on key features. Data mining is not usually conducted on transactional data, but on decision support data. This data may not be updated often by transactions. So, functions such as transaction management could be removed from a mining DBMS, and one could focus on additional features such as providing data integrity and quality. Note that there are cases where transactional data has to be mined, i.e., mining credit card transactions.

In general, in the case of a mining DBMS, all functions may be impacted by mining. These include query processing, storage manager, transaction manager, metadata manager, security and integrity manager. Therefore, we have added a data miner as part of a mining DBMS, as illustrated in Exhibit 4.

Next, let us focus on data modeling. The type of model used may have some impact on mining. In Appendix B, we discuss object models and object-relational data models for data representation. If such object databases are to be mined, we need to develop techniques for mining object databases and object-relational databases. Exhibit 5 illustrates an example of mining an object database where the relationships between the objects are extracted first and stored in a relational database, and then the mining tools are applied to the relational database.

Database design plays a major role in mining. For example, in the case of data warehousing, various approaches have been proposed to model and subsequently design the warehouse. These include multidimensional data models and online analytical processing models. Various schemas such as the star schema have been proposed for data warehousing. As mentioned, organizing the data effectively is critical for mining. Therefore, such models and schemas are also important for mining.

Database administration is also impacted by mining. If one is to integrate mining with a DBMS, the following questions prevail:

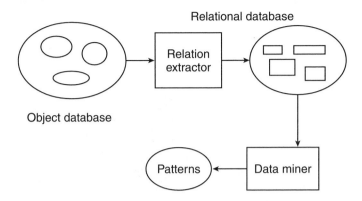

Exhibit 5.   Mining Object Databases

- How often should the data in the databases be mined?
- Can mining be used to analyze the audit data?
- If the data is updated frequently, then how does it impact mining?

These are interesting questions, and we expect answers as more information is obtained about integrating mining with the DBMS functions.

Let us now examine the impact of data mining on the functions of a DBMS, especially in the case of tight integration between the DBMS and the data miner. In this case, there is an impact on the various database system functions. For example, consider query processing. There are efforts to examine query languages such as SQL to determine if extensions are needed to support mining (for example, see [ACM96]). If there are additional constructs and queries that are complex, then the query optimizer has to be adapted to handle such cases. Closely related to query optimization is efficient storage structures, indexes, and access methods. Special mechanisms may be needed to support data mining in the query process.

In the case of transaction management, as mentioned earlier, mining may have little impact, because mining is usually done on decision support data and not on transactional data. However, there are cases where transactional data is analyzed for anomalies such as credit card and telephone card anomalies. Some of us have been notified by our credit card or telephone companies about abnormal patterns in usage. This is usually done by analyzing the transactional data. Such data could also be mined.

In the case of metadata, one could mine metadata to extract useful information in cases where the data cannot be analyzed. This may be the situation for unstructured data whose metadata may be structured. On the other hand, metadata could be a very useful resource for a data miner. Metadata could give additional information to help with the mining process.

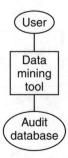

Exhibit 6.   Mining an Audit Database

Security, integrity, data quality, and fault tolerance are impacted by data mining. Privacy issues are discussed in Chapter 25. While data mining could be a threat to privacy, data mining can be used to detect intrusions as well as to analyze audit data. Furthermore, data mining may also help to handle terrorism and identity theft. In the case of auditing, the data to be mined is the large quantity of audit data. One may apply data mining tools to detect abnormal patterns. For example, suppose an employee makes an excessive number of trips to a particular country and this fact is known by posing some queries. The next query to pose is whether the employee has associations with certain people from that country. If the answer is positive, then the employee's behavior is flagged. The use of data mining for analyzing audit databases is illustrated in Exhibit 6. Note that we will revisit this topic in Part III when we discuss counter-terrorism, security, and privacy.

Note that data mining has many applications in intrusion detection and in analyzing threat databases. One can use data mining to detect patterns of intrusions and threats. This is an emerging area called *information assurance.* Not only is it important to have quality data, it is also important to recover from faults, malicious or otherwise, and to protect the data from threats or intrusions. While research in this area is just beginning, we can expect to see much progress. Part III addresses this topic in more detail.

In the case of data quality and integrity, one could apply mining techniques to detect bad data and improve the quality of the data. Mining can also be used to analyze safety data for air traffic control systems, nuclear systems, and weapons systems. This is illustrated in Exhibit 7.

Next, let us examine data warehousing. A data warehouse assembles the data from heterogeneous databases so that users query only a single point. The responses that a user gets to a query depend on the contents of the data warehouse. The data warehouse in general does not attempt to extract information from the data in the warehouse. While data warehousing formats and organizes the data to support management functions, data

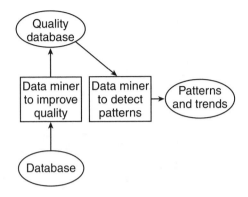

Exhibit 7. Data Quality and Data Mining

mining attempts to extract useful information and predicts trends from the data. Exhibit 8 illustrates a data warehouse. Exhibit 9 illustrates the relationship between data warehousing and data mining. Note that having a warehouse is not necessary to do mining, as data mining can be applied to databases also. However, a warehouse structures the data in a way that facilitates mining, so in many cases it is highly desirable to have a data warehouse to carry out mining. The relationship between warehousing, mining, and database systems is illustrated in Exhibit 10.

When giving various tutorials on data warehousing and mining, we are often asked the question: where does warehousing end and mining begin? For example, is there a clear difference between warehousing and mining? The answer, we think, is subjective. There are certain questions that warehouses can answer. Furthermore, warehouses have built-in decision sup-

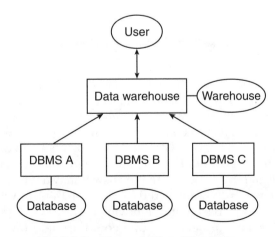

Exhibit 8. Example Data Warehouse

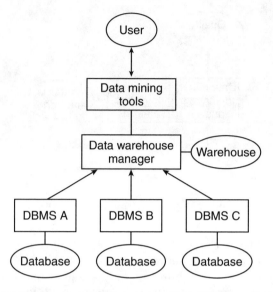

Exhibit 9.   Data Mining versus Data Warehousing

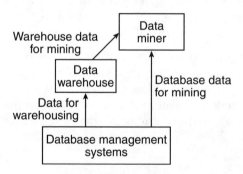

Exhibit 10.   Database Systems, Data Warehousing, and Data Mining

port capabilities. Some warehouses carry out predictions and trends. In this case, warehouses carry out some of the data mining functions. In general, we believe that in the case of a warehouse, the answer is in the database. The warehouse has to come up with query optimization and access techniques to get the answer. For example, consider the following question: "How many red cars did physicians buy in 1990 in New York?". The answer is in the database. However, the answer may not be in the database for a question such as "how many red cars do you think physicians will buy in 2005 in New York?". Based on the buying patterns of physicians in New York and their salary projections, one could predict the answer to this question. In the case of video data, the question is, can you find the number

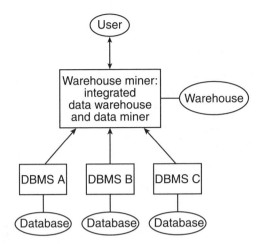

Exhibit 11.   Integrated Data Warehousing and Data Mining

of times the President of the United States appears with the Prime Minister of England?

Essentially, a warehouse organizes the data effectively so the data can be mined. The question then is, do you absolutely have to have a warehouse to mine the data? The answer we give is that it is very good to have a warehouse, but it does not mean we must have a warehouse to mine. A good DBMS that manages a database effectively could also be used. Also, with a warehouse one often does not have transactional data. Furthermore, the data may not be current, therefore the results obtained from mining may not be current. If one needs up-to-date information, then one could mine the database managed by a DBMS that also has transaction processing features. Mining data that keeps changing often is a challenge. Typically, mining has been used for decision support data. Therefore, there are several issues that need further investigation before we can carry out what we call real-time data mining. For now at least, we believe that having a good data warehouse is critical to do good mining for decision support functions. Note that one could also have an integrated tool that carries out both data warehousing and data mining functions. We call such a tool a data warehouse miner (Exhibit 11). We will revisit data warehousing for the Web in Chapter 5 when we discuss Web database management. Mining Web data warehouses as well as mining Web databases will be discussed in Chapter 11.

STATISTICAL REASONING

Statistical reasoning techniques and methods have been around for several decades. They were the sole means of analyzing data in the past.

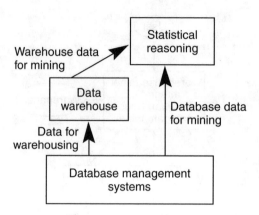

Exhibit 12.   Statistical Packages Operating on Databases

Numerous packages are now available to compute averages, sums, and various distributions for several applications. For example, a census bureau uses statistical analysis and methods to analyze the population in a country. More recently, statistical reasoning techniques are playing a major role in data mining. Some argue that the various statistical packages that have been around for a while are now being marketed as data mining products. For us this is not an issue, as statistical reasoning plays just one role. For data mining, you need the support of various other technologies to organize and structure the data. Many of the older statistical packages did not work with large relational databases. However, the packages that are being marketed today are integrated with various databases, as illustrated in Exhibit 12.

As mentioned in [CARB98], the statistical techniques that are being employed for data mining include those based on linear models as well as those based on nonlinear models. Linear regression techniques are employed for prediction. Prediction is a data mining task that predicts variables from available data. For example, one could predict the salary of an employee in five years based on his current performance, his education, and market trends. Linear discriminate analysis techniques are used for classification. Classification is another data mining task where an object is placed in a group based on some classifier. For example, John is placed in a class with others who earn more than 100K. Nonlinear techniques are used to estimate values of new variables based on the data already available and characterized. Estimation is also a data mining task where the various values are estimated based on data that is available. Sampling is another statistical technique used for data analysis. For example, in many cases it will be impossible to analyze all of the data. Therefore, one draws samples such as every *nth* row in a relation, forms a sample, and analyzes the sample. There has been some criticism of using samples for data mining.

In general, one cannot categorically state that linear models are used for classification while nonlinear models are used for estimation. There is no well-defined theory in this area. The point is that statistics play a major role in data analysis. Even in machine learning, statistics play a key role. Unless one understands statistics and some operations research, it will be difficult to appreciate machine learning. Because of this, we cannot study data mining without a good knowledge of statistics.

This section has discussed statistical reasoning only very briefly. We refer to the numerous texts on this subject should the reader require in-depth knowledge. A useful book is one by DeGroot [DEGR86]. In Mitchell's book on machine learning [MITC97], there is a good introduction to the statistical terms and techniques needed for data mining. These include random variables, probability distribution, standard distribution, and variance. We need to determine how statistical reasoning may be applied for multimedia databases.

MACHINE LEARNING

Machine learning is all about learning rules from the data. Essentially, machine learning techniques are the ones that are used for data mining. So the question is, while machine learning has been around for a while, what is new about its connection to data mining? Again, the answer is in the data. It is only recently that the various machine learning techniques are being applied to data in databases. These machine learning techniques are becoming data mining techniques.

Machine learning is all about making computers learn from experience. As Mitchell describes in his excellent text on machine learning [MITC97], machine learning is about learning from past experiences with respect to some performance measure. For example, in computer games applications, machine learning could be learning to play a game of chess from past experiences, which could be games that the machine plays against itself with respect to some performance measure such as winning a certain number of games.

Various techniques have been developed on machine learning. These include concept learning where one learns concepts from several training examples, neural networks, genetic algorithms, decision trees, and inductive logic programming. Each technique is essentially about learning from experience with respect to some performance measure. We discuss the various techniques in more detail later in this chapter. Several theoretical studies have also been conducted on machine learning. These studies attempt to determine the complexity of machine learning techniques [MITC97].

Machine learning researchers have grouped some of the techniques into three categories: (1) active learning, which deals with interaction and ask-

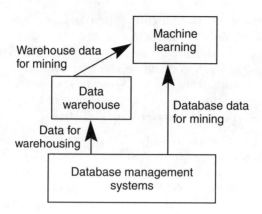

Exhibit 13.   Machine Learning and Data Mining

ing questions during learning; (2) learning from prior knowledge; and (3) learning incrementally. There is some overlap between the three methods. Various issues and challenges on machine learning and its relationship to data mining were addressed in a recent workshop on machine learning [DARP98].* There is still much research to be done in this area, especially on integrating machine learning with various data management techniques, as shown in Exhibit 13. Such research will significantly improve the whole area of data mining. Some interesting machine learning algorithms are given in [QUIN93].

VISUALIZATION

Visualization technologies graphically display the data in the databases. Much research has been conducted on visualization, and the field has advanced a great deal, especially with the advent of multimedia computing. For example, the data in the databases could be rows and rows of numerical values. Visualization tools take the data and plot it in some form of a graph. The visualization models could be two-dimensional, four-dimensional, or even higher. Recently, several visualization tools have been developed to integrate with databases, and workshops are devoted to this topic [VIS95]. An example illustration of integration of a visualization package with a database system is shown in Exhibit 14.

More recently, there has been much discussion on using visualization for data mining. There has also been some discussion on using data mining to help the visualization process. However, when considering visualization as a supporting technology, it is the former approach that is getting considerable attention (for example, see [GRIN95]). As data mining techniques mature, it will be important to integrate them with visualization tech-

* This effort has now evolved into DARPA's Evidence Extraction and Link Detection program.

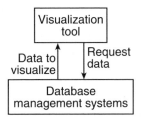

Exhibit 14. Database and Visualization

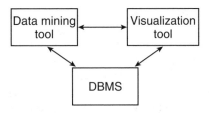

Exhibit 15. Interactive Data Mining

niques. Exhibit 15 illustrates interactive data mining. Here, the database management system, visualization tool, and machine learning tool all interact with each other for data mining.

Let us reexamine some of the issues on integrating data mining with visualization. There are four possible approaches here:

1. Using visualization techniques to present the results that are obtained from mining the data in the databases. These results may be in the form of clusters, or they could specify correlations between the data in the databases.
2. Applying data mining techniques to visualization. The assumption here is that it is easier to apply data mining tools to data in the visual form. Therefore, rather than applying the data mining tools to large and complex databases, one captures some of the essential semantics visually, and then applies the data mining tools.
3. Using visualization techniques to complement the data mining techniques. For example, one may use data mining techniques to obtain correlations between data or detect patterns. However, visualization techniques may still be needed to obtain a better understanding of the data in the database.
4. Using visualization techniques to steer the mining process.

In summary, visualization tools help interactive data mining, as was illustrated in Exhibit 15. As illustrated in this exhibit, visualization tools can be used to visually display the responses from the database system directly so that the visual displays can be used by the data mining tool. On the other hand, the visualization tool can be used to visualize the results of the data mining tool directly. There is little work on integrating data mining and visualization tools. Some preliminary ideas were presented at the 1995 IEEE Databases and Visualization Workshop (for example, see, [VIS95]). However, more progress has been reported in [VIS97]. There is still much work to be done on this topic.

PARALLEL PROCESSING

Parallel processing is a subject that has been around for a while. The area has developed significantly from single processor systems to multiprocessor systems. Multiprocessor systems could be distributed systems or they could be centralized systems with shared memory multiprocessors or with shared-nothing multiprocessors. There has been much work on using parallel architectures for database processing (for example, see [IEEE89]). While considerable work was carried out, these systems did not take off commercially until the development of data warehousing. Many of the data warehouses employ parallel processors to speed up query processing.

In a parallel database system, the various operations and functions are executed in parallel. While research on parallel database systems began in the 1970s, it is only recently that we are seeing these systems being used for commercial applications. This is partly due to the explosion of data warehousing and data mining technologies where performance of query algorithms is critical.

Let us consider a query operation that involves a join operation between two object-relations. If these object-relations are to be sorted first on some attribute before the join, then the sorting can be done in parallel. We can take it a step further and execute a single join operation with multiple processors. Note that multiple tuples are involved in a join operation from both relations. Join operations between the tuples may be executed in parallel.

Many of the commercial database system vendors are now marketing parallel database management technology. This is an area we can expect to grow significantly over the next decade. One of the major challenges here is the scalability of various algorithms for functions such as data warehousing and data mining. We also need to determine how these algorithms may handle multimedia data.

Recently, parallel processing techniques are being examined for data mining. Many of the data mining techniques are computationally intensive. Appropriate hardware and software are needed to scale the data mining techniques. Database vendors are using parallel processing machines to carry out data mining. The data mining algorithms are parallelized using various parallel processing techniques. This is illustrated in Exhibit 16.

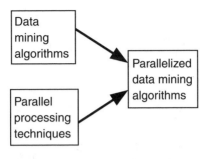

Exhibit 16.   Parallel Data Mining

Vendors of workstations are also interested in developing appropriate machines to facilitate data mining. This is an area of active research and development, and corporations such as Silicon Graphics and Thinking Machines have developed such products. We can expect to see much progress in this area during the next few years.

DECISION SUPPORT

While data mining deals with discovering patterns from the data, machine learning deals with learning from experiences to do predictions as well as analysis. Decision support systems are tools that managers use to make effective decisions. They are based on decision theory. One can consider data mining tools as special kinds of decision support tools, as are tools based on machine learning, and tools for extracting data from data warehouses. Decision support tools belong to a broad category (for example, see [DECI]).

In general, decision support tools could also be tools that remove unnecessary and irrelevant results obtained from data mining. These pruning tools could also be spreadsheets, expert systems, hypertext systems, Web information management systems, and any other system that helps analysts and managers to effectively manage large quantities of data and information. More recently, an emerging area called knowledge management deals with effectively managing an organization's data, information, and knowledge (see [MORE98a] and [MORE01]). This includes storing the information, managing it, as well as developing tools to extract useful information. Some knowledge management tools also help in decision support.

In summary, we believe that decision support is a technology that overlaps with data mining, data warehousing, knowledge management, machine learning, statistics, and other technologies that help to manage an organization's knowledge and data. We illustrate this in Exhibit 17. Exhibit 18 illustrates the relationship between data warehousing, database management, mining, and decision support.

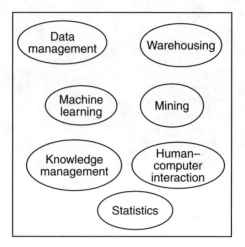

Exhibit 17.   Decision Support Technologies

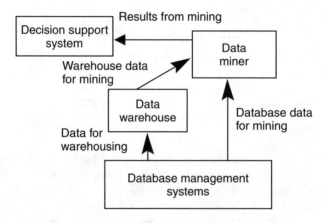

Exhibit 18.   Decision Support and Data Mining

ARCHITECTURAL SUPPORT FOR DATA MINING

Overview

As in data management, data mining also needs architectural support. This section discusses various aspects of architectural support for data mining. Note that architecture will be discussed throughout this book. In particular, we will discuss federated architectures and the notion of federated data mining for counter-terrorism.

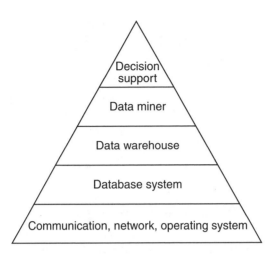

Exhibit 19. Pyramid for Data Mining

Technology Integration Architecture

One needs architectural support for integrating the technologies discussed earlier in this chapter. Exhibit 19 shows a pyramid-like structure which illustrates how the various technologies fit with one another. As shown in Exhibit 19, there are communications and system-level support at the lowest level. Then there is middleware support, followed by database management and data warehousing. Then there is the various data mining technologies. Finally, there is the decision support systems that take the results of data mining and help users such as managers, analysts, and programmers to effectively make decisions.

When one builds systems, the various technologies involved may not fit the pyramid exactly as we have shown. For example, we could skip the warehousing stage and go straight to mining. One of the key issues here is the interfaces between the various systems. At present, we do not have any well-defined standard interfaces except some of the standards and interface definition languages emerging from various groups such as the Object Management Group. However, as these technologies mature, one can expect standards to be developed for the interfaces.

The different data mining technologies have to work together. For example, one possibility is shown in Exhibit 20, where multiple databases are integrated through some middleware and subsequently form a data warehouse, which is then mined. The data mining component is also integrated into this setting so that the databases are mined directly. Some of these issues will be discussed in the section on system architecture.

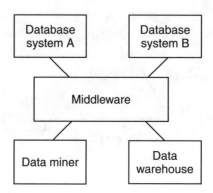

Exhibit 20.   Revisiting the Data Mining Architecture

Exhibit 21 illustrates a three-dimensional view of data mining technologies. Central to this is the technology for integration. This is the middleware technology such as distributed object management and Web technology for integration and access through the Web. On one plane, we have all the basic data technologies such as multimedia, relational and object databases, and distributed, heterogeneous, and legacy databases. On another plane, we have the technologies that do data mining. We have included warehousing as well as machine learning such as inductive logic programming and statistical reasoning here. The third plane has technologies such as parallel processing, visualization, metadata management, and secure access, which are important to carry out data mining.

Functional Architecture

The steps to data mining were discussed in Chapter 2 and will be elaborated in Part II. These steps also describe the functional components of data mining. These functional components are the subject of this section. A data miner could be part of a DBMS. Such a DBMS is a mining DBMS. This is illustrated in Exhibit 22 (note that a slight variation of a mining DBMS was illustrated in Exhibit 4). In this approach, we consider data mining as an extension to the query processor. That is, the query processor modules such as the query optimizer could be extended to handle data mining. Note that in this diagram, we have omitted the transaction manager, as data mining is used mostly for online analytical processing.

The question is, what are the components of the data miner? As illustrated in Exhibit 23, a data miner could have the following components: a learning-from-experience component that uses various training sets and learns various strategies, a data-analyzer component that analyzes the data based on what it has learned, and a results-producing component that does classification, clustering, and other tasks such as associations. There is interaction between all three components. For example, the component

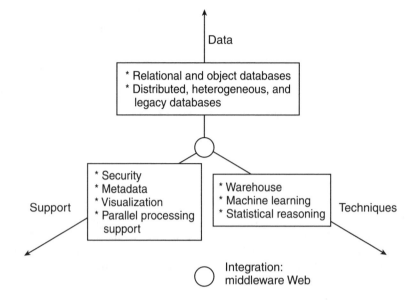

Exhibit 21. Three-Dimensional View

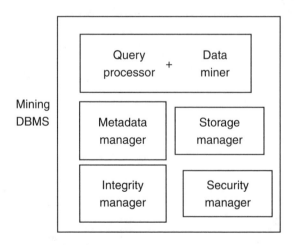

Exhibit 22. Data Mining as Part of Query Processor

that produces results then feeds the results back to the training component to see if this component has to be adapted. The training component feeds information to the data-analyzer component. The data-analyzer component feeds information to the results-producing component.

Note that we have not included components such as data preprocessor and results pruner into the data mining modules. These components are also needed to complete the entire process. The data preprocessor for-

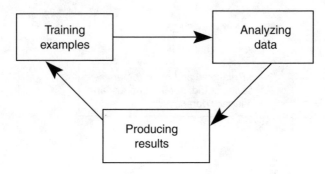

Exhibit 23. Data Mining Functions

mats the data. In a way, the data warehouse may do this function. The results-pruning component may extract only the useful information. This could be carried out by a decision support system. All of these steps will be integrated into the data mining process discussed later.

System Architecture

In Part I, we discussed various architectures for multimedia database management and interoperability. We examine these architectures and discuss the impact of mining.

Consider the architecture of Exhibit 24. In this example, the data miner could be used as a server, the database management system could be another server, while the data warehouse could be a third server. The client issues requests to the database system, warehouse, and the miner as illustrated in this exhibit.

One could also use an ORB for data mining. In this case, the data miner is encapsulated as an object. The database system and warehouse are also

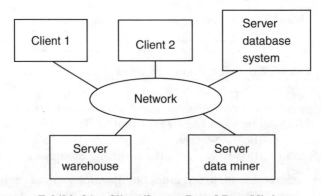

Exhibit 24. Client/Server-Based Data Mining

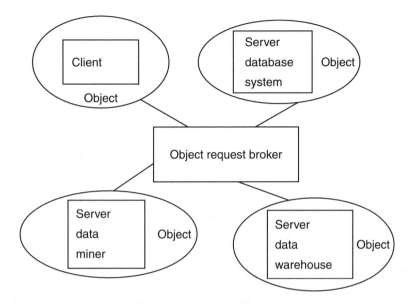

Exhibit 25. Data Mining through ORB

objects. This is illustrated in Exhibit 25. The challenge here is to define IDLs (Interface Description Language) for the various objects.

Note that client/server technology does not develop algorithms for data management, warehousing, or mining. This means that the algorithms are still needed for these areas. What client/server technology and, in particular, distributed object management technology such as CORBA do for you is facilitate interoperation between the different components. For example, the data miner, the database system, and the warehouse communicate with each other and with the clients through the ORB.

Note that the three-tier architecture is becoming very popular (see the discussion in [THUR97]). In this architecture, a thin client does minimum processing, the server does the database management functions, and the middle tier carries out various business processing functions. In the case of data mining, one could also utilize a three-tier architecture where the data miner is placed in the middle tier, as illustrated in Exhibit 26. The data miner could be developed as a collection of components. These components could be based on object technology. By developing data mining modules as a collection of components, one could develop generic tools and then customize them for specialized applications.

Another advantage of developing a data mining system as a collection of components is that one could purchase components from different vendors and assemble them together to form a system. Furthermore, compo-

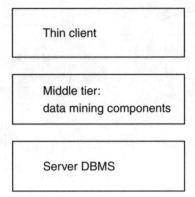

Exhibit 26.   Three-Tier Architecture for Data Miner

nents can be reused. Consider that the data source integrator, the data miner, the results pruner, and the report generator can be encapsulated as objects, and one could use ORBs to integrate these different objects. As a result, one can use a plug-and-play approach to developing data mining tools. Exhibit 27 illustrates the encapsulation of the various data mining modules as objects. One could also decompose the data miner into multiple modules and encapsulate these modules as objects. For example, consider the modules of the data miner illustrated in Exhibit 27. These modules are part of the data miner module and could themselves be encapsulated as objects and integrated through an ORB.

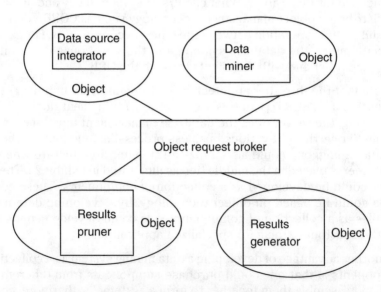

Exhibit 27.   Encapsulating Data Mining Modules as Objects

RELATIONSHIP TO WEB DATA MINING

All of the technologies that we are discussing in Part I are supporting technologies for Web data mining. Exhibit 1 illustrates the relationship. That is, while machine learning, database management, visualization, and decision support are core supporting technologies for data mining, data mining and Web database management are supporting technologies for Web data mining. This also means that machine learning, visualization, and statistical reasoning are supporting technologies for Web data mining.*

Essentially, Web data mining is about data mining on the Web. In addition, Web data mining also includes areas that are specific to the Web: mining usage and access patterns and customer profiles for targeted marketing on the Web. Machine learning and statistical reasoning techniques can be used to form patterns and trends for databases on the Web as well as to obtain usage patterns and trends. Visualization techniques will help one to understand the Web data better and, as a result, apply more effective data mining techniques. In addition, the various data mining techniques can be used to detect and find out about the various resources on the Web. That is, one of the challenges in Web searching is to determine where to go for the information. Various search engines could use machine learning and statistical reasoning techniques to determine the location of the resources and databases on the Web.

Exhibit 28 illustrates the application of supporting technologies for Web data mining. We have only scratched the surface here. There is still a lot of research to be done. That is, can we apply standard machine learning techniques or do we develop techniques specifically for Web data mining? We hope that as we make progress we can get better answers and solutions. One thing to note is that in the future we can expect much of the data about individuals as well as newspapers, events, and other entities to be on the Web. This Web may be based on public networks or private networks. Therefore, data mining alone may not suffice. That is, while data mining will be needed, we may need to go beyond and develop data mining techniques that will work for the Web.

SUMMARY

In this chapter, we have discussed some of the core data mining technologies, including data warehousing, machine learning, statistical reasoning, visualization, and decision support. We also discussed architectures for data mining.

These core data mining technologies are also needed for Web data mining. Note that eventually not only will much of the data be computerized, it will also be available on the Web. Even within organizations and agen-

---

* This is similar to saying that the subpart of a part is a subpart.

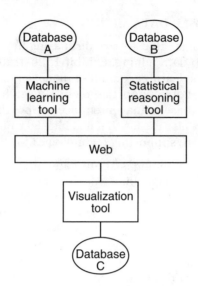

Exhibit 28.   Core Data Mining Technologies for Web Mining

cies there are internal Webs, also called intranets, that manage corporate data. Therefore, we need the various data mining techniques to work on Web databases. The next chapter will provide an overview of Web database management.

Chapter 5
Web Database Management

INTRODUCTION

As mentioned in Chapter 1, Part I describes various key supporting technologies for Web mining. We provided an overview of data mining in Chapter 3 and some more details on core data mining technologies in Chapter 4. There are several other supporting technologies for Web data mining. This chapter describes another major supporting technology for Web mining: Web data management. That is, one has to manage the databases on the Web so that these databases can be mined effectively. In other words, data mining and Web data management are two of the core supporting technologies for Web data mining.

Loosely related to Web data management are digital libraries and Web database management. Digital libraries are essentially digitized information distributed across several sites. The goal is for users to access this information in a transparent manner. The information could contain multimedia data such as voice, text, video, and images. The information could also be stored in structured databases such as relational and object-oriented databases. Sometimes, the terms digital libraries and *Web databases* have been used interchangeably.*

The explosion of the number of users on the Web and the increasing number of Web servers worldwide are rapidly advancing Web data management. Users can access various information sources on the Web. There is no single technology for Web data management. It is a combination of many technologies including heterogeneous database management, query management, intelligent agents and mediators, and data mining. For example, the heterogeneous information sources have to be integrated so that users access the servers in a transparent and timely manner. Security and privacy is becoming a major concern for Web data management. So are other issues such as copyright protection and ownership of the data. Policies and procedures have to be set up to address these issues.

---

* These have also been called Internet databases.

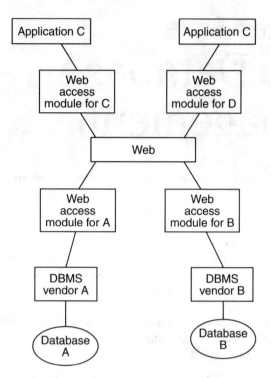

Exhibit 1. Database Access through the Web

Exhibit 1 illustrates recent developments in data management technology for the Web. Database management system vendors are now building interfaces to the Web. Query languages such as SQL are embedded into Web access languages. In the example of Exhibit 1, database management system (DBMS) vendors A and B make their data available to applications C and D. DBMS vendors are also developing interfaces to the Java programming environment (see [THUR00]). Essentially, what this all means is that heterogeneous databases are integrated through the Web.

WEB DATABASES

This section discusses the core concepts in Web data management. As stated earlier, many of the developments for the Web have been influenced by the management of databases on the Web. One of our earlier books was devoted mainly to Web data management and its application to E-commerce [THUR00]. This section summarizes some of the discussions.

Data Representation and Modeling

A major challenge for Web data management researchers and practitioners is coming up with an appropriate data representation scheme. The question is, is there a need for a standard data model for digital libraries and Web database access? Is it at all possible to develop such a standard? If so, what are the relationships between the standard model and the individual models used by the databases on the Web?

Back in 1996 when we gave presentations at various conferences on data representation for Web databases (e.g., Object Management Group's Internet SIG meeting in June 1996), many felt that it would be impossible to come up with a standard notation. Some even felt that because relational representation was popular, one might need some form of relational notation and SQL-like language to access various data sources on the Web. There were also discussions on variations of an object model for the Web. Representation schemes such as UML (for example, see [FOWL97]) were emerging, and it was thought that perhaps such schemes would be popular for Web data modeling. At that time, various data representation schemes such as SGML (Standard Generalized Markup Language), HTML (Hypertext Markup Language), and ODA (Office Document Architecture) were being examined (for example, see [ACM96]). The question at that time was, are they sufficient or is another representation scheme needed?

The significant development for Web data modeling came in the latter part of 1996 when the World Wide Web Consortium (W3C) was formed. This group felt that Web data modeling was an important area and began addressing the data modeling aspects. Then sometime around 1997, interest in XML (Extensible Markup Language) began. This was an effort of the W3C. XML is not a data model. It is a metalanguage for representing documents. The idea is that if documents are represented using XML, then these documents can be uniformly represented and therefore exchanged on the Web. Since 1998, one of the significant developments for the Web is XML. There are now numerous groups working on XML and proposing extensions to XML for different applications (see [THUR02]). Exhibit 2 illustrates the evolution of data model discussions for Web databases.

Web Database Management Functions

Database management functions for the Web include query processing, metadata management, security, and integrity. In [THUR96b], we have examined various database management system functions and discussed the impact of Web database access on these functions. Some of the issues are discussed here. Exhibit 3 illustrates the functions. Querying and browsing are two of the key functions. First of all, an appropriate query language is needed. Because SQL is a popular language, appropriate extensions to SQL may be desired. XML-QL [SIGM01], is moving in this direction. Query processing involves developing a cost model. Are there special cost models for Web database management? With respect to browsing operation, the query processing techniques have to be integrated with techniques for

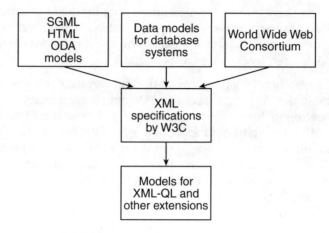

Exhibit 2. Data Modeling for the Web

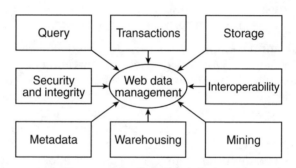

Exhibit 3. Web Database Functions

following links. That is, hypermedia technology has to be integrated with database management technology.

Updating digital libraries or Web databases could mean different things. One could create a new Web site, place servers at that site, and update the data managed by the servers. The question is, can a user of the library send information to update the data at a Web site? The issue here is security privileges. If the user has write privileges, then he could update the databases that he is authorized to modify. Agents and mediators could be used to locate the databases as well as to process the update.

Transaction management is essential for many applications. There may be new kinds of transactions on the Web. For example, various items may be sold through the Web. In this case, the item should not be locked immediately when a potential buyer makes a bid. It has to be left open until several bids are received and the item is sold. That is, special transaction models are needed. Appropriate concurrency control and recovery techniques have to be developed for the transaction models.

Metadata management is a major concern for digital libraries. The question is, what is metadata? Metadata describes all of the information pertaining to the library. This could include the various Web sites, the types of users, access control issues, and policies enforced. Where should the metadata be located? Should each participating site maintain its own metadata? Should the metadata be replicated or should there be a centralized metadata repository? Metadata in such an environment could be very dynamic, especially because the users and the Web sites may be changing continuously. Because of the importance of metadata for Web mining, we will elaborate on metadata management in a later section.

Storage management for Web database access is a complex function. Appropriate index strategies and access methods for handling multimedia data are needed. In addition, due to the large volumes of data, techniques for integrating database management technology with mass storage technology are also needed.

Security and privacy is a major challenge. Once you put the data at a site, who owns the data? If a user copies the data from a site, can he distribute the data? Can he use the information in papers that he is writing? Who owns the copyright to the original data? What role do digital signatures play? Mechanisms for copyright protection and plagiarism detection are needed. In addition, some of the issues discussed in [THUR97] on handling heterogeneous security policies will be of concern.* Security and privacy considerations will be discussed in Part III.

Maintaining the integrity of the data is critical. Because the data may originate from multiple sources around the world, it will be difficult to keep tabs on the accuracy of the data. Data quality maintenance techniques need to be developed for digital libraries and Web database access. For example, special tagging mechanisms may be needed to determine the quality of the data.

Other data management functions include integrating heterogeneous databases, managing multimedia data, and mining. Integrating various data sources will be covered later in this chapter when we address interoperability. Managing multimedia data will be addressed in Chapter 6. Web mining, which is the main focus of this book, will be discussed in all chapters.

---

* Also, there has been much discussion on the notion of a "firewall" to protect the internal information from external users. We do not address firewall issues in this chapter. For more details, the reader is referred to [CHES94] and [FIRE].

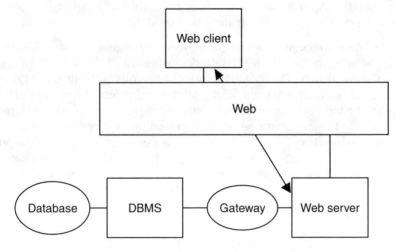

Exhibit 4.   Database Access via Gateways

Web Database Access

In the earlier sections of this chapter, we gave a high level illustration of database access. One approach is to embed SQL calls into Java programs and access relational databases via ODBC (open database connections). The approaches have been extended to include object databases as well as object-relational databases.

While JDBC-based approaches are the way of the future, unfortunately many of the Web clients cannot understand the concepts in relational databases. That is, Web clients only understand the results of Web servers, and database management systems are not Web servers in general. Therefore, as discussed in the various papers in the June 1998 issue of the *IEEE Data Engineering Bulletin,* one of the approaches currently being adopted for Web database access is to use gateways between the database system and the Web servers. These gateways will take the output of the database systems and then format it in a way that the Web servers can manage. Then Web clients and Web servers can communicate with each other through the various protocols discussed in [THUR00] (see also Chapter 2). That is, as illustrated in Exhibit 4, when a client issues a request to the server, the data from the databases is retrieved via the gateway. The results are then delivered to the user.

One of the advantages of standards such as XML is to eliminate the need for such gateways. That is, if all of the documents are expressed in XML, then the database outputs will be represented using XML, which can then be interpreted by Web servers as well as clients. This way, the need for gateways can be eliminated. This is illustrated in Exhibit 5.

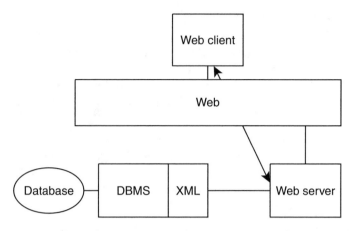

Exhibit 5. Database Access without Gateways

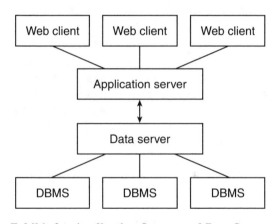

Exhibit 6. Application Server and Data Server

When numerous applications have to access databases on the Web, performance becomes a major consideration. One of the trends today is to use various application servers based on Enterprise Java Beans (EJB) technology. Application servers can coordinate between the various applications. These application servers communicate either directly with the database systems or go through a data server. That is, a data server has two parts: one is access to the back-end database systems, and the other is access to the application servers. The data server can schedule various transactions and access the back-end database system. We illustrate such a system in Exhibit 6. This technology is becoming very popular, and we are now seeing various application and data servers on the market.

SEMISTRUCTURED DATABASES

Since Codd published his paper on the relational data model [CODD70], there has been much work on developing various data models. These models mainly represent structured data. By structured data, we mean data that has a well-defined structure such as data represented by tables. Here, each element belongs to a data type such as integer, string, real, or Boolean.

However, with multimedia data, there is very little structure. Text data could be many characters with no structure. Images could be a collection of pixels. Video and audio data also have no structure. That is, there is no organized way to represent such multimedia data. This type of data has come to be known as unstructured data.

It is nearly impossible to represent unstructured data. Therefore, to better represent such data, one introduces some structure to it. For example, text data could be represented as title, author, affiliation, and paragraphs. Such data are called semistructured data. That is, semistructured data is not fully structured like relational structures, but it has partial structure.

During the past five years or so, researchers have focused on developing models to represent semistructured data. Some of the early models were object-based. Object-relational models were also being proposed for semistructured data. However, with the advent of the Web and W3C, there is much interest to develop models for text data. One of the most popular representation schemes is XML. Note that, as stated in [THUR02], XML is not a data model, but it is a metamodel to represent various documents. That is, documents such as memos, letters, books, and journal articles are represented with XML. In other words, XML defines the structure to represent such textual documents. The approach taken to represent text data with XML is being adopted to represent various types of data such as video, chemical structures, financial securities information, and medical imagery. XML extensions are also being proposed for E-commerce. In a way, all of these representations can be regarded as representations for semistructured data. Essentially, semistructured data models can be used as the global data models in the integration of structured data with, for instance, text data, as shown in Exhibit 7, or they can be used to directly represent semistructured databases (see the discussion in [THUR02]). Some extensive research on semistructured databases has been carried out at Stanford University in the Lore project [WIDO98]. Various research efforts on semistructured databases have also been reported (see [IEEE98] and [SIGM01]). With the advent of XML, we can expect research and practice of semistructured databases to grow tremendously.

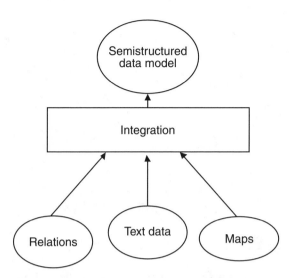

Exhibit 7. Integration of Structured and Semistructured Data

METADATA, ONTOLOGIES, AND THE WEB

We discussed some of the metadata management issues for Web database management. Maintaining appropriate metadata is critical for intelligent browsing. As one goes through the cyberspace, the metadata, which describes the navigation patterns, should get updated. This metadata is consulted periodically so that a user can have some idea where he is. Metadata becomes like a map of sorts. Furthermore, the Web metadata manager should continually give advice to the users.

Appropriate techniques are needed to manage the metadata. These include querying and updating the metadata. The Web environment is very dynamic. This means that the metadata must be updated continually as users browse through the Web, as well as when data sources get updated. Furthermore, as new data sources get added, the changes have to be reflected in the metadata. Metadata may also include various security policies. The metadata must also be available to the users in a timely manner. Finally, appropriate models for the metadata are also needed. These models may be based on the various data models or may utilize the models for text and multimedia data.

Metadata repositories may be included with the various data servers, or there may be separate repositories for the metadata. A scenario having multiple data servers and metadata repositories is illustrated in Exhibit 8.

There is much research being carried out on metadata management for the Web (for example, see [AIPA95], [AIPA96], and [META96]). However, much

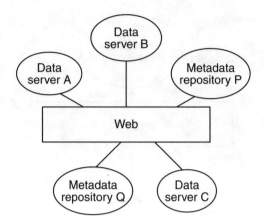

Exhibit 8. Metadata Repositories on the Web

remains to be done before efficient techniques are developed for metadata representation and management. Defining the metadata is also a major issue.

Special types of metadata are ontologies. During recent years, we have been hearing a lot about ontologies. What is an ontology? Fikes has defined an ontology as a specification of concepts to be used for expressing knowledge. This would include entities, attributes, relationships, and constraints (see the discussion in [ONTO] about this work).

One may argue that we have been talking about entities and relationships for more than two decades. So what additional benefits do ontologies give us? Ontologies are essentially an agreed-upon way to specify knowledge. Fikes states that ontologies are distinguished not by their form but by the role they play in representing knowledge. One can have ontologies to represent persons, vehicles, animals, and other general entities such as tables, chairs, and chemistry. For example, a group of people could define an ontology for a person, and this ontology could be reused by someone else. Another group may want to modify the ontology for a person and have its own ontology. That is, different groups could have different ontologies for the same entity. Once these ontologies are used repeatedly, a standard set of ontologies may evolve. There are efforts to standardize ontologies by different programs. In addition, standards organizations are also attempting to specify ontologies.

Why are ontologies useful? They are needed whenever two or more people have to work together. For example, ontologies are very important for collaboration, agent-to-agent communication, or knowledge management, and for different database systems to interoperate with each other. Ontologies are also useful for education, training, genetics, as well as modeling and simulation. In summary, many fields require ontologies. A good exam-

Problem: interoperation of databases A, B, and C

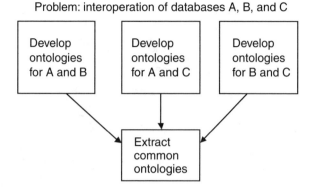

Exhibit 9.   Common Ontologies from Domain-Specific Ontologies

ple is different groups collaborating on a design project. They could define ontologies so that they all speak the same language. If ontologies are previously defined by other design groups, they could reuse these ontologies to save time.

We often hear about domain-specific ontologies. The question is, what are they? One can arbitrarily come up with ontologies for aircraft. But groups working in various Air Force organizations may have their own specialization for aircraft. These are domain-specific ontologies. One challenge when interoperating heterogeneous databases is whether one can come up with a common set of ontologies for semantic integration of the databases, or is each pair of databases to be treated separately? In order to come up with a common set of ontologies, it is sometimes necessary to examine various pairs and develop ontologies for these pairs, and then see if a common set of ontologies can be extracted. The goal for integrating heterogeneous databases is to come up with a common set of ontologies from the domain-specific ontologies. This is illustrated in Exhibit 9.

E-commerce applications and Web data management will define a new set of ontologies. For E-commerce applications, ontologies will include specifications for Web pages to set up E-commerce sites as well as ontologies for specifying various goods. There are Web sites emerging that specify ontologies. These ontologies can be used for various activities such as collaboration and integration.

There is extensive research on ontologies by computer scientists as well as logicians and philosophers. Uncertain reasoning, probabilities, and other heuristics are being incorporated into ontology research. This is a very dynamic area, and we urge the reader to visit various Web sites specifying ontologies and to keep up with the developments. We will revisit ontologies when we discuss the semantic Web in Chapter 8. A discussion of ontology mining will be given in Chapter 23.

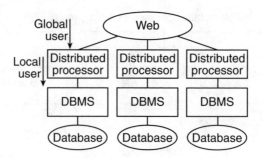

Exhibit 10.   Distributed Data Management on the Web

DISTRIBUTED, HETEROGENEOUS, AND LEGACY DATABASES ON THE WEB

While the previous sections discussed various aspects of Web data management functions, this section will focus on distributed, heterogeneous, and legacy databases on the Web. For example, the databases on the Web may be distributed. Therefore, distributed database functions such as distributed query processing and transaction management have to be extended for Web distributed data management. The Web will have numerous heterogeneous databases with different data formats and models. These databases have to be integrated. Finally, legacy databases may have to be migrated to take advantage of new architectures.

Distributed Data Management on the Web

Large databases may be distributed on the Web for the reasons we discuss in Appendix B, where we provide an overview of distributed databases. These distributed databases may be queried from different locations and the distribution of the data should be transparent to the user. Furthermore, distributed transactions may have to be carried out on the Web. This may especially be the case for E-commerce transactions. We need to ensure that these distributed transactions preserve the integrity and the accuracy of the distributed database.

Exhibit 10 illustrates an architecture for distributed data management on the Web. Essentially, we have adapted the architecture for distributed database systems (discussed in Appendix B) for the Web. This means that the distributed processor, which includes the distributed query processor, distributed transaction management, and the distributed metadata manager have to interface to the Web. Another approach is to use the various components for distributed data management, as illustrated in Exhibit 11. There is still much research that is needed to determine the feasibility of this approach. We have only discussed some of the preliminary points in

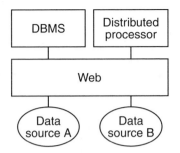

Exhibit 11.   Component-Based Approach for Distributed Data Management

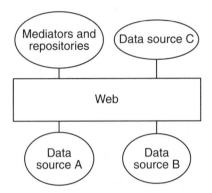

Exhibit 12.   Integrating Data Sources on the Web

this section. Essentially, what we need to do is to see how the various concepts in distributed data management can be adapted to work on the Web.

Heterogeneous Database Integration on the Web

One can expect to have numerous heterogeneous databases connected to the Web. The various heterogeneous data sources have to be integrated to provide transparent access to the user, as illustrated in Exhibit 12. In some cases, the data sources have to be integrated into a warehouse. Data mining helps the users to extract meaningful information from the numerous data sources. Because the data in the libraries could have different semantics and syntax, it will be difficult to extract useful information. Sophisticated data mining tools are needed for this purpose.

One way to interoperate heterogeneous databases is to use ORBs (see Exhibit 13). A major challenge in ORB-based interoperability is to develop an appropriate interface between the ORB and the Web. That is, extensions to IDL are needed for Web database access. Another challenge with the Web is to connect different components of the database management system. Dif-

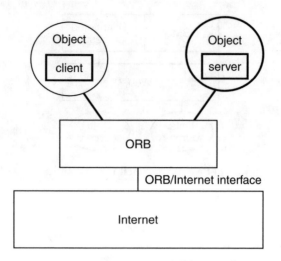

Exhibit 13. Internet-ORB-Based Interoperability

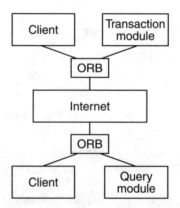

Exhibit 14. ORB-Based Component Integration

ferent vendors may provide different components. For example, a query module may be developed by vendor A, and a transaction module (possibly with real-time processing capability) may be developed by vendor B. The two modules may need to be accessed through the Web. ORB technology would facilitate such integration also. This is illustrated in Exhibit 14. Object Management Group (OMG)'s Internet SIG is focusing on ORB interfaces to the Web. Alternatives to OMG's CORBA technology, such as Microsoft's Distributed OLE/COM, are also viable technologies for Web database access.

Migrating Legacy Databases on the Web

In Appendix B, we discuss various aspects of migrating legacy databases. We describe migrating databases as well as applications. For data-

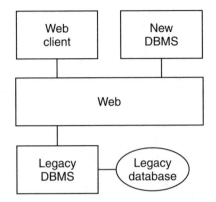

Exhibit 15.   Initial Phase of Migration

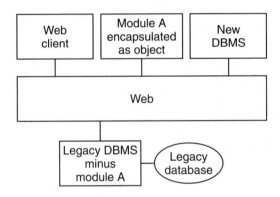

Exhibit 16.   Intermediate Phase of Migration

base migration, one needs to develop schemas for the new environment and then migrate the data. This is the easier part of the migration effort. Migrating applications is more difficult. The applications could be based on complex code and have many relationships. The challenge is to extract the relationships, and then migrate the applications to run on the new environment.

The question is, what impact does the Web have on migrating legacy databases and applications? At this point, it does not appear that the Web has any significant impact on the migration process itself. Exhibits 15 through 17 illustrate the steps to migrating a legacy database accessed on the Web. As in the case of a non-Web environment, the module that is to be migrated may be extracted as objects and then integrated with the new database. Various issues on migrating databases and applications and the role of object technology for migration is discussed in [THUR97]. The impact of the Web needs to be investigated.

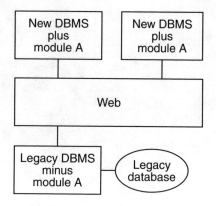

Exhibit 17.   Final Phase of Migration

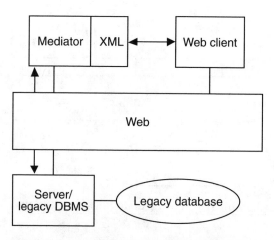

Exhibit 18.   Mediator Approach to Migration

Data modeling will be impacted by the Web. For example, how can XML be used to represent module A that is extracted for the legacy database? Can XML or similar technology be used to access the legacy databases? That is, does one need a mediator that can understand XML at the client side and can access the legacy databases, as illustrated in Exhibit 18? We are just at the beginning of the migration revolution on the Web, and we can expect to find answers to some of these questions within the next couple of years. However, at this time we feel that legacy migration on the Web is still premature.

DATA WAREHOUSING ON THE WEB

We discussed data warehousing in Chapter 4. Data warehousing is an important supporting technology for data mining. Data warehousing is essentially an integration of various data sources for decision support and

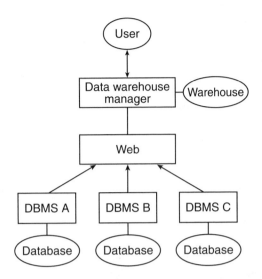

Exhibit 19. Data Warehousing on the Web

analysis. Several of these data sources may be on the Web, and therefore one needs to build data warehouses on the Web so that these warehouses can be mined effectively. As we stress throughout the book, much of the data will be on the Web, whether it is on the Internet or on an intranet. Even in the case of classified databases, there may be a need to build a classified version of the Web to access the databases. Therefore, integrating the various data sources on the Web to carry out analysis will be critical.

As we have stressed, we need good data so that we can obtain useful results from mining. That is, we need to build effective data warehouses on the Web. Exhibit 19 illustrates an approach to data warehousing on the Web. All of the issues and challenges discussed for data warehousing in Chapter 4 apply for Web data warehousing. There are also additional challenges. For example, how can we find the various data sources on the Web to integrate? What sort of interfaces should we build for integration on the Web? There is some research on data warehousing on the Web. There is still much to be done.

ARCHITECTURAL ASPECTS

There are various dimensions to Web data management architectures which will be discussed in the remainder of this chapter. Architectures include publish and subscribe, client/server, and federation, among others.

Three-Tier Computing

Another concept that is extremely popular for the Web is three-tier computing. We discussed some of these aspects in [THUR00]. The front end has

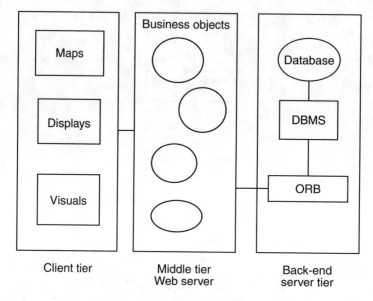

Exhibit 20. Three-Tier Computing

the client and the logic for presentation. The middle tier is the Web server. The third tier is the database server.

We have used three-tier computing in a number of applications for data management as well as knowledge management. Exhibit 20 illustrates such an example. The client displays maps to the user. The Web server is based on EJB technology and is a collection of business objects to carry out the functions of the application. One could use a database system to manage the Web server objects. The back end may be a relational database system.* Other aspects of middleware include transaction processing monitors (TP) and message-oriented middleware (MOM). As mentioned earlier, in the future we can expect ORBs, TPs, and MOMs to be integrated.

A Note on Federated Computing

Another computing model that is worth mentioning is the federated computing model. In Appendix B, we discuss federated databases. This model for computing is becoming popular for the Web. Each group or domain may form its own federation. Various federations have to communicate with each other. As we mention in Appendix B, with federated computing one needs to ensure that collaboration as well as autonomy are maintained. Exhibit 21 illustrates federated computing on the Web. Many of the techniques and issues we discuss in Appendix B apply here.

---

* I thank Eric Hughes and Tim Frangioso for discussions and information on three-tier computing for the Web.

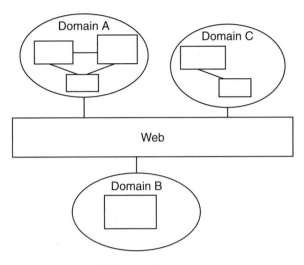

Exhibit 21.   Federated Computing on the Web

However, the details of the impact of the Web on federated computing are not well understood at present. This is an area that needs more research. For example, how can users share data and collaborate with one another? What about security concerns? How can data quality be maintained? Some of the issues are discussed in the chapters on knowledge management and collaboration. We will discuss federated data management and federated data mining for counter-terrorism in Part III.

Models of Communication

In this section, we examine various models for communication on the Web. By "communication," we do not mean networking. We mean the paradigms for communicating data between the client and the server. Essentially, the server here is the producer of the data and the client is the consumer. So the communication is between the producer and the consumer via the Web.*

In the first model of communication, the consumer requests for data. The Web agents search for the appropriate producers of the data and get the data for the consumer. This model is illustrated in Exhibit 22. In the second model, sometimes referred to as the push model, the consumer does not request for the data. As the producer produces the data, it is pushed to the consumer. This model is illustrated in Exhibit 23. A variation of this model is when the consumer publishes a need for the data. As the data gets produced, the producers push the data to the consumer. Another variation is when the producer pushes the data to the consumer based on consumer

* I thank Mike Hebert for discussions on push/pull models.

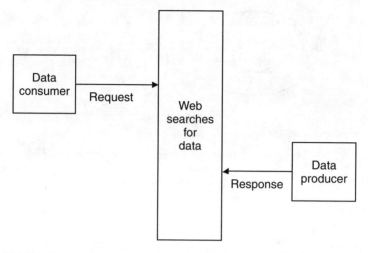

Exhibit 22.   Request-Response between Producer and Consumer

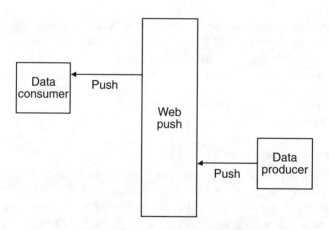

Exhibit 23.   Push Data to Consumer

profiles. In this case, the consumer gets personalized services. A third model is a pull model where the consumer pulls the data from the producers. Producers may place the data at a certain repository, and the consumers may only pull the data from the repository. This model is illustrated in Exhibit 24. Several variations of these models have been proposed. While the different models necessitate different processing routines, some of the essential routines are the same. These routines are for processing queries, executing transactions, extracting metadata, as well as accessing complex storage media. As we get to know more about the Web, the number of models of communication will also grow.

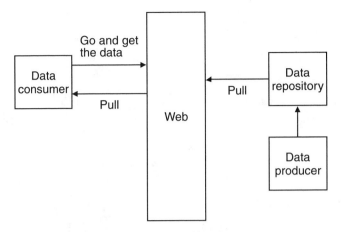

Exhibit 24.   Consumer Pulls Data

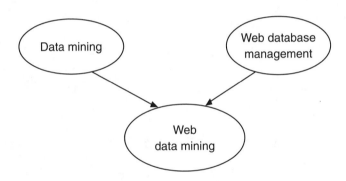

Exhibit 25.   Relationship to Web Mining

RELATIONSHIP TO WEB DATA MINING

In Part II, we will elaborate on Web data management and mining. Essentially, the databases on the Web have to be mined to extract useful information and hidden patterns and trends. Therefore, much of the discussion in Chapters 3 and 4 on data mining applies here. That is, Web data mining integrates data mining and Web data management, as illustrated in Exhibit 25. In Exhibit 26, we show how the databases on the Web can be mined.

Several technologies have to work together for Web data mining. These include database management, machine learning, information retrieval, and Web technologies. We will discuss them in more detail in Part II. Part III will focus on counter-terrorism.

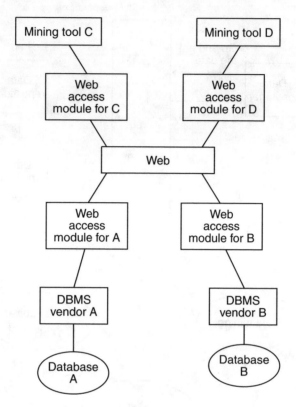

Exhibit 26.   Mining the Web Databases

SUMMARY

This chapter has discussed various aspects of Web database management. We first provided an overview of Web database management functions. This was followed by discussions of metadata and semistructured databases. Next, we discussed distributed, heterogeneous, and legacy databases on the Web. We provided an overview of data warehousing on the Web, and discussed some architectural aspects. We ended the chapter with a discussion of the relationship of Web database management to Web data mining.

Managing the databases on the Web is the first step to good Web data mining. We need to ensure that the data on the Web is accurate and of high quality. This chapter has provided some direction toward Web database management and Web data mining. Part II will explore Web data mining in more detail. Applications to counter-terrorism will be the subject of Part III.

Chapter 6
Information Retrieval Systems

INTRODUCTION

In this chapter, we continue with the discussion of supporting technologies for Web data mining. In particular, we discuss information retrieval systems. Information retrieval systems essentially provide support for managing documents. The functions include document retrieval, document update, and document storage management, among others. These systems are essentially database management systems for managing documents. There are various types of information retrieval systems for text, images, audio, and video data.

Markup languages such as XML, HTML, and SGML have played an important role in information retrieval. XML evolved from HTML and SGML. SGML was developed specifically for tagging text. HTML was developed for tagging text on the Web. Therefore, XML was conceived for tagging text data. Essentially, it provides support for exchanging text documents on the Web. However, over the years XML has provided support for not only managing text documents, but also for images, video, and all types of structured and unstructured documents on the Web.

TEXT RETRIEVAL

A text retrieval system is essentially a database management system for handling text data. Text data could be documents such as books, journals, magazines, etc. There are various issues that need to be considered. We discuss some of them in this section.

First of all, one needs a good data model for document representation. A considerable amount of work has gone into developing semantic data models and object models for document management. For example, a document could have paragraphs, and a paragraph could have sections, etc., as shown in Exhibit 1. Then an architecture is needed for the system. A functional architecture would have the following modules: query manager, browser, editor, update manager (which may overlap with the editor), storage manager, and metadata manager. In addition, you need an integrity and

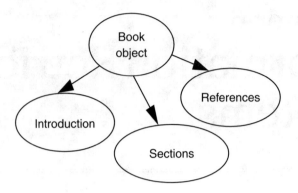

Exhibit 1. Data Model for Text

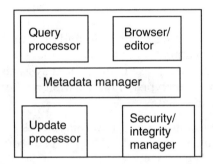

Exhibit 2. Functional Architecture for Text Processing System

security manager to maintain integrity and security. An architecture for a text processing system is illustrated in Exhibit 2.

Querying documents could be based on many factors. One could specify keywords and request the documents with the keywords to be retrieved. One could also retrieve documents that have some relationship with one another. Recent research on information retrieval is focusing on querying documents based on semantics. For example, "retrieve documents that describe scenic views" or "retrieve documents that are useful to children under ten years" are examples of such queries.

Much of the information is now in textual form. This could be data on the Web, library data, electronic books, etc. One of the problems with text data is that it is not structured as relational data. In many cases, it is unstructured, and in some cases, it is semistructured. Semistructured data, for example, is an article that has a title, author, abstract, and paragraphs. The paragraphs are not structured, while the format is structured (see [CLIF97]).

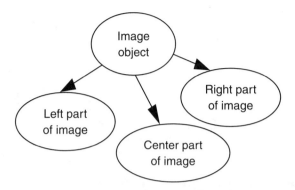

Exhibit 3.   Data Model for Image

Information retrieval systems and text processing systems have been developed for more than a few decades. Some of these systems are quite sophisticated and can retrieve documents by specifying attributes or key words. There are also text-processing systems that can retrieve associations between documents. So we are often asked what the difference is between information retrieval systems and text mining systems.

We define text mining to be data mining on text data. Text mining is all about extracting previously unknown patterns and associations from large text databases. The difference between text mining and information retrieval is analogous to the difference between data mining and database management. There is really no clear difference. Some of the recent information retrieval and text processing systems do discover associations between words and paragraphs, and therefore can be regarded as text mining systems.

IMAGE RETRIEVAL

An image retrieval system is essentially a database management system for handling image data. Image data could be x-rays, pictures, satellite images, and photographs. There are various issues that need to be considered. We discuss some of them in this section.

First of all, one needs a good data model for image representation. Some work has gone into developing semantic data models and object models for image management (for example, see [THUR93]). For example, an image could consist of a right and a left image, as shown in Exhibit 3 (an example is an x-ray of the lungs). Then you need an architecture for the system. A functional architecture would have the following modules: query manager, browser, editor, update manager (which may overlap with the editor), a storage manager, and a metadata manager. In addition, you need

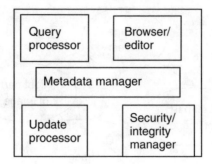

Exhibit 4.   Functional Architecture for Image Processing System

an integrity and security manager to maintain integrity and security. An architecture for an image processing system is illustrated in Exhibit 4.

Querying images could be based on many factors. One could extract text from images and then query the text. One could tag images and then query the tags. One could also retrieve images from patterns. For example, an image could contain several squares. With a picture of a square, one could query the image and retrieve all the squares in the image. We can also query images based on content. For example, "retrieve all images that illustrate sunset" or "retrieve images that illustrate Victorian buildings" are examples of queries.

If text mining is still in the early research stages, image mining is an even more immature technology. Image processing has been around for quite a while. We have image processing applications in various domains, including medical imaging for cancer detection, processing satellite images for space and intelligence applications, and also handling hyperspectral images. Images include maps, geological structures, biological structures, and many other entities. Image processing has dealt with areas such as detecting patterns that deviate from the norm, retrieving images by content, and pattern matching.

The main question here is, what is image mining? How does it differ from image processing? Again, we do not have clear-cut answers. One can say that while image processing is focusing on detecting abnormal patterns as well as retrieving images, image mining is all about finding unusual patterns. Therefore, one can say that image mining deals with making associations between different images from large image databases.

VIDEO RETRIEVAL

A video retrieval system is essentially a database management system for handling video data. Video data could be documentaries, films, and television shows. There are various issues that need to be considered. We discuss some of them in this section.

First of all, one needs a good data model for video representation. Some work has gone into developing semantic data models and object models for video data management (see [WOEL86]). For example, a video object could have advertisements, a main film, and coming attractions, as shown in Exhibit 5. Then you need an architecture for the system. A functional architecture would have the following modules: query manager, browser, editor, update manager (which may overlap with the editor), a storage manager, and a metadata manager. In addition, you need an integrity and security manager to maintain integrity and security. An architecture for the video processing system is illustrated in Exhibit 6.

Querying documents could be based on many factors. One could extract text from the video and query the text. One could also extract images from the video and query the images. One could store short video scripts and carry out pattern matching. That is, "find the video that contains the following script." Examples of queries include "find films where

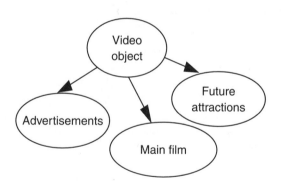

Exhibit 5.   Data Model for Video

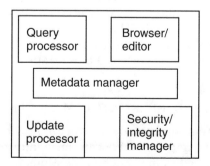

Exhibit 6.   Functional Architecture for Video Processing System

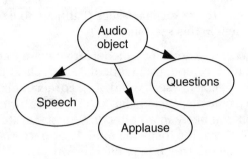

Exhibit 7. Data Model for Audio

the hero is John Wayne" or "find video scripts that show two presidents shaking hands."

AUDIO RETRIEVAL

An audio retrieval system is essentially a database management system for handling audio data. Audio data could be speeches and voice recordings. There are various issues that need to be considered. We discuss some of them in this section.

First of all, one needs a good data model for audio representation. Some work has gone into developing semantic data models and objects models for audio data management (see WOEL86]). For example, an audio object could have speeches, questions, and applause, as shown in Exhibit 7. Then you need an architecture for the system. A functional architecture would have the following modules: query manager, browser, editor, update manager (which may overlap with the editor), a storage manager, and a metadata manager. In addition, you need an integrity and security manager to maintain integrity and security. An architecture for the audio processing system is illustrated in Exhibit 8.

Querying documents could be based on many factors. One could extract text from the audio and query the text. One could store short audio scripts and carry out pattern matching. That is, "find the audio that contains the following script." Examples include "find audio tapes containing the speeches of President Bush" or "find audio tapes of poems recited by female narrators."

MULTIMEDIA DATA AND INFORMATION MANAGEMENT

The previous sections discussed retrieval for individual data types such as text, images, video, and audio. We call these information retrieval systems. However, we need to manage combinations of data types, and the systems that manage them are multimedia database systems.

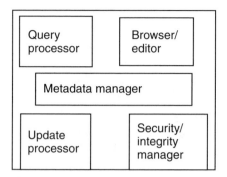

Exhibit 8. Functional Architecture for Audio Processing System

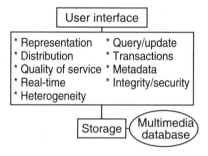

Exhibit 9. Functional Architecture for MM-DBMS

A multimedia database management system (MM-DBMS) provides support for storing, manipulating, and retrieving multimedia data from a multimedia database. In a sense, a multimedia database system is a type of heterogeneous database system, as it manages heterogeneous data types. Heterogeneity is due to the medium of the data such as text, video, and audio.

An MM-DBMS must provide support for typical database management system functions. These include query processing, update processing, transaction management, storage management, metadata management, security, and integrity. In addition, in many cases the various types of data, such as voice and video, have to be synchronized for display, and therefore, real-time processing is also a major issue in an MM-DBMS. Exhibit 9 illustrates the functions of an MM-DBMS.

Various architectures are being examined to design and develop an MM-DBMS. In one approach, the DBMS is used just to manage the metadata, and a multimedia file manager is used to manage the multimedia data. Then there is a module for integrating the DBMS and the multimedia file manager. In this case, the MM-DBMS consists of the three modules: the

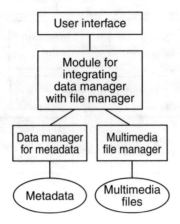

Exhibit 10.   Loose Coupling Architecture

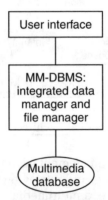

Exhibit 11.   Tight Coupling Architecture

DBMS managing the metadata, the multimedia file manager, and the module for integrating the two. The loose coupling architecture is illustrated in Exhibit 10.

The second architecture is the tight coupling approach illustrated in Exhibit 11. In this architecture, the DBMS manages both the multimedia database as well as the metadata. That is, the DBMS is an MM-DBMS. The tight coupling architecture has an advantage because all of the DBMS functions could be applied on the multimedia database. This includes query processing, transaction management, metadata management, storage management, and security and integrity management. Note that with the loose coupling approach, unless the file manager performs the DBMS functions, the DBMS only manages the metadata for the multimedia data.

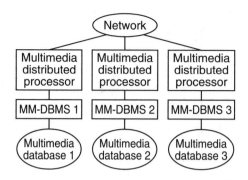

Exhibit 12.   Distributed MM-DBMS

There are other aspects to architectures, as discussed in [THUR97]. For example, a multimedia database system could use a commercial object-oriented database system to manage multimedia objects. However, relationships between objects and the representation of temporal relationships may involve extensions to the database management system. That is, a DBMS together with an extension layer provide complete support to manage multimedia data. In the alternative case, both the extensions and the database management functions are integrated so that there is one database management system to manage multimedia objects as well as the relationships between the objects. Further details of these architectures as well as managing multimedia databases are discussed in [THUR01]. Multimedia databases could also be distributed. In this case, we assume that each MM-DBMS is augmented with a multimedia distributed processor (MDP). The distributed architecture is illustrated in Exhibit 12.

There is news all over the world: the British Broadcasting Corporation, the American Broadcasting Corporation, the *Financial Times* of London, the *Wall Street Journal,* and the Cable News Network, to name a few. Many of the organizations that are producers of such multimedia information now want to put their information on the Web. But there is so much data that it is almost impossible to get quality presentations of multimedia data on the Web. This is especially true with continuous media such as video and audio.

There are network communication problems that have to be overcome. While there is progress, and hardware is becoming less expensive, developing good software to ensure quality of service, timely access, and presentation of this data remains the challenge. We have come a long way over the past few years in implementing delayed broadcast services. For example, important speeches by heads of countries are posted on the Internet within minutes. But we still are a long way from live video broadcast and

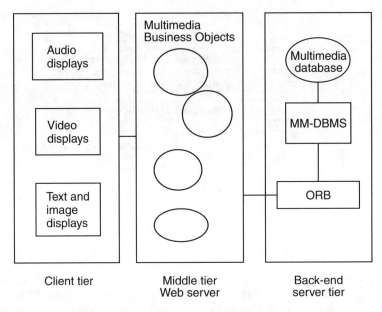

Exhibit 13.   Three-Tier Multimedia Computing on the Web

movies on the Web. This does not mean live entertainment is not yet possible. The service we get today is not of good quality.

The biggest consumers of multimedia data on the Web are the entertainment, broadcasting, and journalism industries. There is a huge market for this, and these industries have tapped into only a small portion of it. As technology becomes more mature, we can expect major players in the entertainment industry to become very active. In a way, this is all part of E-commerce. Although this does not deal with buying and selling music and video on the Internet, it deals with playing video and music on the Internet. Some of the technical challenges for data management include synchronizing presentation with storage, security, and ensuring that quality of service is maintained. Exhibit 13 illustrates multimedia on the Web with a three-tiered approach where the middle tier does all the Web-based multimedia data processing. Another application area for multimedia on the Web is training and distance learning. We will discuss this application in the next chapter.

QUESTION ANSWERING SYSTEMS

Question answering systems are sort of the early information retrieval systems developed in the late 1960s. They would typically give yes/no answers. Since then, there have been many advances in information retrieval systems including text, image, and video systems. However, with

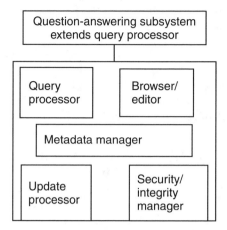

Exhibit 14. Question Answering and Text Retrieval

the advent of the Web, the question answering systems have received much attention. They are not just limited to a yes/no answer. They give answers to various complex queries such as "what is the weather forecast today in Chicago?" or "retrieve the flight schedules from London to Tokyo that make at most one stop."

Various search engines such as Google are capable of executing complex searches. But they are yet to answer complex queries. The research on question answering systems is just beginning and we can expect search engines to have this capability. Question answering systems integrate many technologies, including natural language processing, information retrieval, search engines, and data management (Exhibit 14).

MARKUP LANGUAGES

Markup languages provide the support to tag any entity of interest. These entities could be person, place, or object. Markup languages can provide structure to unstructured data such as text. One of the first markup languages is SGML (Standard Generalized Markup Language). Details of this language can be found in numerous texts, including [SGML]. We briefly discuss some of the essential points in this section.

SGML is a descriptive language rather than a procedural language. Essentially, it uses markup codes to mark up the document. Note that procedural languages specify the processing to be carried out. In SGML, instructions to process the document are separated from the descriptive markup, which is the set of markup codes. With descriptive markup, the document can be independent of the system, which processes it. One can mark up names, places, or entities, and the processing program can handle various parts of the document.

Document type and document type definitions (DTDs) were introduced in SGML and are now used in XML. Documents have types, defined by the structure of the document. For example, a book document type may contain title, front matter, introduction, chapters, references, appendixes, and index. A document parser can check that the document conforms to its specified type.

The design goal of SGML was to ensure that documents written in one system could be transported to another without any loss of information. This means that there has to be a way of representing strings, numbers, etc., in a machine-independent way. SGML provokes support for such representations. Essentially, there has to be a way to consistently represent various strings, letters, and characters.

It is impossible to give an overview of SGML in a few paragraphs. Nevertheless, we have discussed some of the key points. XML has been much influenced by the developments with SGML. XML evolved from HTML and SGML. Furthermore, XML was primarily developed to tag text. However, XML is now being used to tag all kinds of documents, including images, video, audio, and multimedia documents. XML is also being used for music, math, and E-business documents. Essentially, XML has become key to the exchange of not only text documents but other types of documents as well, including relational databases on the Web. More details on XML and its relationship to databases was discussed in our earlier book [THUR02]. The next step to markup languages is RDF (Resource Description Framework). Some details are given in [THUR02]. However, we will briefly discuss XML and RDF in Chapter 7. The evolution of markup languages is illustrated in Exhibit 15. Note that various XML and RDF documents will also have to be mined so that useful information is extracted.

RELATIONSHIP TO WEB DATA MINING

Web mining has important relationships to all of the technologies we have discussed here. Consider, for example, text retrieval. One could ask the question, what is the difference between text mining and text retrieval? The answer is subjective. Text mining finds associations and relationships between documents and within a document, while text retrieval returns documents and paragraphs based on some criteria. There is lot of text on the Web. This text has to be mined so that one can extract patterns and trends. This is where Web mining comes in.

Similar arguments can be given for video, image, and audio mining. There is a lot of image data on the Web, for example, maps and drawings. This image data has to be mined to find unusual occurrences. Finally, we

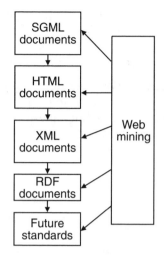

Exhibit 15. Markup Languages and Web Mining

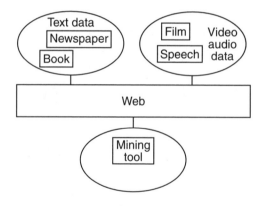

Exhibit 16. Web Mining and Information Retrieval

need to mine and extract patterns from multimedia databases. Many of these databases are now on the Web. Mining information retrieval systems on the Web is illustrated in Exhibit 16.

We will explore information retrieval and Web mining in more detail in Part II. We will first discuss search engines and how they may incorporate Web mining. Then we will discuss some other aspects of mining text, images, and video on the Web.

SUMMARY

In this chapter, we have mainly addressed information retrieval systems. We first discussed text, image, video, and audio retrieval systems.

Then we addressed multimedia data management. This was followed by a discussion of question answering systems. Next, we provided a brief introduction to markup languages that have a close relationship to information retrieval. Finally, we discussed the relationship to Web mining.

Now that we have provided an overview of information retrieval and Web data management, we can explore information management technologies, which are also supporting technologies for Web mining. This will be the subject of Chapter 7. Part II will elaborate on information retrieval and Web mining.

Chapter 7
Information
Management
Technologies

INTRODUCTION

Chapter 5 described Web databases and Chapter 6 described information retrieval. This chapter focuses on information management technologies such as collaboration, knowledge management, and agents, among others. Then we will focus on the relationship to Web mining. Note that Web mining and information management will be elaborated further in Part II.

We have tried to separate data management and information management. That is, data management focuses on database systems technologies such as query management, transaction management, and storage management. Information management is much broader than data management, and we have included many topics in this category. Note that information retrieval is also a particular aspect of information management. We have devoted a separate chapter to information retrieval systems such as text retrieval, image retrieval, and video retrieval as they have a special relationship to search engines and Web mining, to be elaborated in Part II.

COLLABORATION AND DATA MANAGEMENT

Although the notion of computer-supported cooperative work (CSCW) was first proposed in the early 1980s, it is only recently that much interest is being shown in this area. Several research papers have now been published in collaborative computing, and prototypes and products have been developed. Collaborative computing enables groups of individuals and organizations to work together with one another in order to accomplish a task or a collection of tasks. These tasks could vary from participating in conferences, solving a specific problem, or working on the design of a system. Specific contributions to collaborative computing include the development of team workstations (where groupware creates a shared workspace supporting dynamic collaboration in a workgroup), multimedia communication systems supporting distributed workgroups, and collaborative computing systems supporting cooperation in the design of an entity (such as an electrical or mechanical system).* Several technologies including multimedia, artificial intelligence, networking and distributed processing, and database systems, as well as disciplines such as organizational behavior and human–computer interaction have contributed significantly toward the growth of collaborative computing.

One aspect of collaborative computing of particular interest to the database community is workflow computing. Workflow is defined as the automation of a series of functions that comprise a business process such as data entry, data review, and monitoring performed by one or more people. An example of a process that is well suited for workflow automation is the purchasing process. Applications can range from simple user-defined processes such as document review to complex applications such as manufacturing processes. Original custom-made workflow systems developed over the past 20 years for applications such as factory automation were built using a centralized database. Many commercial workflow system products targeted for office environments are based on a messaging architecture. This architecture supports the distributed nature of current work teams. However, the messaging architecture is usually file-based and lacks many of the features supported by database management systems such as data representation, consistency management, tracking, and monitoring. Although the emerging products show some promise, they do not provide the functionality of database management systems.

Exhibit 1 illustrates an example where teams A and B are working on a geographical problem such as analyzing and predicting the weather in North America. The two teams must have a global picture of the map as well as any notes that go with it. Any changes made by one team should be instantly visible to the other team, and both teams communicate as if they are in the same room.

To enable such transparent communication, data management support is needed. One could utilize a database management system to manage the data or some type of data manager that provides some of the essential features such as data integrity, concurrent access, and retrieval capabilities. In this example, the database may consist of information describing the problem the teams are working on, the data that is involved, historical data, and the metadata information. The data manager must provide appropriate concurrency control features so that when both teams simultaneously access the common picture and make changes, these changes are coordinated.

One possible scenario for the data manager is illustrated in Exhibit 2, where each team has its own local data manager and there is a data manager to maintain any global information, including the data and the meta-

---

* See the discussions in [ACM91a].

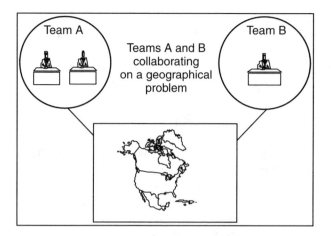

Exhibit 1.   Collaboration Example

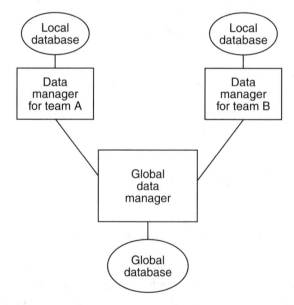

Exhibit 2.   Database Support

data. The local data managers communicate with the global data manager. The global data manager illustrated in this exhibit is at the logical level. At the physical level, the global data manager may also be distributed. The data managers coordinate their activities to provide features such as concurrency control, integrity, and retrieval.

The Web has increased the need for collaboration even further. Users now share documents and work on papers and designs on the Web. Corporate information infrastructures promote collaboration and sharing of information and documents. Therefore, the collaborative tools have to work effectively on the Web. While the Web promotes collaboration, collaboration also benefits the Web. That is, it is a key information technology to enhance the Web. Therefore, the two technologies can benefit from each other.

The challenge is to use these tools to work effectively on the Web. In the simple case, Web interfaces can be built. However, many of the tools were not developed with the Web in mind. This was the case with the database systems, and building Web access is the easy part. The many challenges such as data formats, transactions, and metadata management on the Web are also present for collaboration. Some of the collaborative tools work with the understanding that the people are located in the same building. While for corporate Intranets this may not be a problem, with the Internet this could pose some major problems. Scalability of the tools is also an important issue. Typically, the tools have been developed for dozens of users. With the Web, these tools have to work for thousands of users. These requirements have to be taken into consideration.

We believe that collaboration and the Web will go hand in hand. In the future, collaboration tools will have to work with multimedia data. Therefore, we address multimedia data in the next section. In recent years, there have been some interesting articles published on collaboration and the impact of the Web on the collaboration tools [IEEE99].

KNOWLEDGE MANAGEMENT

Knowledge management is the process of using knowledge as a resource to manage an organization. It could mean sharing expertise, developing a learning organization, teaching the staff, learning from experiences, as well as collaboration. Essentially, knowledge management will include data management and information management. However, this is not a view shared by everyone. Various definitions of knowledge management have been proposed. A good text on knowledge management is that by Davenport [DAVE97]. Knowledge management is a discipline invented mainly by business schools. The concepts have been around for a long time. But the term *knowledge management* was coined as a result of information technology and the Web.

In the collection of papers on knowledge management by Morey et al. [MORE01], knowledge management is divided into three areas, as shown in Exhibit 3: (1) strategies such as building a knowledge company and making the staff knowledge workers; (2) processes such as techniques for knowledge management, including developing a method to share documents and tools; and (3) metrics that measure the effectiveness of knowledge management. In the *Harvard Business Review,* there is an excellent collection of

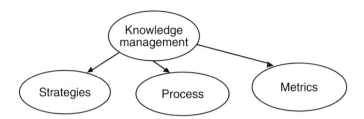

Exhibit 3.   Knowledge Management Components

articles on knowledge management describing a knowledge-creation company, building a learning organization, and teaching people how to learn [HARV96]. Organizational behavior and team dynamics play major roles in knowledge management.

Knowledge management essentially changes the way an organization functions. Instead of competition, it promotes collaboration. This means managers have to motivate employees by giving awards and other incentives to share ideas and collaborate. Team spirit is essential for knowledge management. People are often threatened with imparting knowledge because their jobs may be on the line. They are reluctant to share expertise. This type of behavior could vary from culture to culture. It is critical that managers eliminate this kind of behavior, not by forcing the issue but by motivating the staff and educating them of all the benefits that can occur with good knowledge management practices

Teaching and learning are two important aspects of knowledge management. Both the teacher and the student have to be given incentives. The teacher can benefit by receiving thank-you notes or write-ups in the company newsletter. The student may be rewarded by certificates, monetary awards, and other similar gestures. Knowledge management also includes areas such as protecting the company's intellectual properties, job sharing, changing jobs within the company, and encouraging change in an organization. Effective knowledge management eliminates the dictatorial management style and promotes a more-collaborative management style. Knowledge management follows a cycle of creating knowledge, sharing the knowledge, integrating the knowledge, evaluating the performance with metrics, and then giving feedback to create more knowledge. This is illustrated in Exhibit 4. Variations of this cycle have been proposed in the literature [MORE98b].

The major question is, what are knowledge management technologies? This is where information technology comes in. Artificial intelligence researchers have carried out a considerable amount of research on knowledge acquisition. They have also developed expert systems. These are also knowledge management technologies. Other knowledge management

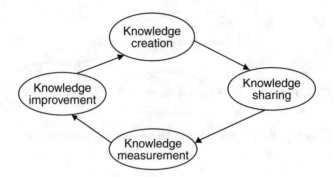

Exhibit 4.   Knowledge Management Cycle

technologies include collaboration tools, tools for organizing information on the Web, and tools for measuring the effectiveness of the knowledge gained, such as collecting various metrics. Knowledge management technologies essentially include data management and information management technologies. Exhibit 5 illustrates some of the knowledge management technologies. As can be seen, Web technologies play a major role in knowledge management. The impact of the Web will be the subject of the next subsection.

Knowledge management and the Web are closely related. While knowledge management practices have existed for many years, it is the Web that has promoted knowledge management. Remember knowledge management is essentially building a knowledge organization. No technology is better than the Web for sharing information. You can travel around the world in seconds with the Web. As a result, a tremendous amount of knowledge can be gained by browsing the Web.

Many corporations now have intranets and this is the single most powerful knowledge management tool. Thousands of employees are con-

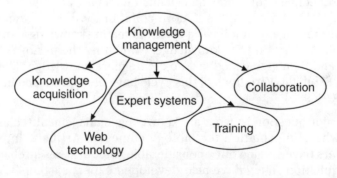

Exhibit 5.   Knowledge Management Technologies

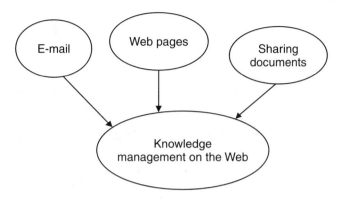

Exhibit 6. Knowledge Management on the Web

nected through the Web in an organization. Large corporations have sites all over the world, and the employees are becoming well connected with one another. E-mail can be regarded as one of the early knowledge management tools. Now there are many tools such as search engines and E-commerce tools.

With the proliferation of Web data management and E-commerce tools, knowledge management will become an essential part of the Web and E-commerce. Exhibit 6 illustrates knowledge management activities on the Web, such as creating Web pages, building E-commerce sites, sending e-mail, and collecting metrics on Web usage. A collection of papers on knowledge management experiences including strategies, processes, and metrics is given in [MORE01]. Collaborative knowledge management is discussed in [GUPT02].

AGENTS FOR THE WEB

Since the development of the Web in the early 1990s, we have heard the term *agents*. The problem is that it has been very difficult for people to agree on what the term means. Some say agents are simply processes; others say agents are Java applets. A third group says that agents are processes that can jump from machine to machine and can execute everywhere. Yet a fourth group says that agents are processes that have to communicate according to some well-defined protocol.

In fact, all of these definitions are correct. That is, agents are essentially processes that function on behalf of other processes and users. But they have to satisfy some agreed-upon method of communication.

Agents carry out many functions, including locating resources on the Web or otherwise, retrieving data, filtering data for security purposes, as well as executing code. Agents also may be self-describing, they may be

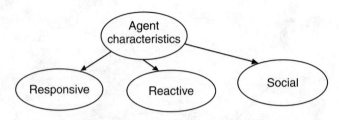

Exhibit 7. Agent Characteristics

decentralized and autonomous, or they may be distributed and heterogeneous. Various agent architectures have been proposed. These architectures essentially describe frameworks for agent communication. Commutation also occurs based on well-defined protocols and languages. While agents carry out security features such as performing access controls and filtering, the agents themselves have to be secure. Furthermore, recent research investigates real-time and fault-tolerant aspects of agents. That is, agents have to react in a timely manner and recover from failures gracefully.

After examining the various definitions of agents, DiPippo et al. give the following definition in [DIPI99]:

> *An agent is a computer system, situated in some environment, that is capable of flexible autonomous action in order to meet its design objectives.*

DiPippo also defines agents as having three major characteristics, as illustrated in Exhibit 7:

1. *Responsive:* React to environment
2. *Proactive:* Opportunistic, goal-directed, take initiative
3. *Social:* Interact with other agents (and users)

For example, agents have to take certain actions when certain situations occur, such as getting data to the right users when it becomes available, as described in the push model in Chapter 3.

Various types of agents have been proposed, including:

1. *Data retrieval agent:* Retrieves data and knows when a user (or other agent) requires certain data; autonomously retrieves the data on behalf of the user (or agent).
2. *Data filtering agent:* Sorts incoming data (e-mail, news, etc.) to determine relevant place in appropriate location.
3. *Resource locating agent:* Locates various resources such as database and files.
4. *Situation monitoring agent:* Monitors a situation and executes triggers when an event occurs.
5. *Mobile agent:* Migrates from machine to machine and executes code in different environments.

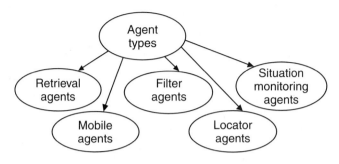

Exhibit 8.   Basic Agent Types

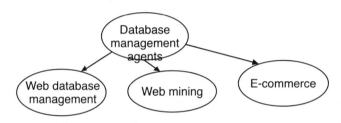

Exhibit 9.   Agent Functions

6. *Data management agent:* Executes various functions such as queries, transactions, mining, and E-commerce.

Note that the first five types can be regarded as basic agents and may carry out activities for database management, data mining, and E-commerce. Exhibit 8 illustrates the basic agent types, while Exhibit 9 illustrates the functions of the database management agents. Note that agents do not necessarily have to function on the Web. However, the Web has really expanded agent technology. Agents now perform Web mining, Web database management, and E-commerce. The relationship between agents and the Web is illustrated in Exhibit 10.

Mobile agents are essentially agents on the Web that execute at different locations and sites. These are processes that migrate from one environment to another and execute in a new environment. An example of a simple mobile agent is a Java applet. An applet is essentially piece of code that resides in the server. It executes in the browser environment when requested by a Web page. Another alternative is a servlet, which executes in the server environment and the results are brought to the client.

An applet is a mobile agent because it migrates to the client environment from a server environment and executes in the client environment. Security is a major consideration for applet execution. An applet may be untrusted, and therefore could corrupt the client resources. This is why

111

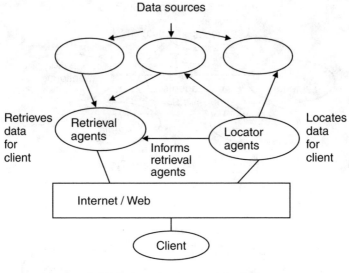

Data sources

Retrieves
data
for
client

Retrieval
agents

Informs
retrieval
agents

Locator
agents

Locates
data
for
client

Internet / Web

Client

Exhibit 10.   Agents and the Web

applets generally execute in what is called a sandbox, and cannot corrupt the client's resources.

Mobile code is not just restricted to applets. It is essentially any process that exists on any machine, either client or server, and executes in any environment. The advantages of this approach are that you need to execute processes in the server environment and bring the results to the client. This could have a performance impact. By bringing the process into the client environment, speed may be enhanced, especially if the server environment is slow. Also, a server may execute many requests, and priority may not be given to a client's request. By bringing the process into the client, this problem is avoided. Mobile code can execute between servers. For example, a mobile agent can move from one server to another.

Various aspects of mobile code are being examined. Most important is security, we believe, for the reasons mentioned earlier. In addition to trusting mobile code, other security issues include access control and execute permissions. That is, appropriate access control and execution rules have to be enforced. The challenge is, who is to enforce these rules in a Web environment? When code migrates from system to system, what privileges does it have? Does it use the privileges originally granted to it or does it modify the privileges, based on the execution environment. A good discussion of secure mobile agents is given in [CORR99], which focuses on not only securing the agents, but also ensuring that untrusted hosts do not corrupt the agents or spy on the agents. That is, protecting the agents is also an issue. Other research issues for mobile agents include real-time comput-

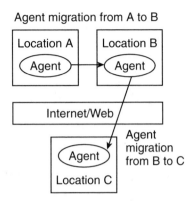

Exhibit 11. Mobile Agents

ing where these agents have to migrate, execute, and give results within a certain timeframe. Fault tolerance is also a major consideration, as the mobile agents have to recover from faults.

Ultimately, we feel there is little difference if an agent is a mobile agent or another type, such as a retrieval agent. For example, a mobile agent can perform retrieval facilities. A retrieval agent can migrate to different environments. We expect that research and practice on mobile agents and code will continue to explode. Java and similar developments are just the beginning. Exhibit 11 illustrates an example of mobile agents.

The ideal goal is to get the right information at the right time to the users. This could be achieved either through the push model, where information is pushed to the user, or a pull model, where the user goes out and gets the data, or a combination of push and pull. In Chapter 5, we discussed various models for communications, including the push and pull models. Essentially, it all comes down to information dissemination. That is, all kinds of information is produced. This information has to be disseminated to the users in an appropriate manner.

Now that we have examined various aspects of agents, we discuss the role of agents in information dissemination.

As stated earlier, agents could be locator agents that locate the resources, retrieval agents that retrieve data either by monitoring or when requested, situation monitoring agents that monitor for events, and filtering agents that filter unwanted information. All of these agents play a role in information dissemination. Exhibit 12 illustrates a situation where situation agents monitor for information production, and this information is retrieved and filtered, and then given to the consumer. Exhibit 13 illustrates the case where the consumer requests information, the locator agent locates the producers, and then the retrieval agents retrieve the information.

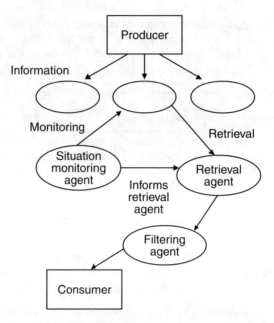

Exhibit 12.   Pushing Information to Consumer

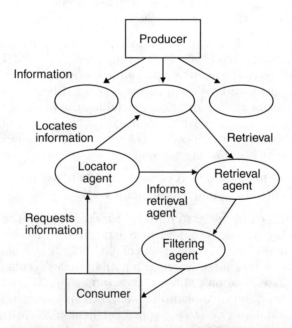

Exhibit 13.   Pulling Information from Producer

Information dissemination technologies have expanded due to the Web. The challenge is to get the information to the user without overloading him. Because this is such a big challenge, we cannot expect this problem to be solved completely. However, technologies being developed show much promise so that information dissemination is enhanced.

TRAINING AND DISTANCE LEARNING

Computer-based training (CBT) is a hot topic today. CBT is all about preparing course materials and making it available electronically so that trainees can learn at their own pace. Because the instructor is often not present, there are several user interface issues and human–computer interaction aspects that come into play here. The challenge is to provide a personalized service to the trainee. For example, in a course on data management, financial workers may want information on E-commerce while defense workers may want information on data management for government applications. Instructors have to interview users, gather requirements, and prepare the material according to the requirements.

A closely related form of distance learning is CBT on the Web. We now see various universities offering degrees on the Web, based on distance learning. The challenge is not only preparing the material to satisfy the users, but also delivering the material in a timely manner. Multimedia on the Web is an important technology for this application, as live teaching may be desirable at times. That is, while CBT is extremely useful, from time to time students may want contact with the instructor, who may be thousands of miles away. Distance learning is not restricted by geography; it is now being implemented across continents. Exhibit 14 illustrates CBT on the Web. Several technologies have to work together in CBT: multimedia, real-time processing, and all of the technologies for Web data management. We can expect to hear much about CBT on the Web and distance learning over the next several years.

WIRELESS INFORMATION MANAGEMENT AND PERVASIVE COMPUTING

During the past decade, we have heard a lot about mobile information management or wireless information management. While mobile agents are an important aspect of wireless information management, there are many other issues that have to be taken into consideration.

Today's world is becoming more and more wireless with handheld devices and personal digital assistants. Managing the information and representing the information displayed on wireless devices is becoming critical. Various standards for networking and information management are being proposed for wireless technology. For example, WAP (Wireless Access Protocol) enables information to be displayed on wireless devices

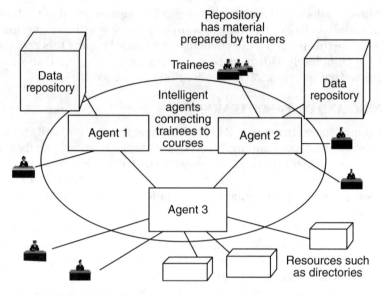

Exhibit 14. Computer-Based Training on the Web

such a mobile phones. More recently, there are the 3G (third-generation) wireless protocols. Finally, XML extensions have also been proposed for wireless technologies.

The database community has been examining data management issues for mobile computing for the past decade [IMIE92]. However, information management technologies have not kept up with the wireless technologies. We need a research and development program to ensure that appropriate data management and information management technologies are developed. These include query processing techniques as well as indexing strategies. In addition, data modeling and display technologies are also important. Exhibit 15 illustrates wireless information management technologies.

In a way, pervasive computing encompasses wireless technologies. We assume here that there are computers everywhere, embedded or otherwise. There are sensors all over the place and information, sometimes in the form of streams, is gathered and managed. Because sensor information management has received much attention lately and there is a lot of sensor data to be mined, we discuss this as a special section.

SENSOR INFORMATION MANAGEMENT

As mentioned at the end of the previous section, there are sensors all over the place. For example, transportation services use sensors. Various government agencies use sensors to track individuals, vehicles, and other

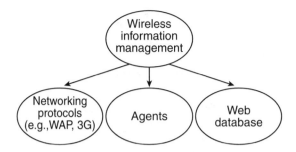

Exhibit 15.   Wireless Information Technologies

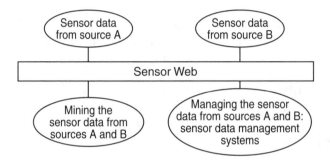

Exhibit 16.   Sensor Information Management

entities. A lot of data is emanating from sensors. This data is in the form of streams and is continuous.

There is much research now on managing sensor data. Various efforts have been reported in developing sensor database management systems. Query processing and optimization for sensor data processing has also received much attention (for example, see [SIGM01]). All of these data streams have to be mined. That is, sensor data and information mining is becoming an important area. We will discuss this topic further in Part II. Exhibit 16 illustrates the notion of the sensor Web.

QUALITY OF SERVICE ASPECTS

There are many Web data management technologies, such as database management, security, multimedia, and integrity, that it will be a challenge to make all of them work together effectively. For example, how can we guarantee that stock information meets the timing constraints for delivery to the trader and yet maintain 100 percent security? This will be very difficult. If we add the tasks of ensuring integrity of the data, and techniques for recovering from faults, and presenting multimedia data in a timely manner, the problem becomes nearly impossible to solve. So the question

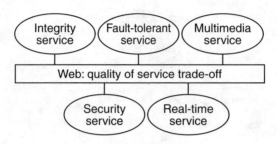

Exhibit 17.   Quality of Service Trade-Offs

is, what do we do? This is when quality of service (QoS) comes in. It is almost impossible to satisfy all of the requirements all of the time. So, QoS specifies policies for trade-offs. For example, if security and real-time are constraints that have to be met, then perhaps in some instances it is not absolutely necessary to meet all the timing constraints, and we need to focus on security. In other instances, meeting timing constraints may be crucial. As another example, consider multimedia presentation. In some instances, we can live with low resolution and other times we may need perfect pictures.

Recently, there has been much work on QoS. But we are yet to find a model that takes into consideration all factors for quality of service. This is a difficult problem, but with so many research efforts underway we can expect to see progress. Essentially, the user specifies what he wants, and his requirements are mapped down to the database system, operating system, and the networking requirements. Exhibit 17 illustrates an approach to QoS on the Web. The ideas are rather preliminary and there is much work to be done.

SOME DIRECTIONS

This chapter has discussed various technologies and services for the Web. Much of our discussion focused on collaboration, knowledge management, agents, training, wireless information management, and sensor information management. Some other related technologies, such as decision support and visualization, were discussed in Chapter 4.

Many of the technologies, such as data, information, and knowledge management, are being used ultimately for managers, policymakers, and other authorities to make effective decisions. Therefore, decision support is an important technology area for the Web, as in the future we can expect these managers and policymakers to access the Web to make effective decisions based on the information they get.

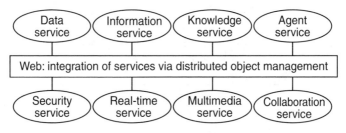

Exhibit 18. Integration of Services on the Web

Technologies for accessing the resources on the Web as well as for processing these resources are critical for effective data management on the Web. The technology that is vital for these services is agent technology. There are different types of agents. Some agents locate resources, some carry out mediation, and some are mobile and execute in different environments. A Java applet can be considered a simple agent.

Therefore, in addition to data, information, and knowledge management technologies, there are other technologies for Web data management and mining, including collaboration, visualization real-time processing, training, and multimedia. We have discussed them in Part I. There are several other technologies we have not mentioned, including data quality, fault tolerance, mass storage, fuzzy systems, machine translation, multilingual data mining, and data administration. All of these technologies and services have to work together to make Web information management and mining a success. Exhibit 18 illustrates how a distributed object management system can integrate the various technologies and services to provide effective Web data and information management. Impact of Web mining will be discussed in Part II.

RELATIONSHIP TO WEB DATA MINING

This chapter has described a number of information management technologies for the Web. The question is, what is the relationship between these technologies and Web mining? Exhibit 19 illustrates one concept. Here we show the relationship between the various information management technologies and Web mining. For example, we need special agents to carry out Web mining. One needs collaborative data mining to mine the data scattered across several locations. Web mining is a tool for effective knowledge management. Finally, sensor data has to be mined also.

In Part II, we will explore the relationship between information management and Web mining in more detail. The information gathered from sensors and streams has to be mined. On the other hand, Web mining can enhance information management technologies.

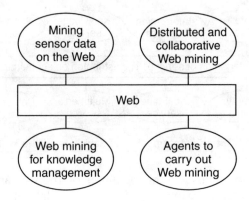

Exhibit 19.   Information Management and Web Mining

SUMMARY

This chapter has provided an overview of a number of information management technologies, including collaboration, knowledge management, training, and agents as well as technologies such as sensor information management and wireless information management. We then briefly examined the relationship of these technologies to Web mining. Note that some other information management technologies, such as multimedia processing, visualization, and decision support, were discussed in previous chapters.

This chapter essentially provides the background for a more in-depth exploration of Web mining in Part II. In particular, we will discuss Web mining for a number of information management technologies. The applications of information management and Web mining for counter-terrorism will be the subject of Part III.

Chapter 8
The Semantic Web

INTRODUCTION

In this chapter, we conclude the discussion of the supporting technologies for Web mining. In particular, we discuss the semantic Web. While the ideas about the semantic Web are still somewhat fuzzy, we expect the Web to evolve into the semantic Web.

One often asks the question, what is the difference between the Web and the semantic Web? Languages such as XML enable one to focus on the syntax of the documents. The Web has objects with complicated relationships. We need a way to specify all these relationships. Furthermore, the Web pages currently are for human consumption and manipulation. One needs the Web pages to be understood by machines. This is the idea behind the semantic Web. A semantic Web is not a single entity. It is a collection of XML documents, semistructured databases, and the millions of objects on the Web whose rich semantics need to be described. Furthermore, based on information on the Web, the machines and agents need to carry out actions and make decisions. Work in semantic Web is just beginning. But we need to master this technology to carry out effective E-business on the Web.

The idea of the semantic Web was conceived by Tim Berners-Lee. In his book on weaving the Web, he explains his ideas on going from the Web to the semantic Web [LEE99]. Perhaps one of the best articles on the semantic Web was published by Berners-Lee et al. in May 2001 [LEE01]. The authors explain clearly how with the semantic Web, agents are able to effectively carry out all operations from coordinating the activities to keeping appointments and schedules.

The idea behind the semantic Web is to make the Web as intelligent as possible. Therefore, in addition to storing and managing data and information, the Web should enable people to carry out their daily activities. Each individual could have his own personal space on the Web and carry out various activities from learning to teaching to providing and obtaining services from the Web. The ultimate goal is for users to get the right information at the right time displayed on their personal digital assistants (PDAs). Users should also be able to get the information they want from the Web using their PDAs. Although wireless technology and Web technology have come a long way, we still have much work to do before this goal can be realized.

121

While Web mining is now a reality, semantic Web mining is just beginning. All of the challenges and issues related to Web mining also relate to semantic Web mining. Semantic Web mining has additional challenges. For example, if the machine is to understand the Web pages, some mining has to be done to make things easier. That is, semantic Web mining will become a key technology for the semantic Web. In addition, semantic Web mining is a tool that could be used by the users of the semantic Web.

This chapter explores the various aspects of the semantic Web. The technologies for the semantic Web include RDF (resource description framework) and ontologies. We also discuss the DAML program at DARPA, and then describe how the Web can be viewed as a huge database. Note that Web mining has many applications in E-commerce, and we will briefly discuss them in Part II.

SEMANTIC WEB CONCEPTS

While the semantic Web as a concept is still evolving, there have been many developments in this area. These include RDF, ontologies, agents, and databases. Exhibit 1 illustrates the technologies for the semantic Web. We illustrate a model for the semantic Web in Exhibit 2. One could envisage a publish-and-subscribe model for the Web, where producers publish the services while consumers subscribe for the services.

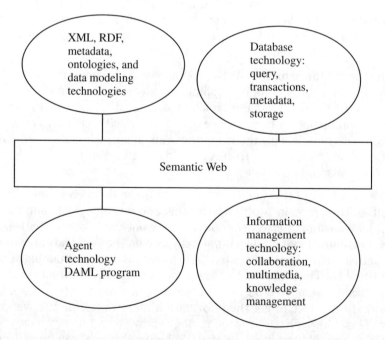

Exhibit 1.   Technologies for the Semantic Web

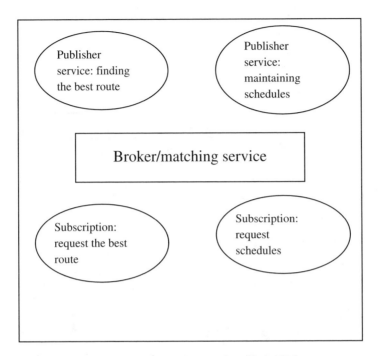

Exhibit 2.   Model for the Semantic Web

Exhibit 3 illustrates an example concept of operation for the semantic Web. As shown here, agents act on behalf of users. There are various types of agents, including brokers who negotiate the best deals for their customers. These services could be managing schedules and appointments, giving advice, and essentially managing all of the activities for a customer.

Consider a hypothetical example of John, who is a physician. The Web will wake him up, depending on the day of the year. Then he will be informed of his entire schedule and appointments. He could get information about the optimal routes to get to his destinations. He could also be informed of where his personal accessories are. Then as the day progresses, the Web will manage dynamic situations such as accidents, unexpected traffic, and other unanticipated events. Then the Web also gives him information about his patients, such as patient history; when his work is complete for the day, the Web makes arrangements for John to meet his wife for dinner and the theater.

One could say that the Web has completely taken over John's life and, yes, that is the ultimate goal. It would certainly make things a lot easier for John, and in the end it is up to John to follow the advice and directions. In the end, John will decide how he should proceed for the day.

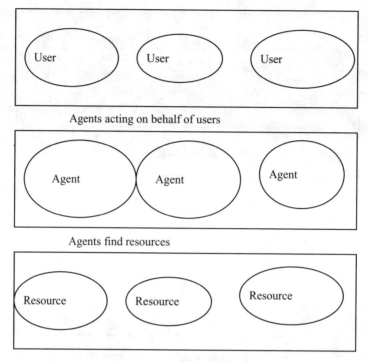

Agents acting on behalf of users

Agents find resources

Exhibit 3. Concept of Operation for the Semantic Web

Now that we have provided a brief overview of what the semantic Web is, we will be able to explore some of the technologies. In the next four sections we discuss RDF, ontologies, agents, and databases — all relating to the semantic Web.

RDF

RDF (resource description framework) is the foundation of the semantic Web. RDF is essentially the foundation for processing metadata (see [RDF] for an excellent tutorial). While XML is limited in providing machine-understandable documents, RDF handles this limitation. As a result, RDF provides better support for interoperability, searching, and cataloging. It also describes contents of documents and relationships between various entities in the document. As stated in the tutorial, RDF complements XML. That is, while XML provides syntax and notations, RDF supplements this by providing semantic information in a standardized way. RDF is the work of many communities collaborating together to represent metadata in a standardized way. These communities include the Web Standardization Community and those working on XML, HTML, SGML and other related standards.

Let us now examine the basic RDF model and some advanced concepts. The basic RDF model has three types: resources, properties, and statements. A resource is anything described by an RDF expression. It could be a Web page or a collection of pages. Property is a specific attribute used to describe a resource. RDF statements are resources together with a named property plus the value of the property. Statement components are subject, predicate, and object. So, for example, if we have a sentence of the form "John is the creator of xxx," then "xxx" is the subject or resource, "creator" is the property or predicate, and "John" is the object or literal. There are RDF diagrams very similar to ER (entity relationship) diagrams or object diagrams to represent statements. RDFs describe what is intended (such as John is the creator of xxx) in the following form:

```
<rdf:RDF>

</rdf:RDF>
```

There are various aspects specific to RDF syntax, and for more details we refer to the various documents on RDF published by the World Wide Web Consortium (W3C). Also, it is very important that the intended interpretation is used for RDF sentences. This is accomplished by RDF schemas. A schema is a dictionary of sorts that has interpretations of various terms used in sentences. RDF and XML name spaces may be used to resolve conflicts in semantics.

More advanced concepts in RDF include the container model and statements about statements. The container model has three types of container objects: bag, sequence, and alternative. A bag is an unordered list of resources or literals used to indicate that a property has multiple values, but the order is not important. A sequence is a list of ordered resources; here the order is important. Alternative is a list of resources that represent alternatives for the value of a property. Various tutorials in RDF describe the syntax of containers in more detail.

RDF also provides support for making statements about other statements. For example, with this facility one can make statements of the form, "the statement A is false," where A is the statement, "John is the creator of xxx." Again, one can use object-like diagrams to represent containers and statements about statements. Exhibit 4 illustrates the various aspects of RDF.

RDF also has a formula model associated with it. This model has a formal grammar and is the result of logicians and theoreticians working on RDF. Essentially, RDF is the work of theoreticians and practitioners. For further information on RDF, we refer to the work of W3C and, in particular, the work of the RDF Model and Syntax Working Group. As in the case of any language or model, RDF will continue to evolve. Therefore, we encourage the reader

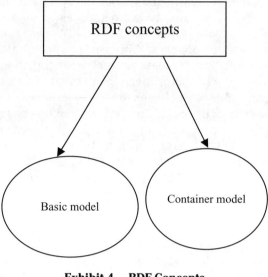

Exhibit 4.   RDF Concepts

to keep up with the latest developments with RDF and check the W3C Web page from time to time for new developments and pointers.

ROLE OF ONTOLOGIES

Let us examine the role of ontologies. As we mentioned in Chapter 5, ontologies essentially describe entities and relationships among entities. As we have pointed out, the concept of metadata has evolved over the years, starting from data dictionaries to database schemas and now to ontologies, XML, XML schemas, RDF, and RDF schemas. XML and RDF are special ways of representing the various ontologies. Ontologies could describe vehicles, people, animals, and relationships between people, events, and many other things. While XML has limitations and has less semantic power to represent ontologies, RDF attempts to overcome the limitations. XML and RDF are not the only way to represent ontologies. One can use semantic networks, frames, object models, hypersemantic data models, and many other presentation schemas for ontologies.

Exhibit 5 shows how ontologies can be represented using XML and RDF schemas. As illustrated, ontologies resulted from various metadata concepts. Ontologies can also be represented by semantic nets and other models such as frames. That is, ontologies are essentially semantics about various entities, events, and the relationships between the entities. There are several representational schemes for ontologies and RDF is one of them.

In summary, ontologies are essential for developing the semantic Web. As we have mentioned, semantic Web is the Web that consists of agents

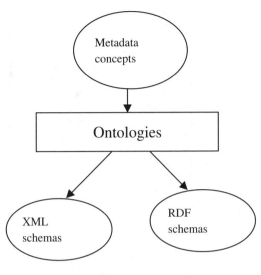

Exhibit 5. Ontologies

that can manage the numerous resources, including the Web pages, and handle activities for people. Therefore, semantic representation and managing the semantics of applications are essential for the semantic Web. Ontologies are a means of describing semantics. The specific syntax chosen could be one of many. Nevertheless, ontologies are at the heart of the semantic Web. There have been many efforts and discussions on integrating ontologies and transforming ontologies. We will discuss them in Chapter 16 when we discuss some directions for building the semantic Web.

AGENTS AND THE DAML PROGRAM

The DAML (DARPA Agent Markup Language) Program was initiated by Dr. James Hendler when he was the program manager at DARPA (Defense Advanced Research Projects Agency). The program officially began in 2000 and is ongoing. The goal of this program is to develop a markup language for agents. The idea is for agents to understand the Web information and process the information. This essentially is the goal of the semantic Web. Although DAML and the semantic Web initially developed independently, the goals are the same. Therefore, one can say that DAML is currently developing technologies for the semantic Web.

DAML researchers are investigating various aspects, including RDF, data models, ontologies, logics for RDF, and metadata processing. Note that RDF was also being developed independently by W3C working groups. However, the DAML research output is being examined by the W3C and, as a result, DAML is influencing the development of RDF a great deal. The relationship between DAML and W3C is illustrated in Exhibit 6.

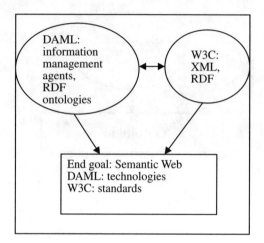

Exhibit 6.   DAML and W3C

While W3C is involved with coming up with specifications, DAML complements the work by investigating many of the research issues, including
ontologies and logics. We need more programs like DAML to develop the
semantic Web. That is, the work of W3C alone is not sufficient. More recently,
the National Science Foundation is working collaboratively with research
agencies in Europe to further identify research topics for the semantic Web.

In summary, the semantic Web technologies are in their infancy. Various
data and information management technologies have to be investigated to
develop the semantic Web. The DAML program is moving in the right direction. The relationship between DAML and W3C is also moving in the right
direction. There is still much to be done.

SEMANTIC WEB AS A DATABASE

We have found that there is no standard definition of a semantic database. We have adopted the view presented by Berners-Lee et al. [LEE01].
Some say that it is the Web where agents process the information. Others
say it is based on the publish-and-subscribe model. There is another group
that says that it is an intelligent database and therefore all of the techniques developed for managing intelligent databases apply here as well.
This section examines the latter view.

One could consider the semantic Web as a collection of information
sources that are interconnected and have to be managed by a database
management system. The challenges include modeling the database, integrating the heterogeneous information sources, querying the information
and sources, and accessing information, which means developing appropriate indexing techniques. One needs to understand the schemas of the

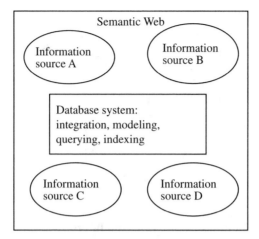

Exhibit 7. Semantic Web as a Database

information sources and integrate the schemas. One could think of using XML or RDF to represent the schemas. Schema integration issues include handling semantic heterogeneity. We need to examine the developments on integrating heterogeneous data and information sources (see [ACM90]) and then apply them for the semantic Web. Exhibit 7 illustrates the semantic Web as a database.

XML, RDF, AND INTEROPERABILITY

There have been discussions about how XML supports interoperability. As we have mentioned, XML supports common representation of documents. As a result, it is possible for different systems to interpret the document the same way. Common representation is key to interoperability. However, XML does not support semantics. Therefore, various aspects such as semantic heterogeneity cannot be handled by XML. One proposal is to use RDF to facilitate semantic heterogeneity, as illustrated in Exhibit 8. That is, RDF, with the use of ontologies, supports semantics. This way, one can handle syntactic and semantic heterogeneity.

In the case of database interoperability, with both XML and RDF one can represent the schemas of various databases including legacy databases. This in turn supports interoperability, as illustrated in Exhibit 9. That is, XML and RDF are essential technologies for interoperability. Whether it will be XML or RDF or some other technology in the end is yet to be determined. However, the Web community is moving in the right direction. What was thought to be almost impossible just a few years ago is possible now. That is, the community has more or less come to an agreement on common terminology and semantics. This was one of the major challenges faced by database researchers in the early 1990s.

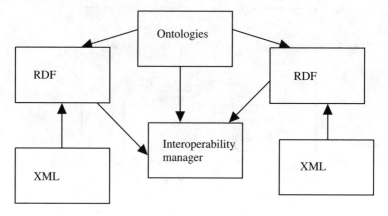

Exhibit 8. XML, RDF, and Interoperability

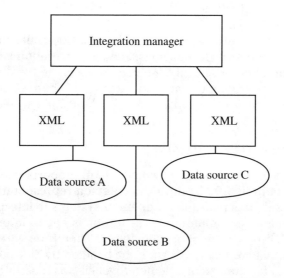

Exhibit 9. XML and Database Interoperability

WEB SERVICES

In [THUR02], we discussed Web Services Description Language (WSDL). We repeat the discussion here and then briefly discuss Web services. There has to be some way to describe the communication on the Web in a structured and organized way. WSDL does this by defining an XML grammar for describing network services. As described in [WSDL], the network services are described as a collection of communication endpoints capable of exchanging messages. A WSDL document has various elements, including types, which is a container for data type definition; message, which is the data being communicated; operation, which is an action supported by the

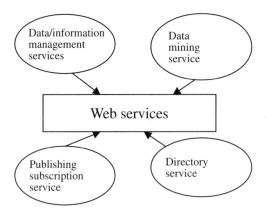

Exhibit 10.   Example Web Services

service; port type, which is a subset of operations supported by the end-points; binding, which is a concrete protocol and data format specification for a particular port type; port, which is an endpoint; and service, which is a collection of endpoints.

So while WSDL is a Web services description language, what are Web services? These are services provided by the Web to its users. These could be publishing services, data management services, information management services, directory services, etc. That is, any service that the Web provides is a Web service, and WSDL provides the means to specify the service. Web services is an area that will expand a great deal in the coming years. These services will form the essence of the semantic Web. Exhibit 10 shows a high level view of Web services. One may need to mine the information to provide relevant Web services to the user. On the other hand, mining service could be a Web service.

We are already on the right path. As we have mentioned in earlier chapters, different domain groups such as the E-commerce Group, the Wireless Group, and the Multimedia Group are developing customized XML specifications. It has been pointed out to us that the geographic information systems community is coming up with its own markup language (e.g., GML, Geographic Markup Language), while the medical community is coming up with its own XML specifications. That is, XML is being customized.

NOTE ON E-COMMERCE, BUSINESS INTELLIGENCE, AND THE SEMANTIC WEB

In [THUR00], we have discussed data mining for E-commerce. That is, data mining in general and Web mining in particular are critical technologies for E-commerce. One can mine information about customers in order to carry out targeted marketing. One can also mine the databases to get

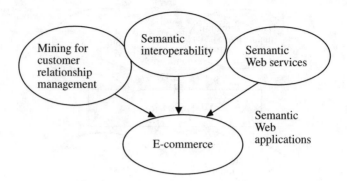

Exhibit 11.   Semantic Web for E-Commerce

information about consumers, customers, and competitors. Furthermore, E-commerce is the killer application for the Web.

The question is, what is the relationship between the semantic Web and E-commerce? If we have machine-understandable Web pages, then the burden placed on the human can be greatly relieved. For example, common ontologies and representations enable semantic interoperability between organizations. As a result, E-commerce can be greatly facilitated. Furthermore, the semantic Web enhances business intelligence as well. Because of machine-understandable Web pages, one semantic Web could improve the gathering of intelligence information for organizations. We will revisit semantic Web mining and E-commerce in Part II of this book. Part III will discuss them again with respect to counter-terrorism. Exhibit 11 provides an overview on the semantic Web for E-commerce.

WEB VERSUS THE SEMANTIC WEB

There have been discussions about the differences between the Web and the semantic Web. Some say that the Web is a system where humans read the Web pages, while the semantic Web is a system where the machine reads and understands the Web pages. Others say that the Web today is the semantic Web of yesterday and the Web tomorrow is the semantic Web of today. That is, we are getting closer to machine-understandable Web pages. However, we are still a long way from achieving this.

One cannot say that the semantic Web will end once we have a system with machine-understandable Web pages. The enhancements will continue forever as new technologies emerge. That is, we cannot say that we have finished building the semantic Web, as we believe that it will continue to evolve forever.

Exhibit 12 illustrates the evolution of the Web to the semantic Web. Yesterday we had HTML, today we have XML, tomorrow we will have RDF, and

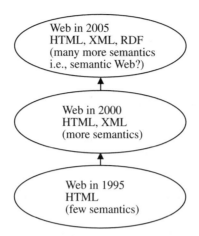

Exhibit 12.   From the Web to the Semantic Web

the day after we will have something else. The biggest challenge for us was to build the initial Web. This was accomplished by pioneers such as Tim Berners-Lee. After that, it appears there is no end in sight. We believe that the Web will continue to evolve forever.

DATA MINING AND THE SEMANTIC WEB

As we have mentioned earlier, Web mining is now a reality. The challenge is to carry out semantic Web mining. The question is, what does it mean to mine the semantic Web? Note that semantic Web is about machine-understandable Web pages so that the Web is more intelligent and can perform useful services to the user. This means that the information in the Web pages may have to be mined so that the machine can understand the Web pages. Essentially, we need to carry out machine learning on the Web pages and other information on the Web.

Another challenge is also to mine the RDF and XML documents and also develop semantic Web services. One can also mine the ontologies and other databases on the Web. We will revisit semantic Web mining in Part II. Exhibit 13 illustrates a high level overview of semantic Web mining.

SUMMARY

This chapter is devoted to a discussion of the semantic Web. We first provided an overview of the semantic Web and showed how it differed from the Web. Then we discussed some technologies related to the semantic Web. Next we provided an overview of agents and DARPA's DAML program. We discussed some issues on treating the semantic Web as a database and examined how the various database concepts could be reused to

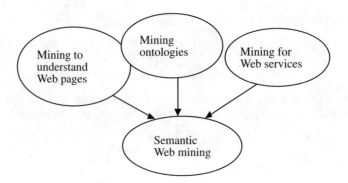

Exhibit 13.   Semantic Web Mining

address the semantic Web. Finally, we discussed interoperability issues and then provided our view of the Web versus the semantic Web. We ended the chapter with a discussion of the relationship between semantic Web and data mining.

Note that we have provided just a brief description of the semantic Web. There are many papers being written on the semantic Web. The area is still relatively new, and we expect significant developments to be made over the next few years. Berners-Lee and coworkers provide a good starting point to understanding the semantic Web ([LEE99] and [LEE01]). While the ideas about the semantic Web are still quite fuzzy, we believe that Web is evolving into the semantic Web (see also [ONTO], [RDF], [W3C], [WML], [WORK1], [WORK2], [XML1], and [XML2]). That is, the technologies will eventually lead us toward machine-understandable Web pages.

With this chapter, we end the discussion of key supporting technologies for Web mining. In Part II, we will elaborate on Web mining. This will set the stage for Part III, which will be devoted on Web mining for counterterrorism.

CONCLUSION TO PART I

Part I has described various supporting technologies. These include the Web and E-commerce, Web database systems, data mining, information retrieval, information management, and the semantic Web.

In Part II we will see how these technologies relate to Web mining. For example, the databases on the Web have to be mined. Furthermore, search engines have incorporated mining techniques. Information management technologies are needed for Web data mining. Finally, semantic Web mining is an emerging area.

With this background we are now in a position to explore the relationship between Web mining and the supporting technologies we have discussed. This relationship will be explored in Part II. Applications in counter-terrorism will be the subject of Part III.

Part II
Web Data Mining: Techniques, Tools, and Trends

INTRODUCTION TO PART II

Part II, consisting of nine chapters, describes techniques, tools, and trends for Web data mining. Chapter 9 provides an overview of Web data mining, and particularly, the various aspects of Web mining, including Web data mining, Web usage mining, and Web structure mining. Chapter 10 describes processes and techniques for Web data mining. We discuss the techniques for data mining and see how they can be adapted for Web data mining.

Chapter 11 discusses issues on mining Web databases. Essentially, it examines the technologies discussed in Chapter 5 and discusses the impact of Web mining. Chapter 12 examines information retrieval techniques, discussed in Chapter 6, and describes the impact of Web mining. Chapter 13 examines the information management technologies, discussed in Chapter 7, and the impact of Web mining. Chapter 14 examines the semantic Web technologies, discussed in Chapter 8, and the impact of Web mining. That is, Chapters 11 through 14 examine the technologies in Part I and discuss the impact of Web mining.

As we will see in Chapter 9, there are three aspects to Web mining. The first is Web data mining, the second is Web usage mining, and the third is Web structure mining. Chapter 15 discusses Web usage and structure mining in more detail. Some tools for Web data mining will be discussed in Chapter 16. Some applications of Web mining, including E-commerce and biotechnology, will be discussed in Chapter 17. Note that while we discuss the applications briefly in Part II, the major application considered, counter-terrorism, will be the subject of Part III. As in Part I, each chapter in Part II begins with an introduction and ends with a summary.

Chapter 9
Data Mining and the Web

INTRODUCTION

Part I discussed supporting technologies for Web data mining; Part II will discuss the impact of Web data mining on these technologies. In this chapter, we provide an overview of Web data mining. Note that Part II also discusses tools and applications for Web data mining. However, the major application considered in this book will be discussed in Part III; that application is counter-terrorism.

With information overload on the Web, it is highly desirable to mine the data and extract patterns and information relevant for the user. This will make the task of browsing on the Internet so much easier for the user. Therefore, there has been a lot of interest in Web mining, which is essentially mining databases on the Web or mining usage patterns so that helpful information can be provided to the user.

Data mining and the Web developed as independent technology areas in the mid-1990s. While it was felt that mining data on the Web would be useful to help the information overload problem, the extent to which Web mining would help key areas such as E-commerce was not well understood until recently. It was only a few years ago that researchers and practitioners seriously started to think about Web mining. The Web Mining Workshop held during the Knowledge Discovery in Databases Conference in 1999 was one of the first [WDM99]. Our initial work on Web mining did not take place until the Web Mining Panel at the International Conference on Tools in Artificial Intelligence Conference in November 1997 [ICTA97].

Cooley ([COOL98]) and Srivastava et al. ([SHR102]) have specified a taxonomy for Web mining. They initially divided Web mining into two categories: (1) getting patterns from Web data and (2) getting Web logs. Then the taxonomy was expanded to include three areas that are known as Web content mining, Web usage mining, and Web structure mining. Web content mining is mining the data which will include text, video, etc., on the Web. Essentially, Web content mining subsumes data mining. Web usage mining is mining information about access to Web pages and includes clickstream

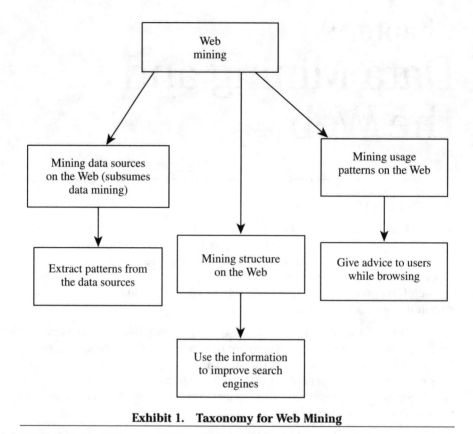

Exhibit 1.   Taxonomy for Web Mining

analysis. Web structure mining is essentially mining the URLs and other Web links to extract structure. Exhibit 1 illustrates this taxonomy.

Closely related to Web usage mining is mining to support E-commerce. There are two aspects here. One is to mine information about competitors and the other is to mine customer profiles, usage patterns, and targeted marketing.

MINING DATA ON THE WEB

Mining the data on the Web is one of the major challenges faced by the data management and mining community as well as those working on Web information management and machine learning. There is so much data and information on the Web that extracting what is useful and relevant to the user is the real challenge. When a user scans through the Web, it can become quite daunting, and soon the user is overloaded with data. The question is, how do you convert this data into information and, subsequently, knowledge so that the user gets only what he wants? Further-

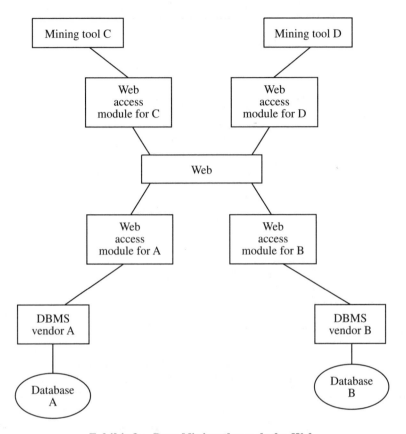

Exhibit 2.   Data Mining through the Web

more, what are the ways of extracting previously unknown information from the data on the Web? In this section, we discuss various aspects of Web mining.

One simple solution is to integrate the data mining tools with the data on the Web. This is illustrated in Exhibit 2. This approach works well, especially if the data is in relational databases. Therefore, one needs to mine the data in the relational databases with the data mining tools that are available. These data mining tools have to develop interfaces to the Web. For example, if a relational interface is provided, as in the Junglee system ([JUNG98]), then SQL-based mining tools could be applied to the virtual relational database, as illustrated in Exhibit 3.

Unfortunately, the Web world is not so straightforward. Much of the data is unstructured and semistructured. There is a lot of imagery data and video data. Providing a relational interface to all such databases may be complicated. The question is, how do you mine such data? In Chapter 12,

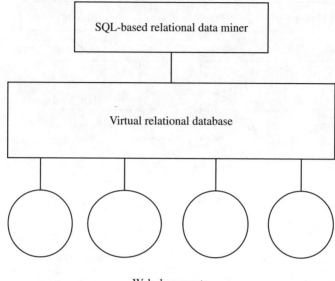

Exhibit 3.   Web Mining on Virtual Relational Databases

we discuss various aspects of mining multimedia data. In particular, we focus on mining text, images, video, and audio data. One needs to develop tools first to mine multimedia data, and then focus on developing tools to mine such data on the Web. We illustrate a scenario for multimedia mining on the Web in Exhibit 4, where multimedia databases are first integrated and then mined.

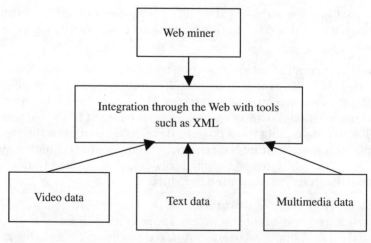

Exhibit 4.   Multimedia Web Mining

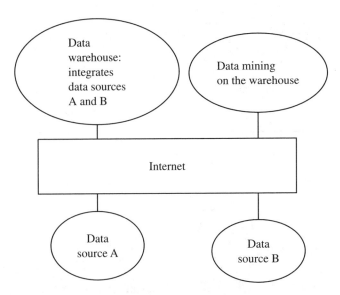

Exhibit 5.   Data Warehousing and Mining on the Internet

Much of the previous discussion has focused on integrating data mining tools with the databases on the Web. In many cases, the data on the Web is not in databases. It is on various servers. Therefore, the challenge is to organize the data on these servers. Some form of data warehousing technology may be needed to organize the data to be mined. A scenario is illustrated in Exhibit 5. There is little work in developing some sort of data warehousing technology for the Web to facilitate mining.

Another area that needs attention is visualization of the data on the Web [THUR96c]. Much of the data is unorganized and difficult to understand. Furthermore, as discussed in [THUR98], mining is greatly facilitated by visualization; therefore, developing appropriate visualization tools for the Web will greatly facilitate mining the data. These visualization tools could aid in the mining process, as illustrated in Exhibit 6.

Recently, various standards have been developed by organizations such as ISO (International Standards organization), W3C (World Wide Web Consortium), and OMG (Object Management Group) for Internet data access and management. These standards include models, specification languages, and architectures. One of the developments is XML (Extensible Markup Language) for writing a Document Type Definition that allows the document to be interpreted by the person receiving the document ([XML1] and [XML2]). Relationships between data mining and standards such as XML are largely unexplored. However, one could expect data mining languages to be developed for the Web.

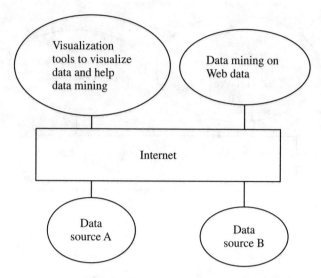

Exhibit 6.   Data Mining and Visualization on the Web

In summary, several technologies have to work together to effectively mine the data on the Web. These include data mining on multimedia data, mining tools to predict trends and activities on the Web, as well as technologies for data management on the Web, data warehousing, and visualization. There is active research in Web mining, and we can expect to see much progress being made here.

MINING USAGE PATTERNS

Another aspect to mining on the Web is to collect various statistics to determine which Web pages are likely to be accessed, based on various usage patterns. Research in this direction is being conducted by various groups (for example, see [MORE98a]). Here, based on usage patterns of various users, trends and predictions are made as to the likely Web pages a user may want to scan. Based on this information, a user can be given guidance as to the Web pages he may want to browse, as illustrated in Exhibit 7. This will facilitate the work a user has to do with respect to scanning various Web pages. Note that while the previous paragraphs in this section focused on developing data mining tools to mine the data on the Web, here we are focusing on using mining to expedite the Web browsing process. We can expect to see many results in this area.

Mining can also be used to give only selective information to the user. For example, many of us are flooded with e-mail messages daily. Some of these messages are not relevant for our work. One can develop tools to discard the messages that are not relevant. These tools could be simple filtering tools or sophisticated data mining tools. Similarly, these data min-

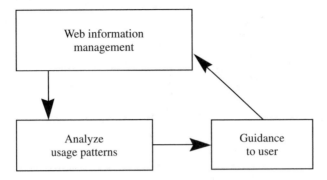

Exhibit 7. Analyzing Usage Patterns and Predicting Trends

ing tools could also be used to display only the Web pages in which a user is interested.

WEB STRUCTURE MINING

Web structure mining is essentially about mining the links on the Web. It is closely related to Web usage mining. For example, giving advice to the user about browsing uses both Web usage mining and Web structure mining. One needs to mine the links to determine where the user is and the Web pages he can access from where he is.

Web structure mining is used in search engines such as Google. For example, the links are mined and one can then determine the Web pages that point to a particular Web page. Then when you search for a string, the Web page with the search string that has the most number of links pointing to it may be listed first. That is, Web pages are listed based on rank, which is determined by the ranks of the Web pages pointing to it.

Web structure mining is essentially about mining graphs and detecting patterns. One can use link analysis techniques to determine patterns in the graphs. We will revisit Web structure mining in a later chapter. The importance of link mining for counter-terrorism will be discussed in Part III.

Exhibit 8 illustrates Web structure mining. In this exhibit, the circles represent Web pages that are linked. We can also see a pattern emerge, as shown on the right. In this example, the pattern is somewhat obvious. In the real world, the graph may be quite complex and, therefore, one needs to mine to extract patterns. Link analysis will be discussed further in Part III.

APPLICATIONS AND DIRECTIONS

One of the major applications of Web mining is E-commerce. Corporations want to have the competitive edge and are exploring numerous ways

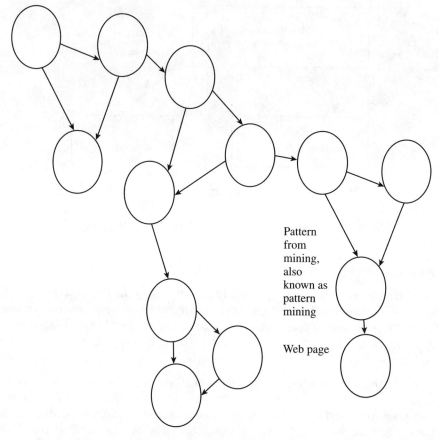

Exhibit 8.   Pattern Mining

to market effectively. Major organizations, including retail stores, have E-commerce sites now. Customers can order products from books to clothing to toys through these sites. The goal is to provide customized marketing. For example, user group A may prefer literature novels whereas user group B may prefer mystery novels. Therefore, new literature novels have to be marketed to group A and new mystery novels have to be marketed to group B. How does an E-commerce site know about these preferences? The answer is data mining. The usage patterns have to be mined. In addition, the organization may mine various public and private databases to get additional information about these users. That is, both types of data mining described in the taxonomy have to be performed. Exhibit 9 illustrates the application of Web mining to E-commerce. Essentially, one mines usage patterns, gathers business intelligence, and makes improvement to the E-commerce site.

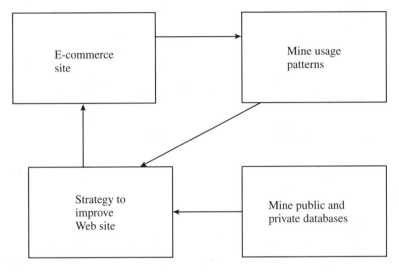

Exhibit 9.   Web Mining for E-Commerce

Web mining can also be used to provide entertainment on the Web. This is another variation of E-commerce. Web access and Web data may be mined for user preferences on movies and record albums and the corporations can carry out targeted marketing.

As more developments are made on data mining and the Web, we can expect better tools to emerge on Web mining both to mine the data on the Web and to mine the usage patterns. We can expect to hear much about Web mining in coming years.

Not only can data mining help E-commerce sites, it can also help users to find information. For example, one E-commerce site manager mentioned to me that that the major problem his site has is that of being found by users. He has advertised in various magazines, but the ads reach only those who have access to the magazines. One solution is to have a third-party agent make the connection between the site and the user. Another solution is to make the search engines more intelligent. Data mining could help here. The data miner could match the requirements of the user to what is being offered by the E-commerce sites. Work is beginning in this area and we still have a long way to go. This is illustrated in Exhibit 10.

We will revisit this application later in Part II. Counter-terrorism, the main application considered in this book, will be discussed in Part III. Note that counter-terrorism includes insider threat analysis, cyber-terrorism, and bio-terrorism. In Part III, we will also draw parallels between E-commerce, business intelligence, and counter-terrorism technologies. Essen-

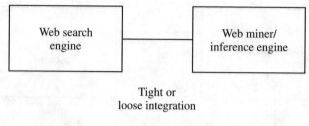

Tight or
loose integration

Exhibit 10.   Web Mining for Search Engines

tially, one needs to gather business intelligence to handle threats and counter-terrorist attacks.

SUMMARY

This chapter has discussed the emerging topic of Web data mining. First we provided some of the challenges in mining Web databases and then we discussed issues on Web usage mining. Finally, we discussed major applications in electronic commerce.

Web mining is still a relatively new area and there is active research on this topic. Various conferences are now including panels on Web mining (for example, see [ICTA97]). As Web technology and data mining technology mature, we can expect good tools to be developed to mine the large quantities of data on the Web. As mentioned earlier, at present many of the data mining tools work on relational databases. However, much of the data on the Web is semistructured and unstructured. Therefore, we need to focus our attention on mining text and other types of nonrelational databases. Unless advances are made in this area, successful Web mining will be difficult to achieve.

As mentioned in [THUR98], for mining to be effective, we need good data. Therefore, to get meaningful results from Web mining, we need to have good data on the Web. In other words, effective Web data management is critical for Web mining. There is much to be done in Web data management. It is only recently that various approaches are being proposed for Web data management (for example, see [IEEE98]). As Web data management and data mining technologies mature, we can expect to see good Web mining tools emerge.

Chapter 10
Processes and Techniques for Web Data Mining

INTRODUCTION

In this chapter, we will discuss processes and techniques for Web mining. In Part III, we will show how these techniques may be applied for counter-terrorism.

Recently, there has been much interest in mining Web databases, including multimedia databases. As mentioned, many of the data mining tools work on relational databases; however, a considerable amount of data is now in multimedia format. There is a large amount of text and image data on the Web. News services provide much video and audio data. This data has to be mined so that useful information can be extracted. One solution is to extract structured data from the multimedia databases and then mine the structured data using traditional data mining tools. Another solution is to develop mining tools to operate on the multimedia data directly. Technologies and techniques for Web data mining are the subjects of this chapter. In particular, we discuss data mining basics and show how they can be adapted for Web data mining. These techniques are important because in Part III we show how these techniques are used for various applications, including intrusion detection and counter-terrorism.

PROCESS OF WEB DATA MINING

Now that we have an understanding of what Web data mining technologies are and how they contribute to data mining, let us next discuss what data mining is all about and how we go about it. As mentioned in Chapter 3, data mining is the process of posing queries and extracting useful, previously unknown information, patterns, and trends from large quantities of data that is possibly stored in databases. That is, not only do we want to get patterns and trends, these patterns and trends must be useful, otherwise we can get irrelevant data that could turn out to be harmful or cause problems with the actions taken. For example, if a data miner finds incorrectly that an individual is involved in fraud and begins to investigate the individual's behavior, this could damage the individual. This is called a false positive. However, we also do not want results that are false negatives. We do not want the data miner to return a result that the individual is well behaved when he is a fraud. So data mining has serious implications. This is why it is critical that we have good data to mine and we know the limitations of the data mining techniques.

We would like to stress to managers and project leaders that they should not rush into data mining. Data mining is not the answer to all questions, and sometimes it has been overemphasized. It is expensive to carry out the entire mining process and, therefore, the decision to use data mining has to be thought out completely. In reality, the mining part is only a small step toward the entire process. We need to ask questions: Is there a need for mining? Do we have the right data in the right format? Do we have the right tools? More importantly, do we have the people to do the work? Do we have sufficient funds allocated to the project? All these questions have to be answered before we embark on a data mining project. Otherwise, we can be extremely disappointed with the results.

This section discusses data mining from start to finish without going into the technical details such as algorithms, approaches, and outcomes. We describe various example applications that would benefit from Web data mining. These are examples we have obtained from various discussions we have had and articles we have read, as well as applying common sense. This would give the reader a good idea as to what data mining and Web data mining are all about. We discuss why we want to do Web data mining. For example, why is data mining such a buzz word right now? What is it about the world that has changed that makes data mining so useful now and not 20 years ago? Then we discuss the steps to Web data mining. These steps include identifying and preparing the data, determining which data to mine, preparing the data to mine, carrying out the mining, pruning the results, taking actions, evaluating the actions, and determining when to do mining next. Note that data mining is not a one-time activity. An organization has to continually do mining as the data changes, the actions may not be beneficial, or the tools may have improved. Then we discuss some of the limitations and challenges to Web data mining. These include incorrect data, incomplete data, insufficient resources such as man power, and inadequate tools. Some user interface aspects are discussed. Note that much of the discussion in this section applies to data mining as well as to Web data mining. We also mentioned the additional challenges for Web data mining. As we have mentioned, we expect much of the data available to be on the Web. The Web can be based on public or private networks. Therefore, Web mining will encompass data mining. In Chapter 9, we discussed three aspects to Web mining: Web content mining, Web usage mining, and Web structure mining.

Some Examples

In this section, we give numerous examples to illustrate how mining can be used. Some of these examples have been obtained from various papers and proceedings (for example, see [GRUP98]) and some others from discussions. While much of the work in data mining is being done to support marketing and sales, it is also useful in other areas. Following are some examples; note that many of these examples are relevant to counter-terrorism applications.

- A supermarket store analyzes the purchases made by various people and arranges the items on the shelves in a way that improves sales. This data usually resides in a structured database; however, there may be some text to mine here.
- A credit bureau analyzes the credit history of various people to determine risk. These histories may be in the form of text.
- An investigation agency analyzes the behavior patterns of people to determine potential threats to protected information. The reports to be analyzed may be in the form of text.
- A pharmacy determines which physicians are likely to buy their products by analyzing the prescription patterns of physicians. While the data is usually in structured databases, it may also be text.
- An insurance company determines which patients might potentially be expensive by analyzing various patient records. These records may be in structured or text databases.
- An automobile sales company analyzes the buying patterns of people living in a specific location, and sends them brochures of cars they are likely to buy. Here again, data may be in structured or text databases.
- An employment agency analyzes employment histories of job candidates and sends them information about potentially lucrative jobs. Data may be in text databases.
- An adversary uses data mining tools to access unclassified databases and deduces potentially classified information. There may be text, images, video, and audio data to mine here.
- An educational institution analyzes students' records to determine who is likely to attend the institution, and sends them promotional brochures. The records are likely to be in structured databases, although there may be text data.
- A nuclear weapons plant analyzes audit records of historical information and determines that there could be a potential nuclear disaster if certain precautions are not taken.
- A command-and-control agency analyzes the behavior patterns of an adversary to determine what weapons the adversary has. Here data may be in the form of text or images.

- A marketing organization analyzes the buying patterns of people and estimates the number of children they have and their income so that potentially useful marketing information can be sent. While data is usually in structured databases, it is likely that there may be some text to mine.
- By analyzing patient history and current medical conditions, physicians diagnose current conditions and predict potential problems. Data may be in image databases (x-rays) and text databases.
- The Internal Revenue Service examines the tax returns of various groups of people and finds abnormal patterns and trends. Data may be in text form.
- By analyzing the travel patterns of various groups of people, an investigative agency determines the associations between the various groups. Data could be in text or image databases.
- An investigative agency analyzes the criminal records to determine who are likely to commit terrorism and mass murder. Data may be in text such as newspaper articles.

Note that we have selected various examples from all types of applications, including financial, intelligence, and medical, to carry out various activities such as marketing, diagnosis, correlations, and fault detection. These application areas are illustrated in Exhibit 1. We will revisit some of them in Chapter 17. All these examples show that a great amount of data analysis is needed to come up with results and conclusions. This type of

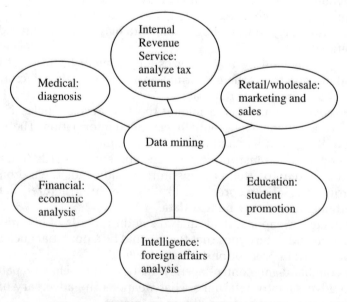

Exhibit 1.   Some Data Mining Application Areas

Data, data, and more data

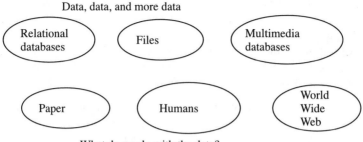

What do we do with the data?
Mine, mine, and mine until we get useful information.

Exhibit 2. Why Data Mining?

data analysis is usually referred to as mining. Note that mining is not always used in a positive manner for the betterment of human society. In many cases, it could be quite dangerous, such as compromising the privacy of individuals. Privacy will be addressed in Chapter 25. In this book, we have provided information not only on the positive aspects, but also on the negative aspects of data mining. In addition, we also discuss the difficulties and challenges to mining.

Why Web Data Mining

So now that we have seen various applications that may need data mining, let us discuss why is it that we are talking about data mining now? We know that many of these problems have existed for many years and data has been around for centuries. The answer is that we are using new tools and techniques to solve these problems. For example, data analysis has been carried out for years in different ways, but it is only now that we call it data mining with improved methods and techniques (see Exhibit 2). In this section, we will discuss the reasons for carrying out data mining and then examine the reasons for carrying out Web data mining.

Although data has been around, it has been on paper and, in many cases, in the minds of people. Typically, clerks spend years recording data, and human analysts go through it to detect various patterns. Eventually, the idea of statistics gave a new way to analyze the data; however, organizing data was still a big problem. Then, with the advent of computers and databases, we started storing the data in computerized files and databases. This was the first big step toward data mining. After that came the area of artificial intelligence with new and improved searching and learning techniques. What has contributed mostly to data mining is the improved way to store and retrieve data, and that is essentially database management systems technology.

More recently, techniques and tools are being developed to focus on improving methods to capture the data and knowledge of organizations. This is going to be even better for data mining. There is still a tremendous amount of data out there that has not been captured. Furthermore, even if it is captured, one does not know of the existence of the data. So, knowledge management techniques will improve these deficiencies [MORE98a].

So now we have large quantities of computerized data in files, relational databases, multimedia databases, and on the World Wide Web. We have very sophisticated statistical analysis packages. Tools have been developed for machine learning. Parallel computing technology is becoming mature for improving performance. Visualization techniques improve the understanding of data. Decision support tools are also maturing. So what better way is there than integrating these various developments to provide improved capabilities for analyzing data and predicting trends? Data mining has become a reality; therefore, we are beginning to prepare for data mining. With respect to Web data mining, it is only recently that we are getting a good handle on managing Web databases. Web data mining technologies are still a few years away.

This section has essentially discussed the need for data mining. However, because of the fact that we expect much of the data to be on the Web, there is also a clear need to mine the data on the Web. As we have stated in earlier chapters with respect to Web data mining, not only do we need to mine the content on the Web, we also need to mine the usage patterns and structures.

Steps to Data Mining

We have given various examples of data mining and established a need for data mining as well as Web data mining. In this section, we will discuss the steps for data mining and the steps for Web data mining. What are the steps to mining? Where do we start and where do we end? Various texts have discussed the steps to data mining and we have found them quite useful (for example, see [BERR97]). Based on what we have read and our experiences, the data mining steps, some of which are as illustrated in Exhibit 3, are as follows:

- Identifying the data
- Preparing the data
- Mining the data
- Getting useful results
- Identifying actions
- Implementing the actions
- Evaluating the benefits
- Determining what to do next
- Carrying out the next cycle

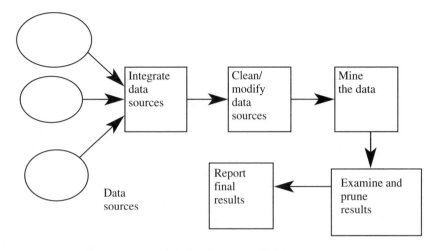

Exhibit 3.   Steps to Mining

First, we need to identify the data. As mentioned in the previous section, data could be all over the world, not just in the enterprise. Data could be distributed. It could be on paper and even in people's heads. Data could be in the form of text, images, video, and audio. We need to figure out what data we need, where to find it, and then get it.

Once we have the data, we need to prepare it. This takes lot of effort. We may have to put it in databases in the right format. Even worse, we may have to build a data warehouse or get a database management system. This is by no means trivial, and people often underestimate this step. We have repeatedly heard it said that this is one of the most difficult tasks in mining.

Now that we have the data in the right format, we need to clean the data, scrub unnecessary items, and get only the data essential for mining. This is also not trivial.

We now have the data we want to mine and we have seen how to go about mining. Next, what outcomes do we want? It is good to have some idea. Do we want the tools to find interesting patterns without letting it know something about what we want? How do we go about getting what we want? Are there tools available? Do we build the tools? This is also very time-consuming.

When we have determined the data and the tool, we use the tool to operate on the data. This is the easy part. The tool could produce a lot of data which may seem like a foreign language to many. What do we do with the patterns? Do we have an application specialist analyze the patterns? Are there analysts who can figure out what the data is all about? Do we have

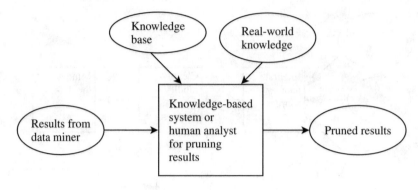

Exhibit 4.   Pruning the Results

tools to analyze the results and get useful patterns? That is, we need to figure out how to effectively prune the results for what is most useful. The
pruning process is illustrated in Exhibit 4.

Now we think we have useful results. We need to examine the results and
identify actions that can be taken. For example, by analyzing various purchases in a supermarket, we decide that milk and moisturizing cream
should be in close proximity. We then identify the actions we think will be
beneficial and discuss procedures to implement the actions.

When the actions have been implemented, we wait to see the results.
The results may be immediate or may take a very long time. Once we are in
a position to determine the benefits and costs of our actions, we then
reevaluate the whole procedure. By then, the data may have changed. New
tools may be available. We may have to do things differently. So we plan for
the next mining cycle and determine how to go about it.

Note that this discussion does not bring the human element into the process. Humans play a major part. First of all, we do need management buy-
in, so we must be very careful not to oversell the project. Be realistic as to
what mining can and cannot do. Once management is convinced, we need
to determine whether we have the manpower. Do we train employees or
bring in contractors? We also need to discuss these issues with the client.
Another question is, what about the tool developers? Again, do we train
employees or bring in contractors? The client, contractor, and tool devel-
oper have to work very closely to make mining a success.

If the project has failed, do not point a finger at one person or a group of
people. Remember this is still a new technology, so the likelihood of success may not be high. Learn from your experience. Talk to people who have
had similar experiences. See what can be done differently. In many cases,
it might be good to start a small pilot project or prototype effort before
going into full-scale mining.

These steps are relevant for Web data mining also. The main challenge here is locating and preparing the data. Data may be scattered all over the Web, and different groups may own the data and may not want to share it. Therefore, it is critical that organizations negotiate to share data. We will see the importance of data sharing in Part III when we address counter-terrorism.

Challenges

Why we are mining, and what are the steps involved? What are the difficulties, technical and otherwise? The nontechnical difficulties include insufficient management support and resources such as trained individuals and low budgets. The technical challenges are many.

We have stressed that getting the right data in the right format is critical. But there are many problems in this area. First of all, the data may not be accurate. What do we do then? How do we track down the source, as data may have passed many levels? This is one of the major challenges. The data may be incomplete and there may be many missing values. How do we fill in the blanks? It may be uncertain how accurate the data is. Here again, do we track down the source? So, missing, inaccurate, and uncertain data are major challenges.

Next, do we have the right tools? If not, do we adapt existing tools or develop them from scratch? This is a big problem because the tools are still not mature. Another challenge is developing adaptive techniques. That is, many of the tools only do one type of data mining such as classification or clustering. Can we develop tools that can adapt to the situation and carry out a particular type of mining? Can a tool use multiple mining techniques and handle different outcomes? There is research in this area, but we are a long way from robust commercial tools.

We have named a few of the challenges and some of them are illustrated in Exhibit 5. The good news is that there is much research in data mining and new initiatives are being formed. So, as time goes by, we feel that we will be getting good answers to many of the questions we have posed.

User Interface Aspects

As in any system, having a good user interface is critical to mining. Note that some of the early database management systems had very primitive user interfaces. Therefore, users had to spend a great deal of time writing SQL queries and applications programs. After much work, current database systems have excellent user interface tools. User interface tools are also being developed for multimedia databases. These include tools for generating queries, applications programs, and reports. Various multimodal interfaces are also being provided for database management.

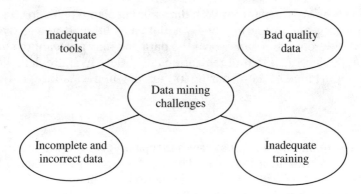

Exhibit 5.   Some Data Mining Challenges

User interface support for current data mining systems is fairly primitive. As mentioned earlier, visualization tools are being developed to help with data mining, but tools for generating queries, application programs, and reports are not sophisticated. To make data mining a success, we need better user interface tools. Computer scientists and technologists are not the only ones who should be involved in developing such tools. Interactions between technologists, scientists, psychologists, and computer specialists are necessary to develop better tools. Exhibit 6 illustrates an example user interface for data mining. The interface has buttons not only for generating queries, applications, and reports, but also for selecting the outcomes desired, approaches to be followed, and the techniques to be utilized.

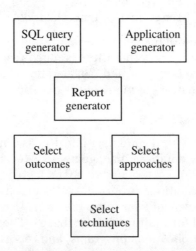

Exhibit 6.   Example User Interface for Mining

WEB DATA MINING OUTCOMES, APPROACHES, AND TECHNIQUES

This section focuses on concepts in data mining. In particular, what possible outcomes can one expect, what are the approaches or methodologies used, and what are the data mining techniques used? Various data mining and machine learning textbooks, such as [ADRI96], [BERR97], and [MITC97] have focused mainly on the topics discussed in this chapter. In particular, Berry and Linoff [BERR97] have provided an excellent discussion on the outcomes, approaches, and techniques for data mining.* Therefore, we will discuss only the essential points in this chapter. For further reading, we refer the reader to the references we have mentioned. Many of the techniques discussed here can be applied for Web data. For example, one can find associations in text as well as anomalies in images.

The outcomes of data mining are also referred to as the data mining tasks or types. These are the results that one can expect to see from data mining. We discussed some of the tasks in Chapter 3. The data mining outcomes include classification, clustering, prediction, estimation, and affinity grouping. It should be noted that there is no standard terminology. Therefore, various papers and texts have used different terms sometimes to mean the same concept.

There are top-down, bottom-up, or hybrid approaches to data mining, also referred to as methodologies. In addition, the methods could also be directed or undirected. Directed techniques are also sometimes called supervised learning, and undirected techniques are called unsupervised learning.

Data mining techniques are the algorithms employed to carry out data mining. There has been some confusion between techniques and outcomes. For example, a collection of data mining techniques is used for market basket analysis. However, market basket analysis is also an application. This is all about determining which items are purchased together in a supermarket. Therefore, there is some confusion within the community as to what these terms mean. We expect progress to be made with respect to terminology as the technology matures and standards are developed.

In general, to carry out data mining for a specific application, first we have to decide on the type of outcome expected from the process. Then we have to determine the techniques to be employed to get the expected outcome. Finally, we have to determine whether to steer the process in a top-down, bottom-up, or hybrid fashion. Exhibit 7 illustrates these steps.

This chapter is devoted to the outcomes, approaches, and techniques for data mining.

---

* In fact, Berry and Linoff call these terms *data mining tasks, methodologies, and techniques* [BERR97]. As we have mentioned, there is no standard terminology for data mining. We hope that the data mining community will eventually standardize various terms.

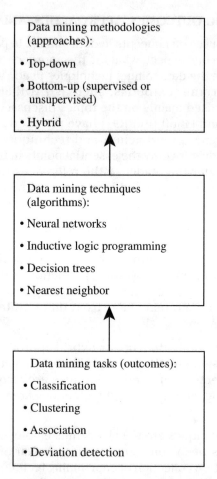

Exhibit 7. Data Mining Tasks, Techniques, and Methodologies

Outcomes of Web Data Mining

The outcomes of data mining are also referred to as data mining tasks or types. In a task called classification, the tool examines the features of a new entity, examines a predefined set of classes, and classifies the entity as belonging to a particular class if common features are extracted. For example, a class of mammals could have attributes that describe a mammal. If a living entity has to be classified and satisfies the properties for a mammal, then it can be classified as a mammal. Classification is carried out by developing training sets with preclassified examples and then building a model that fits the description of the classes. Then this model is applied to the data not yet classified and results are obtained. In summary, with classification a group of entities is partitioned, based on a predefined value of some attribute. For example, one could classify text and images based on the content.

Estimation and prediction are two other data mining tasks. In the case of estimation based on a person's spending patterns and his age, one can estimate his salary or the number of children he has. Prediction tasks predict the future behavior of some value. For example, based on the education of a person, his current job, and the trends in the industry, one can predict that his salary will be a certain amount by year 2005. Another example, depending on the patterns observed in newspaper articles, one could predict certain events in the future.

One task that is extremely useful is affinity grouping. This is also sometimes referred to as making associations and correlations. Essentially, this determines the items that go together. Who are the people that travel together? What are the items that are purchased together? While prediction is some future value and estimation is an estimated value, affinity grouping makes associations between current values.

Clustering is a data mining task that is often confused with classification. While classification classifies an entity based on some predefined values of attributes, clustering groups similar records not based on some predefined values. That is, when we classify a group of people, we essentially have predefined classes based on values of some attributes. In the case of clustering, we do not have these predefined classes; instead we form clusters by analyzing the data. For example, suppose we want to find something interesting about a group of people in a community, but we do not have any predefined classes. We analyze their spending patterns for automobiles, and we form the following clusters based on the analysis: group X prefers Volvos, group Y prefers Saabs, and group Z prefers Mercedes. Once the clusters are obtained, each cluster can be examined and mined further for other outcomes such as estimation and classification.

Other data mining tasks include deviation analysis and anomaly detection. For example, John usually goes shopping after he goes to the bank, but last week he went shopping after going to church. Anomaly detection is a form of deviation detection used for applications such as fraud detection and medical illness detection. Some consider summarization and semantic content exploration (for example, understanding the data) data mining tasks.

Here are some of our observations. While one can see differences between the different tasks, often there are similarities. When we teach a data mining course, the students frequently ask questions such as "what is the difference between affinity grouping and estimation?" There is still no theory behind data mining where one can be precise with the notions and definitions. It is still rather *ad hoc*. For example, while neural net-

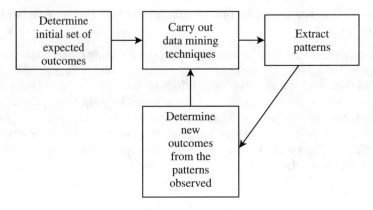

Exhibit 8.   Data Mining Outcomes

works are good for clustering, one cannot make definite statements such as technique A is used for task X and technique B is good for task Y. It is largely trial and error, and one gets better with experience. Therefore, unless you do a lot of data mining, it is difficult to determine what is best for a particular situation. Exhibit 8 illustrates the process of getting data mining outcomes.

Approaches to Web Data Mining

Berry and Linoff have clearly explained the approaches to data mining, which they call methodologies [BERR97]. These methodologies are not the outcomes nor are they the techniques. They are the steps we would take to do mining. Once the outcomes are determined, how do we go about doing the mining? Where do we start? This section addresses some of these issues.

Essentially, there are two approaches: top-down and bottom-up. We can combine the two and have a hybrid approach. In the top-down approach, we have to start with some idea or a pattern or a hypothesis. For example, a hypothesis could be "all those who live in Concord, Massachusetts, earn a minimum of $50K." Then we start querying the database to test our ideas and hypothesis. If we find something that does not confirm our hypothesis, then we have to revise our hypothesis. A lot of statistical reasoning is used for this purpose. In general, hypothesis testing is about generating ideas, developing models, and evaluating the model to determine if the hypothesis is valid or not. Developing the model is a major challenge. If the model is not a good one, then one cannot rely on the outcome. The models could simply be a collection of rules of the form "if a person lives in New York, then he owns a house worth more than $300K." To evaluate the model, one needs to query the database. In this example, one could pose a query to select all those living in New York in homes costing less than $300K.

In the bottom-up approach to data mining, there is no hypothesis to test. This is much harder because the tool has to examine the data and come up with patterns. The bottom-up approach could be directed or undirected. In directed data mining, also referred to as supervised learning in the machine learning literature, you have some idea what you are looking for. For example, who often travels with John to New York? What item is often purchased with milk? As in the top-down approach, models are developed and evaluated based on the data you analyze. With undirected data mining, also called unsupervised learning in the machine learning literature, you have no idea what you are looking for. You ask the tool to find something interesting. For example, in image data mining, the data mining tool can go about finding something that it thinks is unusual. As before, you develop a model and evaluate the model with the data. Once something interesting is found, then you can conduct directed data mining.

The hybrid approach is a combination of both top-down and bottom-up mining. For example, you can start with bottom-up mining, analyze the data and then discover a pattern. This pattern could be a hypothesis and you can do top-down mining to test the hypothesis. As a result, you can find new patterns, which become a new hypothesis. The tool can switch between top-down and bottom-up mining and between directed and undirected mining. Data mining approaches are illustrated in Exhibit 9.

Web Data Mining Techniques and Algorithms

Now we come to the important part of data mining: the algorithms and techniques employed to do the mining. There are numerous data mining techniques such as statistical analysis, machine learning, and other reasoning techniques. We discuss only a few of them. It should be noted that we have not distinguished between techniques and algorithms. One can argue that while techniques describe a broad class of procedures to carry out mining, algorithms go into more detail. For example, while link analysis can be regarded as a data mining technique, one could employ various algorithms, such as intelligent searching and graph traversal, to carry out link analysis. The outcome of link analysis is to make associations between various entities. We will see in Part III that link analysis is an important data mining technique for counter-terrorism applications.

One popular class of data mining techniques is market basket analysis. These are techniques that group items together. For example, which items go together, who travels with whom together, and what events occur together? The actual techniques employed to do market basket analysis are intelligent searching and pruning the search. Many of the intelligent search techniques that were developed for artificial intelligence are being employed for market basket analysis. If one were to search the entire search space, then it would become combinatorially explosive. Therefore,

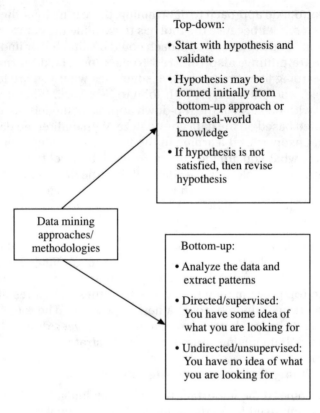

Exhibit 9.   Some Data Mining Approaches

the challenge here is to determine how to search and eliminate unnecessary items from the search space.

Various papers and books have given examples of market basket analysis from supermarket purchases. The idea is to make a list of all purchases for a certain period and then analyze these purchases to determine which items are often purchased together. There will be some obvious patterns such as bread and milk, bread and cheese, etc. What the decision maker is looking for is some of the less-obvious patterns such as bread and soy sauce.

Another data mining technique is a decision tree. This is a machine learning technique and is used extensively for classification. Records and objects are divided into groups based on some attribute value. For example, the population may be divided into groups based on annual income; each of the groups can then be divided into subclasses based on some value, such as age; and each of the subclasses can be divided based on marital status. Subsequently, a tree structure is formed with leaves at the end; the decision tree is then used for training. Then as new data appears for analysis, the training examples are used to classify the data.

A neural network is another popular data mining technique that has been around for a while. A neural network is essentially a collection of input signals, nodes, and output signals. They are first trained with training sets and examples. Once the learning is completed, new patterns are given to the network. The network then uses its training experience to analyze the new data. It may be used for clustering, identifying entities, deviation analysis, and other data mining tasks. Neural networks have been used to detect abnormal patterns in images. For details, we refer to [THUR01].

Inductive logic programming is a machine-learning technique that is of special interest to us because of our own research. It originated from logic programming. Instead of deducing new data from existing data and rules, inductive logic programming is all about inducing rules from analyzing data. It has theory behind it and uses a variation of the resolution principle in theorem proving for discovering rules. Because inductive logic programming is of interest to us, we have devoted the next chapter to this topic.

Several other data mining techniques are in use today, including link analysis techniques, which are a collection of techniques to find associations and relationships between records; automatic cluster detection techniques, which are a collection of techniques to find clusters; techniques to find association rules that are similar to link analysis; and nearest-neighbor techniques, which are a collection of techniques for analyzing new data based on its neighbors. For example, in the nearest-neighbor techniques, if a situation has to be analyzed, the database is examined to see if there are neighbors with similar properties, and conclusions are drawn about the new situation. The techniques employ distance functions to determine the closeness between the data entities. It is assumed that points in space that are close together have similar properties. So for new data, compute its point in space based on some predefined computation, find out how close it is to known data points, and then determine its properties. Association rule-based techniques are popular among the database researchers. These techniques essentially examine the data in the database and come up with associations between the entities. In many ways, the techniques are similar to those used for link analysis.

Other data mining techniques include those based on genetic algorithms, fuzzy logic, rough sets, concept learning, and simple rule-based reasoning. For a detailed discussion of these techniques, we refer to [BERR97], [HAN01], [LIN97], and [MITC97]. As mentioned, there is some overlap between the different techniques that have been proposed. These techniques have been taken from statistics, data management, and machine learning. As we make progress toward integrating the various data mining technologies, we can expect more and more sophisticated

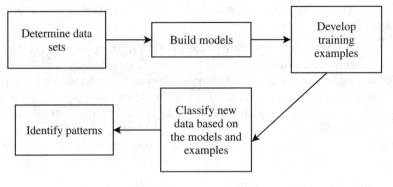

Exhibit 10. Operation of Data Mining Techniques

techniques to be developed. Exhibit 10 illustrates the way data mining techniques operate.

WEB DATA MINING VS. DATA MINING

Much of the information we have discussed in this section is general enough to be applicable for data mining, Web data mining, and multimedia data mining. So, the main question is, what are the special considerations for Web data mining? First of all, what we have discussed in the previous sections applies for Web data mining also. This is because there is a lot of data on the Web, including multimedia data and semistructured data. As we have stated throughout this book, we feel that Web data mining is more general than just data mining and encompasses data mining. As far as the differences are concerned, one of the main challenges for Web data mining is to get the data ready for mining. For example, Web data may not be easy to find, gather, and manager. That is, we need to find and organize the data sources. We need technologies for managing Web data. We need to apply information management techniques for Web data. Furthermore, we need to migrate from Web data mining to semantic Web data mining. Note also that Web data mining is not only about Web content mining, it also includes Web usage mining and Web structure mining. As we have stressed in this book, we expect much of the data to be on the Web. The Web includes the Internet as well as corporate intranets.

There are also additional considerations for Web mining. First of all, we can mine the data on the Web as well as mine usage patterns and structures. That is, we need to collect data about the usage of the Web, the Web pages frequently browsed, build profiles of users, etc. Then we need to develop techniques to mine and manage the usage data. Other considerations include privacy. When we mine data in a closed environment, such as within an agency, we may not give much consideration to privacy. But in an open environment such as the Internet, we need to make sure that pri-

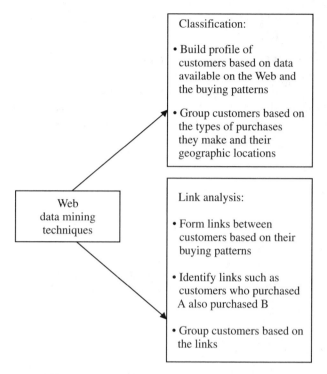

Exhibit 11.   Web Mining Techniques for E-Commerce

vacy of individuals is not violated. Also, as we have stressed throughout this book, much of the data will be Web-based, either through intranets or on the Internet. Therefore, Web data mining will dominate and can be expected to subsume data mining.

As far the processes and techniques are concerned, we feel that much of the information discussed in the previous sections apply for Web data mining. That is, we need to get the data ready, mine the data, create pilot projects, and perhaps carry out large-scale data mining. Also, techniques such as neural networks, decision trees, and link analysis apply for Web mining. Exhibit 11 illustrates Web data mining techniques applied to an application in E-commerce. We will elaborate on Web data mining for counter-terrorism in Part III.

SUMMARY

This chapter has taken various data mining prerequisites and examined their impact on Web data. We started with a discussion of the need for data mining. We gave several examples. Next, an overview of data mining techniques was described. Many of these techniques may also be applied for Web data mining. Finally, we discussed the similarities and differences between data mining and Web data mining with respect to the information provided in this chapter.

Now that we have some background on Web data mining, including technologies and techniques for Web data mining, we are ready to use the technologies discussed in Part I to examine the impact of Web data mining. For example, we will discuss mining Web databases and issues in mining text, images, video, and audio data. This topic will be addressed in the next few chapters.

Chapter 11
Mining Databases on the Web

INTRODUCTION

While Chapters 9 and 10 provided an overview of Web data mining, this chapter discusses aspects of mining the databases on the Web. Essentially, we use the technologies discussed in Chapter 5 to describe the impact of Web mining.

As we have mentioned, there is a lot of data on the Web, some in databases, some in files or other data sources. The databases may be semistructured or they may be relational, object, or multimedia databases. These databases have to be mined so that useful information is extracted.

CONCEPTS IN WEB DATABASE MINING

A simple illustration of Web database mining is shown in Exhibit 1. Note that we also discussed this figure in Chapters 3 and 5. The idea is that there are databases on the Web and these databases have to be mined to extract patterns and trends.

While we could use many of the data mining techniques to mine the Web databases, the challenge is to locate the databases on the Web. Furthermore, the databases may not be in the format that we need for mining the data. We may need mediators to mediate between the data miners and the databases on the Web. This is illustrated in Exhibit 2.

In Chapter 5, we discussed other aspects of Web database management, including processing queries and carrying out transactions, as well as metadata management, data warehousing, and data distribution. We discuss metadata mining as well as mining distributed databases later in this chapter. In the next section, we discuss Web database functions and data mining.

Web Database Management Functions and Data Mining

We discussed Web data representation and Web database functions in Chapter 5. In this chapter, we examine the impact of data mining. As mentioned previously, data could be in relational, object, or semistructured

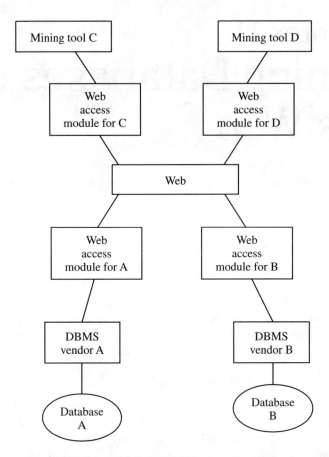

Exhibit 1. Mining Databases on the Web

databases. Mining semistructured databases is discussed in the next section. In the case of relational, object, and object-relational databases, we may apply the data mining tools directly on the database or we may extract key information from the data and then mine the extracted information. This is not different from what we have mentioned in our previous books (for example, see [THUR98]). However, because Web data may be coming from numerous sources, it may be incomplete or inconsistent. Therefore, we will have to reason under incompleteness and inaccuracy. An example of mining object-relational databases is illustrated in Exhibit 3.

In Chapter 5, we also discussed database functions, including query processing and transaction management. Query processing includes special optimization techniques and languages for the Web. We need to include data mining constructs into the languages as well as data mining techniques into the query optimization algorithms. Data mining can contribute in two ways for transaction management on the Web: mining Web transac-

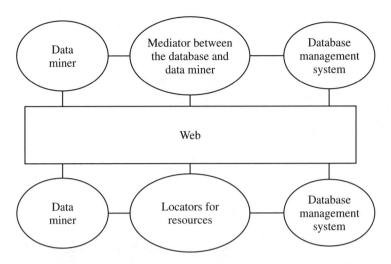

Exhibit 2.   Mediation and Location for Web Database Mining

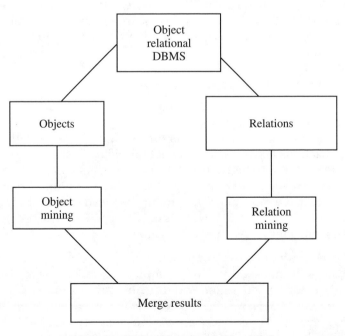

Exhibit 3.   Object-Relational Data Mining

Data mining integrated into Web query optimization	Data mining for mining Web transaction logs

Data mining for storage management and organization

Exhibit 4.   Web Database Functions and Mining

tion logs and mining when the transaction is being executed in real-time. There is little work on real-time data mining because data mining is usually carried out for analysis and it is difficult to build models in real-time. But we will see that for certain applications such as intrusion detection, we need to mine real-time databases. Building models in real-time will be a major challenge. Managing storage is also a function of Web database management. Here, data mining could help to determine the organization and structure of databases. We need more research in this area. Exhibit 4 illustrates some of the applications of data mining to Web database management functions.

Data Sharing vs. Data Mining on the Web

As we have stressed, one of the challenges in data mining is to get the data ready for mining. This means that organizations have to be willing to share the data. In many cases, data is private and may be sensitive. Therefore, organizations and agencies may not be willing to share all of the data. As we have stated, with bad data one cannot have good data mining results even if using excellent data mining tools. So the question is, how can we share data so that we can mine? Essentially, we need to carry out federated data mining. This aspect will be discussed in Part III. We will see that federated data mining may have applications in counter-terrorism.

We discuss federated data mining in a later section. We discuss some preliminaries in this section. For example, in a federated environment, organizations form a federation with the objective to share data and still have autonomy. That is, we need federated data management practices for data sharing and mining. There are various ways to carry out federated data mining. In one approach, we can export certain data and schema to

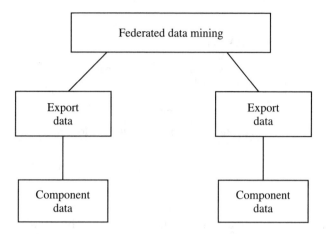

Exhibit 5.   Federated Data Mining: Approach I

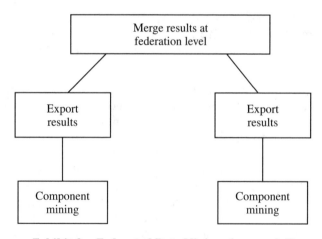

Exhibit 6.   Federated Data Mining: Approach II

the federation and then carry out mining, as illustrated in Exhibit 5. In another approach, we carry out mining at the component level and then put the pieces together at the federation level. This latter approach is illustrated in Exhibit 6. We address distributed, heterogeneous, legacy, and federated database mining in a later section.

MINING SEMISTRUCTURED DATABASES

Chapter 5 discussed semistructured databases. We elaborated on semistructured databases as well as XML databases in [THUR02]. Essentially, we use the terms *semistructured databases* and *XML databases* interchange-

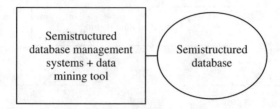

Exhibit 7.   Tight Integration between Data Miner and DBMS

ably, although semistructured databases are much broader and include RDF document databases.

In our example of object-relational database mining, we gave some idea of how to mine objects and relations and merge the results. With semistructured database management, there are two approaches to managing the semistructured documents. One is to develop a database management system to manage the semistructured documents, known as the tight coupling approach. The other approach is to build an interface, for example, over relational databases to manage the semistructured documents, known as the loose coupling approach. We discussed these approaches in [THUR02].

In the case of data mining, there are various approaches. In one approach, we can extend the semistructured database management system with a data miner to mine the documents (see Exhibit 7), or we can build an interface to the semistructured database management system (see Exhibit 8). The former is the tight coupling between the data miner and the database management system (DBMS), and the latter is the loose coupling between the data miner and the DBMS. In the loose coupling approach to semistructured database management, we can mine the relations and the semistructured documents and then integrate the results (see Exhibit 9). Another approach is to extract structure from the semi-

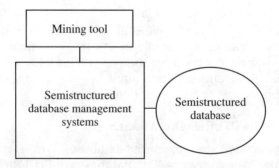

Exhibit 8.   Loose Integration between Data Miner and DBMS

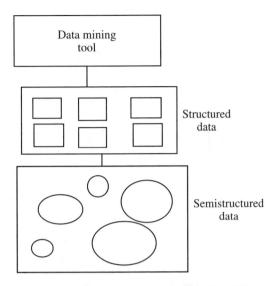

Exhibit 9.   Extract Structure and then Mine

structured documents and then mine the structured documents (Exhibit 10). Note that there are various permutations and combinations of these approaches. For example, even in the loose coupling approach to semistructured database management, we can build a data miner as an interface to the database management system (Exhibit 11). The point we are making is that there are two ways to manage the semistructured databases: the loose coupling approach and the tight coupling approach. Also, in the case of data mining, we can have a tight coupling or a loose coupling with the data miner.

With respect to data warehousing, there are two aspects. One is that XML documents, semistructured databases, relational databases, and other data sources have to be integrated into a warehouse. Much of the work until now has been in integrating relational databases into a warehouse, also based on a relational model. When the databases are XML documents as well as semistructured databases, the question is, how do we integrate them into a warehouse? What is an appropriate model for a warehouse? Because there are now mappings between SQL and XML, can we still have an SQL-based model for the warehouse? The second aspect is representing the warehouse as a collection of XML documents. In this case, for example, we need mappings between the data sources based on relational and object models, to XML data models. We also need to develop techniques for accessing, querying, and indexing the warehouse. Both aspects of data warehousing are illustrated in Exhibits 12 and 13.

175

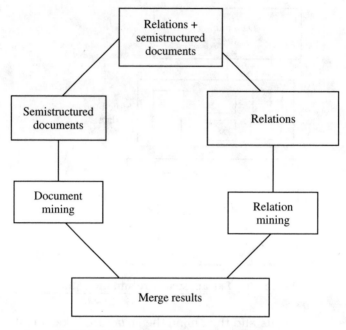

Exhibit 10.   Mining and then Merging

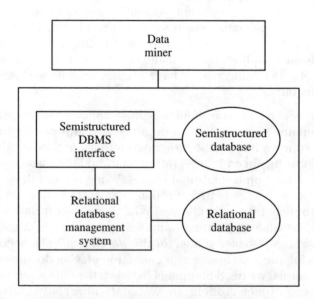

Exhibit 11.   Data Miner as an Interface to a Loose Coupling Semistructured DBMS

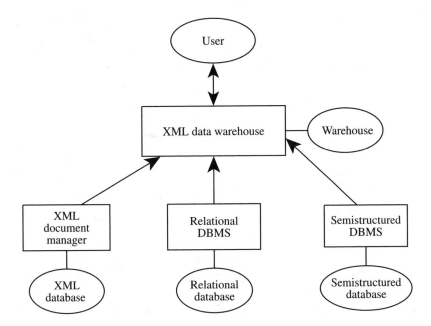

Exhibit 12. XML Data Warehouse: Approach I

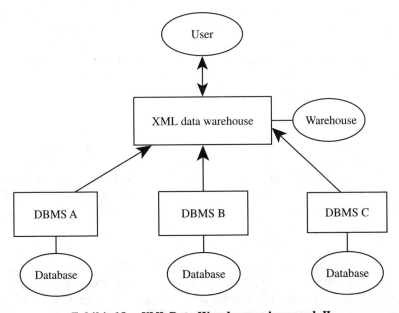

Exhibit 13. XML Data Warehouse: Approach II

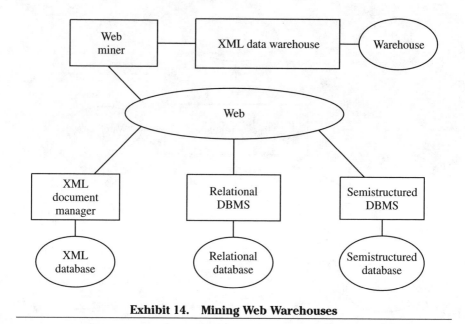

Exhibit 14.   Mining Web Warehouses

Mining XML documents is receiving more attention recently. There are two aspects here. One is to mine the documents to extract useful information such as patterns and trends. For example, XML documents may be mined for business intelligence. One could also mine these documents for customer relationship management. The other aspect is to mine the links in an XML document and extract some information from these links. There is still much to be done here. Exhibit 14 illustrates mining the XML-based warehouses shown in Exhibits 12 and 13.

METADATA AND WEB MINING

As discussed previously, metadata by itself is becoming a key technology for various tasks such as data management, data warehousing, Web searching, multimedia information processing, and data mining. Because metadata has been so closely aligned with databases in the past, we have included a discussion of the impact of metadata technology on Web data mining in this book.

Metadata plays an important role in data mining. It could guide the data mining process. That is, the data mining tool could consult the metadatabase and determine the types of queries to pose to the DBMS. Metadata may be updated during the mining process. For example, historical information as well as statistics may be collected during the mining process, and the metadata has to reflect the changes in the environment. The role of metadata in guiding the data mining process is illustrated in Exhibit 15.

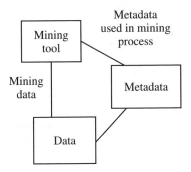

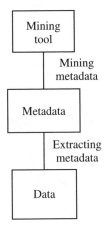

Exhibit 15. Metadata Used in Data Mining

Exhibit 16. Metadata Mining

Extracting metadata from the data and then mining the metadata is illustrated in Exhibit 16.

There has been much discussion on the role of metadata for data mining [META96]. There are many challenges here. For example, when is it better to mine the metadata? What are the techniques for metadata mining? How does one structure the metadata to facilitate data mining? Researchers are working on addressing these questions.

Closely associated with the metadata notion is that of a repository. A repository is a database that stores possibly all the metadata, the mappings between various data sources when integrating heterogeneous data sources, the information needed to handle semantic heterogeneity such as "ship X and submarine Y are the same entity," the enforced policies and procedures, as well as information on data quality. So the data mining tool

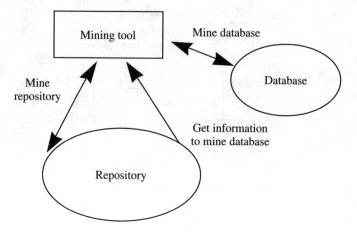

Exhibit 17.   Repository and Mining

may consult the repository to carry out the mining. On the other hand, the repository itself may be mined. Both scenarios are illustrated in Exhibit 17.

Metadata plays an important role in various types of mining. For example, in the case of mining multimedia data metadata may be extracted from the multimedia databases and then used to mine the data. For example, as illustrated in Exhibit 18, the metadata may help in extracting the key entities from the text. These entities may be mined using commercial data mining tools. Note that in the case of textual data, metadata may include information such as the type of document, the number of paragraphs, and other

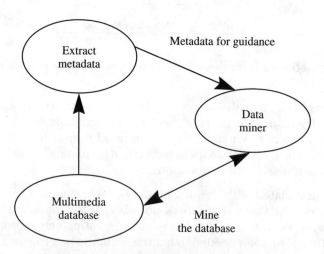

Exhibit 18.   Metadata for Multimedia Mining

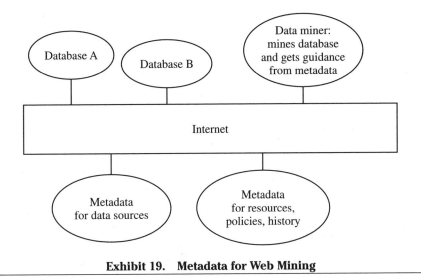

Exhibit 19.   Metadata for Web Mining

information describing the document, but not the contents of the document itself.

Metadata is also critical in the case of Web mining, which is the main focus of this book. Because there is so much information and data on the Web, mining this data directly could become quite challenging. Therefore, we may need to extract metadata from the data, and then either mine this metadata or use this metadata to guide in the mining process. This is illustrated in Exhibit 19. Note that languages such as XML, which we will briefly discuss in the next section, will play a role in describing metadata for Web documents.

In Part III, we will address privacy issues for data mining. Policies and procedures will be a key issue for determining the extent to which we want to protect the privacy of individuals. These policies and procedures can be regarded as part of the metadata. Therefore, such metadata will have to guide the process of data mining so that privacy issues are not compromised through mining.

In almost every aspect of mining, metadata plays a crucial role. Even in the case of data warehousing, which we have regarded as a preliminary step to mining, it is important to collect metadata at various stages. For example, in the case of a data warehouse, data from multiple sources has to be integrated. Metadata will guide the transformation process from layer to layer in building the warehouse (see the discussion in [THUR97]). Metadata will also help in administering the data warehouse. Also, metadata is used in extracting answers to the various queries posed.

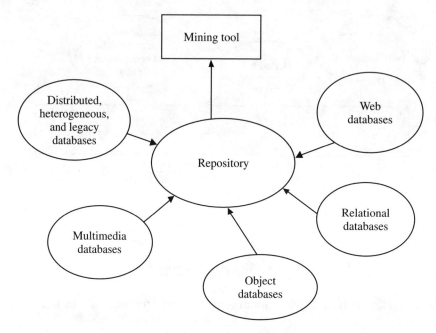

Exhibit 20.   Metadata as the Central Repository for Mining

Because metadata is key to all kinds of databases including relational, object, multimedia, distributed, heterogeneous, legacy, and Web databases, one could envisage building a metadata repository that contains metadata from the different kinds of databases and then mining the metadata to extract patterns. This approach is illustrated in Exhibit 20 and could be an alternative if the data in the databases is difficult to mine directly.

MINING DISTRIBUTED, HETEROGENEOUS, LEGACY, AND FEDERATED DATABASES ON THE WEB

In [THUR97], we placed much emphasis on heterogeneous database integration and interoperability. Many applications require the integration of multiple data sources and databases. These data sources may need to be mined to uncover patterns. Furthermore, interesting patterns may be found across the multiple databases. Mining heterogeneous and distributed data sources is a subject that has received little attention.

In the case of distributed databases, one approach is to have the data mining tool as part of the distributed processor where each distributed processor (DP) has a mining component also, as illustrated in Exhibit 21. This way, each data mining component could mine the data in the local database and the DP could combine all the results. This will be quite chal-

182

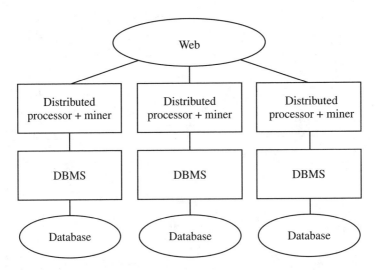

Exhibit 21.   Distributed Processing and Mining

lenging, as the relationships between the various fragments of the relations or objects have to be maintained in order to mine effectively. Also, the data mining tool could be embedded into the query optimizer of the DQP (distributed query processor). Essentially, with this approach the DP has one additional module, a distributed data miner (DDM), as shown in Exhibit 22.

We illustrate distributed data mining with an example shown in Exhibit 23. Each DDM mines data from a specific database. These databases contain information on projects, employees, and travel. The DDMs can mine and get the following information: John and James travel together to London on project XXX at least 10 times a year. Mary joins them at least four times a year.

An alternative approach is to implement the data mining tool on top of the distributed system. As far as the mining tool is concerned, the data-

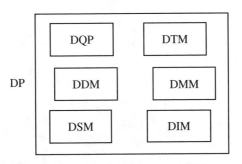

Exhibit 22.   Modules of DP for Data Mining

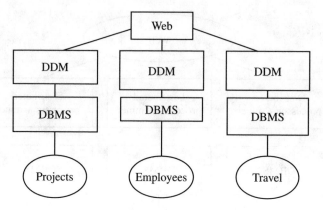

Exhibit 23.   Example Distributed Data Mining

base is one monolithic entity. The data in this database has to be mined and useful patterns have to be extracted as illustrated in Exhibit 24.

In the case of heterogeneous data sources, we can either integrate the data and then apply data mining tools as shown in Exhibit 25, or apply data mining tools to the various data sources and then integrate the results, as shown in Exhibit 26. Note that if we integrate the databases first, then integration methods for interoperating heterogeneous databases are different from those for providing an integrated view in a distributed database. Some of these issues are discussed in [THUR97]. Furthermore, for each data mining query, one may need first to send that same query to the various data sources, get the results, and integrate the results, as shown in

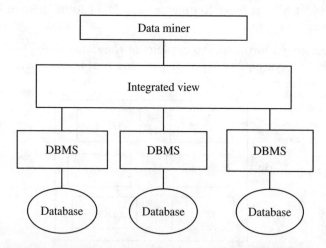

Exhibit 24.   Data Mining Hosted on a Distributed Database

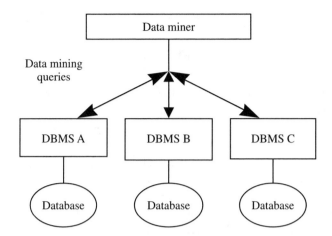

Exhibit 25.   Data Mining on Heterogeneous Data Sources

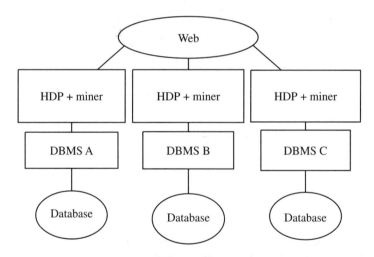

Exhibit 26.   Mining and then Integration

Exhibit 25. If the data is not integrated, then a data miner may need to be integrated with the heterogeneous distributed processor (HDP), as illustrated in Exhibit 26. If each data source is to have its own data miner, then each data miner is acting independently. We are not sending the same query to the different data sources as each data miner will determine how to operate on its data. The challenge here is to integrate the results of the various mining tools applied to the individual data sources so that patterns may be found across data sources.

If we integrate the data sources and then apply the data mining tools, the question is, do we develop a data warehouse and mine the warehouse, or

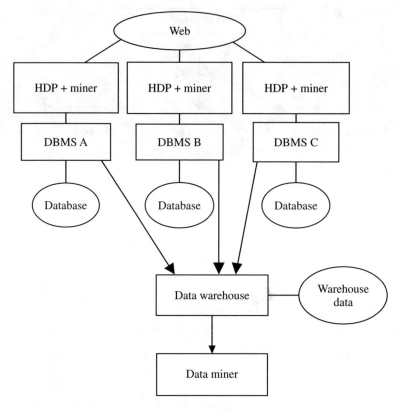

Exhibit 27.   Mining, Interoperability, and Warehousing

do we mine with interoperating database systems? Note that in the case of a warehouse approach, not all of the data in the heterogeneous data sources is brought into the warehouse. Only decision support data is brought into the warehouse. If interoperability is used together with warehousing, then the data miner could augment both the HDP and the warehouse, as illustrated in Exhibit 27.

One could also use more sophisticated tools such as agents to mine heterogeneous data sources, as illustrated in Exhibit 28 where an integration agent integrates the results of all the mining agents. The integration agent may give feedback to the mining agents so that the mining agents may pose further queries to the data sources and obtain interesting information. There is two-way communication between the integration agent and the mining agents. Another alternative is to have no integration agent, but have instead the various mining agents collaborate with each other and discover interesting patterns across the various data sources. This is illustrated in Exhibit 29. This latter approach is also called collaborative data

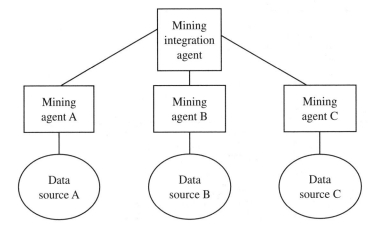

Exhibit 28.   Integrating Data Mining Agents

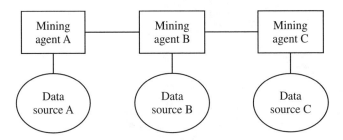

Exhibit 29.   Collaboration among Mining Agents

mining. In this approach, collaborative computing, data mining, and heterogeneous database integration technologies have to work together.

The specific approach to mining heterogeneous data sources, whether to use an integration agent or have the mining agents collaborate, is yet to be determined. One may need both approaches or there may be yet another approach. Note also that heterogeneity may exist with respect to data models, data types, and languages. This could pose additional challenges to the data mining process. There is much research to be done in this area.

Another scenario for collaborative data mining is illustrated in Exhibit 30. Here, two teams at different sites use collaboration and mining tools to mine the shared database. One could also use mediators to mine heterogeneous data sources. Exhibit 31 illustrates an example where we assume that general purpose data miners and mediators are placed between the data miners and the data sources. We also use a mediator to integrate the results from the different data miners.

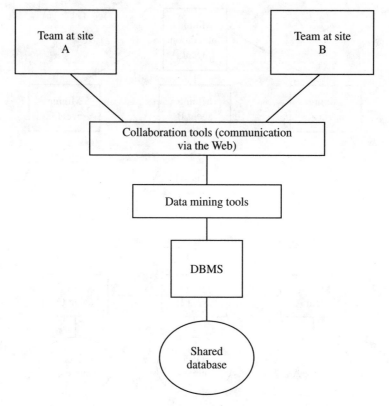

Exhibit 30.   Teams Conducting Mining on Shared Database

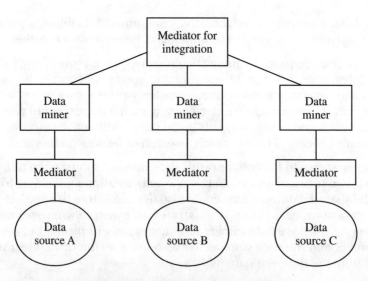

Exhibit 31.   Mediator for Integration

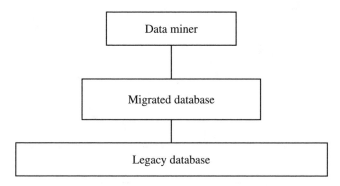

Exhibit 32. Migration and then Mining

Next, let us focus on legacy databases. One of the challenges here is how the legacy databases are to be mined. Can we rely on the data in these databases? Is it worth organizing and formatting this data, especially if it has to be migrated to newer systems? Is it worth developing tools to mine the legacy databases? How easy is it to integrate the legacy databases to form a data warehouse? There are some options. One is to migrate the legacy databases to new systems and mine the data in the new systems (see Exhibit 32). Another approach is to integrate legacy databases and form a data warehouse based on new architectures and technologies, and then mine the data in the warehouse (see Exhibit 33). In general, it is not a good idea to directly mine legacy data, as this data could soon be migrated, or it could be incomplete, uncertain, and therefore expensive to mine. Note that

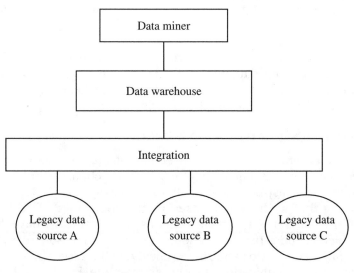

Exhibit 33. Mining Legacy Databases

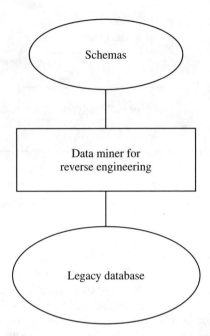

Exhibit 34.   Extract Schemas from Legacy Databases

mining could also be used to reverse engineer and extract schemas from the legacy databases (see Exhibit 34 and the discussions in [THUR98]).

Finally, we will examine federated architectures and data mining. We call this federated data mining. Here, the data miners at the local sites need some autonomy and also need to share information with the foreign sites. As we have stated in our previous book [THUR97], Sheth and Larson [SHET90] came up with this very interesting schema architecture for federated databases. We adapted this architecture for security policies. Now we need to adapt it for data mining. Exhibit 35 illustrates our preliminary ideas on federated data mining. Note that we also discussed some approaches when we discussed data sharing and data mining.

ARCHITECTURES AND WEB DATA MINING

There are several dimensions to Web data management architectures. We discussed many of them in Chapter 5. In this section, we focus on some of the data mining aspects. First of all, the three-tier architecture for Web data mining that we have discussed in our books (see [THUR00] and [THUR01]) is illustrated in Exhibit 36. In this architecture, we have the Web server which includes the data miner in the middle tier. Note that parts of the data miner could also reside in the client and the server DBMS. That is, there are various combinations for this architecture. Exhibit 37 illustrates

Layer 5

> External results: views
> for the various classes of users

Layer 4

> Federated data mining: integrate export
> results of the components of the federation

Layer 3

> Export results for the components:
> (e.g., export results for components A, B, and C)
> (<u>Note:</u> component may export different results
> to different federations)

Layer 2

> Generic representation of mining results
> (e.g., results for components A, B, and C)

Layer 1

> Mining at the component
> level, (e.g., component schemas
> for components A, B, and C)

Exhibit 35.   Five-Level Architecture for Federated Data Mining

> Thin client

> Middle tier web server:
> data mining

> Server DBMS

Exhibit 36.   Three-Tier Architecture for Data Miner

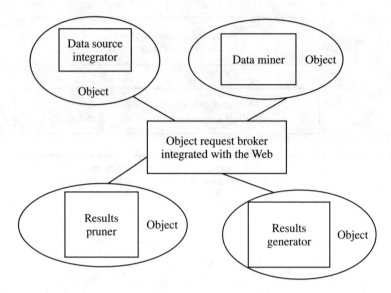

Exhibit 37. Encapsulating Data Mining Modules as Objects

the use of objects for data mining. Here, various data mining components are encapsulated as objects and an object request broker (ORB) is used to integrate the objects via the Web.

In Chapter 4, we also discussed various push/pull architectures. The question is, where does the data miner reside? In the case of pulling the data and pushing it to the consumer, we could have a data miner to carry out selective pulling as well as selective pushing of the data, as illustrated in Exhibit 38. Essentially, data mining is used as a Web service. We will discuss this further in Chapter 13. Another example of data mining from an architectural perspective is the application server/data server architecture discussed in Chapter 4. We can place a data miner to mine data at the server level as well as the application level, as illustrated in Exhibit 39. Note that there are several dimensions to architectures, and we have discussed just a few in this section.

SUMMARY

This chapter has discussed various aspects of mining Web databases. Essentially, we examined the concepts in Chapter 5 and discussed the impact of data mining. First we discussed issues on mining databases such as integrating data mining into Web query optimization. Then we addressed mining semistructured databases. Metadata mining was discussed next. This was followed by a broad overview of mining distributed and heterogeneous databases. We also discussed approaches to

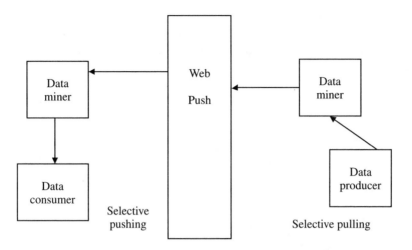

Exhibit 38.   Push/Pull and Data Mining: An Example

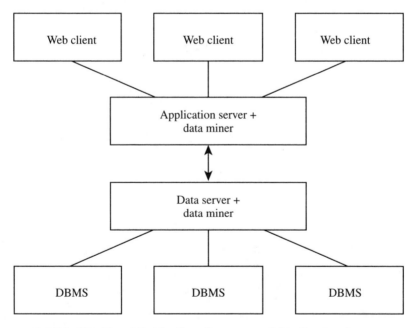

Exhibit 39.   Data Mining, Data Servers, and Application Servers

federated data mining. Finally, we discussed architectural aspects of Web data mining.

As we have stressed in this book, our goal is to give the essential information at a high level. We have not given the details of algorithms for query optimization and metadata mining. For details, we refer the reader to the various articles in journals and conference proceedings (see Appendix D). Our goal is to provide enough detail so that the reader can start thinking about applying the technologies to critical applications such as counter-terrorism.

Chapter 12
Information Retrieval and Web Data Mining

INTRODUCTION

Chapter 6 discussed information retrieval. Essentially, we provided an overview of text retrieval, image retrieval, video retrieval, and multimedia information retrieval. This chapter will examine the information retrieval systems discussed in Chapter 6 and the impact of Web mining. It will also provide an overview of search engines and Web mining.

As we have stressed throughout this book, much of the data on the Web is in the form of text. There is also structured and semistructured data as well as image and video data. For example, consider the search engine, Google™, which can be used to search for text (www.google.com) as well as images (www.images.google.com). However, the text search is far more sophisticated than the image search. There is still a lot to be done on image search and audio/video search on the Web.

SEARCH ENGINES AND WEB DATA MINING

Since the early 1990s, numerous search engines have been developed. They have origins in the information retrieval systems developed in the 1960s and beyond. Typically when we invoke a browser such as Netscape or Microsoft's Explorer, we have access to several search engines. Some of the early search engines were AltaVista, Yahoo, Infoseek, and Lycos. These systems were around in 1995 and were fairly effective for their times. They are much improved now. Since around 1999, Google has been one of the most popular search engines. It started as a Stanford University research project funded by organizations, such as the National Science Foundation and the Central Intelligence Agency, and was later commercialized. Systems such as Google provide intelligent searches. However, they still have a long way to go before users can get exact answers to their queries.

Note that we are not intending to provide a complete overview of search engines. We provide only a high-level overview. Details on an individual search can be obtained from the Web itself. For example, if we type "white papers about Google" on www.google.com, we get many results. When we click on some of them, we get useful information about Google.

Note that the various search engines we have listed here are trademarks of various corporations. As mentioned in the preface, we have not listed all the trademarks because they often change as corporations merge. For example, Netscape was a product of Netscape Corporation until it was purchased by AOL (www.aol.com). AltaVista was originally a product of what used to be Digital Equipment Corporation, which later was purchased by Compaq, which has now merged with Hewlett Packard.

Search Engines

Note that we have discussed various types of search engines. In this section, we discuss some of the ideas behind the search engines.

As we have stated, a search engine is accessed via the browser. When we click on the search engine, we get a window that allows us to request a search by entering keywords. The keywords search returns a list of various Web pages that match our request. The question is, how does a search engine find the Web pages? It essentially uses information retrieval on the Web.

The rating of a search engine is determined by the speed at which it produces results and, more importantly, the accuracy or relevancy of the results. For example, when we type a query for "lung cancer," does the search engine provide the relevant information we are looking for with respect to lung cancer? For example, it can list resources about lung cancer or list information about who has had lung cancer. Usually, people want a list of resources about lung cancer. If they want to find out who has lung cancer, then they could type in "people with lung cancer."

Although extremely useful, the problem with many searches is that they often provide a lot of irrelevant information. Very sophisticated indexing techniques have to be built to get accurate results. They also may cache information from Web servers for frequently posed queries. Exhibit 1 illustrates the connection between search engines and Web servers. Some typical modules of a search engine are illustrated in Exhibit 2.

Search engines have a directory about the various Web servers they have to search. This directory is updated as new servers come online. Then the search engines build indices for the various keywords. When a user poses a query, the search engine will consult its knowledge base, which consists of information about the Web servers and various indices. It also examines any caches it might have, and searches the Web servers for the information. All this activity has to be carried out in real-time.

Unless some form of intelligence is built into the search engine, it will return a lot of irrelevant results. For example, a search engine could list Web pages that have a lot of occurrences of the keyword entered by the user, or it could list Web pages that have had many hits. It would also be nice for search engines to list Web pages that have been accessed fre-

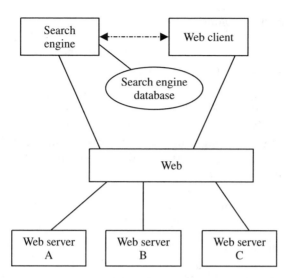

Exhibit 1.   Search Engines and Web Servers

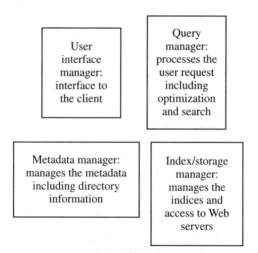

Exhibit 2.   Modules of the Search Engines

quently by the user. That is, search engines build user profiles and then list the Web pages favored by the user. We do have some of these features in search engines today, but there is still a lot of work to be done before a user gets exactly what he wants. This is where Web mining will help.

Web Data Mining for Search Engines

As we have stated, for search engines to be useful, they have to list results that are most relevant to the user. For example, if the user requests information on "lung cancer," the search engine can randomly select Web pages with the keywords in them or it can use techniques such as "most recently used" or "most frequently used" to return results. Web mining can help a great deal with intelligent searches.

With Web mining, we can mine the user log and build profiles for various users. Note that there are millions of users, and building profiles is not straightforward. We need to mine the Web logs to find users' preferences. Then we list those Web pages for the user. Furthermore, if a user is searching for some information, from time to time the search engines can list Web pages that could be relevant to the user's request. That is, search engines will have to dynamically carry out searches based on what the user wants. We will revisit this topic later when we discuss question answering systems; mining Web logs will be discussed in Part II.

Another challenge with search engines is to examine the relevant Web servers. There may be many Web servers that have irrelevant information for the user. Here again, Web mining could help to group or classify the Web servers. For example, a Web server at the National Institutes of Health (NIH) will have information about diseases and other medical information. A Web server at General Motors will have information about vehicles. If a user wants information about vehicles, then it may not be effective to search the NIH Web server. If a user who lives in an upscale neighborhood requests information about cars, it may not be effective to search the General Motors Web pages, as this user may prefer expensive cars.

To achieve intelligence and effective searching, we need effective Web mining. A Web miner would be part of the search engine, as illustrated in Exhibit 3, or it could be an interface to the search engine, as illustrated in Exhibit 4. In the latter case, the Web miner may also have a direct interface to the Web. In the tight integration approach, the Web miner may be part of the query manager, the metadata manager, and the index/storage manager. That is, the Web miner may be well integrated with the functions of the search engine. These Web miners are also needed to locate resources. For example, how can a search engine find all the relevant servers on the Web? That is, how do we find all the data sources? In many cases, the data could be in databases, which may not be known to the search engines. Effective Web mining techniques are needed to search what is called the "deep Web." Note also that search engines such as Google use a form of structure mining to determine the rank of a Web page. As discussed in Chapter 9, the Web links are mined and the rank of a Web page is determined by the rank of the Web pages that point to it. When the search engine searches for a string, the Web page with the search string and with the highest rank is displayed. Mining Web structures is still an emerging area, and it is sometimes difficult to separate Web structure mining from Web usage mining.

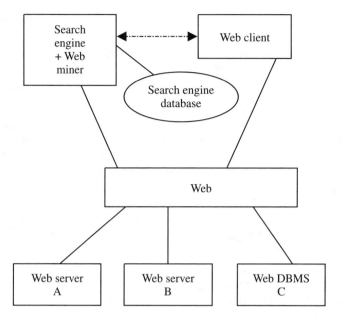

Exhibit 3. Tight Integration between Web Miner and Search Engine

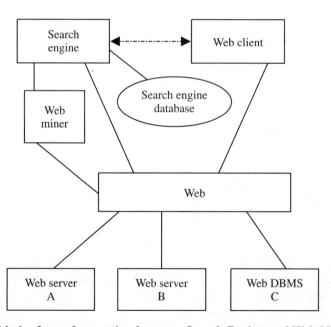

Exhibit 4. Loose Integration between Search Engine and Web Miner

As we have stated, there is tremendous improvement in search engines in recent years. They became popular in the mid-1990s, and although they were useful, they were also premature. The quality of search engines has improved a great deal. But we still have a long way to go before the user gets exactly what he wants.

Other concerns include security, privacy, and data quality. We want to make sure that search engines list Web pages that can be accessed by the user. Furthermore, they have to ensure that the user's privacy is maintained. Finally, search engines have to ensure that the information they provide is of high quality. For example, a Web server may have incorrect information. Then the question is, who is responsible for the information given to the user? There are legal issues involved here. Although there have been discussions on security, privacy, and data quality, there is little actual work reported. That is, search engines at present do not enforce access control rules. Essentially, access control is maintained by those providing the services. The question is, should the search engines enforce security also? There are many questions that need answers, and Web mining is one of the technologies that could help toward finding useful and relevant searches on the Web.

MULTIMEDIA DATA MINING AND THE WEB

We previously provided an overview of search engines as well as incorporating Web mining into search engines. We will now discuss the issues involved in mining and extracting information from text, images, video, and audio data. Note that the techniques discussed here will eventually be helpful for better Web searches.

As stated earlier, multimedia data includes text, images, video, and audio. Text and images are considered still media, while audio and video are continuous media. The issues surrounding still and continuous media are somewhat different and have been explained in various texts and papers such as [PRAB97]. In this section, we will consider text, image, video, and audio and how such data can be mined. First of all, what are the differences between mining multimedia data and topics such as text, image, and video retrieval? What is meant by mining such data? What are the developments and challenges?

Data mining has an impact on the functions of multimedia database systems discussed in [THUR01]. For example, the query processing strategies have to be adapted to handle mining queries if a tight integration between the data miner and the database system is the approach taken. This will then have an impact on the storage strategies. Furthermore, the data model will also have an impact. At present, many of the mining tools work on relational databases. However, if object-relational databases are to be used for multimedia modeling, then data mining tools have to be developed to handle such databases.

Text Mining

Information retrieval systems and text processing systems have been developed for more than a few decades. Some of these systems are quite sophisticated and can retrieve documents by specifying attributes or keywords. There are also text-processing systems that can retrieve associations between documents. So, we are often asked what the difference is between information retrieval systems and text mining systems

We define text mining as data mining on text data. Text mining is all about previously unknown extracting patterns and associations from large text databases. The difference between text mining and information retrieval is analogous to the difference between data mining and database management; there is really no clear difference. Some of the recent information retrieval and text processing systems do discover associations between words and paragraphs, and therefore can be regarded as text mining systems.

Next, let us examine the approaches to text mining. Note that many of the current tools and techniques for data mining work for relational databases. Even for data in object-oriented databases, rarely do we hear about data mining tools for such data. Therefore, current data mining tools cannot be directly applied to text data. Some of the current directions in mining unstructured data include the following:

- Extract data and metadata from the unstructured databases possibly by using tagging techniques, store the extracted data in structured databases, and apply data mining tools on the structured databases. This is illustrated in Exhibit 5.
- Integrate data mining techniques with information retrieval tools so that appropriate data mining tools can be developed for unstructured databases. This is illustrated in Exhibit 6.
- Develop data mining tools to operate directly on unstructured databases. This is illustrated in Exhibit 7.

When converting text data into relational databases, one has to be careful that there is no loss of key information. As we have stated before, unless we have good data, we cannot mine the data effectively and expect to get useful results. We first need to create a sort of warehouse before mining the converted database. This warehouse is essentially a relational database that has the essential data from the text data. In other words, we need a transformer that takes a text corpus as input and outputs tables that have, for example, the keywords from the text.

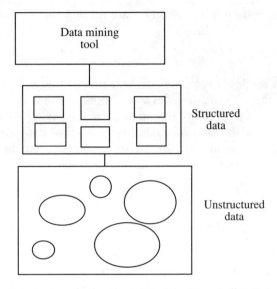

Exhibit 5.   Converting Unstructured Data to Structured Data for Mining

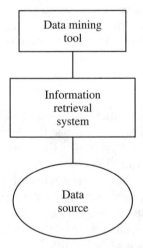

Exhibit 6.   Augmenting an Information Retrieval System

As an example, in a text database that has several journal articles, one could create a warehouse with tables containing the following attributes: author, date, publisher, title, and keywords. From the keywords, one can form associations. The keywords in one article could be "Belgium, nuclear weapons" and the keywords in another article could be "Spain, nuclear weapons." The data miner could make the association that authors from Belgium and Spain write articles on nuclear weapons.

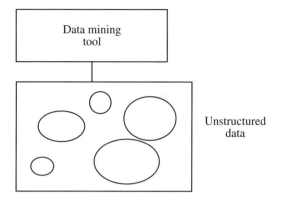

Exhibit 7.   Mining Directly on Unstructured Data

Note that we are only in the beginning of text mining. In the longer-term approach, we would want to develop tools directly to mine text data. These tools have to read the text, understand the text, put out pertinent information about the text, and then make associations between different documents. We are far from developing such sophisticated text mining tools. However, the work reported in [TSUR98] and [CLIF98] is the first step toward text mining. Some interesting early work on text mining is reported in [FELD95].

A taxonomy of text retrieval and text mining is illustrated in Exhibit 8. At the bottom is text retrieval, at the top is true text mining systems, and in between there may be multiple levels. At one level, there may be an intelligent text mining system that may make deductions and inferences. At another level, there may be a text understanding system. At a third level, there may be a semitext mining system that may make partial correlations. At a fourth level, there may be a system that extracts structured data from text and mines the structured data. As we go higher and higher, we get to a true text mining system where text is mined directly.

Note that this text mining taxonomy is somewhat subjective and depends on whose viewpoint it is. Nevertheless, there is a slight distinction between text mining and text retrieval. At the one end, we have a simple query system for retrieving documents. At the other end, we have a true text mining system. Between the two ends, we have many layers with increasing levels of sophistication.

Image Mining

If text mining is still in the early research stages, image mining is an even more immature technology. In this section, we will examine this area and discuss the current status and challenges.

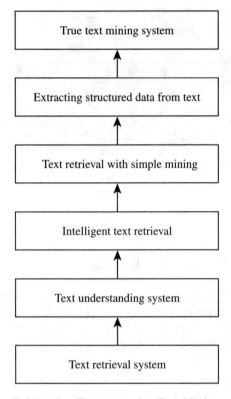

Exhibit 8.   Taxonomy for Text Mining

Image processing has been around for quite a while. We have image processing applications in various domains, including medical imaging for cancer detection, processing satellite images for space and intelligence applications, and also handling hyperspectral images. Images include maps, geological structures, biological structures, and many other entities. Image processing has dealt with areas such as detecting patterns which deviate from the norm, retrieving images by content, and pattern matching.

The main question here is, what is image mining? How does it differ from image processing? Again, we do not have clear-cut answers. One can say that while image processing is focusing on detecting abnormal patterns as well as retrieving images, image mining is all about finding unusual patterns. Therefore, one can say that image mining deals with making associations between different images from large image databases.

Clifton et al. [CLIF98] have begun work in image mining. Initially, the plan was to extract metadata from images and then carry out mining on the metadata. This would essentially be mining the metadata in relational databases. However, after some consideration, it was felt that images could be

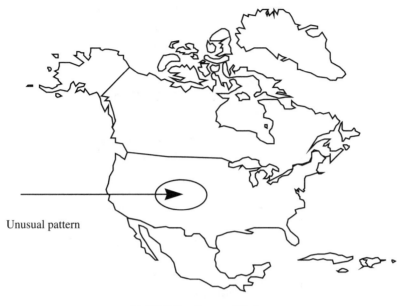

Unusual pattern

Exhibit 9.   Image Mining

mined directly. The challenge then is to determine what type of mining out-come is most suitable. One could mine for associations between images, cluster images, and classify images, as well as detect unusual patterns. One area of research being pursued by Clifton et al. is mining images to find any-thing unusual. So the approach is to develop templates that generate sev-eral rules about the images, and from there, apply the data mining tools to see if unusual patterns can be obtained. However, the mining tools will not tell us why these patterns are unusual. Exhibit 9 shows an image with some unusual patterns.

Note that detecting unusual patterns is not the only outcome of image mining. However, this is just the beginning. We need to conduct more research on image mining to see if data mining techniques could be used to classify, cluster, and associate images. Image mining is an area with appli-cations in numerous domains, including space images, medical images, and geological images

A taxonomy for image retrieval and image mining is illustrated in Exhibit 10. At the bottom is image retrieval; at the top are true image mining sys-tems; between the two there may be multiple levels. At one level, there may be an intelligent image mining system that may make deductions and infer-ences. At another level, there may be a semiimage mining system that may make partial correlations. At a third level, there may be a system that extracts structured data from an image and mines the structured data. As we go higher and higher, we get to a true image mining system.

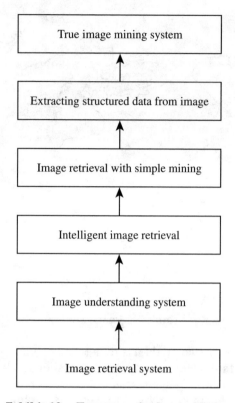

Exhibit 10.   Taxonomy for Image Mining

Note that this image mining taxonomy is somewhat subjective and depends on viewpoint. Nevertheless, there is some distinction between image mining and image retrieval. At the one end, we have a simple query system for retrieving documents; at the other end, we have a true image mining system; in between the two ends, we have many layers with increasing levels of sophistication.

Video Mining

Mining video data is even more complicated than mining image data. One can regard video as a collection of moving images, much like animation. Video data management has been the subject of much research. The important areas include developing query and retrieval techniques for video databases, including video indexing, query languages, and optimization strategies. The first question one asks is, what is the difference between video information retrieval and video mining? Unlike image and text mining, we do not have a clear idea of what is meant by video mining. For example, one could examine video clips and find associations between different clips. Another example is to find unusual patterns in video clips.

But how is this different from finding unusual patterns in images? The first step to successful video mining is to have a good handle on image mining.

Let us examine pattern matching in video databases. Should we have predefined images and then match these images with the video data? Is there any way we can do pattern recognition in video data by specifying what we are looking for and then do feature extraction for the video data? If this is video information retrieval, what then is mining video data? To be consistent with our terminology, we can say that finding previously unknown correlations and patterns from large video databases is video mining. By analyzing a video clip or multiple video clips, we come to conclusions about some unusual behavior. People in the video who are unlikely to be there, yet have appeared two or three times could mean something significant. Another way to look at the problem is to capture the text in video format and make the associations one would make with text using the video data instead.

Unlike text and image mining where our ideas have been less vague, the discussion here on video mining is quite preliminary. This is mainly because there is so little known about video mining. Even the term *video mining* is something very new, and to date we do not have any concrete results reported in this area. We do have a lot of information about analyzing video data and producing summaries. One could mine these summaries, which would amount to mining text, as shown in Exhibit 11. One good example of this effort is the work by Merlino et al. [MERL97] on summarizing video news. Converting the video mining problem to a text mining problem is reasonably well understood. However, the challenge is mining video data directly and, more importantly, knowing what we want to mine. With

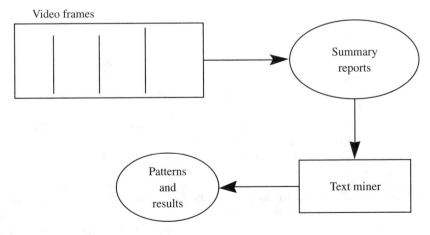

Exhibit 11.   Mining Text Extracted from Video

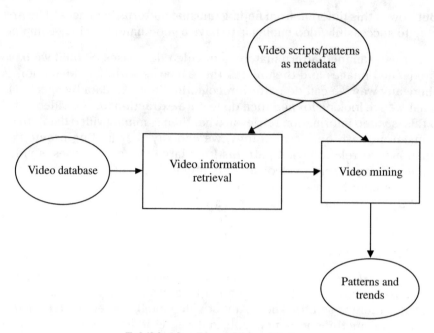

Exhibit 12. Direct Video Mining

the emergence of the Web, video mining becomes even more important. An example of direct video mining is illustrated in Exhibit 12.

Another point to note here is that one could use techniques from image mining for video mining. That is, one could detect abnormal patterns in video data. Here, one may use neural networks to train normal video, such as who usually appears with whom, and when something abnormal occurs, such as "John appearing with Mary for the first time," the system will flag this event as something abnormal. Anomaly detection for video mining needs further investigation.

A taxonomy for video retrieval and video mining is illustrated in Exhibit 13. At the bottom is video retrieval; at the top is true video mining systems; in between the two there may be multiple levels. At one level, there may be an intelligent video mining system that may make deductions and infer- ences. At another level, there may be a semivideo mining system that may make partial correlations. At a third level, there may be a system that extracts structured data from video and mines the structured data. As we go higher and higher, we get to a true video mining system.

Note that this video mining taxonomy is somewhat subjective and depends on viewpoint. Nevertheless, there is some distinction between video mining and video retrieval. At the one end, we have a simple query system for retrieving documents. At the other end, we have a true video

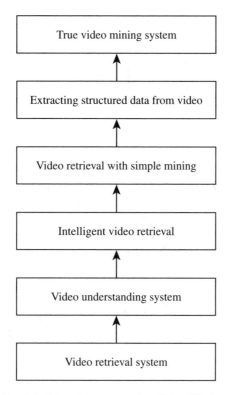

Exhibit 13. Taxonomy for Video Mining

mining system. Between the two ends, we have many layers with increasing levels of sophistication.

Audio Mining

To mine audio data, one could convert it into text using speech transcription techniques and other techniques such as keyword extraction and then mine the text data, as illustrated in Exhibit 14. On the other hand, audio data could also be mined directly by using audio information processing techniques and then mining selected audio data. This is illustrated in Exhibit 15.

In general, audio mining is even more primitive than video mining. While a few papers have appeared on text mining as well as image and video mining, work on audio mining is just beginning. Another point to note here is that one could also use techniques from image mining for audio mining. That is, one could detect abnormal patterns in audio data. Here, one may use neural networks to train normal audio data, and when something abnormal occurs for the first time, the system will flag this event as something abnormal. Anomaly detection for audio mining needs further investigation.

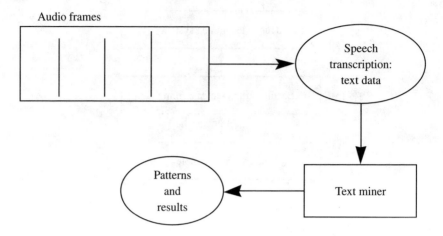

Exhibit 14.   Mining Text Extracted from Audio

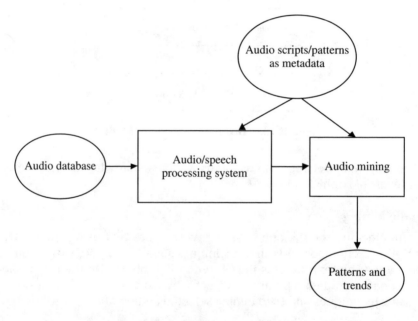

Exhibit 15.   Direct Audio Mining

A taxonomy for audio retrieval and audio mining is illustrated in Exhibit 16. At the bottom is audio retrieval; at the top is true audio mining systems; in between there may be multiple levels. At one level, there may be an intelligent audio mining system that may make deductions and inferences. At another level, there may be a semiaudio mining system that may make partial correlations. At a third level, there may be a system that extracts struc-

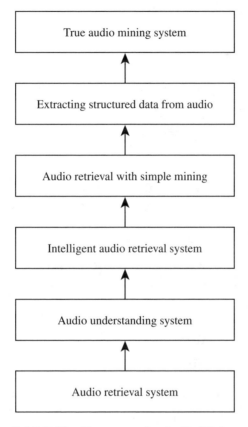

Exhibit 16.   Taxonomy for Audio Mining

tured data from audio and mines the structured data. As we go higher and higher, we get to a true audio mining system.

Note that this audio mining taxonomy is somewhat subjective and depends on viewpoint. Nevertheless, there is some distinction between audio mining and audio retrieval. At the one end, we have a simple query system for retrieving documents. At the other end, we have a true audio mining system. Between the two ends, we have many layers with increasing levels of sophistication.

Mining Multimedia Data Types

The previous sections discussed mining for individual data types such as text, images, video, and audio. These are what we call information retrieval and mining systems. However, we need to manage combinations of data types. The systems that manage them are multimedia database systems.

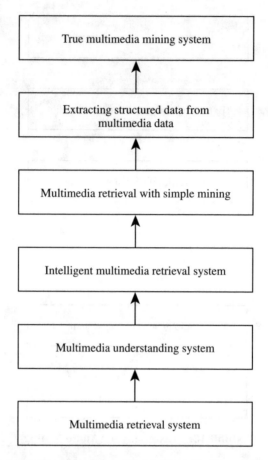

Exhibit 17.   Taxonomy for Multimedia Data Mining

If we are to mine multimedia data, then we need to mine combinations of two or more data types such as text and images, text and video, or a combination of text, audio, and video. In this section, we will briefly discuss some of the issues in multimedia data mining. Exhibit 17 illustrates a taxonomy for multimedia data mining.

Handling combinations of data types is very much like dealing with heterogeneous databases. For example, each database in the heterogeneous environment could contain data belonging to multiple data types. These heterogeneous databases could be first integrated and then mined, or one could apply mining tools on the individual databases and then combine the results of the various data miners. These two scenarios are illustrated in Exhibits 18 and 19. In both cases, the distributed multimedia processor (DMP) plays a role. If the data is to be integrated before being mined, then

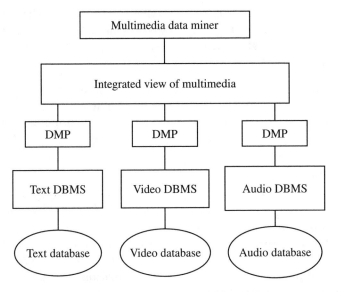

Exhibit 18.   Integration and Then Mining

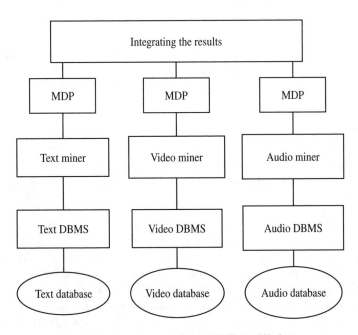

Exhibit 19.   Integration and Then Mining

this integration is carried out via the DMPs. If the data is to be mined first, the data miner augments the corresponding MM-DBMS (multimedia database management system) and the results of the data miners are integrated via the DMPs.

Because there is much to be done on mining individual data types such as text, images, video, and audio, mining combinations of data types is still a challenge. Once we have a better handle on mining individual data types, we can focus on mining combinations of data types.

Impact of the Web

Much of the discussion in the previous sections apply to mining multimedia data, whether it is on the Web or not. As we have mentioned, much of the data on the Web is in the form of text, images, video, and audio. There is also structured data and semistructured data. That is, there are Web databases as well as data in Web servers and other sources. This could be relational data, object data, object-relational data, or multimedia data. There could also be multimedia data, which consists of various combinations of data types. Therefore, all of the discussions in the previous sections apply for Web multimedia data mining also.

The question is, what are the additional challenges for mining multimedia data on the Web? We have mentioned that Web mining has to be incorporated into the search engines. Therefore, we need to develop special Web mining techniques that would help toward more intelligent and relevant searches. These techniques could be based on clustering, link analysis, or decision trees. For example, we could mine the data to obtain various links between different data in different Web servers. That is, one Web server could have information about people enrolled in flight training schools, and another Web server could have information about people purchasing firearms. The challenge is to find links between these two groups of people. While the techniques may be the same whether it is data mining or Web mining, the data may often reside on Web servers. Therefore, Web mining is critical for many applications to make links and associations.

Exhibit 20 illustrates an approach to augmenting multimedia data miners with Web miners. Essentially, these Web miners have interfaces to the Web and can be accessed via the Web. On the other hand, the Web miners could be tightly integrated with the MM-data miners, which in turn could be tightly integrated with the multimedia DBMS, as illustrated in Exhibit 21. Note there are various architectural configurations for integrating multimedia data miners with Web miners. In this section, we have illustrated only two of these configurations.

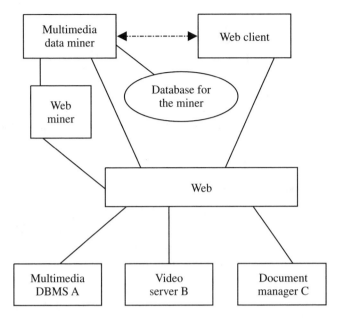

Exhibit 20. Loose Integration between Multimedia Data Miner and Web Miner

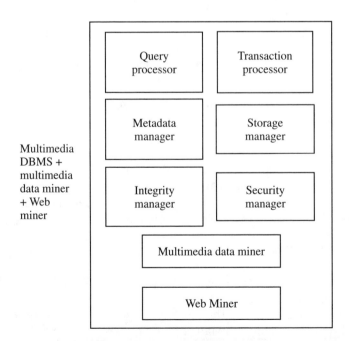

Exhibit 21. Tight Integration between Multimedia DBMS + Multimedia Data Miner + Web Miner

SOME OTHER ASPECTS

In Chapter 6, we discussed some other aspects such as question answering systems and markup languages. In this section, we discuss the impact of Web mining on these technologies.

A question answering system goes beyond the search engine. Not only does it carry out searches, it also guides the user to the answers that he wants. For example, when we type "lung cancer," a search engine will list Web pages that have lung cancer on them. However, a question answering system will ask the user, "do you want information about lung cancer or information about who has lung cancer?" That is, there is dialogue between the question answering system and the user.

Markup languages such XML, RDF, SGML, and HTML were developed specifically for the Web. For example, several extensions to XML have been proposed for images, video, and domain-specific applications such as finance and medical. These XML documents may have to be mined to extract hidden information and patterns.

The next two sections examine the impact of Web mining on question answering and markup languages.

Question Answering and Web Data Mining

We have mentioned in the previous section that a question answering system is much more than just a search engine. It not only lists Web pages but also conducts dialogue with the user. That is, it questions the user until it obtains answers that are relevant to the user's query.

A question answering system even answers questions such as "who is the best surgeon in Boston for heart transplants?" The system will then search the databases for heart transplant surgeries, examine the success rate of these surgeries, find the surgeons who have performed these surgeries, and then provide the answers. While this may sound simple, a lot of analysis is needed. This is where Web mining plays a role. With Web mining, the system will examine all the relevant databases and search for specific criteria such as success rates and qualifications of surgeons, the number of operations performed, etc. For example, if a surgeon has had a success rate of 80 out of 100, the surgeon may be considered better than another surgeon with a success rate of one out of one. The system may also ask the user to define "the best surgeon." That is, does the definition depend on the percentage of successful surgeries or on the actual number of surgeries carried out by the surgeon? Does the definition depend on whether the surgeon uses the latest techniques?

Various Web mining techniques could be used for question answering. For example, the system could form clusters of surgeons based on geo-

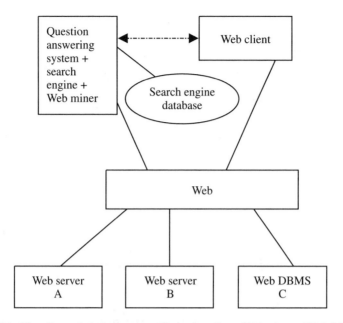

Exhibit 22.   Question Answering System + Search Engine + Web Miner

graphic area or number of surgeries performed. The system may also use profiles of customers in its searches, and may form links and associations between the surgeons, the primary care physicians, and other specialists to give the best answers.

Essentially, what we need are semantic Webs with machine-understandable Web pages incorporated with Web mining. We discuss semantic Web and Web mining in Chapter 14. Exhibit 22 illustrates the incorporation of Web mining with question answering systems.

Markup Languages and Web Data Mining

We discussed markup languages in Part I. XML is now one of the most popular markup languages. It has become the *de facto* standard for document interchange on the Web. There are now XML databases on the Web. These databases could be native XML databases or relational databases with XML interfaces. These databases have to be mined.

In Chapter 11, we discussed Web mining for semistructured databases. An XML database is an example of a semistructured database. One can incorporate a data miner with a query optimizer or build a data miner as an interface to an XML database. Exhibits 23 and 24 illustrate both approaches. Mining XML databases are a combination of mining relational databases and text databases. Many of the concepts and issues discussed

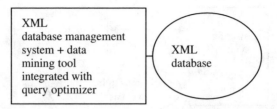

Exhibit 23.   Tight Coupling between XML DBMS and Data/Web Miner

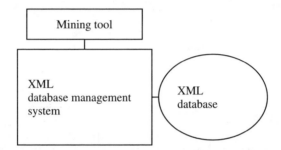

Exhibit 24.   Loose Integration between XML DBMS and Data/Web Miner

in Chapter 11 and in the previous sections of this chapter also apply here. One may also mine the various ontologies to extract hidden patterns and trends. We will revisit this subject in Chapter 14 when we discuss semantic Web and Web mining.

SUMMARY

In this chapter, we have mainly addressed information retrieval and Web mining. We started with a discussion of search engines and Web mining, and showed the need for incorporating Web mining into search engines so that they can perform intelligent searches. Next, we discussed multimedia data mining. Finally, we provided an overview of incorporating Web mining into question answering systems, and discussed mining XML documents.

Throughout this book, we have discussed concepts at a high level. One of our main goals is to show the relevance of the technologies discussed in Parts I and II to applications in counter-terrorism, which is the focus of Part III. For further details of the techniques, we refer to the references we have provided. There are also workshops and conferences now on Web mining. We encourage the reader to keep up with the developments and to start using the data mining and Web mining tools on various information retrieval systems.

Chapter 13
Information Management and Web Data Mining

INTRODUCTION

In this chapter, we examine the various information management technologies discussed in Chapter 7 and the impact of Web mining.

COLLABORATIVE DATA MINING

We discussed collaborative data mining as part of heterogeneous database mining in Chapter 11. In the case of federated and heterogeneous database mining, the various systems may have to work together and mine data collaboratively. In this section, we revisit the discussion in Chapter 11 as it is also very relevant for the discussion on collaborative data mining.

In collaborative data management, the idea is for different users to collaborate with each other on a project and share data. With collaborative data mining, different users or agents acting on behalf of users collaboratively mine the data. The data could be in multiple data sources or there could be shared databases. Exhibit 1 illustrates the idea of various mining agents collaborating with each other and discovering patterns across the various data sources. In this approach, collaborative computing, data mining, and heterogeneous database integration technologies have to work together.

Another scenario for collaborative data mining is illustrated in Exhibit 2. Here, two teams at different sites use collaboration and mining tools to mine the shared database. Exhibit 3 illustrates another approach to collaborative data mining, where Web miners collaboratively mine the various data sources on the Web. That is, in the scenario illustrated in Exhibit 1 each agent is responsible for mining a data source, however, in the scenario illustrated in Exhibit 3, the agents mine multiple data sources collaboratively. Note that there are different ways for data miners to carry out collaborative data mining. We have illustrated just a few of them. Research on collaborative data mining is still in its infancy. There is still a lot of work to be done.

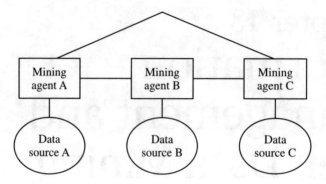

Exhibit 1.   Collaboration among Mining Agents

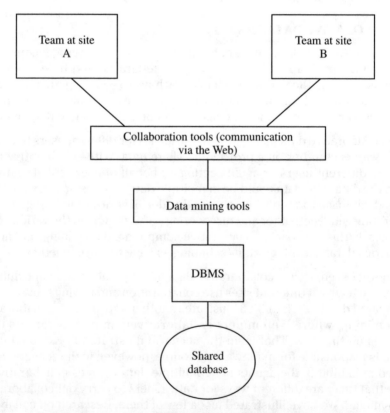

Exhibit 2.   Teams Conducting Mining on Shared Database

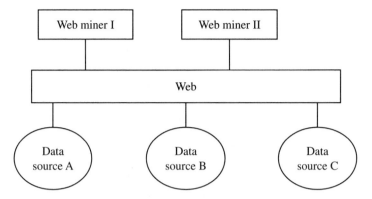

Exhibit 3. Multiple Miners and Multiple Data Sources

KNOWLEDGE MANAGEMENT AND WEB DATA MINING

Chapter 7 discussed knowledge management in some detail. Knowledge management is essentially about corporations using resources effectively to run their day-to-day business, including information sharing and collaboration. That is, information sharing and collaboration are tools for knowledge management. One needs to effectively manage the data, information, and knowledge of a corporation. The Internet in general and corporate intranets in particular play a major role.

The question is, what is the relationship between knowledge management and Web mining? Knowledge management is a very useful technology for Web mining. That is, one needs to organize and structure the data sources so that they can be mined. This is known as knowledge mining, where one mines the data to extract knowledge. As we have stated in the Preface, data, information, and knowledge are nebulous terms and, unless otherwise stated, we do not distinguish between them in this book. However, there do exist some distinctions between these terms. Knowledge is information that one can use. Therefore, to carry out knowledge mining, we need effective knowledge management. We need people to share data and information as well as collaborate with each other. Then we can mine the data and information that we have assimilated to extract useful knowledge for the corporation. For example, suppose we want to determine who is likely to leave the company within the next five years. We want to gather information about the projects they have worked on, their associations with professional organizations, their interactions with their peers and management, and many other aspects without violating their privacy. Then we develop a repository or warehouse of this data/information/knowledge and mine the repository to extract what we want. Knowledge management will help us to develop the repository. While knowledge management is a tool for Web mining, Web mining can also help knowledge management.

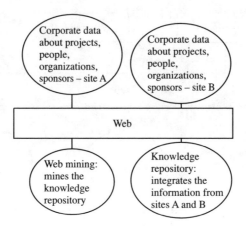

Exhibit 4.   Knowledge Management and Web Data Mining

Using this same example, this information is something new and can go into our knowledge repository. That is, the data/information/knowledge that we extract as a result of Web mining will contribute toward obtaining knowledge about the corporation, thereby improving the knowledge management capabilities of the corporation. In other words, this is a cyclic operation. Knowledge management is needed to build knowledge repositories. These knowledge repositories are mined and the extracted patterns are put back into the knowledge repository. Exhibit 4 illustrates Web mining and knowledge management.

This means that Web mining and knowledge management both contribute to each other. That is, effective knowledge management is needed to carry out Web mining. The knowledge gained from Web mining contributes to knowledge management. We will see that for many of the information management technologies, there is a two-way contribution between the technology and Web mining.

TRAINING AND WEB DATA MINING

The previous sections discussed the relationship between Web mining and collaboration as well as between Web mining and knowledge management. In this section, we will address Web mining and training.

Training can be both computer-based training (CBT) and more-traditional forms of training, such as training military personnel for combat. Training contributes to Web mining by essentially teaching various groups and individuals all about Web mining. We could have electronic or more-traditional courses on Web mining. While the idea is quite simple, it is still about teaching and training, and we need to train various individuals about data and Web mining.

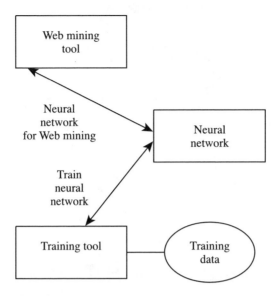

Exhibit 5.   Training and Web Data Mining

The question is, how can Web mining contribute to training? There are many ways Web mining can contribute. We need to mine the data on the Web to determine who needs training in what area. We may anticipate that a certain area will be very popular in the near future and want to train staff or develop high school and college courses. That is, by effectively mining the data on the Web or otherwise we can get a lot of hidden information about what is likely to happen in order to prepare ourselves for an event. Let us suppose through data mining we get information that certain buildings are going to be attacked in a certain way. Then we can prepare emergency response teams for the best response.

Exhibit 5 illustrates an example of how training can be used for Web mining. Here, a training tool trains a neural network to carry out Web mining. Our ideas are preliminary, but it is still a start. We need to determine how to effectively use both Web mining and training to provide safety as well as to run better organizations.

AGENTS AND WEB DATA MINING

In this section, we will examine the relationship between Web mining and agents. In Chapter 7, we provided an overview of agents. Agents are essentially processes that have well-defined interfaces and communicate with each other through well-defined protocols. So, the question is, what is the relationship between agents and Web mining? One is that agent technology can be used for Web mining. That is, we could use agents to mine the data on the Web. While we could use simple processes for data and

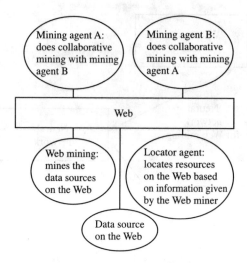

Exhibit 6.   Agents and Web Data Mining

Web mining, with agents we can have protocol-based communication between the agents. That is, a mining agent could communicate with a resource manager agent and a resource manage agent could communicate with a locator agent, all through well-defined protocols.

How can Web mining support agents? With Web mining, we can find various resources, patterns, and trends. This in turn could help toward constructing various types of agents. We can use Web mining to support a variety of agents to carry out their jobs. These will include locator agents, resource management agents, as well as agents for knowledge management and collaboration, etc.

Exhibit 6 illustrates agents mining data on the Web, as well as using Web mining to locate resources on the Web. Here again, our ideas are preliminary, but we need to start somewhere.

WIRELESS COMPUTING AND WEB DATA MINING

In Chapter 7, we discussed wireless computing and information management. The question is, what is the relationship between Web mining and wireless computing? Web mining is an important technology for wireless computing. There are now many individuals with mobile telephones, palm pilots, and other devices traveling around the world. They need to get the right information at the right time to carry out their tasks. Web mining mines the data on the wireless Web and gives useful feedback to these individuals.

For example, suppose someone wants to travel to a certain place in six months. With data mining, one could extract information not only about

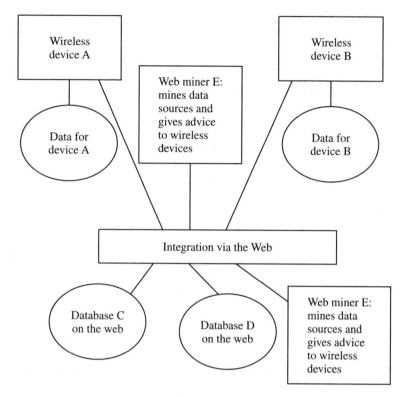

Exhibit 7. Wireless Information Management and Web Data Mining

the climate, but also about potential political problems, terrorist attacks, and travel options. Another example is a situation where a traveler needs immediate help with a medical situation. With intelligent search techniques, he could perhaps get the needed information. But when effective Web mining capabilities are added to the information retrieval systems, he can go further and get information on the most likely areas to get help even if it is not available in the town that he is visiting.

The other question is, how can wireless computing help Web mining? The answer is more nebulous here. One could think of wireless technologies providing the backbone for mobile communications and wireless information management. This information has to be mined so that useful information can be extracted. That is, we build Web mining on top of wireless information management, which is built on top of wireless technologies. That is, we can see a two-way relationship between Web mining and wireless computing. There is little work reported on wireless data mining. But we can expect to see lot of progress in this area. Exhibit 7 illustrates the relationship between Web mining and wireless information management.

SENSOR WEB MINING

Next, we examine the relationship between sensor Web and Web mining. As we have mentioned in Chapter 7, the sensor Web is about millions of sensors connected through a network and forming some sort of Web. Streams emanate from sensors and, we need to develop effective information management technologies for managing these streams. The question here is, what is the relationship between sensor Web and Web mining?

First of all, the streams that emanate from the sensors are data, and the stream data will have to be mined to extract useful information. Sensor data could be information about tracking various individuals or information from sensors tracking the temperature in a manufacturing plant. We need to mine the data to determine potential problems. For example, if law enforcement officials see that an individual is making frequent trips to a shop that sells chemicals and one that sells firearms, they may want to place that individual on a list of suspicious persons. That is, with appropriate mining of the data emanating from the sensors placed in the various shops, we could make connections, links, and associations.* The next question is, how can sensors help with Web mining? As in the case of wireless computing, the answer is more nebulous. One can perhaps think of having very effective sensors and sensor information management technologies to carry out sensor data and information mining. As in the case of wireless information mining, sensor Web data mining is also a very new area where research is just beginning. Exhibit 8 illustrates the relationship between sensor Web and Web mining. The task of mining sensor data is known as sensor Web mining.

QUALITY OF SERVICE AND WEB DATA MINING

Next, we discuss the important topic of quality of service (QoS) and Web mining. Quality of service is about making trade-offs between various parameters such as precision, accuracy, safety, security, timeliness, etc. We discussed QoS in Chapter 7. Here we discuss the relationship between QoS and Web mining.

With data mining as well as with Web mining, we need good training data. The question is, how many examples do we need to train a neural network? Do we need hundreds or thousands of examples? Again, having good training data or good warehouse data is critical for good data mining. If we do not have good data, the results of data mining may not be useful. Because it may take a very long time to get good data, we need to make QoS decisions. Do we sacrifice accuracy for timeliness?

---

* Note that when shops that sell firearms and chemicals inform law enforcement officials about their sales, they may violate the privacy of the purchasers. This privacy issue is discussed in Part III in general and in Chapter 25 in particular.

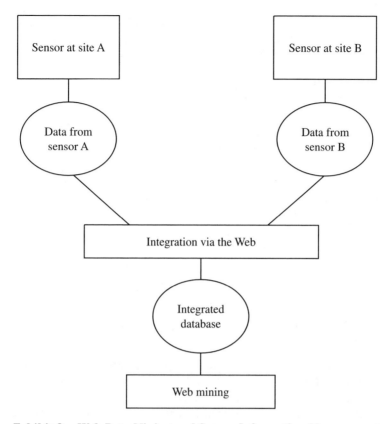

Exhibit 8. Web Data Mining and Sensor Information Management

Timeliness also has other connections to Web and data mining. Currently, we hear much about real-time data mining. The question is, what do we mean by real-time data mining? Data mining is supposed to carry out analysis of data that has been accumulated over a period. Also, the models for data mining are not built in real-time. Some are skeptical about real-time data mining and building real-time models. Nevertheless, we need to carry out some form of real-time analysis for applications such as intrusion detection. The challenge here is to develop QoS measures so that we can use some prior knowledge and experience and yet carry out the analysis in real-time.

Web and data mining may also help toward developing QoS measures. That is, we can mine data to get information about various applications and give advice to users on getting appropriate QoS parameters. The ideas here are very preliminary and much thought is needed.

Finally, while we are carrying out data mining, we can enforce QoS. That is, when do we stop the mining process? When do we know that we have

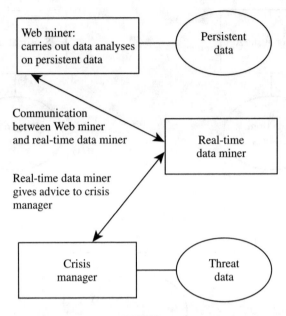

Exhibit 9. QoS and Web Data Mining

obtained all the answers? Can we stop after we obtain some partial answers? Note that data mining is an expensive process and, therefore, we need to enforce some QoS measures. Here again, the trade-off is between timeliness and accuracy. Exhibit 9 illustrates the relationship between QoS and Web mining. In this example, real-time data mining is carried out for crisis situations. The Web miner will work together with the real-time data miner for less critical situations.

OTHER ASPECTS

This chapter has discussed various information technologies and services for the Web and then discussed the impact of Web mining. Essentially, we examined the technologies in Chapter 7 and the impact of Web mining on technologies such as collaborative data management, training, knowledge management, agents, quality of service, and sensor and wireless information management.

As we have stated in Chapter 7, many of the technologies such as data, information, and knowledge management are being used ultimately for managers, policymakers, and other authorities to make effective decisions. Therefore, Web mining is a critical technology for decision makers, managers, and policy makers.

In Chapter 7, we listed some other technologies that are important for information management. These technologies include fault tolerance, data

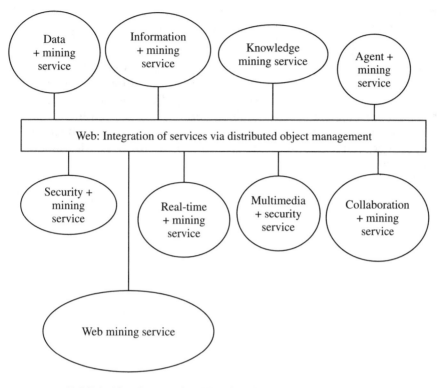

Exhibit 10.   Integrating Web Services and Data Mining

quality, multilingual data mining, data and information administration, etc. The relationship between Web mining and these information management technologies has to be examined also. Because of the breadth and depth of information management, it is almost impossible to list all of the technologies and examine the impact of Web mining for them. We have discussed only some of them in this chapter. Exhibit 10 illustrates the integration of various technologies with Web mining. Essentially, we have taken the information in Exhibit 18 from Chapter 7 and inserted Web mining for the various services. Note that we can have a separate Web mining component, or Web mining can be integrated into the services. This is related to semantic Web mining, which will be discussed in the next chapter.

SUMMARY

This chapter has examined the various information management technologies discussed in Chapter 7 and the impact of Web mining. For example, we examined collaborative data management, knowledge management, training, agents, wireless information management, sensor information management, quality of service aspects, and the relationship between Web mining and these technologies. Many of the ideas on Web mining technologies are still in development. Nevertheless, we have presented some direction for Web mining.

In the next chapter, we will examine the semantic Web technologies discussed in Chapter 8 and examine the impact of Web mining. This area is known as semantic Web mining (see [NGDM]). In particular, we will discuss the concept of semantic Web mining and examine technologies such as XML document mining and semantic Web mining services. In the future, we can expect Web mining technologies to evolve into semantic Web mining technologies.

Chapter 14
Semantic Web Mining

INTRODUCTION

As mentioned in Chapter 8, although the ideas are still somewhat fuzzy, the Web is evolving into the semantic Web. The technologies that are being developed will eventually give us machine-understandable Web pages. Furthermore, Web mining is now a reality. The challenge therefore is to carry out semantic Web mining. That is, we need to mine the semantic Web. The question is, what does it mean to mine the semantic Web? Note that the semantic Web is about machine-understandable Web pages to make the Web more intelligent and able to provide useful services to the user. This means that the information on Web pages may have to be mined so that the machine can understand the content. Essentially, we need to carry out machine learning on the Web.

Another challenge is to mine the RDF and XML documents to develop semantic Web services. One can also mine the ontologies and other databases so that the Web is made more intelligent. While we briefly discussed semantic Web mining in Chapter 8, we will explore this topic in some detail in this chapter. In particular, we will examine each of the technologies discussed in Chapter 8 and discuss the impact of Web mining.

CONCEPTS IN SEMANTIC WEB MINING

Chapter 8 discussed the semantic Web and provided an example concept of operation. In this section, we discuss semantic Web mining. It is essentially mining the information pertaining to the semantic Web. This means mining Web pages so that the machine can better understand the information. It also means mining the data sources to develop an effective semantic Web.

Exhibit 1 illustrates semantic Web mining. It is essentially mining various XML and RDF documents as well as mining ontologies and metadata. It also includes mining the data sources on the Web and mining the information relating to the information management technologies. Note that in Chapter 7, while we discussed semantic Web, it was difficult to give a definition of the semantic Web. That is, it is not possible to say that this is where the Web ends and the semantic Web begins. The semantic Web is essentially an evolution of the Web. We will not end with the semantic Web. It will evolve as far as we can see. In the same way, semantic Web mining

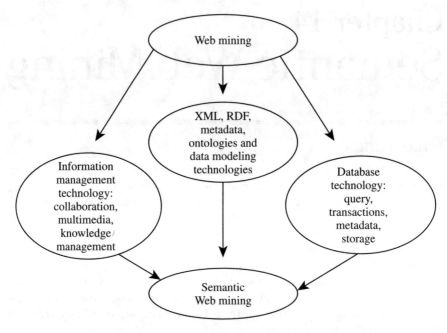

Exhibit 1. Semantic Web Mining Technologies

will evolve from Web mining. The ultimate goal is to make the Web easier to use. In addition, we want to mine the large quantities of information on the Web so that humans can better perform their tasks.

Exhibit 2 illustrates a semantic Web mining concept of operation. As we have mentioned in Chapter 8, the brokering service matches subscribers and publishers. With semantic Web mining, the brokering services use Web mining to determine the best publishers for the subscribers and to advise them. That is, it is not just a matching service; it mines the information and data sources, finds the best match, and provides advice for future services and enhancements.

Exhibit 3 shows how Web mining agents can be integrated with the locator agents and user agents. That is, the Web mining agents give advice to the user agents as well as to the locator agents in terms of finding the resources.

XML, RDF, AND WEB DATA MINING

As we have mentioned in Part I, the Web has both structured and unstructured documents. That is, while some of the data may be in relational databases, XML is becoming the *de facto* standard for Web documents. The W3C (World Wide Web Consortium) has developed standards for RDF. Therefore, we can expect both XML and RDF documents to become the standard document exchange languages for the Web. This

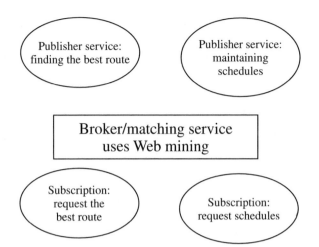

Exhibit 2. **Concept of Operation for Semantic Web Mining**

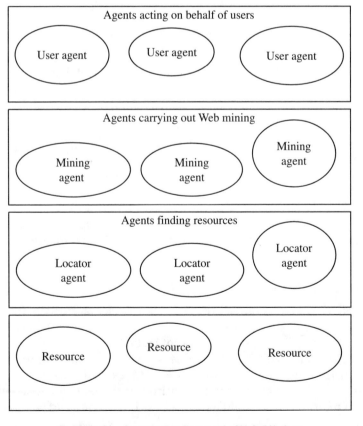

Exhibit 3. **Agents for Semantic Web Mining**

Exhibit 4. Tight Integration between Data Miner and XML/RDF Database

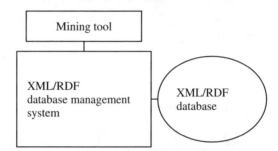

Exhibit 5. Loose Integration between Data Miner and XML/RDF Database

means that there will be XML and, eventually, RDF databases on the Web. One can think of the semantic Web in terms of different kinds of databases such as XML, RDF, multimedia, relational, and object databases, which also have to be mined.

Exhibits 4 and 5 illustrate the tight coupling and loose coupling approaches for semantic Web mining. In the tight coupling approach, the Web miner and XML data manager are tightly integrated. In the loose coupling approach, the data miner is an interface to the XML data manager. Note that, as illustrated in Exhibit 6, one can extract structure from the XML and RDF documents and mine the structured database. Some of the key points were discussed in the previous chapters on mining semistructured databases.

ONTOLOGIES AND WEB DATA MINING

In Chapter 8, we discussed ontologies for the semantic Web. Ontologies were also discussed in Chapter 5 when we addressed metadata for Web data management. The question is, what is the relationship between ontologies and Web mining? We feel that this is a two-way relationship. Web mining can help to develop ontologies. Note that ontologies are somewhat standard definitions about various entities and events such as vehicles, wines, animals, etc. One could mine the data on the Web and develop ontol-

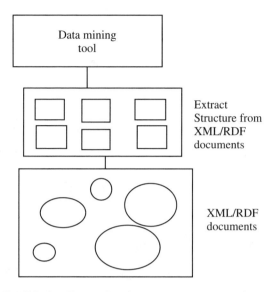

Exhibit 6.   Extracting Structure and then Mining

ogies. For example, by mining the data we may find that there is a special kind of wine. This type of wine can then be included in the wine ontology.

One can also mine the ontologies on the Web so that it is made more intelligent. This is illustrated in Exhibit 7. While ontologies are developed from metadata and ontologies in turn generate, for example, RDF schemas, one could mine the metadata, ontologies, and RDF schemas toward developing the semantic Web. That is, the information mined from ontologies and schemas can be used perhaps to better understand Web pages. There is still much to be done here.

AGENTS AND WEB DATA MINING

In Chapter 13, we discussed agents and Web mining. Agents are a key technology for the semantic Web. Therefore, we will revisit agents for completeness. As we have mentioned earlier, agents are essentially processes that have well-defined interfaces, and communicate with each other through well-defined protocols. The question is, what is the relationship between agents and Web mining? One is that agent technology can be used for Web mining. That is, we could use agents to mine the data on the Web. While we could use simple processes for data and Web mining, with agents we can have protocol-based communication between the agents. A mining agent could communicate with a resource manager agent and a resource manage agent could communicate with a locator agent, all through well-defined protocols.

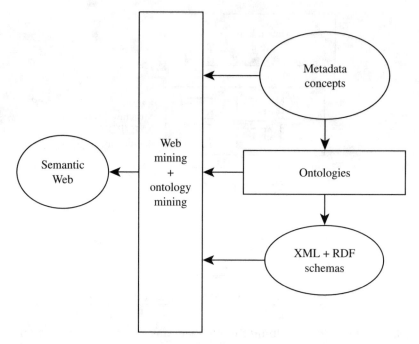

Exhibit 7.   Ontologies and Web Data Mining

How can Web mining support agents? With Web mining, we can find various resources, patterns, and trends. This in turn could help toward constructing various types of agents. We can use Web mining to support a variety of agents to carry out their jobs. These will include locator agents, resource management agents, and agents for knowledge management and collaboration, among others.

Exhibit 8 illustrates agents mining data as well as using Web mining to locate resources on the Web. The ideas discussed here also apply for the semantic Web. That is, we need agents to mine the data on the Web as well as Web pages so that the machine can understand the Web pages better. Eventually, this means that the burden placed on the human could be eased.

WEB MINING AND THE SEMANTIC WEB AS A DATABASE

In Chapter 8, we discussed an alternative way to view the semantic Web. In this view, the semantic Web is considered a database management system managing millions of objects. This means that the semantic Web can query and manage the data in a large distributed database.

In Exhibit 7, Chapter 8, we illustrated how database functions can be applied to the semantic Web. In Exhibit 9, we illustrate how data mining can

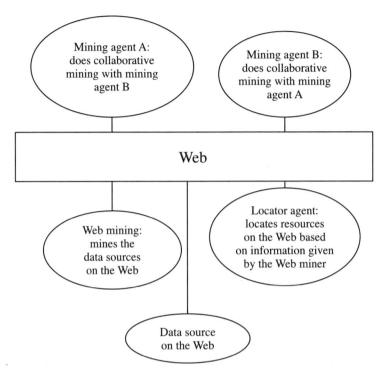

Exhibit 8.   Revisiting Agents and Web Mining

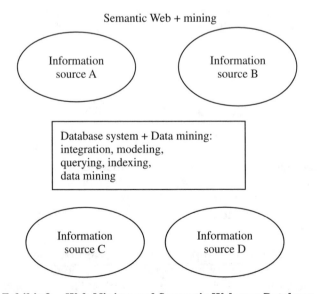

Exhibit 9.   Web Mining and Semantic Web as a Database

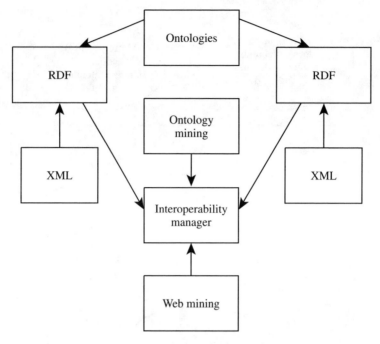

Exhibit 10. Web Mining and Semantic Interoperability

be included as part of the semantic Web function. That is, the database system which is the semantic Web can carry out data mining to extract often previously unknown patterns and trends. There is still a lot of research to be done in considering the semantic Web as a large heterogeneous database system. For example, we need to examine schema integration, federated database concepts, and many other issues. We also need to include data mining as part of this research.

SEMANTIC INTEROPERABILITY AND WEB MINING

In Chapter 8, we discussed semantic interoperability. Here, the various RDF and XML documents have to interoperate. The database researchers have carried out extensive research on semantic heterogeneity in heterogeneous and federated databases. Many of the concepts are also applicable to the semantic Web. Note that this is essentially what we discussed in Chapter 8 when we considered the semantic Web as a large heterogeneous databases manager.

Exhibit 10 illustrates an approach for the interoperability of RDF documents. Note that there may be several interpretations of the same entity and the same interpretation for different entities. The interoperability man-

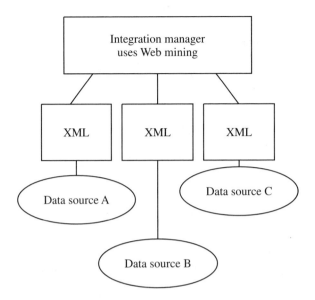

Exhibit 11. Mining for Semantic Interoperability of XML Databases

ager has to handle such heterogeneity. This is where Web mining could help. The various ontologies could be mined to support interoperability.

In addition, the data sources on the Web could be mined. The information extracted from mining could be given as input to the interoperability manager. Exhibit 11 illustrates an example of integrating XML documents. Here again, the interoperability manager uses Web mining to handle semantic heterogeneity.

WEB SERVICES AND WEB MINING

In Chapter 8, we provided an overview of Web services. This is one of the rapidly growing areas in Web technology. The idea is essentially to provide a number of Web services, including publishing, subscription, directory, and many others, to Web users, who make use of the services by calling appropriate service routines.

Exhibit 12 illustrates the concept of incorporating data mining not only as a Web service but also using it to enhance the Web services. For example, one could have a data mining service mine the data sources on the Web. Data mining can also be used to broker the information. That is, the broker service could use data mining to match publishers with subscribers. This is an area that is still largely unexplored. While we have the various pieces such as Web services and Web mining, we need to integrate the two to provide better quality services to the users.

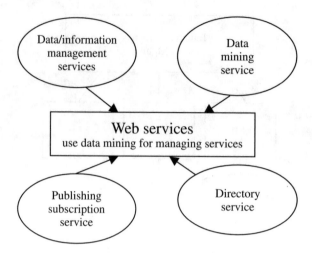

Exhibit 12.   Web Services and Web Mining

WEB MINING VS. SEMANTIC WEB MINING

In Chapter 8, we discussed the evolution of the Web to the semantic Web. As we have mentioned, we cannot say at which point the Web ends and the semantic Web begins. It will be a continuous process. The Web will continually evolve to become the semantic Web and, some say, the knowledge Web eventually. There is only one Web, and as we make progress with technologies and applications, the Web will continue to be enhanced. We also stress that applications as technologies alone will not be sufficient. Applications will drive the way the Web evolves. This is why we provide a brief overview of various applications in Chapter 16. While our focus is on Web mining for these applications, we will discuss how these applications are driving the Web.

Exhibit 13 illustrates semantic Web mining. We started with data mining in the mid-1990s. At that time, many of the data mining tools mined only relational databases. In 2000, we began to see multimedia data mining tools, especially text mining tools, and Web mining tools appear. These tools will eventually evolve into semantic Web mining tools. That is, semantic Web mining is about data mining on the Web to make the Web more intelligent. By 2005, we should begin to see such tools emerge. For example, these tools will mine Web pages and give advice to both the system and the users.

A NOTE ON E-COMMERCE, BUSINESS INTELLIGENCE, AND SEMANTIC WEB MINING

E-commerce is the killer application for the Web. We have provided an overview of E-commerce in Chapter 2, and we have discussed the semantic

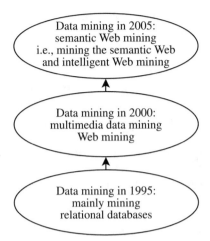

Exhibit 13.   Evolution of Semantic Web Mining

Web and E-commerce in Chapter 8. We revisit E-commerce in this chapter for completion. E-commerce is about carrying out transactions on the Web between the consumer and the business or between businesses. In [THUR00], we discussed how Web data management technologies could be used for E-commerce. We also briefly illustrated how Web mining could help business intelligence. We revisit this topic in this section.

Web mining is one of the key technologies to gather business intelligence. It is illustrated in Exhibit 14. With Web mining, one can develop customer profiles and buying trends, and carry out targeted marketing. We can use many of the mining techniques such as classification, clustering, and

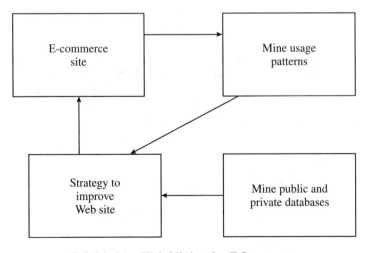

Exhibit 14.   Web Mining for E-Commerce

link analysis to develop profiles of customers. We can extract information, such as "customers who bought X also bought Y," and "customers who purchased X and Y are likely to purchase Z." This way, we could market Z products to customers who have purchased X and Y.

We will discuss the various applications of Web mining in Chapter 17. As we have stated, applications drive the development of the Web. That is, applications drive technologies, and technologies in turn generate new applications. There are many similarities between gathering business intelligence and gathering intelligence for counter-terrorism. This is one of the reasons we have discussed business intelligence analysis throughout this book. We will focus on counter-terrorism in Part III, and will revisit business intelligence in Chapter 27.

SUMMARY

This chapter has provided a broad overview of semantic Web mining. We examined the semantic Web concepts discussed in Chapter 8 and described the impact of Web mining. We started with a discussion of semantic Web mining concepts and discussed a concept of operation. Then we discussed mining XML and RDF documents as well as the semantic interoperability of these documents. We also discussed the use of agents in semantic Web mining and described the notion of incorporating mining into the semantic Web when the semantic Web is considered to be a heterogeneous database manager. Finally, we discussed the evolution of the semantic Web and also examined the use of Web mining in E-commerce.

The previous four chapters essentially examined data management, information retrieval, information management, and semantic Web technologies and discussed the impact of Web mining. The next three chapters will address some related topics. Chapter 15 will discuss Web usage and structure mining, which is another major component of Web mining. Web mining prototypes and products will be the subject of Chapter 16. We provide a broad overview of applications in Chapter 17. This will then set the stage for discussion in Part III of counter-terrorism as one of the critical applications for data and Web mining. Web mining is used to gather business intelligence so that organizations can get information about competitors and improve their business practices. Similarly, business intelligence can be used to learn about the strategies of the adversary to counter terrorism.

Chapter 15
Mining Usage Patterns and Structure on the Web

INTRODUCTION

The previous discussions have focused mainly on mining the data and information on the Web. In this chapter, we discuss Web usage mining and Web structure mining.

As mentioned in Chapter 9, three aspects of mining on the Web are (1) mining Web logs and usage patterns, (2) mining Web links to extract structure, and (3) mining Web content, including data, text, images, video, etc. Research in these areas is being conducted by various groups, including Morey et al. [MORE98a] and Shrivastava et al. [SHRI02]. A good start to Web mining was the ICTAI conference panel on Web mining [ICTA97] and later the KDD workshop on Web mining [KDD99].

In Web usage mining, usage patterns of various users and trends of usage are tracked, and predictions are made about what users want, in the interest of targeted marketing efforts. Users may also be given advice as to what to browse on the Web (Exhibit 1). This facilitates the work a user has to do with respect to scanning various Web pages. With Web structure mining, one mines various links and perhaps extracts patterns and gives advice to search engines. Note that while previous chapters have focused on developing Web data mining tools, here the focus is on mining usage patterns and structures on the Web.

Mining can also be used to provide only selected information to the user. For example, many of us are bombarded daily with e-mail messages, some of which are not relevant to our work. One can develop simple filtering tools or sophisticated data mining tools to discard unwanted e-mail messages. Similarly, these data mining tools could also be used to display only the Web pages in which a user is interested.

Web structure mining is somewhat related to usage mining as one needs to mine the links and structure to determine the links between Web pages.

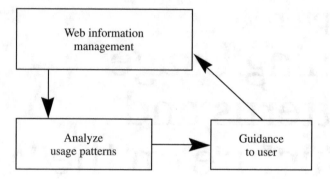

Exhibit 1. Analyzing Usage Patterns and Predicting Trends

This information can be used to give advice to users, as well as to improve the capability of search engines. We will discuss Web structure mining later in this chapter,

WEB USAGE MINING OUTCOMES AND TECHNIQUES

Many of the techniques discussed in Chapter 3 can be applied for Web usage mining and traffic analysis. We will examine some of them.

First, what outcomes do we desire for Web usage mining? We may want to classify groups of people who use certain Web pages. For example, people living in New York often search the Web for apartments in Manhattan. But surprisingly, so do people living in Fargo, North Dakota. To create this classification, data is gathered about Web usage and intelligent searching is used to discover patterns. Then an analysis may produce information that a bank in Manhattan has a major branch in Fargo, North Dakota. Therefore, those who travel often between Fargo and New York lease apartments in Manhattan.

Another outcome we may desire is associations. That is, based on Web usage, we find associations such as people who visit tennis Web pages also visit golf Web pages. This may not be unusual. However, we may find that people who visit tennis Web pages are also interested in shoes because they may get ideas about the brands the tennis players are endorsing. Even more unusual is that those who visit tennis Web pages also visit Web pages discussing chocolates. Such an unusual pattern may need some analysis.

Other outcomes for Web usage mining are detecting anomalies. For example, John is always visiting Web pages on religion. Occasionally, we see that he is visiting Web pages about film stars. This could be unusual because usually very religious people are not too interested in film stars. The reverse may also be true. That is, James is always visiting Web pages on films, film stars, and fashions, and once in awhile he will visit Web pages selling religious books.

By mining, we can carry out predictions and estimations. For example, based on John's Web usage patterns, if a new tennis event is announced, we could predict that he will be visiting that Web page. Another example is in marketing and sales. Suppose a shoe sales company builds customer profiles and gets the information that John visits tennis Web pages as well as shoes Web pages. The company may market the fact that they are developing a new brand and have tennis star Bill endorsing the new product. This information could be sent to John periodically over the Web.

We will see in the next section that quite a few of the Web mining products carry out traffic analysis, clickstream analysis, business intelligence analysis, or Web usage analysis. In a way, Web usage analysis is central to other types of usage. For example, Web traffic is essentially about Web usage. With Web traffic analysis, one could get the information that there is a lot of traffic Wednesday between 3:00 and 5:00 A.M. This could be somewhat unexpected, and the organization can then take appropriate actions such as marketing certain brands at that time.

In this section, we have provided a brief overview of the various techniques that could be employed to carry out Web usage mining. For example, we listed the desired outcomes and then discussed the searching and other techniques that could be used. One could also train decision trees and neural networks to carry out classification and clustering. Market basket analysis techniques could be used for making associations. Link analysis could be used to make links between different entities and activities of terrorists. For example, one could follow the links of the money trail between terrorists by following the links between Web pages and other nodes containing information, and may determine that the funds for terrorist activities actually originated from the President of country X. Exhibit 2 illustrates this discussion.

WEB USAGE MINING ANALYSIS

While the previous section discussed some outcomes of Web usage mining, in this section we will discuss the types of analysis that may be carried out. To illustrate the ideas, we will use some Web mining products. Note that a more-detailed list of products will be given in the next chapter. These products are listed on the kdnuggets Web page (www.kdnuggets.com). We have selected a few of these products to illustrate some of the key ideas. As we have stressed, we are not endorsing any of the products. Here are some products for Web usage mining:

- *Clementine:* Sequence association and clustering used for Web data analysis.
- *eNuggets:* Real-time click analysis and refines models automatically
- *MicroStrategy Web Traffic Analysis Module:* Web site analysis, Web traffic analysis

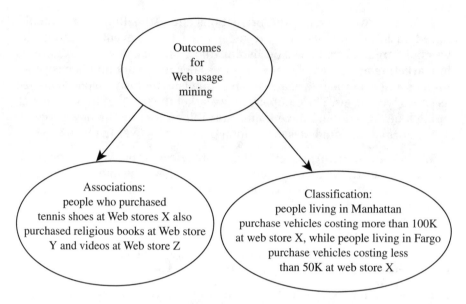

Exhibit 2. Data Mining Outcomes and Techniques

- *net.Analysis (from net.Genesis):* Mines for business intelligence
- *123LogAnalyzer:* Analyzes Web logs

The above tools carry out various activities related to Web usage mining. For example, Clementine analyzes Web data and forms associations and clustering of various groups of people accessing the Web, as we have discussed in the previous section. eNuggets is interesting because it carries out analysis in real-time. That is, every new click (which means a new user entering the site) is taken into consideration. We discussed some real-time data mining challenges in Chapter 13. The product from MicroStrategy analyzes Web traffic and generates reports for the Web site managers. The LogAnalyzer product analyzes the Web logs and extracts information that will be useful to those managing the Web site.

Eventually, Web usage mining and analysis will help those managing the Web sites. If they are corporations, then it will give them insights into their customers and their buying trends. Data mining tools could also be developed specifically for customers who want to find information about corporations. Suppose I want to find a job on the Web. I can list my credentials, and the data mining tool will review the information posted on the Web by corporations and suggest best matches for me.

We will see in Part III that Web usage mining products will be very useful for counter-terrorism activities. We could find out which Web pages these groups are accessing. For example, suppose a group of people frequently visits Web pages of tall buildings and flight training schools. The analyst

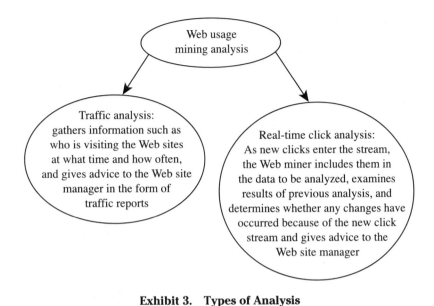

Exhibit 3.   Types of Analysis

may correlate planes with tall buildings. Then one could carry out further mining to get information about this group of people to determine whether they could be planning terrorist acts. Note that when one queries further, this is where privacy issues come in. That is, we may violate the privacy of an individual by extracting too much information about him, especially if he is not a terrorist. However, we need the complete picture to get useful results from mining. We will discuss privacy in Part III.

While the previous section discussed the various techniques, in this section we discussed the types of analyses one could carry out. It is often difficult to separate the techniques from the analyses. Therefore, this section and the one that follows are closely related. Some of the analysis discussions are illustrated in Exhibit 3.

CRM AND BUSINESS INTELLIGENCE APPLICATIONS

We have discussed CRM (customer relationship management) and business intelligence (BI) in many sections because they are important applications of Web mining. Several CRM products are now on the market. Some of them are listed in Exhibit 4. Note that we have obtained this list from kdnuggets.com at the time this book went to press. As we have stressed, we are not endorsing any of the products. These products can also be regarded as Web mining products. However, Web mining products listed under kdnuggets.com are mainly about Web usage mining. It should also be noted that CRM products, while closely associated with the Web, may not necessarily be involved with the Web. Some of the CRM products can be

247

Exhibit 4.   Customer Relationship Management and Products

Product/Manufacturer	Description
absoluteBUSY	Web-based application for contact management and project tracking
Achiever CRM	Provides an integrated CRM solution
AngelexCRM.com	Provides Web-based solutions for sales and intelligence contacts
Applied Predictive Technologies (APT)	Clicks-and-Mortar Personalization™; one-to-one communication with customers
Applix iCustomer.Advantage	Integrates CRM BI
Ardexus	Provides CRM software
Astea International	CRM for productivity improvement; improving productivity, revenue, and customer interaction
ATG	Java-based solution for CRM online
Baan	Enterprise Resource Management system; CRM for supply chain
Broadbase	Integrates customer information from Internet into business intelligence
Chordiant	CRM applications integrating Web and call center operations
Clarify	Provides front-office solutions
Commence RM	CRM for sales and marketing
CRM Central	U.K.-based newsletter focusing on CRM
CRM Forum	Center for CRM resources
CRM Impact	From KnowledgeBase, CRM for marketing, analytics, consulting
CRMXchang	Community site for CRM
cs-live	A division of 800 America, interactive CRM
Cyber Dialogue	Technology platform for CRM
Data Distilleries	Open analytical CRM solutions
Delano	CRM for personalizing customers
Deuxo	Provides lead optimization
Epiphany	Integrated suite of software for CRM
Graham Technology	Infrastructure services for CRM
Harte-Hanks	CRM with real-time personalization
Hyperion	CRM analysis applications
IBM Customer Relationship Services	Provides customer value services
Insightful Corporation Software and Services	Predictive analysis for customer lifecycles
ITtoolbox	CRM knowledge base and service for CRM professionals
Kana Communications	Customer communication software for E-business
KnowledgeSync 2000	From Vineyardsoft, support for alerts, Web cast, etc., of events
LogMetrix	Web-based CRM
MarketMiner	Formerly AbTech Corporation; provides tools for direct marketing applications

Exhibit 4.   Customer Relationship Management and Products *(Continued)*

Product/Manufacturer	Description
MarketSwitch	Database marketing products
Mywice	Web-based knowledge management
NCR Relationship Optimizer	Provides a methodology for CRM
Netmining NV	Web-based sales and marketing
Norkom Technologies	Customer intelligence solutions
OMEGA Active Decision Management Solution	Developed by KiQ, provides predictive modeling of strategies and business monitoring
Onyx Software	Web-based CRM systems
Pivotal	Business Relationship Management (E-BRM) for marketing and sales
Portal Software	Customer management and billing software
Prime Response	Provides marketing automation solutions (U.K.-based)
Quadstone	Provides model development as well as deployment of customer model
Quaero	CRM for maximizing profitability
Recognition Systems	Ideas and solutions for CRM
Salentica Analytics	Web-based dashboard with messages and alerts
SalesLogix	Division of Interact Commerce Corporation; intelligence tools for sales
Sales Management Expert	Web-based sales force automation and contact management software
SAS e-Discovery	CRM solution for predicting customer behavior
searchCRM.com	Search engines for CRM
Searchspace	Develops intelligent enterprise systems
SellWin	Java client/server application for sales force automation
Siebel	Entire focus is on CRM and provides complete integrated solutions
Sightward	Online marketing through pattern recognition
Simera	Develops KM, CRM software
Soffront	Web-based CRM
SPSS	Customer-centric CRM
Talisma	Provides electronic CRM solutions
Target Database	CRM for direct marketing, provides predictive modeling and advanced statistical E-commerce
thinkCRA	From thinkAnalytics, an integrated suite of customer relationship analytics for CRM and business intelligence solutions
TouchPoint	From Broadway & Seymour, CRM system to the financial/legal/services markets
Unica Affinium	CRM with personalization
Update.com	E-CRM solutions in Europe
Vantive	E-Customer Relationship Management
Verbind LifeTime system	Software for corporations to analyze attrition
Xchange	Formerly Exchange Applications; provide E-CRM
YOUcentric	Formerly Salesvision; Web-based CRM

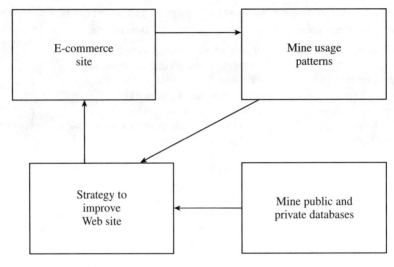

Exhibit 5.   Web Mining for E-Commerce

applied for non-Web-based sales and marketing. That is, while the products listed here are general CRM and BI products that often work on the Web, in the next chapter we list products that carry out Web mining.

Now that we have listed the CRM various products, we will complete our discussion on CRM and BI from the previous chapters. As we have stressed, one of the major applications of Web mining is E-commerce. Corporations want to have the competitive edge and are exploring numerous ways to market effectively. Major corporations, including retail stores, have E-commerce sites now. Customers can order products from books to clothing to toys through these sites. The goal is to provide customized marketing. For example, user group A may prefer literature novels, whereas user group B may prefer mystery novels. Therefore, new literature novels have to be marketed to group A and new mystery novels have to be marketed to group B. How does an E-commerce site know about these preferences? The solution is in data mining. The usage patterns have to be mined. In addition, the company may mine various public and private databases to get additional information about these users. That is, both types of data mining described in the taxonomy have to be performed. Exhibit 5 illustrates the application of Web mining for E-commerce.

Web mining can also be used to provide entertainment on the Web. This is also a variation of E-commerce. Web access and Web data may be mined for user preferences on movies and record albums, and the corporations can carry out targeted marketing.

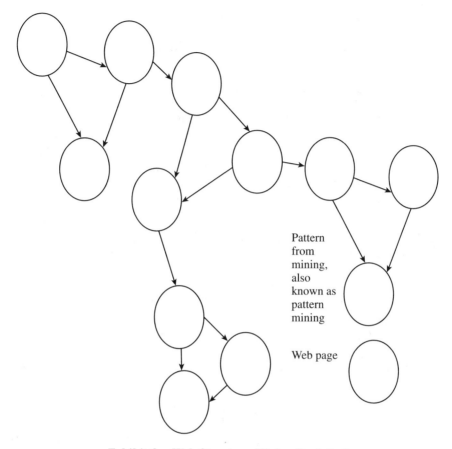

Exhibit 6.   Web Structure Mining Revisited

As more developments are made, we can expect better tools to emerge to mine the data on the Web and to mine the usage patterns. We can expect to hear much about Web mining in coming years.

Not only can data mining help E-commerce sites, data mining can also help the users to find information. For example, one E-commerce site manager mentioned to me that that the major problem his site has is that of being found by users. He has advertised in various magazines, but those who do not have access to the magazines find it difficult to access his sites. One solution here is to have a third-party agent making the connection between the site and the user. Another solution is to make the search engines more intelligent. Data mining could help here. The data miner could match the user's requirements to what is being offered by the E-commerce sites. Work is beginning in this area and we still have a long way to go.

We will revisit this application in Chapter 16. Counter-terrorism, the main application considered in this book, will be discussed in Part III. Note that counter-terrorism includes insider threat analysis, cyber-terrorism, and bio-terrorism.

MINING STRUCTURE ON THE WEB

In Chapter 9, we discussed Web structure mining. In this section, we will discuss more details. First of all, with Web structure mining, one mines the links and obtains patterns. Essentially, one mines the graph structure to extract patterns. We duplicate the exhibit shown in Chapter 9 for Web structure mining in Exhibit 6. As can be seen, the Web links are mined to obtain patterns. The circles represent the Web pages.

Next, we will analyze the types of outcomes one can expect for Web structure mining. One could mine the links and cluster Web pages with similar patterns. In the example shown in Exhibit 6, we can form a cluster with the linked Web pages with the same pattern. Each element in this cluster will consist of the three linked Web pages. Although it is not shown in the example, with complex graphs and links, one could form more clusters. One could also have associations between the Web pages. For example, the purpose of data mining is to extract previously unknown relationships. One could find two Web pages with no connection but with similar patterns surrounding them. These patterns may be quite unusual. Then we may possibly need to examine the content of these two Web pages.

When we mine the links and get some patterns, we can then use Web content mining to get information about the contents of the Web pages associated with the patterns. For example, consider the example in Exhibit 6. Once we form the cluster, we can then examine the contents of the Web pages in the cluster to see if they are related to similar topics or have anything in common. Exhibit 7 illustrates some outcomes of Web structure mining.

SUMMARY

This chapter has provided an overview of Web usage mining. We started with a discussion of various outcomes and techniques for Web usage mining. Then we discussed various types of analysis, customer relationship management and business intelligence, and listed a number of products from kdnuggets.com. As we have mentioned, customer relationship management and business intelligence are key applications for Web mining. In fact, many of these tools can also be applied for counter-terrorism, although more investigation is needed.*

* In fact, at a meeting at the White House on February 8, 2002, on data mining for counter-terrorism, the CEO of MicroStrategy gave an interesting presentation showing how his company's product may help counter-terrorism efforts. Essentially, he was showing how business intelligence could help counter-terrorism.

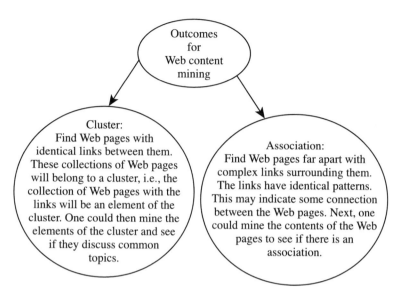

Exhibit 7. Outcomes for Web Structure Mining

The next two chapters will discuss tools and applications for Web mining. Note that we have discussed some tools in this chapter. However, a broader view of prototypes, tools, and standards will be the subject of Chapter 16. Then we discuss various applications in Chapter 17. We will focus on the applications for counter-terrorism in Part III.

Chapter 16
Prototypes, Products, and Standards for Web Data Mining

INTRODUCTION

The previous chapters have provided some information on Web data management and Web data mining. We discussed Web data mining with respect to data management, information retrieval, information management, and semantic Web technologies. We also provided an overview of multimedia data mining on the Web. Many of the concepts addressed in this book have been influenced by various research prototyping activities, which also influence commercial products. Research does not stop when the products are developed. Researchers and standards organizations examine products, figure out ways to make improvements, and develop more prototypes and standards. Therefore, this is a cyclic operation.

This chapter examines prototypes and products for Web data mining. We start with a discussion of data mining prototypes and products, as these can be used for Web mining. Then we will discuss prototypes and products for Web mining. Finally, we will discuss some standards activities for Web mining. Exhibit 1 illustrates the three topics to be addressed in this chapter. Note that standards for Web mining as well as data mining are just emerging; therefore, our discussions here are rather preliminary.

It should be noted that we are not endorsing any of the products. We discuss a prototype or a product mainly due to our familiarity with it. It does not mean that a particular prototype or product is superior. Furthermore, due to rapid developments in the field, the information about these products may soon be outdated. Therefore, we urge the reader to take advantage of the various commercial and research material available on these products.

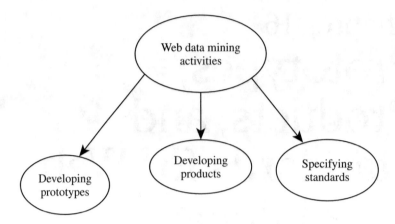

Exhibit 1.   Web Data Mining Activities

PROTOTYPES AND PRODUCTS FOR DATA MINING

We first start with a discussion of data mining prototypes and products. Note that these prototypes and products can also be used on the Web and that some of the research prototypes have evolved into products. We will discuss some specific Web data mining products. As stated earlier, all of the information on these products has been obtained from published material as well as from vendor product literature. Because commercial technology is advancing rapidly, the status of these products as described here may not be current. Again, our purpose is to give an overview of what has recently been out there and not the technical details of these products.

We discuss only some of the key features of the commercial products and prototypes. Note that various data management texts and conferences, including data management/mining magazines, books, and trade shows such as *Database Programming and Design* (Miller Freeman Publishers), the *Data Management Handbook* series ([DMH94]–[DMH98]), and DCI's Database Client Server Computing Conferences have several articles and presentations discussing the commercial products. We urge the reader to take advantage of the information presented in these magazines, books, and conferences and keep up with the latest developments in the vendor products. Furthermore, in areas such as Web mining, we can expect developments to be happening very rapidly. The various Web pages are also a useful source of information.

We have chosen a particular product or prototype to explain a specific technology. We would have liked to have included discussions of many more products and prototypes, but such discussions are beyond the scope of this book. In recent years, various documents have provided a detailed survey of data mining products and prototypes. An example is the docu-

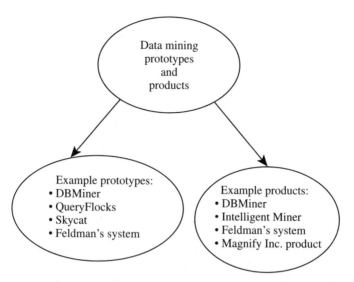

Exhibit 2.   Web Data Mining Prototypes and Products

ment on data mining products by the Two Crows Corporation. This corporation periodically puts out detailed surveys of the products, and we encourage the reader to take advantage of such up-to-date information. There are also tutorials on comparing the various products (see, for example [KDD98]). Exhibit 2 illustrates the prototypes and products discussed here. Note that while many of these systems work for structured data, they are being adapted for unstructured data also.

Prototypes

In recent years, prototype data mining tools have emerged from various universities and research laboratories. Some of these tools are now commercially available. A discussion of all of these tools and systems is beyond the scope of this book. We have discussed tools that we are familiar with. Our discussion has been influenced by the work by Grupe and Orang [GRUP98] (see also [DMH98]).

There are tools that attempt to develop new models for data mining. In particular, they work on relational as well as on text data and provide frameworks for data mining. They are developed by projects involved in developing new functional models. Example projects are underway at Stanford University, the MITRE Corporation, Hitachi Corporation, and Rutgers University.

The projects that attempt to develop new functional models essentially integrate data mining and database management. In particular, the tight integration discussed in Part II is taken by these initiatives. The project at

Stanford University, the MITRE Corporation, and Hitachi Corporation is called Queryflocks [TSUR98]. The idea here is to develop a query methodology and optimization techniques to handle flocks of queries to support data mining. In particular, these queries attempt to produce associations between entities in the database.

The project at Rutgers University also integrates data mining with database management and has formulated query languages for data mining queries. This project also attempts to find associations between the entities. A discussion of this work is given in [ACM96].

The projects that work on new information services essentially mine different types of data such as multimedia data. That is, multimedia data mining is the focus of the projects that fall under this category. We discuss some of them here.

Data mining on text is being attempted by the Queryflocks project at Stanford University, the MITRE Corporation, and Hitachi Corporation. The technique for finding associations can be applied not only to relational databases, but also to text databases once the tagged entities are extracted from the text. Another example of text mining is the work at the University of Arizona by Cheng and Ng. This project searches documents based on colocation of terms in documents. A third example is the work by Feldman at Bar-Ilan University in Israel that finds association rules between identified concepts in text. Note that this tool is also now available as a commercial product.

There is also some work on image mining. Most notable is the SKICAT project by JPL (Jet Propulsion Laboratory). This work detects unusual objects from images in space [ACM96]. Another example of image mining work is that of Clifton et al., at the MITRE Corporation [CLIF98]. This work finds unusual patterns from hyperspectral images. There is also work on image mining at the University of British Columbia [NG97]. The technique used here is distancE-based reasoning.

There is also some work on Web mining that has been reported. Examples include projects at the University of Michigan and at the University of Minnesota (see, for example [ICTA97]). In addition, there are several efforts reported in Web mining that can be found in [WDM99]. With respect to video mining, MITRE has applied Queryflocks to the output BNN (Broadcast News Navigation) system. Essentially, this is about video mining. BNN outputs stories. Queryflocks mines these stories to find correlations.

Scalability of the algorithms in data mining is still a largely unexplored area. The Massive Digital Data Systems Project has focused on scalability of various data management and data mining techniques to handle very large databases [MDDS94]. Scalability could be determined by using larger and larger data sets, by conducting theoretical studies as well as simulation studies.

Scalability of data mining algorithms needs a lot of work. There is some work at Magnify Inc. to determine the scalability of specific data mining techniques. These algorithms handle terabytes of data. Other products focusing on scalability of data mining techniques include those by Thinking Machines Corporation and SGI (Silicon Graphics, Inc.). The work at IBM's Yorktown Heights research laboratory also addresses scalability issues.

In Part II, we discussed the data mining process. After cleaning the data and mining the data, one needs to extract only the useful information. Therefore, understanding the data becomes very important. Some research projects focus on this aspect of data mining. We discuss a few.

GTE (General Telecommunications and Equipment, not part of Verizon) Laboratories has worked on data mining for a number of years. The focus is on the understanding of the data by producing domain-specific reports. Medical cost mining is an application area for this work. Another effort is being carried out at Simon Fraser University. This is one of the prominent places for data mining. One aspect of this work is integration with visualization tools so that the data mining results can be better understood [HAN98]. A third effort is the work at the University of Massachusetts–Lowell [GRIN95]. This work also focuses on integrating data mining with visualization techniques. While these efforts focus mainly on relational data, we feel that understanding the results is very important for multimedia data mining.

At present, much of the focus has been on applying data mining tools to extract patterns. Many say that this is what data mining is all about. Understanding the results is the responsibility of some other area. However, if data mining is to be useful, we need to focus on understanding the data as well as mining the data.

Two very prominent projects in data mining include IBM's Quest project by Agarwal et al., and Simon Fraser University's DBMINER product by Han et al. Numerous papers have been published on this work (for example, see [SIGM]). We discuss only the essential points.

IBM's Quest project uses multiple data mining techniques and finds sequential associations as well as time-series associations. The work is influenced by database systems technology and builds data mining techniques to work with relational database systems. Some of this research has been transferred to IBM's products. Simon Fraser University's DBMiner is now available as a product and focuses on mining relational data that has been warehoused and includes end-user support, visualization capabilities, and understanding of results. Mining association rules is the major focus of both efforts. While these projects initially focused on relational data, more recently they are focusing on multimedia data.

The two large-scale projects that we have discussed here have influenced several other efforts that have emerged. Describing all of these efforts is beyond the scope of this book. However, recent conferences such as the ACM SIGMOD, IEEE Data Engineering, VLDB, as well as various data mining conferences we listed earlier produced many research papers that describe other emerging large-scale projects (for example, see [AFCE], [ICDE], [KDD], [PAKD], [SIGM], and [VLDB]). Additional research papers in data mining can be found in [FAYY96]. Up-to-date information on products can be found at kdnuggets.com.

Products

Many data mining commercial tools are now emerging. These include IBM's Intelligent Miner, Information Discovery's IDIS, and Neo-Vista's Decision Series. While many of them work on relational data, they are being adapted to handle nonrelational data. This section provides an overview of some of the tools.

Other data mining products include Whizsoft's WHIZWHY product, which is an end-user association rule-finding tool that uses rule-based reasoning. Hugin's product, HUGIN, uses Bayesian reasoning and is good for prediction. DATA LOGIC/R, the product of Reduct Systems, uses rough sets as a data mining technique. NICEL by Nicesoft uses fuzzy logic as a data mining technique. SGI's MINESET integrates data mining with visualization and focuses on high performance data mining. DARWIN by Thinking Machines Corporation also illustrates high-performance data mining. SRA Corporation's product finds patterns for fraud detection. MRJ Corporation's data mining product does mining on large data sets. Other notable products include SAS Institute's Enterprise Miner and Redbrick's Datamind. There are also many more products on the market and, as mentioned earlier, describing all of them is beyond the scope of this book. A good tutorial comparing the various products was presented at the Knowledge Discovery in Databases Conference in 1998 [KDD98].

IBM's Intelligent Miner is a popular data mining product on the market. This product incorporates some of the research that has come out of IBM's Almaden Research Center. In particular, the Quest research project at Almaden has some of the origins of the Intelligent Miner product. The techniques used by this product are many. It is a multistrategy data miner. In particular, it uses association rules, decision trees, neural networks, and nearest-neighbor methods for mining. It selects the methods as appropriate for the particular task. The outcomes it handles include missing values, anomaly detection, and categorization of continuous data, and it has applications in various domains. One of the conditions for this product is that the data has to reside in IBM's database system product, called DB2. However, this may change with time. The product is available for PC as well as mainframe environments. There is work on adapting this tool for text data.

Information Discovery's IDIS, one of the earlier data mining tools running on Microsoft's Windows™ and NT™ environments, is an end-user information discovery tool. It provides natural language reports and uses various induction and machine learning techniques. It operates on smaller relational databases. Producing natural language reports of the data mining activities will help to understand the data mining results. Essentially, IDIS hypothesizes rules and then tests to see if the hypotheses are valid. It outputs unusual patterns as well as patterns that deviate from the norm. It has been used for a variety of applications in fields such as financial, medical, scientific, research, and marketing.

Neo-Vista's Decision Series product attempts to provide a framework for integrating multiple data mining products. It supports several data mining techniques such as association rules, neural networks, nearest-neighbor algorithms, and genetic algorithms. This framework has tight integration with ODBC on the server side. ODBC provides the glue for integrating the various data mining products. The data miners can access data from multiple relational database systems, which are integrated via ODBC. Neo-Vista's product essentially focuses on middleware for data mining. This is one of the first products to provide such capability. We need this capability if multiple data mining strategies and products are to be integrated to develop more-sophisticated data mining tools.

WEB DATA MINING PRODUCTS

This section discusses Web data mining products. As we have stressed in this book, to carry out Web data mining, many technologies have to work together effectively. Therefore, we will also examine various Web infrastructure products such as products for Web database management, Web knowledge management, and Web information management. These products provide the infrastructure to carry out Web mining.

In this section, we will list the various Web data mining products and discuss their applications. Note that some of these products carry out Web usage mining and clickstream analysis, while some other products carry out Web data mining. Then we will discuss some Web infrastructure and mining products.

Web Data Mining Tools

The most up-to-date list of products can be found at www.kdnuggets.com. The data mining products have been divided into various groups, including Web mining, mining for bioinformatics, and other appli-

Exhibit 3.　Web Data Mining Tools

Manufacturer/Product	Description
Accrue HitList	Internet reporting and analysis
Amadea Web Mining	Web mining product for CRM
ANGOSS KnowledgeWeb-Miner	Web mining and knowledge management tool for clickstream analysis
Blue Martini Customer Interaction System's Micro Marketing module	Collects clickstream analysis into a data warehouse and carries out mining
Clementine	Sequence association and clustering used for Web data analysis
CustomerConversion from Quadstone	Customer-centric analysis
Data Mining Suite	Web sites activity analysis
eNuggets	Real-time click analysis and refines models automatically
OK-log	Web site activity analysis
Lumio ReCognition (formerly MineIT Easyminer)	Carries out cross-section analysis and clickstream analysis for sales
Megaputer WebAnalyst	Carries out data and text mining of Web data
MicroStrategy Web Traffic Analysis Module	Web site analysis, Web traffic analysis
net.Analysis (from net.Genesis)	Mines for business intelligence
NetTracker family	Tracks Internet usage
prudsys ECOMMINER	Clickstream and database analysis for E-commerce
SAS Webhound	Web traffic analysis
WebTrends	A suite for data mining of Web traffic analysis
XAffinity	Affinity analysis for transactions
XML Miner	Mines XML documents
123LogAnalyzer	Analyzes Web logs

cations. At the time this book is being written, the products listed at the kdnuggets Web site include those shown in Exhibit 3. Note that these products are trademarks of various corporations; details can be found under the individual products.

In order for Web mining to be effective, we need to provide an infrastructure for Web mining. The next subsection discusses the various Web infrastructure as well as Web mining products. Note that we have discussed the products only to illustrate the key points. As we have mentioned, we are not endorsing nor are we evaluating any product.

Web Infrastructure and Data Mining Tools

In this section, we discuss various Web infrastructure and data mining tools. Note that we need to use the infrastructure tools to get the data

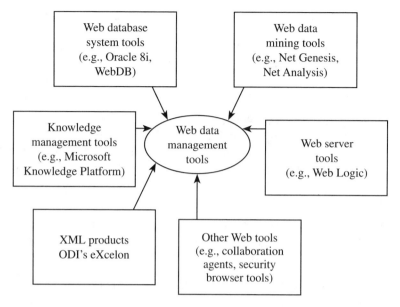

Exhibit 4.   Tools Discussed in this Section

ready and to manage the information so that the data can be mined effectively. The tools discussed in this section are illustrated in Exhibit 4.

Web Databases. Web databases are a key part of Web data management. Almost every major database system vendor now has access to the Web. That is, relational, object-oriented, and object-relational systems have Web access. Web clients can now access these databases. XML is becoming a standard language for formatting the responses from database systems so that the Web clients can understand the results.

This section describes a sample database system and discusses how it can be interfaced to the Web. The database system that we have selected is Oracle's recent Web database system product. As mentioned earlier, we selected this product only because we are more familiar with this product than some of the other products. This does not mean that this is the best product or we are endorsing this product. As we stated, every major database system vendor, including Oracle, Sybase, Informix, and Object Design, has designed its products with Web interfaces. We are most familiar with Oracle's product, but there are other good products as well. For example, recently there have been write-ups about Sybase's ASE product for the Web and enterprise information management [INFO02].

Let us examine the features of Oracle's 8i and WebDB. Oracle 8i (as described in [ORAC1]) combines Internet database capabilities with traditional warehousing and transaction processing capabilities. The Internet

File System feature of Oracle 8i enables users to move their data into Oracle's database. In addition, the interMedia module supports the management of multimedia data. WebDB (to be described later) is a tool to build HTML-based Web pages with data from Oracle databases. Oracle 8i integrates the Java Virtual Machine into its server and this way can deploy Java programs at various tiers (such as client and middle tiers).

In addition to supporting Web data management, Oracle 8i also supports various database management functions. It has enhanced features for transaction processing and warehouse management, database administration, indexing, parallel server management, replication, caching, fine-grained access control, as well as support for objects. Oracle 8i also provides rich support for enterprise data management.

Oracle WebDB (see the description in [ORAC2]) is essentially a Web browser that builds Web pages from various types of data in the Oracle databases. For example, Oracle 8i supports the management of multimedia data such as video and text. With the Web browser, the multimedia data can be viewed efficiently. Essentially, WebDB enables the visualization of the data in the database via the Web. The Web pages can be personalized and can provide multiple views of the same data. For example, some users may want to see graphs while others may want to see just numbers. WebDB provides support for both views.

Oracle 8i, WebDB, and many of the other tools that are emerging make Web data management a reality. As we have stressed, we have chosen products in this book mainly due to our familiarity with them. It should be noted that various database vendors such as Sybase, Microsoft, Informix, and Object Design have developed various Web database management products. This is one of the fastest growing areas in Web information management. Note that Oracle 8i has evolved into 9i and beyond. Nevertheless, 8i was the first product that we discussed on Web data management.

Web Application Server Tools. Various server tools have emerged over the years since the mid-1990s. These server tools perform various functions, including access to database management systems as well as legacy databases. As descried in Chapter 8, the application servers are often based on Enterprise Java Beans (EJB) technology. There are also data servers that access the database systems.

Many application server tools are on the market, and an overview is given in [INFO1]. We illustrate some of the concepts with the tool called WebLogic, a product of BEA Systems (www.beasys.com). BEA states that its E-commerce application server products include WebLogic and BEA Tuxedo. They are used to build rapid E-commerce applications and transactions. They use the latest distributed technologies, including EJB and ORB (Object Request Broker). BEA's eLink integrates new and existing applications for office systems. BEA's products are based on multitier client/server computing with business logic for E-commerce applications in the middle tier.

BEA's WebLogic application server is based on component technology. Its goals are to provide a complete set of tools for enterprise applications and ensure scalability and security. It interfaces to Web applications on the one side and server technologies on the other. That is, through products such as WebLogic, client application to legacy databases are made less complex. Associated with WebLogic is BEA's WebLogic Enterprise, which provides support for manipulating business logic to multiple servers and multiple heterogeneous databases.

Web Knowledge Management Tools. Numerous tools for knowledge management are emerging. These include collaboration and decision support tools as well as Web information management tools. Note that the term *knowledge management* is still rather vague and, therefore, various types of tools have been grouped together as knowledge management tools.

We describe a suite of tools for knowledge management, called the Knowledge Management Platform by Microsoft and its industry partners (see, for example [MICR]). This platform has five components:

1. Knowledge Desktop is essentially a collection of tools to seamlessly access and use Microsoft's knowledge assets through products such as Office 2000.
2. Knowledge Services include collaboration services such as meeting facilities, content management services that capture and manage various experiences and ideas, analysis services that turn data into knowledge, and tracking and workflow services that capture best practices.
3. The System component essentially consists of a Microsoft server that provides a complete set of services to the user.
4. The Connected Devices component supports knowledge workers through partnerships with other companies, e.g., telecommunications.
5. Partner Solutions components enable Microsoft to team with various industry partners to produce various tools such as digital dashboards.

Essentially what we have described here is a collection of tools by Microsoft to support the various knowledge management, collaboration, and decision support functions that we have described in earlier chapters. There are also several smaller companies specializing entirely in knowledge management products. This is an area we can expect numerous products to be developed within the next few years. Furthermore, as definitions of knowledge management become clearer, we can also decide which of these products really performs knowledge management.

Web Metadata/XML Tools. Various XML tools have emerged recently. One of the prominent tools is eXcelon by Object Design. Much information about this tool can be obtained from [ODI]. eXcelon is an application development environment for integrating structured, unstructured, and semistructured data. The goal of eXcelon is to support a variety of E-business Web information management activities for the enterprise. Toward achieving its goal, the company is providing a toolbox to support various XML tools.

One of the key components of this product is eXcelon Stylus, a visual XSL editor for XML. eXcelon's Data Server stores and manages XML documents. Therefore, Object Design provides a complete solution to XML, i.e., the server to manage the data and the tools to edit and manipulate the XML data.

Object Design has discussed various applications for eXcelon, including Web E-commerce, knowledge management, business-to-business, and enterprise application integration. Web E-commerce is about carrying out transactions on the Web. Typically, one has to advertise the company's products. Object Design's eXcelon enables the specification of the company's products whose descriptions may be structured, unstructured, or semistructured. Knowledge management is enhanced by eXcelon by capturing the knowledge assets of the corporation in various data formats. Business-to-business applications are enhanced by eXcelon by its support for XML extensions. Traditional EDI-type (electronic data interchange) information exchange is rather limiting for such applications, and one needs richer representation schemes. The data server component facilitates enterprise application integration. That is, one needs to efficiently integrate the corporation's data, and query the data effectively for enterprise application management. Object Design's eXcelon provides this support.

In summary, XML tools such as eXcelon are in their infancy. Although they provide many critical capabilities for E-business, there is much to be done. As progress is made on XML, we can expect these tools to also advance.

Other Web Information Management Tools. We have briefly discussed various Web data management tools in this chapter. There are numerous other tools that we have not mentioned. We name some of these tools.

Several tools for Web security have emerged, including firewall products, secure Java, and Microsoft's ActiveX. In addition, various secure transaction systems have also emerged for the Web. These include the secure payment protocols. Encryption products are also a type of Web security product.

Other Web tools include tools for collaboration. We discussed knowledge management tools, which included collaboration. Corporations such as Lotus have developed various collaboration tools that enable users to share information and collaborate with one another. Another example of a prototype collaborative system is given in [JONE99]. We discussed Web browser tools such as Oracle's WebDB. This is only one such tool where database data is transformed into Web pages. There are numerous other tools such as Netscape's* browsers and other browser tools to perform visualization. Web agent tools include the various types of Web crawlers and knowbots that locate various resources and enable information sharing and collaboration.

Other Web tools include tools for distance learning, multimedia information processing, and decision support. Some of these functions are already provided by the tools we have discussed. For example, Oracle 8i supports multimedia information management. Microsoft's knowledge platform provides support for collaboration, decision support, and training. In addition to these large corporations, many smaller corporations are all specializing in collaboration, multimedia, decision support, and training. Distance learning and training will become key components of E-business and, therefore, we can expect to see many tools emerge in this area.

In addition to the data management tools for the Web, we can also see various components and infrastructures emerging for the Web. We can expect plug-and-play-based component technology as well as specialized framework and infrastructures to emerge for the Web. Object Management Group (OMG)'s ORB-based tools are the first step toward such infrastructures.

In summary, during recent years the number of Web data management tools has grown almost exponentially. We cannot expect to see a slowdown in the near future. In fact, we believe that this exponential growth will continue well into the 21st century.

Web Mining Tools. We previously listed several Web mining tools. As mentioned earlier, numerous resources to data mining are given at www.kdnuggets.com. These include references to Web mining products. Some of the recent Web mining products include Easy Miner for Web by MINEit Software, which carries out cross-section analysis (which is now called Lumio ReCognition); HitList by Accrue Software, which carries out server log analysis; net.Analysis by net.Genesis, which carries out E-business intelligence analysis; and NetTracker by Sane Solutions, which is an

---

* Netscape is now part of AOL.

Internet usage tracking program. In addition to products, there is also free software listed at kdnuggets.com. A leading research prototype is Imperial College, University of London's Kensington Data Mining tool (see [GUO00].

The products attempt to carry out data mining on the Web as well as Web usage mining and traffic analysis. For example, net.Analysis attempts to provide customer intelligence to the E-business enterprise so that customers can be retained. For example, different segments of shoppers are evaluated and analyzed so that the E-business organization can carry out customized marketing. These products also enable the enterprise to identify the key drivers of the business, and how they can provide competitive advantage. It also helps the organization to understand the nature of the different shoppers and why they behave the way they do, and gives reasons as to why they purchase certain products.

The Web mining products have advanced quite a lot since we wrote our earlier book on Web data management [THUR00]. As mentioned, details of these products can be obtained from www.kdnuggets.com. As we demand more and more Web mining, we can expect much progress to be made. For example, recent innovations in bioinformatics have advanced data mining and Web mining a great deal. While general-purpose data mining tools can be applied for a variety of applications, we are beginning to see the need for domain-specific tools. The various applications will be briefly discussed in the next chapter.

STANDARDS FOR WEB MINING

To handle all of the challenges and make progress in data mining and Web data mining, one needs effective standards for various aspects of data mining. Clifton and Thuraisingham have discussed some aspects of data mining standards in [CLIF01]. We discuss some of them in this section. In particular, we discuss standards for data mining processes, languages, architectures, and E-business. Exhibit 5 illustrates the standards activities.

Data Mining Process

First of all, what do we mean by a "data mining standard"? As we have seen, there are many different tasks that fall under the heading of "data mining." Standardizing the tasks and results becomes difficult. For example, if we define a standard classification model, we ignore a variety of other types of pattern discovery, such as rule discovery or clustering, that also qualify as data mining. The result is that there is currently no attempt at a single "standard" for data mining; instead, there are numerous standards to support different aspects of data mining. These can broadly be divided into:

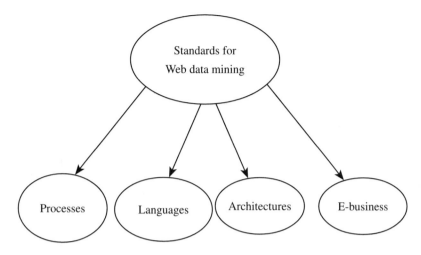

Exhibit 5.   Areas for Standardization

- Standards for the task to be performed (e.g., a formal definition of inputs to and outputs from the training and use phases of a classifier)
- Standards for supporting technology (e.g., SQL as a standard for data access)
- Process standards (e.g., what is the sequence of events in performing a data mining project?)

In this section, we will present some of the ongoing standards efforts in these areas. First of all, can we standardize the data mining process? Exhibit 6 illustrates this process. The first step is to integrate the various data sources, clean the sources, and get the data ready for mining. The second step is to mine the data and get results. The third step is to prune the results to get useful patterns. The fourth step is to take some actions such as carrying out a pilot project. Finally, we need to analyze the results and determine whether to proceed with the next cycle. Currently, these steps are carried out in an *ad hoc* fashion. There are no software engineering methods for mining. The question is, can we apply various models, such as the waterfall model or the spiral model, for data mining?

There is some progress on developing process models for data mining. Notable is the CRISP-DM effort: cross-industry standard process for data mining. CRISP-DM is a consortium of industry partners developing process models for data mining. It examines the knowledge discovery processes and attempts to standardize them. The industry partners include NCR, DaimlerChrysler, Integral Solutions Limited (ISL), and OHRA (an independent insurance company in the Netherlands). For further information on this consortium, see [CRIS].

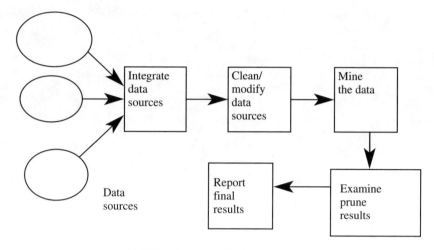

Exhibit 6.   Data Mining Process

Other areas for applying standards include extending SQL for data mining and developing standard architectures for data mining. Because mining for E-commerce and customer intelligence is becoming a big area, we can expect standards to be developed here. We will discuss them in the next few sections.

SQL and Data Mining

SQL (Structured Query Language) is a long-standing standard for database access, which has spawned a number of other standards such as ODBC (open database connectivity) and JDBC (Java database connectivity). These provide a way for tools to get at data. However, SQL is designed for transaction-oriented access to data: retrieval or update of small data sets based on a query. Data mining operates over large data sets. While SQL can easily generate such data sets, the actual application programming interfaces (APIs), such as ODBC and JDBC, are poorly equipped for retrieval of huge quantities of data.

There have been several proposals to add operations to SQL to support data mining. The most common of these is based on the notion of a data cube [GRAY96], a collection of data, where each axis represents a particular "selection criteria," and a point in the cube is the value where all selection criteria meet.

The key to a data cube is that it quickly provides answers to aggregates; for example, we may want sales for all months for New England and the produce department. This sort of aggregation is a useful building block in many data mining algorithms. The idea is that data mining algorithms could use the data cube to get only the needed aggregate information, instead of retrieving the entire set of information from the database. Commercial products (particularly those intended for data warehouse applications) are beginning to include data cube concepts; however, a standard for these extensions does not yet exist.

There is also progress in using SQL-based standards to make the results of data mining tools more accessible. A coalition of organizations headed by Microsoft is addressing this with OLE DB for Data Mining [OLE], an extension of Microsoft's OLE DB database access standard. The idea is to represent the output of a data mining tool as a table. This "prediction table" is created by providing a tool and an input table. This runs the tool on the input. The structure of the prediction table is defined by the input table and a formal definition associated with the tool that defines the output in terms of input for that tool. OLE DB DM has been working with the Data Mining Group to incorporate their Predictive Model Markup Language [PMML], an XML-based specification language for predictive models. This works well for predictive modeling (classification), but extension to other types of data mining may need work. SQL is being extended for Web queries. We need to examine the impact of Web mining for such SQL extensions.

Architecture Standards and Data Mining

In the area of architecture standards for data mining, there are various dimensions. One is the relationship between data mining and related technologies such as database systems, decision support, and data warehousing. What are the interfaces, for example, between a data manager and a data miner? Can one standardize these interfaces? Another area is to standardize the functional architecture for data mining. What are the data mining functions and how can we develop standards? The third area is to develop a three-tier middleware system. The front tier is the client tier. The middle tier is the business objects tier, which consists of business objects for data mining. This tier may be the database server tier. One could use distributed object systems to integrate the various layers.

Exhibit 7 illustrates the three-tier architecture for mining. Such an architecture can be applied for Web data mining also where the client is the Web client and the server is the Web server. There is still very little discussion about standardizing the data mining architecture. However, the OMG is specifying object-based standards for data mining. For further details, see [OMG].

E-Business, XML, and Data Mining Standards

While data mining has been developing over the past decade, E-commerce and E-business have advanced rapidly with the advent of the Web. We often hear the term E-business. Many companies prefer E-business to E-

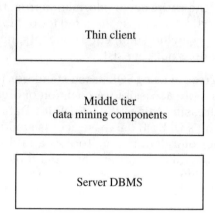

Exhibit 7. Three-Tier Architecture for Data Mining

commerce because they feel E-business encompasses E-commerce. Those who differentiate between the two state that E-commerce is all about carrying out transactions on the Web, but E-business is much broader and includes various activities on the Web, such as learning and training, entertainment, putting up Web pages, hosting Web sites, conducting procurement, carrying out supply chain management, handling help for telephone repairs or other services, and almost anything that can be conducted on the Web. For the purposes of this book, we use the terms *E-business* and *E-commerce* interchangeably. Some background information was given in Chapter 2.

Web mining, which in a way encompasses data mining according to our assumption stated throughout this book, is about:

- Mining the data on the Web to make it more manageable for the user by making associations and patterns (content mining)
- Mining usage patterns (usage mining) to help users to carry out E-business, and to support E-business sites, brokers, and merchants
- Mining the Web links (structure mining)

Corporations want to maintain the competitive edge and are exploring numerous ways to market effectively. Major corporations, including retail stores, have E-business sites, and customers can now order products from books to clothing to toys through these sites. E-business sites collect massive amounts of data on customer purchases, browsing patterns, usage times, and preferences; each site can also collect information on competitors' offerings and prices. Based on the information, a site can adjust its assortments, prices, and promotions quickly and dynamically in response to changing trends, competitors' strategies, and personalization rules.

We can expect to see standards emerge for E-business. Because data mining is a critical technology for E-business, one may need to standardize the data mining processes for E-business. Then each company could use these standard processes and perhaps tailor them for personalized services. XML is becoming a standard for document representation and specification on the Web. XML is being examined for E-commerce activities, as one needs a standard way to specify the documents and product descriptions on the Web. One direction that is yet to be explored is the connection between XML and data mining. How can one mine documents expressed in XML? What are the challenges? What information can be uncovered? Can one mine the XML documents and extract some information about the content? We need to explore these questions. We also need to keep up with the developments with the XML Group and the Query Group at the World Wide Web consortium [W3C].

SUMMARY

This chapter started with a discussion of prototypes, products, and standards for Web data mining. We first started with a discussion of data mining prototypes and products, and then discussed Web mining products. This was followed by a discussion of standards for Web mining. As mentioned earlier, we are not endorsing any of the products. Furthermore, due to rapid developments in the field, the information about these products may soon be outdated. Therefore, we urge the reader to take advantage of the various commercial and research material available on these products.

The developments in data mining in general and Web data mining in particular over the last few years have shown a lot of promise. Although some of the products have been around for a while, they are now being integrated with Web information management systems. As mentioned previously, we need the integration of multiple technologies to make Web data mining work. Furthermore, having good data is critical. Therefore, in the future we will see more and more mining tools being integrated with various types of Web database systems as well as warehouses and information retrieval systems.

As we have stressed in this book, as more and more applications demand the need for Web mining, we can expect more progress to be made on prototypes, products, and tools. The next chapter will review some of the key applications; counter-terrorism applications will be discussed in Part III.

Chapter 17
Some Applications for Web Mining

INTRODUCTION

This chapter describes some examples of Web data mining applications. While we focus on Web data mining, many of these applications also need data mining. As we have assumed in this book, Web data mining encompasses data mining. That is, the data on the Web has to be mined using data mining techniques. In addition, we also need special tools for mining Web usage and Web traffic data.

While the chapters in this part have focused on data management and Web mining, information management and Web mining, information retrieval and Web mining, and semantic Web and Web mining, we want to provide a brief overview of the various applications to set the stage for the main application discussed in this book, counter-terrorism.

The applications we have discussed include E-commerce and E-business, business intelligence, customer relationship management, telecommunications, marketing and sales, and medical, biotechnology, and enterprise resource management. Note that these applications overlap. For example, you need business intelligence to carry out marketing and sales. Business intelligence is also needed for customer relationship management. Customer relationship management is a key aspect of E-commerce. Nevertheless, we address these applications separately and point out the overlap.

Exhibit 1 illustrates the applications we will consider in this chapter.

E-COMMERCE AND E-BUSINESS

While the next two sections focus on business intelligence (BI) and customer relationship management (CRM), in this section we discuss E-commerce and E-business. Note that BI and CRM are essential components of E-commerce and E-business. However, one does not need the Web for BI and CRM. That is, BI and CRM are functions of any business whether it is or is not on the Web. Therefore, in this section we focus on those aspects of Web mining applied to E-commerce. While we cannot avoid discussing BI

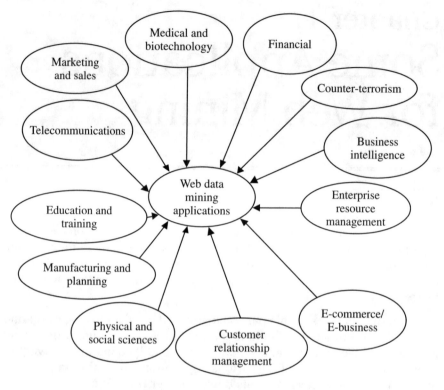

Exhibit 1. Web Data Mining Applications

and CRM when we discuss Web mining for E-commerce, we will also focus on some other aspects of Web mining applications in E-commerce.

As we have mentioned in Chapter 2, E-commerce or E-business can be conducted business-to-consumer or business-to-business. If an organization wants to get on the Web (i.e., build a Web portal), it has to determine what information to put on the Web. Data mining can help identify the types of information that will be most suitable to put on the Web. This would mean conducting an analysis of competitors and potential customers, and determining the expertise of an organization. Consider an organization that sells books. It can put all of its books for sale on the Web. However, it needs to determine how best to market its books. It will be very difficult for a customer to search through all the books. The organization should determine the segments of interest to the customer and develop portals accordingly. The idea here is to make it easy and useful for the customer.

Consider E-business between organizations. That is, organizations want to conduct business and transactions with each other. Before embarking

Exhibit 2.   Data/Web Mining Applications in E-Commerce

- Determining partner organizations
- Analyzing customer profiles
- Determining which products to market online

on any expensive venture, organizations have to mine the information to determine the best partners and competitors; also when an organization wants to set up pricing for its products and services, it should mine the information out there to determine its competitors' strategies and then set up prices to be as profitable as possible.

A lot of thought has to go into Web and data mining for E-commerce and E-business. First of all, an organization has to determine the areas for which mining would be useful. As we have stated, mining is an expensive process. Therefore, an organization has to determine which areas to apply data mining. Then it has to gather the data to mine. For example, in the case of getting information about customers, the organization should search its internal and external knowledge bases. There may be information about customers on public Web sites. Once the data is gathered, the organization has to decide what types of mining to carry out. That is, should the organization form clusters of customers and competitors, and should it find associations between competitors, customers, and partners? Finally, verification and validation methods have to be developed to test the outcome of the results, and plans have to be developed to take appropriate actions.

As we have mentioned, we can see that BI and CRM are important aspects of E-commerce and E-business. Therefore, the next sections will discuss the application of Web mining to BI and CRM. Exhibit 2 illustrates data and Web mining applications for E-commerce.

BUSINESS INTELLIGENCE

We have discussed business intelligence directly and indirectly throughout this book. Business intelligence is essentially getting intelligence to carry out a business. This business can be a commercial business or a military business. To run a business effectively, one needs intelligence about competitors, partners, customers, and employees as well as intelligence about market conditions, future trends, government policies, and much more.

Let us consider some examples. Consider competitor intelligence information. This information will include competitors' strategies, including marketing and sales policies, customer information, how they manage customers, and information about their employees and partners. Then an organization can analyze this information and determine whether to

- Analyzing competitor strategies
- Analyzing customer profiles
- Determining business strategies

develop or launch a product, how to attract new customers, and perhaps better manage existing customers.

Military intelligence is also business intelligence. This is the intelligence that the military needs to carry out its operations. It needs information about the adversary, the resources that the adversary has, the tactics used by the adversary, and many more details. Then military strategies and analysts can use this information to plan their own strategies to defeat the enemy or adversary.

We have addressed only a few aspects of business intelligence. Nevertheless, it gives some idea as to how a business operates. Note that BI is needed whether we are carrying out business on the Web or not. Recently, many BI products have been emerging for E-commerce and E-business. In the next section, we will address the aspect of getting information about customers and managing the customers. Exhibit 3 illustrates data and Web mining applications for BI.

CUSTOMER RELATIONSHIP MANAGEMENT

Customer relationship management is one of the key applications of business intelligence. It is about mining information about customers from public as well as private databases and building customer profiles. For example, it is also about mining buying patterns and buying preferences of customers living in the same area as the targeted customer. Essentially, CRM is about using the information mined and serving the customer in the best possible way.

Note that to carry out CRM, it does not necessarily mean that we need the Web. CRM could be carried out by any organization. However, more and more organizations are carrying out CRM on the Web. That is, customer profiles are collected based on E-commerce carried out by the organization, and these profiles are used to best serve the customer.

Customer profiles include "customers who purchased X also purchased Y," as well as information such as "customers living in Manhattan prefer to buy cars costing more than $100K." Other profile information includes "customer X typically makes his purchases on the Web between 10 and 11 P.M.," or "customer X has a preference for brand Y." Based on these profiles, when customer X logs in, he can get information displayed about

**Exhibit 4.   Data Mining and Web Mining
Applications in CRM**

- Building and analyzing customer profiles
- Developing customer-specific products

brand Y. If CRM is not carried out on the Web, then information about brand Y can be sent to customer X via regular mail.

In Chapters 15 and 16, we discussed various BI, CRM, and Web mining products. For example, the product by Siebel provides solutions for CRM on the Web. There are many more products listed on the kdnuggets Web site (www.kdnuggests.com). As we have stated, we are not endorsing any product or tool. These products provide a variety of services. We encourage the reader who is interested in CRM to become familiar with them. Exhibit 4 illustrates data/Web mining applications for CRM.

MARKETING AND SALES

One of the major areas of applications for data mining is marketing and sales, whether on the Web or otherwise. In [BERR97], a detailed discussion of data mining for marketing and sales is given. In particular, many of the data mining techniques such as market basket analysis, decision trees, neural networks, and genetic algorithms are described from a marketing-and-sales-applications viewpoint. That is, marketing and sales were two of the early applications that drove data mining. Similarly, E-marketing and E-sales have driven Web mining.

Consider, for example, market basket analysis. Using this tool, a store can get information such as "X and Y are purchased together." Then the store could arrange X and Y in the aisles in a way that maximizes sales and profits. Closely related to marketing and sales is advertising. Consider, for example, television commercials. The challenge for an organization is to determine which commercial to air and at what time. For this, the organization has to mine information about audience preferences. For example, during the day an organization may want to target women, while early evening it may want to target children, and air commercials at various channels accordingly.

Here again BI is a key tool. That is, BI plays a major role in marketing and sales whether on the Web or otherwise. With BI, one can get intelligence information about customers and then carry out targeted marketing accordingly. Marketing and sales are closely related. One mines the information, carries out marketing, and then sees how the sales are. Sales in turn influence marketing and, based on sales numbers, an organization can remine the information and carry out further targeted marketing. An organization also determines what the competitors' strategies are through BI

**Exhibit 5.   Data Mining and Web Mining
Applications in Marketing and Sales**

- Carry out targeted marketing
- Determine competitor marketing strategies
- Predict sales trends

and perhaps redirects the sales and marketing strategies. Essentially, the four areas that we have discussed, namely BI, CRM, marketing, and sales are closely interrelated. Key to all of them is BI. With good BI, one can carry out effective CRM, marketing, and sales. Again, whether these activities are on the Web or otherwise, data mining and Web mining will play a major role. Various data mining and Web mining products for marketing and sales have also been listed on the kdnuggets Web page. Some of them have been listed in our discussions in Chapters 14 and 15. Exhibit 5 illustrates data mining and Web mining applications in marketing and sales.

ENTERPRISE RESOURCE MANAGEMENT

Data mining and Web mining have applications for managing the resources of an organization. This area is called enterprise resource management (ERP). The resources of an organization may be human, inventory, expertise, or anything that is of value to an organization.

ERP systems such as products from SAP, Oracle, PeopleSoft, JD Edwards, and Baan typically provide enterprise resource management capabilities. Various human resources organizations use ERP to manage functions such as salary administration, payroll, benefits, and other support for employees. Closely related to enterprise resource management is supply chain management, where an organization has to effectively manage its supplies and inventories. Some of the ERP products such as SAP also provide capabilities for supply chain management.

The question is, how do data mining and Web mining help? With data mining and Web mining, one has a better understanding of the resources of an organization and various features of the resources that may not be obvious otherwise. Consider, for example, employee retention. An organization may mine the data to determine which employees are likely to leave, based on the employees' qualifications, the market conditions, and other factors. Then the organization can decide how to provide better incentives to the employees it wants to retain. In a way, data mining provides special employee care. What would be ideal is for an organization to provide individualized employee care. This is not easy to do, especially if the organization has thousands of employees. However, with effective data mining and Web mining (e.g., mining the information on corporate intranets), the data mining tools can give information to managers and HR specialists on benefits to provide to each employee. We are somewhat far from providing

Exhibit 6.   Data Mining and Web Mining Applications in ERP

- Analyzing human resources for employee retention benefits and payroll
- Analyzing enterprise resources or supply chain management

such individualized attention. But we are moving in that direction. In a way, this is closely related to CRM. That is, while CRM is about managing the relationships with customers, ERP is about managing the relationship with employees. This can be extended to managing other resources and supplies as well.

Here again, BI plays a role. With effective BI, an organization can determine its needs as well as competitors' strategies. For example, what resources does the competitor have? The organization can hire employees to meet its current and future needs. That is, data mining can also be used to predict future trends, which is extremely useful to an organization for its planning and strategizing activities. Exhibit 6 illustrates data mining and Web mining for ERP.

MANUFACTURING AND PLANNING

Another application for data and Web mining is manufacturing and planning. In particular, data mining could help with scheduling, plant monitoring, and several other functions of manufacturing. For example, by mining data pertaining to a particular product, an organization can determine the best way to assemble the product and when to manufacture it.

We will illustrate data mining for manufacturing with some examples. Consider, for example, an automobile manufacturing company attempting to assemble a particular brand of vehicle. While the general assembly of the vehicle will follow the designs, the manufacturing plant has to determine the features that customers want and the best way to assemble the vehicle to suit the customers' needs. Here again, BI and CRM will play a role. That is, with BI and CRM, one can predict customer preferences and carry out targeted assembly of the vehicle.

Mining can also help with scheduling. Based on information about the designs — marketing/sales data and production engineers — the plant can schedule manufacturing at appropriate dates and times. Suppose the preference for a particular vehicle is during winter; the manufacturing plant has to take that information into consideration and assemble the vehicle early enough in the year to be available for sale in winter. Closely related to manufacturing and planning is plant monitoring. Here, data mining could be used to monitor the plant to detect anomalies and unusual patterns. Suppose there are dangerous chemicals that can cause serious injuries to the plant engineers. The data mining tools can monitor the environment to detect and predict potential dangers.

Exhibit 7.   Data Mining and Web Mining Applications in Manufacturing and Planning

- Analyzing and developing schedules
- Determining assembly routines
- Monitoring plants

There are many ways data mining and Web mining can help. We have listed just a few. Web mining will be increasingly useful, as many operations are now controlled through the Web. While Web mining for manufacturing is still in its infancy, we can expect to hear much more about this application in the future. Exhibit 7 illustrates Web mining applications for manufacturing and planning.

EDUCATION AND TRAINING

We briefly discussed Web mining and computer-based training in Chapter 13. We will revisit them in this section. While training is useful for teaching data mining and Web mining courses, Web mining has applications in education and training. For example, by mining the data, one can determine which troops to train and what sort of training courses to prepare. The same is true for education. By mining the needs of corporations and government, one may develop special courses at universities and schools.

We will illustrate with some examples. At present, counter-terrorism is an important area. With mining, we can extract information on what aspect of counter-terrorism will be needed in the future. This way we can prepare appropriate training material to develop technologies for counter-terrorism. A few years ago, there was some interest in genome-related projects. At that time, one could have perhaps predicted with data mining that bioinformatics and biotechnology would be very critical areas for us. This way, certain organizations could have invested in training and education in biotechnology.

We see the use of BI over and over again. With BI, we can obtain useful information about current practices and future trends to develop education and training material and plan for the education and training for the future. Exhibit 8 illustrates data mining and Web mining in education and training.

Exhibit 8.   Data Mining and Web Mining Applications in Education and Training

- Developing courses and schedules
- Predicting future trends in education

Exhibit 9.   Data Mining and Web Mining Applications in Telecommunications

- Determine travel routes and give advice to wireless user
- Critical infrastructure protection of telecommunications lines
- Fault detection of telecommunications lines

TELECOMMUNICATIONS

We briefly discussed Web mining and wireless computing in Chapter 13. In this section, we will expand the applications to telecommunications in general.

In Chapter 12, we discussed how Web and data mining could help the wireless telephone user. With Web mining, one can get information about travel guides, weather predictions, and other data, and give advice to the wireless user. The techniques can also help a user with a landline telephone. That is, by mining the information out there, one could periodically send messages to customers about weather conditions and travel information. There may be an issue here, as customers may not want to be disturbed with too many calls; therefore, one needs to respect the privacy of the customers. If the customer requests this information, then periodic messages may be sent to the user through the Web or otherwise.

Data mining could also help with network intrusion detection and fault monitoring. Telecommunication lines are part of the national infrastructure. Therefore, damaging the communication could cost billions of dollars to businesses and organizations. Effective measures to prevent malicious intrusions and faults occurring through natural disasters should be detected and prevented. We will revisit some of these issues when we discuss terrorism and threats in Part III. Exhibit 9 illustrates data mining and Web mining applications in telecommunications.

FINANCIAL

Financial applications can benefit a great deal from data and Web mining. BI and CRM play a major role here as well. For example, one could mine the data again about customers' investment patterns and carry out targeted marketing about financial services and insurance information. If a customer has preferences for flying airplanes, then he could be given information about various types of insurance such as personal insurance and flight insurance.

Other financial services include providing current stock quotes and future predictions. Predicting how the stock market will perform is key to financial success for investment organizations. These organizations need to predict the market fairly accurately in order to advise customers about

**Exhibit 10.   Data Mining and Web Mining
Applications in Financial Services**

- Analyzing stock quotes
- Predicting stock performance
- Customized investment advice

various choices to enhance the customers' stock portfolio. Data mining and Web mining will be of much use here. Various data mining products for financial services are emerging. Some of them are listed on the kdnuggets Web page.

In our discussion, we have used the terms *data mining* and *Web mining* interchangeably. While data mining typically works for data in general, Web mining works for data on the Web and helps with usage and traffic analysis on the Web. In a way, Web mining encompasses data mining, or one can argue that data mining could include Web mining also. Nevertheless, we have taken a very broad perspective on data mining. Much of the data is on the Web, either in private or public databases. Private databases could be in intranets or special secure networks. Much of the financial data, such as stock quotes, are now on the Web. With Web mining, one could analyze the stocks over a certain period, examine the performance of various business sectors, and make predictions to determine future trends. While much progress has been made on data mining and Web mining for financial applications, we can expect to see much more progress in this area. Exhibit 10 illustrates data mining and Web mining applications for financial services.

PHYSICAL SCIENCES, SOCIAL SCIENCES, AND ENGINEERING

The physical sciences, social sciences, and engineering encompass several disciplines. For example, physical sciences include physics, chemistry, and geology. Social sciences include sociology, psychology, humanities, and anthropology. Engineering includes civil, mechanical, electrical, chemical, and petroleum engineering.

Data mining has many applications in all of these areas. Consider, for example, astronomy. With data mining, one could perhaps detect new planets and stars. In chemistry, data mining could be used to detect new elements. Social scientists typically carry out many surveys and analyze the data. Data mining could help toward analysis of this data. For example, with data mining, one could determine that certain ethnic groups have a preference for honey and cabbage, which are somewhat unrelated food items. Data mining can also help in various engineering disciplines. For example, neural networks could help in the detection of anomalies in process plants.

Exhibit 11.   Data Mining and Web Mining Applications in Physical Sciences, Social Sciences, and Engineering

- Identifying stars and planets
- Identifying chemical elements
- Analyzing social behavior
- Chemical plant monitoring

We have only scratched the surface here. We need to examine each discipline to determine the applications for data mining. For example, in chemistry there are many disciplines such as atomic, organic, physical, and so on. Data mining may have applications in all of these areas. We need interdisciplinary research to determine the various data mining techniques that could be applied to physical sciences, social sciences, and engineering. Exhibit 11 illustrates data mining and Web mining applications in physical sciences, social sciences, and engineering.

MEDICINE AND BIOTECHNOLOGY

One area where data mining has been applied fairly extensively is in medical and biological sciences. There are now many computer applications in biology and medicine. This area has now come to be known as biotechnology. We will discuss data mining applications with examples.

In the area of medicine, data mining could be used to help physicians with diagnosis as well as prevention. For example, with data mining one could determine that certain groups are in danger of developing cancer. Appropriate preventive measures can be taken. Data mining can also help with image analysis such as analyzing x-rays and scans, as well as detecting unusual patterns in x-rays.

More recently, data mining is being used extensively for analyzing genome data. Data mining is being used to analyze the various biotechnology databases for gene pattern detection, as well as isolating genes that could cause various diseases. Typical applications include sequence detection, genome data analysis, and helping search tools with intelligent information retrieval. Various specialized search tools are being used to retrieve gene data. Data mining could help not just with getting the right data at the right time, but also with predicting future trends and needs. In addition, pharmaceutical companies are examining data mining for drug discovery.

The downside of biotechnology is bio-terrorism. Data mining is being used to detect and prevent bio-terrorism. Experts in computational sciences, biological sciences, and data mining need to work together to get

**Exhibit 12.   Data Mining and Web Mining
Applications in Medicine
and Biotechnology**

- Sequence detection
- Gene identification
- Drug discovery
- Medical diagnosis
- Image analysis

effective solutions. We will discuss counter-terrorism in the next section, and that will prepare us for Part III. Exhibit 12 illustrates data mining and Web mining applications in medicine and biotechnology.

COUNTER-TERRORISM

We are now ready to tackle perhaps one of the most critical areas of data mining and Web mining. We have briefly discussed counter-terrorism in the previous chapters. Data mining tools could be used to detect unusual patterns, suspicious behaviors, and unauthorized intrusions. All these will help toward counter-terrorism measures.

In Part III, we will discuss data mining for counter-terrorism. We will first start with a discussion of various types of terrorism, including bio-terrorism and cyber-terrorism and then discuss how data mining could help with preventing and detecting terrorism. Because we have devoted an entire section of this book to this topic, we have kept this section fairly short. Exhibit 13 illustrates data mining and Web mining applications in counter-terrorism.

SUMMARY

This chapter has discussed a variety of applications for data mining. First we provided an overview of data mining for E-commerce as well as business intelligence and customer relationships management. Closely related to these applications are marketing and sales, enterprise resource management, and supply chain management. We discussed these applications next. Then we provided an overview of data mining for training, telecommunications, manufacturing, and financial applications. Next we dis-

**Exhibit 13.   Data Mining and Web
Mining Applications in
Counter-Terrorism**

- Intrusion detection
- Insider threat analysis
- Identifying terrorists

cussed data mining for physical, social, and engineering sciences. This was followed by a discussion of data mining for medicine and biotechnology. Finally, we touched on counter-terrorism. Note that we have discussed only some of the applications of data mining. Data mining could be applied to almost any application. But it is impossible to discuss all of the applications in this book. We have focused on applications to illustrate some of the key points and to set the stage for the discussion in Part III.

The entire discussion in Part III will focus on data mining for counter-terrorism. We will start with a discussion of various threats and then discuss how the technologies of Parts I and II could help with counter-terrorism. That is, Parts I and II have set the stage for us now to discuss data mining and Web mining for counter-terrorism. Like commercial organizations, military organizations can also use business intelligence to gather information about the adversaries. This business intelligence is analyzed and strategies are developed to combat terrorism.

CONCLUSION TO PART II

Part II, consisting of nine chapters, has described various data mining technologies for the Web. Chapter 9 provided an overview of Web data mining. Some Web data mining techniques were discussed in Chapter 10. Mining the Web databases was the subject of Chapter 11. Information retrieval and Web mining was discussed in Chapter 12. Information management and Web mining was the subject of Chapter 13. Semantic Web mining was introduced in Chapter 14. We elaborated on Web usage and structure mining in Chapter 15. While Chapter 16 discussed tools, Chapter 17 focused on some applications.

The technologies discussed in this part form the foundation for data mining applications for counter-terrorism. That is, while the supporting technologies in Part I prepared us for Part II, the technologies of Part II have prepared us for Part III. We are now in a position to address one of the critical applications of data mining and Web mining — counter-terrorism.

Part III
Web Data Mining for Counter-Terrorism

INTRODUCTION TO PART III

Part III, consisting of ten chapters, describes Web data mining for counter-terrorism. Chapter 18 provides an overview of counter-terrorism. In particular, security threats and counter-measures will be discussed. Then, for each key supporting technology discussed in Part II, we discuss its application to counter-terrorism. For example, the application of Web mining techniques is the subject of Chapter 19. The application of Web database mining will be discussed in Chapter 20. An overview of information retrieval, mining and counter-terrorism will be discussed in Chapter 21. Information management, mining, and counter-terrorism will be discussed in Chapter 22. Application of semantic Web mining will be discussed in Chapter 23. Web usage and structure mining will be discussed in Chapter 24. The role of privacy and civil liberties with respect to national security will be discussed in Chapter 25. Finally, in Chapter 26, we revisit the discussion of threats from Chapter 18 and discuss the applicability of the various solutions previously discussed in Chapters 19 through 24. Finally, in Chapter 27, we will revisit E-commerce and business intelligence and examine how counter-terrorism can take advantage of the developments in E-commerce technologies.

The ten chapters in this part provide only some preliminary information for data mining applications in counter-terrorism. This is a new area and still not much is known about it. Policymakers and technologists have to work together; data miners and counter-terrorism experts have to work together. We hope that this book will spawn many novel ideas and research directions so that we can eventually make this world a safer place to live.

Chapter 18

Some Information on Terrorism, Security Threats, and Protection Measures

INTRODUCTION

We are now ready to embark on a critical application of data and Web mining technologies. This application is counter-terrorism. Counter-terrorism is mainly about developing counter-measures to threats occurring from terrorist activities. In this chapter, we focus on the various types of threats that could occur. In the next few chapters, we will discuss how data mining and business intelligence analysis could help prevent and detect the threats.

Our discussion of counter-terrorism is rather preliminary. We are not claiming to be counter-terrorism experts. The information on terrorist threats we have presented here have been obtained entirely from unclassified newspaper articles and news reports that have appeared over the years. Our focus is to illustrate how data mining could help toward combating terrorism. We are not saying that data mining solves all the problems. But because data mining has the capability to extract often previously unknown patterns and trends, we should certainly explore the various data mining and Web mining technologies for counter-terrorism. Note that we have discussed both data mining and Web mining. As we have stated, for us Web mining goes beyond data mining. It not only includes data mining techniques, but also focuses on Web traffic and usage mining as well as Web structure mining. That is, there are additional challenges for Web mining that are not present for just data mining. Furthermore, Web mining also includes mining structured data as well as unstructured data. Furthermore, we have stated that much of the data will eventually be on the Web, whether in public networks such as the Internet or in private corporate intranets and classified intranets. Therefore, studying Web mining encompasses studying data mining as well.

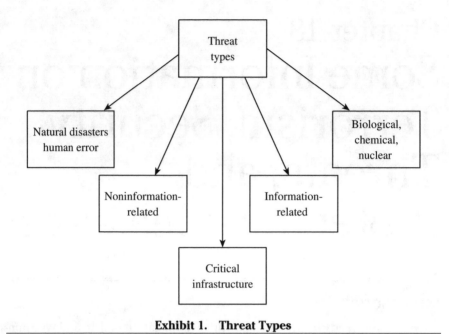

Exhibit 1.   Threat Types

Before we embark on a discussion of counter-terrorism, we need to discuss types of threats. Note that threats could be malicious threats due to terror attacks or nonmalicious threats due to inadvertent errors. While our main focus is on malicious attacks, we also cover some of the inadvertent errors as there may be similar solutions to combat such problems. The types of terrorist threats we discuss include noninformation-related terrorism, information-related terrorism, and biological and chemical attacks. By using the term *noninformation-related terrorism,* we mean people attacking others with bombs and guns. We need to find out who these people are by analyzing their connections and developing counter-terrorism solutions. By using the term *information-related threats,* we mean threats to the existence of computer systems and networks. These are unauthorized intrusions and viruses as well as computer-related vandalism. Information-related terrorism is essentially cyber-terrorism. There are potential biological, chemical, and nuclear attacks. These are not all the types of threats that exist; these are the only threats we will be examining. We will discuss how data mining could perhaps be used to help prevent and detect attacks due to such threats. Exhibit 1 illustrates the types of threats we will discuss in this chapter.

NATURAL DISASTERS AND HUMAN ERRORS

As we have stated, threats could occur due to natural disasters and human error as well as through malicious attacks. While the solutions to the attacks in the near-term may not be that different in terms of emergency responses, the way to combat these threats in the long term will very likely be quite different.

By natural disasters, we mean disasters due to hurricanes, earthquakes, fires, power failures, and accidents. Some of these disasters may be due to human error such as pressing the wrong button in a process plant, causing the plant to explode. Data mining could help detect some of the natural disasters. That is, by analyzing geological data, a data mining tool may predict that an earthquake is about to occur in which case the people in the area could be evacuated beforehand. Similarly by analyzing the weather data, the tool could predict that hurricanes are about to occur. Emergency responses to a building in flames after a natural disaster or a terrorist attack may not be that different. In either case, there will be panic and the danger of structural collapse. We need effective emergency response teams to handle such scenarios. Data mining could be used to analyze previous attacks, train various tools, and advise emergency response teams how to handle the emergency situation. Here again, we need training examples, some of which may not exist. In this case, we may need to train with hypothetical scenarios and simulated examples.

The long-term measures to be taken for natural disasters may be quite different for terrorist attacks. It is not every day that we have an earthquake, even in the most earthquake-prone regions. It is not often that we have hurricanes, even in the most hurricane-prone regions. Therefore, we have time to plan and react. This does not mean that a natural disaster is less complex to manage. It could be devastating and take many lives. Nevertheless, nations usually plan for such disasters mainly through experience.

Human error is also a source of major concern. We need to continually train the operators and advise them to be cautious and alert. We need to take proper actions if humans have been careless. That is, unless there is an absolutely good excuse, human error should not be treated lightly. This way, humans will be cautious and perhaps not make such errors.

Terrorist attacks are quite different. The problem is, one does not know when it will happen and how it will happen. Many of us could never have imagined that airplanes would be used as weapons to bring down the towers of the World Trade Center. We still do not know what the next attack will be like, whether a suicide bomber, a chemical weapon, or cyber-terrorism. The counter-measures for prevention and detection may be quite intense for terrorist attacks. As we have stated, we are not experts on counter-terrorism nor have we studied the nature of the attacks. Our goal is to examine the various data mining techniques to see how they could be applied to handle the various threats that have been discussed almost daily in the newspapers and on television.

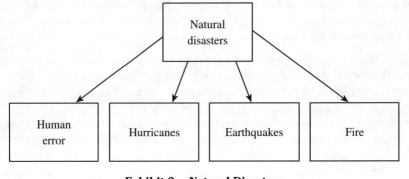

Exhibit 2. Natural Disasters

It should be noted, however, that to develop effective techniques, the data mining specialists have to work together with counter-terrorism experts. That is, one cannot use the techniques without a good understanding of the threats. Therefore, I would urge those interested in applying data mining techniques to solve real-world problems and terrorist attacks to work with counter-terrorism specialists.

In the next few sections, we will discuss various types of terrorism and counter-terrorism measures. We will end the chapter with a discussion of privacy. Exhibit 2 illustrates the types of natural disasters that could occur.

NONINFORMATION-RELATED TERRORISM

In this section, we will provide an overview of various types of noninformation-related terrorism (see Exhibit 3). Note that by information-related terrorism, we mean attacks essentially on computers and networks. That is, information-related terrorism targets electronic information. By noninformation-related terrorism, we mean terrorism due to other means such as attacks, bombings, vandalism, arson, etc.

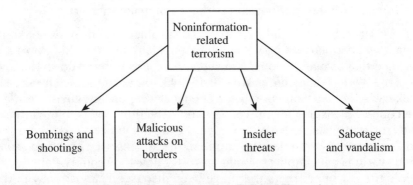

Exhibit 3. Noninformation-Related Terrorism

Terrorist Attacks and External Threats

When we hear the term *terrorism,* it is the external threats that come to mind. Our earliest recollections of terrorism are riots, where one ethnic group attacks another, essentially killing, looting, vandalizing, setting fires, and other violent acts. Later, we heard of airplane hijackings, where a group of terrorists hijacked airplanes and made demands on governments such as releasing political prisoners. Then we heard of suicide bombings, where terrorists carry bombs and blow themselves up as well as others nearby. Such attacks usually occur in crowded places. More recently, we have heard of airplanes being used to blow up buildings.

While these are all terrorist attacks, we hear almost daily about someone shooting and killing someone else when neither party belongs to a gang or terrorist group. This in a way is terrorism also, but these acts are more difficult to detect and prevent because there are always "crazy people" in our society. While the technologies should detect and prevent such attacks also, this book focuses on how to prevent attacks by terrorist groups.

All of the threats we have discussed are external threats, threats occurring from the outside. In general, terrorists are usually neither friends nor acquaintances of the victims involved. But there are also insider threats. We will discuss them in the next section.

Insider Threats

Insider threats are threats from people inside an organization, attacking others around them through sinister mechanisms. Examples of insider threats include employees of a corporation giving information of proprietary products to a competitor. Another example is an intelligence agent committing espionage. A third example is a threat coming from one's own family. For example, a spouse with insider information about assets may give the information to a competitor, to his or her advantage. That is, insider threats can occur at all levels and in all walks of life, and could be quite dangerous and sinister because you never know who these terrorists are. They may be your so-called best friends, your spouse, or your siblings.

We often hear about office shootings. But these shootings are generally not insider threats, as they are not happening in sinister ways. That is, these shootings are external threats although they are coming from people within an organization. We also hear about domestic abuse and violence, husbands shooting wives or vice versa. These are also external threats, although they are occurring from the inside. Insider threats are threats where others are totally unaware until something quite dangerous occurs. We have heard that espionage goes on for years before someone gets caught. While both insider and external threats are very serious and could be devastating, insider threats can be even more dangerous because one never knows who these terrorists are.

Transportation and Border Security Violations

Safeguarding the borders is critical for the security of a nation. There could be threats at borders such as illegal immigration; trafficking in firearms, drugs, and humans; and entering terrorists . We are not saying that illegal immigrants are dangerous or are terrorists. They may be very decent people. However, they have entered a country without the proper authorizations and that could be a major issue. For official immigration into the United States, one needs to pass an interview at the U.S. embassy as well as medical and background checks. It does not mean that people who have entered a country legally are necessarily innocent. They can be terrorists. At least there is some assurance that proper procedures have been followed. Illegal immigration can also cause problems with the economy of a society and violate human rights through illegal labor, etc.

As we have stated, drug trafficking has occurred at borders. Drugs are a danger to society, which could cripple a nation, corrupt its children, cause havoc in families, damage the education system, and cause extensive damage. It is therefore critical that we protect the borders from drug trafficking as well as other types of trafficking including firearms and humans. Other threats at borders include prostitution and child pornography, which are serious threats to decent living. It does not mean that everything is safe inside the country and the problems are only at the borders. Nevertheless, we have to protect our borders so that there are no additional problems to a nation.

Transportation systems' security violations can also cause serious problems. Buses, trains, and airplanes are vehicles that can carry hundreds of people at the same time, and any security violation could cause serious damage and even death. A bomb exploding in an airplane or a train or a bus could be devastating. Transportation systems are also the means for terrorists to escape once they have committed crimes. Therefore, transportation systems have to be secure. A key aspect of transportation systems security is port security. Ports are responsible for ships of the United States Navy. Because these ships are at sea throughout the world, terrorists may have opportunities to attack these ships and their cargo. Therefore, we need security measures to protect the ports, cargo, and our military bases.

INFORMATION-RELATED TERRORISM

This section discusses information-related terrorism. By information-related terrorism we mean cyber-terrorism as well as security violations through access control and other means. Trojan horses and viruses are

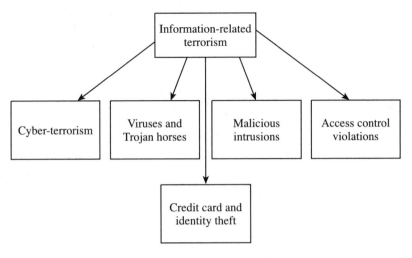

Exhibit 4. Information-Related Terrorism

also information-related security violations, which we group into informa-tion-related terrorism activities.

In the next few sections, we discuss various information-related terror-ist attacks. Because the Web is a major means of information transporta-tion, we give Web security threats special consideration. For an excellent book on Web security that discusses various threats and solutions, see [GHOS98]. Exhibit 4 illustrates information-related terrorist attacks.

Cyber-Terrorism, Insider Threats, and External Attacks

Cyber-terrorism is one of the major terrorist threats posed to our nation today. As we have mentioned earlier, there is now so much information available electronically and on the Web. Attack on computers, networks, databases, and the Internet could be devastating to business. It is esti-mated that cyber-terrorism could cause billions of dollars to business. For example, consider a banking information system. If terrorists attack such a system and deplete accounts, the bank could lose millions and perhaps bil-lions of dollars. By crippling the computer system, millions of hours of pro-ductivity could be lost, which equates to money in the end. Even a simple power outage at work through some accident could cause several hours of productivity loss and, as a result, a major financial loss. Therefore, it is crit-ical that our information systems be secure.

Next we discuss various types of cyber-terrorist attacks. One is spread-ing viruses and Trojan horses that can destroy files and other important documents. Another is intruding the computer networks, which we will discuss in the next section.

297

Note that threats can occur from outside or inside an organization. Outside attacks are attacks on computers from someone outside the organization. We hear of hackers breaking into computer systems and causing havoc within an organization. There are hackers who spread viruses that cause great damage to the files in various computer systems. But a more sinister problem is the insider threat. Just like noninformation-related attacks, there is the insider threat with information-related attacks. There are people inside an organization who have studied the business practices and who develop schemes to cripple the organization's information assets. These people could be regular employees or even those working at computer centers. The problem is quite serious, as someone may be masquerading as someone else and causing all kinds of damage. In the next few chapters, we will examine how data mining could detect and perhaps prevent such attacks.

Malicious Intrusions

We have discussed some aspects of malicious intrusions. These intrusions could be intruding the networks, the Web clients and servers, the databases, operating systems, etc. Many of the cyber-terrorism attacks that we have discussed in the previous sections are malicious intrusions. We will revisit them in this section.

We hear a lot about network intrusions. Intruders tap into networks and get information that is being transmitted. These intruders may be human or Trojan horses set up by humans. Intrusions could also happen on files. For example, an attacker can masquerade as someone else, log into a computer system, and access the files. Intrusions can also occur on databases. Intruders posing as legitimate users can pose queries, and access the data that they are not authorized to have.

Essentially, cyber-terrorism includes malicious intrusions as well as sabotage through malicious intrusions or otherwise. Cyber-security consists of security mechanisms that attempt to provide solutions to cyber-attacks or cyber-terrorism. When we discuss malicious intrusions or cyber-attacks, we need to think about the noncyber-world, i.e., noninformation-related terrorism, and then translate those attacks to attacks on computers and networks. For example, a thief could enter a building through a trap door. In the same way, a computer intruder could enter the computer or network through a trap door that has been intentionally built by a malicious insider and left unattended through careless design. Another example is a masked thief entering a bank and stealing money. The analogy is an intruder masquerading as someone else, legitimately entering the system and taking all the information assets. Money in the real world translates to information assets in the cyber-world. That is, there are many parallels between noninformation-related attacks and information-related attacks. We can proceed to develop counter-measures for both types of attacks.

Credit Card Fraud and Identity Theft

We are hearing much today about credit card fraud and identity theft. In the case of credit card fraud, unauthorized persons steal credit card information and make purchases. By the time the card owner discovers the theft, it may be too late. The thief may have left the country by then. A similar problem occurs with telephone calling cards. Perhaps when using a calling card to make a phone call at an airport, someone may hear the tones and use them later to charge calls to that calling card. Sometimes the telephone company detects these instances and informs the card owner. In these cases, the problem can be dealt with immediately.

A more serious problem is identity theft. Here, one assumes the identity of another person by obtaining a social security number, and carries out transactions under that person's name. This could involve fraudulently selling the victim's home and depositing the funds in a bank account. By the time the victim finds out, it is very likely that he may have lost millions of dollars due to the identity theft.

We need to explore the use of data mining both for credit card fraud detection as well as for identity theft. There have been some efforts in detecting credit card fraud (see [AFCE]). We need to start working proactively on detecting and preventing identity theft.

Information Security Violations

In this section, we provide an overview of various information security violations. These violations do not necessarily mean that they are occurring through cyber-attacks or cyber-terrorism. They could occur through poor security design and practices. Nevertheless, we have included this discussion for completion.

Information security violations typically occur due to access control violations. That is, users are granted access based on their roles (role-based access control) or their clearance level (multilevel access control) or on a need-to-know basis. Access controls are violated usually due to poor design or designer error. For example, suppose John does not have access to salary data. By some error, this rule may not be enforced and, as a result, John gets access to salary values. Access control violations can also occur due to malicious attacks. That is, someone could enter the system by pretending to be the system administrator and delete the access control rule that John does not have access to salaries. Another way is for a Trojan horse to operate on behalf of the malicious users and, each time John makes a request, the malicious code could ensure that the access control rule is bypassed.

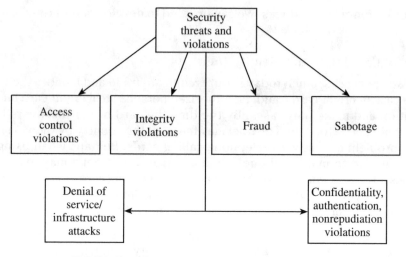

Exhibit 5.   Web Security Threats and Violations

We have provided a brief overview of access control violations. We discuss these violations in Appendix C. Security problems for the Web are discussed in the next section.

Security Problems for the Web

As mentioned previously, there are numerous security attacks that can occur through the Web. These security threats are illustrated in Exhibit 5. As we have mentioned, Ghosh has provided an excellent introduction to Web security and various threats [GHOS98]. Note that while we have focused on Web threats in this section, the threats illustrated in Exhibit 5 are applicable to any information system such as networks, databases, and operating systems.

- *Access control violations:* Traditional access control violations could be extended to the Web. Users may access unauthorized data across the Web. Note that there is so much data on the Web that controlling access to this data is quite a challenge.
- *Integrity violations:* Data on the Web may be subject to unauthorized modifications. This makes it easier to corrupt the data. Also, data could originate from anywhere, and the producers of the data may not be trustworthy. Incorrect data could cause serious damage, such as incorrect bank accounts, which could result in incorrect transactions.
- *Sabotage:* We hear of hackers breaking into systems and posting inappropriate messages. For example, there are reports about the sabotage of various government Web pages [GHOS98]. One needs

only to corrupt one server, client, or network for the problem to cascade to several machines.

- *Fraud:* With so much business and commerce being carried out on the Web without proper controls, Internet fraud could cause businesses to lose millions of dollars. Intruders could obtain the identity of legitimate users and, through masquerading, may empty bank accounts.
- *Privacy:* We have been stressing privacy throughout this book. With the Web, one can obtain all kinds of information collected about individuals. Also, data mining tools facilitate the compromise of privacy.
- *Denial of service and infrastructure attacks:* We hear about infrastructures being brought down by hackers. Infrastructures could be the telecommunication system, power system, and the heating system. These systems are being controlled by computers and often through the Internet. Such attacks cause denials of service.
- *Other threats:* These include violations to confidentiality, authenticity, and nonrepudiation. Confidentiality violations enable intruders to listen to the message. Authentication violations include using passwords without permissions. Nonrepudiation violations enable someone to deny that he sent a message.

All of these threats collectively have come to be known as cyber-war or cyber-terrorism. Essentially, cyber-war is about corrupting the Web and all of its components so that the enemy or adversary system collapses. There is currently much money being invested by the governments of the United States and western Europe to conduct research on protecting the Web and preventing cyber-wars and cyber-terrorism.

The Web threats discussed here occur because of insecure clients, servers, and networks. To have complete security, one needs end-to-end security; that means secure clients, secure servers, secure operating systems, secure databases, secure middleware, and secure networks, and there is much emphasis today on developing security solutions for these environments. Programming languages such as Java and technologies such as Microsoft's ActiveX are being made secure. Sophisticated encryption mechanisms are being developed for network security.

BIOLOGICAL, CHEMICAL, AND NUCLEAR ATTACKS

The previous sections discussed noninformation-related as well as information-related terrorist attacks. By information-related attacks, we mean cyber-attacks; noninformation-related attacks mean everything else. However, we have separated biological and chemical weapons attacks from noninformation-related attacks. We have also given special consideration to critical infrastructure attacks. That is, the noninformation-related attacks are essentially attacks due to fires, explosions, or other similar activities.

While biological, chemical, and nuclear weapons attacks have been discussed at least for several decades, it is only after September 11, 2001, that the public is paying attention to these discussions. The anthrax attacks that occurred during the latter part of 2001 have resulted in increased fear and awareness of the potential dangers of bio-terrorism attacks. More recently, there is increasing awareness of the dangers due to bio-terrorism attacks resulting in the spread of infectious diseases such as smallpox and yellow fever. These diseases are so infectious that it is critical that their spread is detected as soon as they occur. Preventing such attacks is the ultimate goal; technologies would include sensor technology and data mining and data management.

Attacks using chemical weapons are equally deadly. Poisonous gas or chemical agents can be introduced into the air, water, and food supplies. For example, dangerous chemical agents could be sprayed from the air on plants and crops. When these plants and crops enter the food supply, people and animals could suffer. We have to develop technologies to detect and prevent such attacks.

Nuclear attacks could wipe out the entire population of the world. There are various nations developing nuclear weapons. This is what makes the world very dangerous. We have to develop technologies to prevent such deadly attacks from taking place.

There are some good books that are being written about such terrorist activities (see [ELLI99] and [BOLZ01]). As we have stressed, we are not counter-terrorism experts; nor have we studied the various types of terrorist attacks in any depth. Our information is obtained from various newspaper articles and documentaries. Our main goal is to examine various data mining techniques and see how they could be applied to detect and prevent such deadly attacks. Data mining for counter-terrorism will be discussed in Chapters 18 through 24. Exhibit 6 illustrates various biological, chemical, and nuclear attacks.

ATTACKS ON CRITICAL INFRASTRUCTURES

Attacks on critical infrastructures could cripple a nation and its economy. Infrastructure attacks can impact telecommunications lines; electric power, gas, water, and food supplies; and other basic entities that are critical to the operation of a nation.

Attacks on critical infrastructures could occur during any type of attack, whether noninformation-related, information-related, or bio-terrorism attacks. For example, one could attack the software that runs the telecommunications industry and shut down all the telecommunications lines;

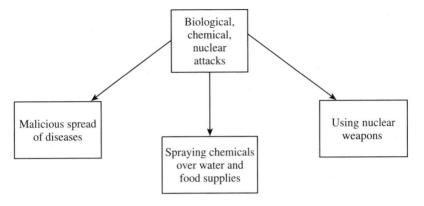

Exhibit 6. Biological, Chemical, and Nuclear Attacks

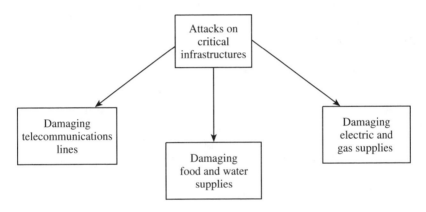

Exhibit 7. Critical Infrastructure Attacks

software that runs the power and gas supplies could be attacked. Attacks using bombs and explosives could be used against telecommunications lines. Attacking transportation lines such as highways and railroads are also attacks on infrastructures.

As we have mentioned previously, infrastructures could also be damaged by natural disasters such as hurricanes and earthquakes. However, our main interest is the malicious attacks. Our goal is to examine data mining and related data management technologies to detect and prevent such infrastructure attacks. Exhibit 7 illustrates various types of infrastructure attacks.

NONREAL-TIME THREATS VS. REAL-TIME THREATS

The threats that we have discussed thus far can be grouped into two categories: nonreal-time threats and real-time threats. In a way, all threats are real-time as we have to act once the threats have occurred. However, while some threats have to be handled immediately, others are analyzed over a period of time. We discuss the various threats here.

Consider, for example, the biological, chemical, and nuclear threats. These threats have to be handled in real-time. That is, the responses to these threats have timing constraints. If the smallpox virus is being spread, then we have to start vaccinations immediately. Similarly, if networks for critical infrastructures are being attacked, the response has to be immediate. Otherwise we could lose millions of lives and millions of dollars.

There are some other threats that do not have to be handled in real-time. For example, consider the behavior of people suspected of belonging to a certain terrorist organization or those enrolling in flight training schools. They may be involved in planning attacks but, sometimes, even they are not sure when the attack will occur. Therefore, these people have to be monitored, their behavior analyzed, and their actions predicted. While there are timing constraints for these threats, the urgency is not as great as for others, for example, the spread of the smallpox virus. But one should also be vigilant about these nonreal-time threats.

In general there is no way to say that A is a real-time threat and B is a nonreal-time threat. A nonreal-time threat could turn into a real-time threat. For example, once the terrorists had hijacked the airplanes on September 11, 2001, the threat became a real-time threat as action had to be taken within an hour. Exhibit 8 illustrates both types of threats.

ASPECTS OF COUNTER-TERRORISM

Now that we have provided some discussion on various types of terrorist attacks including noninformation-related terrorism, information-related terrorism, bio-terrorism, etc., we will discuss what counter-terrorism is all about. Counter-terrorism is a collection of techniques used to combat, prevent, and detect terrorism (see Exhibit 9). Our goal in this book is to examine various data mining techniques to see how we can combat terrorism. In this section, we will briefly discuss what counter-terrorism is all about for the terrorist attacks previously discussed.

Protecting from Noninformation-Related Terrorism

As we have stated, noninformation-related counter-terrorism includes protection from bombings, explosions, vandalism, and other kinds of terrorist attacks not involved with computers. For example, hijacking an airplane and attacking buildings with airplanes are examples of noninformation-related terrorist activity. The question is, how do we protect against such terrorist attacks?

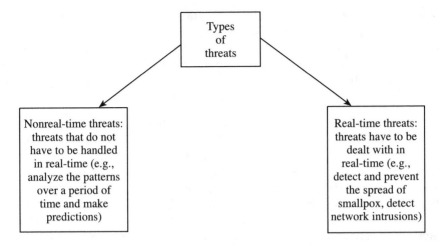

Exhibit 8.   Nonreal-Time vs. Real-Time Threats

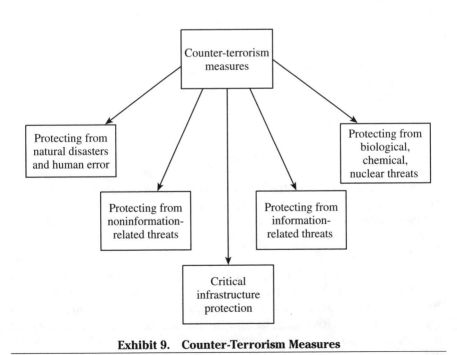

Exhibit 9.   Counter-Terrorism Measures

First of all, we need to gather information about various scenarios and examples. That is, we need to identify all kinds of terrorist acts that have occurred in history starting from airplane hijacking to bombing buildings. We also need to gather information about those under suspicion. All of the data that we have gathered needs to be analyzed to see if any patterns emerge.

We also need to ensure there are physical safety measures. For example, we need to check identity at airports or other places, randomly as well as routinely. We need to check the belongings of a person to see if there are dangerous weapons or chemicals if that person arouses suspicion. We should also use sniffing dogs and sensor devices to see if there are potentially hazardous materials. We need surveillance cameras to see who is entering the building. These cameras should also capture perhaps the facial expressions of various people. The data gathered from the cameras should be analyzed further for suspicious behavior. We also need to enforce access control measures at military bases and seaports.

In summary, several counter-terrorism measures have to be taken to combat noninformation-related terrorism. These measures include information gathering and analysis, surveillance, physical security, and various other mechanisms. In the next few chapters, we will examine data mining techniques and see how they can detect and prevent terrorist attacks.

Protecting from Information-Related Terrorism

We will first provide an overview of counter-terrorism with respect to information-related terrorism. We will give special consideration for security solution for the Web later on.

Essentially, protecting from information-related terrorism involves detecting and preventing malicious attacks and intrusions. These attacks could be attacks due to viruses or spoofing or masquerading and stealing information assets. These attacks could also be attacks on databases and malicious corruption of data. That is, terrorist attacks are not necessarily stealing and accessing unauthorized information. They could also include malicious corruption and alteration of the data so that the data will be of little or no use. Terrorist attacks also include credit card fraud and identity theft.

Various data mining techniques are being proposed for detecting intrusions as well as credit card fraud. We will discuss them in later chapters. Preventing malicious attacks is more challenging. We need to design systems so that malicious attacks and intrusions are prevented. When an intruder attempts to attack the system, the system would figure this out and alert the security officer. There is research being carried out on secure systems design so that such intrusions are prevented. However, there is more focus on detecting than preventing such intrusions.

Enforcing appropriate access control techniques is also a way to enforce security. For example, users may have certificates to access the information they need to carry out the jobs that they are assigned to do. The organization should give the users no more or no less privileges. There is much research on managing privileges and access rights to various types of systems.

We have briefly discussed cyber-security measures. We will discuss security solutions for the Web in more detail next. Note that there are also additional problems such as the inference problem where users pose sets of queries and infer sensitive information. This is also an attack. We will visit the inference problem later when we discuss privacy.

Security Solutions for the Web

Exhibit 10 illustrates the various components that have to be made secure to get a secure Web. We need end-end-end security and, therefore, the components include secure clients, secure servers, secure databases, secure operating systems, secure infrastructures, secure networks, secure transactions, and secure protocols. One needs good encryption mechanisms to ensure that the sender and receiver communicate securely. Ultimately, whether exchanging messages or carrying out transactions, communication between sender and receiver or buyer and seller has to be secure. Secure client solutions include securing the browser, securing the Java virtual machine, securing Java applets, and incorporating various

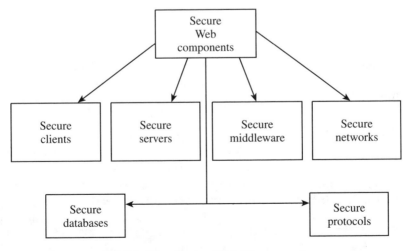

Exhibit 10. Secure Web Components

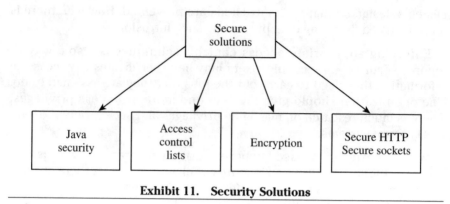

Exhibit 11. Security Solutions

security features into languages such as Java. Note that Java is not the only component that has to be secure. Microsoft has come up with a collection of products, including ActiveX, that also have to be secure. Securing protocols include secure HTTP, and secure SSL. Securing the Web server means the server has to be installed securely and that it cannot be attacked after installation. Various mechanisms that have been used to secure operating systems and databases may be applied here. Notable among them are access control lists that specify which user has access and permissions to Web pages and data. The Web servers may be connected to databases at the back end and these databases have to be secure. Finally, various encryption algorithms are being implemented for networks, and groups such as the OMG (Object Management Group) are envisaging security for middleware such as ORB (object request broker). Exhibit 11 illustrates various security solutions.

One of the challenges faced by Web managers is implementing security policies. One may have policies for clients, servers, networks, middleware, and databases. The question is, how do you integrate these policies? How do you make these policies work together? Who is responsible for implementing these policies? Is there a global administrator or are there several administrators that have to work together? Security policy integration is an area that is being examined by researchers (see [THUR94]).

Finally, one of the emerging technologies for ensuring that an organization's assets are protected is firewalls. Various organizations now have Web infrastructures for internal and external use. To access the external infrastructure, one has to go through the firewall. These firewalls examine the information that comes into and out of an organization. This way, the internal assets are protected and inappropriate information may be blocked. We can expect sophisticated firewalls to be developed in the future. Other security mechanisms include cryptography. We have discussed security mechanisms in more detail in a previous book [THUR00].

Protecting from Biological and Chemical Attacks

In this section, we discuss counter-terrorism measures. First of all, unlike noninformation-related terrorism where bombings and shootings are fairly explicit, biological and chemical attacks are not immediately obvious. Suppose a terrorist spreads the smallpox virus; it takes at least a few days before the symptoms surface and a few more days before the diagnosis is made. By then it may be too late, as millions of people may be infected in trains and planes and large gatherings and meetings. The challenge here is to prevent as well as detect such attacks as soon as possible.

Preventing such attacks could mean developing special sensors to detect certain viruses in the air. The sensors may also have to identify the viruses. A cold virus is not as harmful as a smallpox virus. If the disease has spread, some quick decisions have to be made about who to vaccinate.

Chemical weapons may also be treated similarly. One needs sensors to detect who has these weapons. Once the dangerous chemicals are released, we need to determine what antidotes to use to limit the damage caused by the chemicals. For example, acidic material can be countered by washing with soap-based materials.

In the case of nuclear attacks, we need to determine what nuclear weapons have been used and what actions to take. How do we evacuate large groups of people in an organized fashion? What medications do we give them? These are very difficult challenges. Research activities are proceeding, but it will take a very long time to find viable solutions.

Critical Infrastructure Protection

Our critical infrastructures are telecommunications systems, gas and electric lines, networks, water and food supplies, etc. Attacking the critical infrastructure could cripple business and government. We need to determine the measures to be taken when infrastructures are attacked.

Essentially, the counter-measures include those developed for noninformation-based terrorism as well as for information-based terrorism. For example, one could bomb telecommunications systems or create computer viruses that affect telecommunications software. This means that all communication through phone lines could be crippled. The counter-measures developed for noninformation-related and information-related terrorism could be applied here. We need to gather information about terrorist groups to extract patterns. We also need to detect unauthorized intrusions. Our ultimate goal is to prevent such disastrous acts.

Even biological, chemical, and nuclear weapons could attack the infrastructure of the nation. For example, our food, water, and medical supplies could be damaged by biological warfare. Here again, we need to examine counter-terrorism measures for biological, chemical, and nuclear attacks and apply them.

Protecting from Nonreal-Time and Real-Time Threats

As we have mentioned, it is difficult to state that A is a real-time threat and B is a nonreal-time threat. Over time, a nonreal-time threat could become a real-time threat. Real-time threats have to be handled in real-time. An example of a real-time threat is detecting and preventing the spread of the smallpox virus.

When it comes to counter-measures for handling these threats, one needs to develop techniques that meet timing constraints to handle real-time threats. For example, if data mining is used to detect and prevent the malicious intrusions into corporate networks, then these data mining techniques have to give results in real-time. In the case of nonreal-time threats, the data mining techniques could analyze the data and make predictions that certain threats could occur, for example, in July 2003.

In Chapter 19, we will revisit nonreal-time threats and real-time threats from a data mining perspective. While real-time threats need immediate response, both nonreal-time threats as well as real-time threats could be deadly and have to be taken seriously.

A NOTE ON PRIVACY

The previous sections have discussed terrorism attacks and counter-terrorism measures. Our focus has been on gathering information about terrorists, including information about their activities, whereabouts, and origins. In the case of intrusions, we gather information about which groups are likely to commit computer crimes and develop viruses, etc. While gathering information is necessary as we need good data to carry out mining, this also causes a serious threat to privacy.

Recently at the International Federation for Information Processing (IFIP) 11.3 working conferences in database security, there have been many discussions and panels on national security vs. privacy. Developing counter-terrorism measures does not usually come without sacrificing privacy. So the challenge is to protect the nation and at the same time ensure privacy. While the September 11, 2001, attacks have resulted in many counter-terrorism-related discussions, it has also resulted in privacy awareness. Before that, there was some concern about privacy, especially in protecting medical data. However, all kinds of information is being gathered about us today. The various data mining tools can be used to extract unknown patterns about people and events. This is a serious threat to privacy. In Chapter 25, we will revisit privacy, national security, and civil liberties. We wanted to introduce it in this chapter to raise the privacy issue while we are discussing data mining for national security in the next few chapters.

SUMMARY

This chapter has provided a fairly broad overview of various aspects of threats and counter-terrorism measures. First we discussed natural disasters and human error. Then we divided the threats into various groups, including noninformation-related terrorism, information-related terrorism; and biological, chemical, and nuclear threats. We also discussed critical infrastructure threats.

Next we discussed counter-terrorism measures for all types of threats. For example, we need to gather information about terrorists and terrorist groups, mine the information, and extract patterns. In the case of bio-terrorism, we need to prevent terrorist attacks, for example, with the use of sensors. Finally, we discussed the conflict between national security and privacy. It should be noted that in all cases we need to gather intelligence about attacks, terrorist activities, and other related events, analyze the intelligence and develop countermeasures. That is, carrying out business intelligence analysis is a major activity for combatting terrorism.

Now that we have discussed the various threats, we are ready to discuss how data mining could be applied for counter-terrorism. We take each technology discussed in Parts I and II and discuss how they can be applied for counter-terrorism. That is, we examine Web database mining, information retrieval and mining, information management and mining, semantic Web mining, and Web usage mining and see how it can help counter-terrorism. We also analyze the various data mining techniques for counter-terrorism. Part III will also discuss privacy and civil liberties. We will end Part III with a discussion of the parallels between E-commerce and counter-terrorism. They both need to carry out business intelligence analysis.

Chapter 19

Web Data Mining for Counter-Terrorism

INTRODUCTION

In the previous chapter, we discussed various threats and counter-measures. In particular, we discussed noninformation-related attacks, such as bombings and explosions; information-related attacks, such as cyber-terrorism; biological, chemical, and nuclear attacks, such as the spread of smallpox; and critical infrastructure attacks, such as attacks on electric power and gas lines. Counter-terrorism measures include ways of protecting against these forms of terrorism.

In this chapter, we provide a high-level overview of how Web data mining and data mining could help toward counter-terrorism. Note that we have used the terms *Web data mining* and *data mining* interchangeably because our definition of Web data mining goes beyond just mining structured data. We have included mining unstructured data, mining for business intelligence, Web usage mining, and Web structure mining as part of Web data mining. That is, in a way Web data mining encompasses data mining.

As we have stated, data mining could contribute toward counter-terrorism. We are not saying that data mining will solve all our national security problems. However, the ability to extract hidden patterns and trends from large quantities of data is very important for detecting and preventing terrorist attacks. In this chapter as well as in the ensuing chapters, we will explore how the technologies discussed in Part II can be applied for counter-terrorism.

Note that in the next few chapters we will take each technology discussed in Part II and see how it can be applied for counter-terrorism. For example, Web database mining for counter-terrorism is the subject of Chapter 20. Information retrieval and Web mining for counter-terrorism will be discussed in Chapter 21. Information management and Web mining for counter-terrorism will be discussed in Chapter 22. Semantic Web mining for counter-terrorism will be discussed in Chapter 23. Finally, Web usage and structure mining for counter-terrorism will be discussed in Chapter 24.*

WEB DATA MINING FOR COUNTER-TERRORISM

In Chapter 18, we grouped threats in different ways. One grouping was whether they were information-related or noninformation-related threats. It was somewhat artificial because we need information for all types of threats. However, in our terminology, information-related threats were threats dealing with computers; some of these were real-time threats, some were not. The grouping was somewhat arbitrary because a nonreal-time threat could become a real-time threat. For example, one could suspect that a group of terrorists will eventually perform some act of terrorism. However, when we set time bounds (for example, a threat will likely occur before July 1, 2003), it becomes a real-time threat and we have to take action immediately. If the time bounds are tighter (for example, a threat will occur within two days), then we cannot afford to make any mistakes in our response.

The purpose of this section is to examine both the nonreal-time and real-time threats and see how data mining in general and Web data mining in particular could handle such threats. Again, we want to stress that Web data mining in our terminology also encompasses mining structured and unstructured data. Furthermore, we are assuming that much of the data will be on the Web, either on public networks or private intranets. Therefore, we are using the terms *data mining* and *Web data mining* interchangeably. We will refer to the specific examples that we have mentioned in the previous chapter in our discussions as needed. Topics such as data sharing vs. data mining will be discussed in Chapter 20 when we discuss Web database mining for counter-terrorism. Note that in Part II we gave special consideration for database mining. This is about mining the various databases on the Web or otherwise. Therefore, we will discuss aspects of database management such as data sharing and data mining for counter-terrorism in Chapter 20. Information retrieval, information management, semantic Web, and Web mining for counter-terrorism will be discussed in Chapters 21 through 23. Exhibit 1 illustrates various aspects discussed in this chapter.

* At the June 1998 DARPA workshop on data mining, there was considerable discussion of link analysis for counter-terrorism. Several years prior to that, I had many interesting discussions on link analysis with Dr. Rick Steinheiser of the CIA when we worked on the MDDS project. Subsequently, we had discussions with DARPA about starting an initiative on data mining. This led to the workshop in June 1998, which eventually resulted in DARPA's EELD program in the Information Awareness Office. EELD is also focusing on link analysis among other techniques.

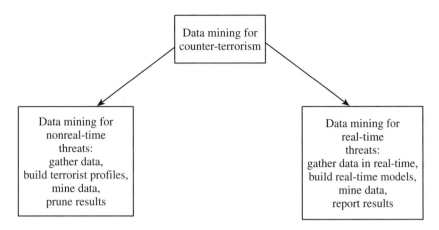

Exhibit 1.   Data Mining for Counter-Terrorism

Nonreal-Time Threats

Nonreal-time threats are threats that do not have to be handled in real-time. That is, there are no timing constraints for these threats. For example, we may need to collect data over months, analyze the data, and then detect or prevent some terrorist attack, which may or may not occur. The question is, how does data mining help toward identifying such threats and attacks?

As we have stressed previously, we need good data to carry out data mining and obtain useful results. We also need to reason with incomplete data. This is the big challenge, as organizations are not often prepared to share the data. This means that the data mining tools have to make assumptions about the data belonging to other organizations. The other alternative is to carry out federated data mining under some federated administrator. For example, the Department of Homeland Security could serve as a federated administrator and ensure that the various agencies have autonomy and at the same time collaborate when needed. We will discuss data sharing and database mining in Chapter 20.

Next, what data should we collect? We need to start gathering information about various people. The question is, who? Everyone in the world? This is quite impossible. Nevertheless, we need to gather information about as many people as possible, because sometimes even those who seem most innocent may have ulterior motives. One possibility is to group the individuals based on say where they come from, what they are doing, who their relatives are, etc. Some may have more suspicious backgrounds than others. If we know that someone has had a criminal record, then we need to be more vigilant about that person.

To have complete information about people, we need to gather all kinds of information about them, including information about their behavior, where they have lived, their religion and ethnic origin, their relatives and associates, their travel records, etc. When this was mentioned at a panel at the July 2002 IFIP 11.3 Conference in Cambridge, England, there were some major concerns from the audience about privacy and civil liberties, especially from prominent European human-rights lawyers. Yes, garnering such information is a violation of privacy and civil liberties. The question is, what alternative do we have? By omitting information, we may not have the complete picture. In this discussion, no sides are being taken; both points of view are represented. Therefore, Part III contains a chapter on privacy and civil liberties. From a technology point of view, we need complete data not only about individuals, but also about various events and entities. For example, suppose information is being gathered about an individual who drives a particular vehicle. This will also include information about the vehicle and how long the individual has driven, his hobbies or interests such as flying airplanes, enrollment in a flight school, and whether the individual has expressed no interest in learning about take-offs or landings, etc.

Once the data is collected, it has to be formatted and organized. Essentially, one may need to build a warehouse to analyze the data. Data may be structured or unstructured. In Chapter 21, we will discuss details on information retrieval and mining for counter-terrorism, and the need for mining unstructured data. Also, there may be data that is warehoused that may not be of much use. For example, the fact that an individual likes ice cream may not help the analysis a great deal. Therefore, we can segment the data in terms of critical data and noncritical data.

Once the data is gathered and organized, the next step is to carry out mining. The question is, what mining tools do we use and what outcomes will we find? Do we want to find associations or clusters? This will determine what the goal is. We may want to find anything that is suspicious. For example, the fact that an individual wants to learn how to fly an airplane, but is not interested in take-off or landing should raise a red flag. Once we determine the outcomes we want, we determine the mining tools to use and start the mining process.

Then comes the very hard part. How do we know that the mining results are useful? There could be false positives and false negatives. For example, the tool could incorrectly produce the result that John is planning to attack the Empire State Building on July 1, 2003. Then the law enforcement officials could go after John, and the consequences could be disastrous. The tool could also incorrectly produce the result that James is innocent, when he is in fact guilty. In this case, the law enforcement officials may not pay much attention to James. The consequence here could also be disastrous. As we

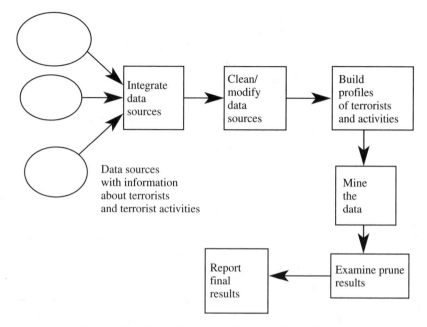

Exhibit 2.   Data Mining for Nonreal-Time Threats

have stated, we need intelligent mining tools. At present, we need the human specialists to work with the mining tools. If the tool states that John could be a terrorist, the specialist will have to do some more checking before arresting or detaining John. On the other hand, if the tool states that James is innocent, the specialist should do some more checking in this case.

Essentially, with nonreal-time threats, we have time to gather data, build profiles if necessary, analyze the data, and take actions. Now, a nonreal-time threat could become a real-time threat. That is, the data mining tool could state that there could be some potential terrorist attacks. But after a while, with some more information, the tool could state that the attacks will occur between September 10 and September 12, 2001. Then it becomes a real-time threat. The challenge will then be to find exactly what the attack will be. Will it be an attack on the World Trade Center, the Tower of London, or the Eiffel Tower? We need data mining tools that can continue with the reasoning as new information comes in. That is, as new information comes in, the warehouse needs to be updated; the mining tools should be dynamic in taking the new data and information into consideration in the mining process. Exhibit 2 illustrates data mining for nonreal-time threats.

Real-Time Threats

In the previous section, we discussed nonreal-time threats where we have time to handle the threats. In the case of real-time threats, there are timing constraints. That is, such threats may occur within a certain time and, therefore, we need to respond to them immediately. Example of such threats are the spread of smallpox virus, chemical attacks, nuclear attacks, network intrusions, bombing of a building before 9 A.M., etc. The question is, what type of data mining techniques do we need for real-time threats?

By definition, data mining works on data that has been gathered over a period of time. The goal is to analyze the data to make deductions and predict future trends. Ideally, it is used as a decision support tool. However, the real-time situation is entirely different. We need to rethink the way we do data mining so that the tools can return results in real-time.

For data mining to work effectively, we need many examples and patterns. We use known patterns and historical data to make predictions. Often, for real-time data mining and terrorist attacks, we have no prior knowledge. For example, the attack on the World Trade Center came as a surprise to many of us. As ordinary citizens, we could not have imagined that these buildings would be attacked by airplanes. Another good example is the recent sniper attacks in the Washington, D.C. area. Here again, many of us could never have imagined that the sniper would shoot from the trunk of a car. So the question is, how do we train the data mining tools, such as neural networks, without historical data? Here we need to use hypothetical data as well as simulated data. We need to work with counter-terrorism specialists and get as many examples as possible. The question is, once we gather the examples and start training the neural networks and other data mining tools, what sort of models do we build? Often the models for data mining are built beforehand. These models are not dynamic. To handle real-time threats, we need the models to change dynamically. This is a big challenge.

Data gathering is also a challenge for real-time data mining. In the case of nonreal-time data mining, we can collect data, clean data, format the data, build warehouses, and then carry out mining. All these tasks may not be possible for real-time data mining because there are time constraints. Therefore the question is, what tasks are critical and what tasks are not? Do we have time to analyze the data? Which data do we discard? How do we build profiles of terrorists for real-time data mining? We need real-time data management capabilities for real-time data mining.

From the previous discussion, it is clear that there is much to be done before we can effectively carry out real-time data mining. Some have argued that there is no such thing as real-time data mining and it will be impossible to build models in real-time. Some others have argued that without real-world examples and historical data, we cannot do effective data mining. These arguments may be true. However, our challenge perhaps is to redefine data mining and figure out ways to handle real-time threats.

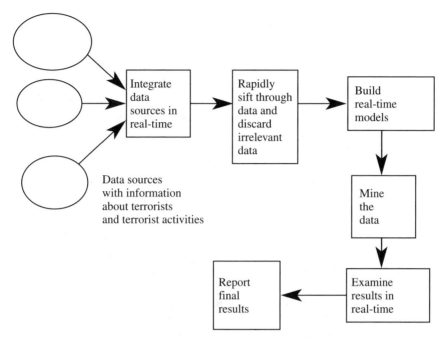

Exhibit 3. Data Mining for Real-Time Threats

As we have stated, there are several situations that have to be managed in real-time. Examples are the spread of smallpox, network intrusions, and even analyzing data emanating from sensors. For example, there are surveillance cameras placed in various locations such as at shopping centers, in front of embassies, and other public places. The data emanating from the sensors have to be analyzed in many cases in real-time to detect and prevent attacks. For example, by analyzing the data, we may find that there are some individuals at a mall carrying bombs. Then we have to alert law enforcement officials so that they can take action. This also raises the questions of privacy and civil liberties. The question is, what alternatives do we have? Should we sacrifice privacy to protect the lives of people? As we will see in Chapter 25, we need technologists, policy makers, and lawyers working together to come up with viable solutions. Exhibit 3 illustrates real-time data mining.

ANALYZING THE TECHNIQUES

As we have mentioned, applying data mining for real-time threats is a major challenge. This is because the goal of data mining is to analyze data and make predictions and trends. Current tools are not capable of making the predictions and trends in real-time, although there are some real-time data mining tools emerging (some of them have been listed in Part II). The challenge is to develop models in real-time as well as get patterns and trends based on real-world examples.

In this section, we will examine the various data mining outcomes and discuss how they could be applied for counter-terrorism. Note that the outcomes include making associations, link analysis, forming clusters, classification, and anomaly detection. The techniques that result in these outcomes are based on neural networks, decisions trees, market basket analysis, inductive logic programming, rough sets, link analysis based on the graph theory, and nearest-neighbor techniques. As we have stated in Part I, the methods used for data mining are (1) top-down reasoning, where we start with a hypothesis and determine whether the hypothesis is true, or (2) bottom-up reasoning, where we start with examples and then come up with a hypothesis.

Let us start with association techniques. An example of these techniques is market basket analysis. The goal is to find items that sell together. For example, we may apply a data mining tool to data that has been gathered, and find that John comes from country X, and he has associated with James, who has a criminal record. The tool also outputs the result that an unusually high percentage of people from country X have performed some form of terrorist attack. Because of the association between John and country X, between John and James, and between James and criminal records, one may conclude that John should be under scrutiny. This is an example of an association.

Link analysis is closely associated with making associations. While association-rule-based techniques are essentially intelligent search techniques, link analysis uses graph theoretic methods for detecting patterns. With graphs (i.e., nodes and links), one can follow the chain and find links. For example, A is seen with B, B is friends with C, C and D travel together often, and D has a criminal record. The question is, what conclusions can we draw about A? Link analysis is becoming a very important technique for detecting abnormal behavior. Therefore, we will discuss this technique in more detail in the next section.

Next, let us consider clustering techniques. One could analyze the data and form various clusters. For example, people from country X who belong to a certain religion may be grouped into cluster I. People from country Y who are less than 50 years old may form cluster II. These clusters are formed based on travel, eating, buying, or behavior patterns. While clustering does not divide the population based on specified conditions, classification does. The condition is found based on examples. For example, we can form a profile of a terrorist using the following characteristics: male, less than 30 years old, of a certain religion, and a certain ethnic origin. This means all males who match these criteria will be classified in this group and could possibly be placed under observation.

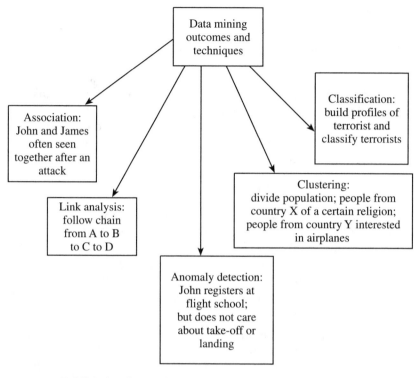

Exhibit 4. Data Mining Outcomes and Techniques for Counter-Terrorism

Another data mining outcome is anomaly detection. A good example here is learning to fly an airplane and expressing no interest in learning take-offs or landings. This is an anomaly. The general pattern is that most people want to get a complete training course in flying. Another example is John always goes to the grocery store on Saturday. But on Saturday, October 26, 2002, he goes to a firearms store and buys a rifle. This is an anomaly and may need some further analysis. Is he nervous after hearing about the sniper shootings or does he have some other motive? If he is living in the Washington, D.C. area, we can understand why he wants to buy a firearm; but if he is living in say Socorro, New Mexico, then his actions may have to be scrutinized further.

As we have stated, all of the discussions on data mining for counter-terrorism have consequences when it comes to privacy and civil liberties. As we have mentioned repeatedly, what are the alternatives? How can we carry out data mining and at the same time preserve privacy? Some of our ideas are discussed in Chapter 25. Exhibit 4 illustrates data mining outcomes and techniques for counter-terrorism.

LINK ANALYSIS

In this section, we discuss a particular data mining technique that is especially useful for detecting abnormal patterns. This technique is link analysis. There have been many discussions in the literature on link analysis. In fact, one of the earlier books on data mining discussed link analysis in some detail [BERR97]. As mentioned in the previous section, link analysis uses various graph theoretic techniques. It is essentially about analyzing graphs. Note that link analysis is also used in Web data mining, especially for Web structure mining. With Web structure mining, the idea is to mine the links to extract Web patterns and structures. As we have mentioned in Part II, search engines such as Google use some form of link analysis for displaying the results of a search.

As mentioned in [BERR97], the challenge in link analysis is to reduce the graphs into manageable chunks. As in the case of market basket analysis, where one needs to carry out intelligent searching by pruning unwanted results, in link analysis one needs to reduce the graphs so that the analysis is manageable and not combinatorially explosive. Therefore, results in graph reduction need to be applied for the graphs that are obtained by representing the various associations.

Exhibit 5 illustrates a scenario where a graph is reduced to a smaller graph. In this example, we assume that the interesting associations are between A and D as well as between A and F. Therefore, one can eliminate the associations between the nodes. The challenge here is to find the interesting associations and then determine how to reduce the graphs. Various graphs theoreticians are working on graph reduction problems. We need to determine how to apply the techniques to detect abnormal and suspicious behavior.*

Another challenge in using link analysis for counter-terrorism is reasoning with partial information. For example, agencies A, B, and C may each have a partial graph. The question is, how do we find the associations between the graphs when no agency has the complete picture? One would argue that we need a data miner that would reason under uncertainty and figure out the links between the three graphs. This would be the ideal solution, and the research challenge is to develop such a data miner. The other approach is to have an umbrella organization over the three agencies that will have access to the three graphs. One can think of this organization as the Department of Homeland Security. In the ensuing chapters, we will dis-

---

* The importance of link analysis for counter-terrorism was pointed out to us by Dr. Rick Steinheiser back in 1996. As mentioned earlier, DARPA's EELD program is conducting research on this topic. Also, Ted Senator, program manager for EELD, has made some very interesting presentations on this topic. He says that connecting all dots in the graph is the challenge. He also states that "finding the needle in the haystack" is not the issue here. He says that the problem is much harder. The challenge is to "find the suspicious needle among millions of needles."

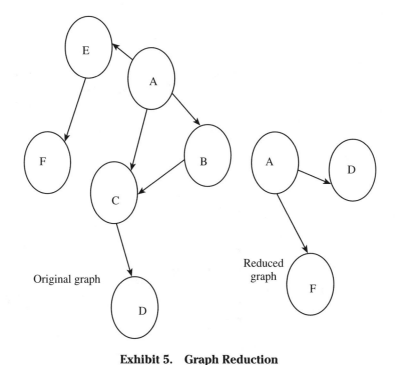

Exhibit 5.   Graph Reduction

cuss various federated architectures for counter-terrorism. Exhibit 6 illustrates the scenario of connecting partial graphs.

We need to conduct extensive research on link analysis as well as on other data and Web mining techniques to determine how they can be applied effectively for counter-terrorism. For example, by following the various links, one could perhaps trace the financing of terrorist operations to the president of country X. Another challenge with link analysis as well with other data mining techniques is having good data. However, much of the data could be classified for the domain that we are considering. If we truly are to get the benefits of the techniques, we need to test with actual data. But not all of the researchers have the clearances to work on classified data. The challenge is to find unclassified data that is a representative sample of the classified data. It is not straightforward to do this, as one has to make sure that all classified information, even through implication, is removed. Another alternative is to find as much good data as possible in an unclassified setting for the researchers to work on. However, the researchers have to work not only with counter-terrorism experts, but also with data mining specialists who have the clearances to work in classified environments. That is, the research carried out in an unclassified setting has to be transferred to a classified setting later to test the applicability of the data mining algorithms. Only then can we get the true benefits of data mining.

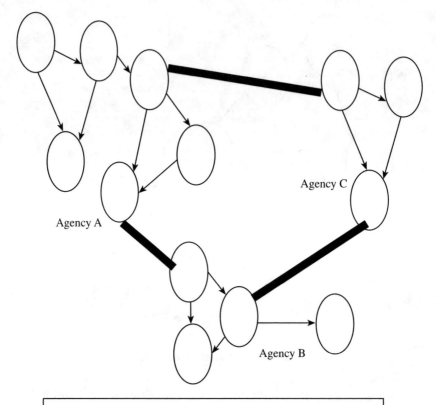

Either a data miner automatically connects the nodes
or a federated administrator combines the graphs, carries out
mining, and connects the nodes. Connections are shown by
darkened lines.

Exhibit 6.   Connecting the Graphs

SUMMARY

This chapter has provided a rather broad overview of data mining for counter-terrorism. As we have stated, we have used the terms *data mining* and *Web mining* interchangeably. Again, we can expect much of the data to be on the Web, whether on the Internet or on corporate intranets. Therefore, mining the data sources and databases on the Web to detect and prevent terrorist attacks will become a necessity. These could be public or private databases.

First we discussed data mining for nonreal-time threats. The idea is to gather data, build profiles, learn from examples, and detect as well as prevent attacks. The challenge is to find real-world examples as in many cases a particular attack has not happened before. Next, we discussed real-time data mining. The challenge is to build models in real-time. Finally, we discussed data mining outcomes and techniques as well as link analysis for counter-terrorism.

Essentially, we have introduced data mining for counter-terrorism. In summary, data mining may be applied to gather business intelligence. Business intelligence analysis may be used to combat terrorism. In the next few chapters, we will take each technology discussed in Part II and show how it can be applied for counter-terrorism. As we have stated, we are not counter-terrorism experts. Our discussions on counter-terrorism are based on various newspaper articles and documentaries. Our goal is to explore how data mining can be exploited for counter-terrorism. We want to raise the awareness that data mining could possibly help detect and prevent terrorist attacks. Again, this is a new area. Much research needs to be done. We hope that this book will encourage interesting ideas so that researchers and practitioners start or continue to work on data mining and apply the techniques for counter-terrorism.

Chapter 20
Mining Web Databases for Counter-Terrorism

INTRODUCTION

The previous chapter introduced the notion of data mining for counter-terrorism. As we have stated, we are not saying that data mining and Web data mining are going to solve all the problems. Nevertheless, data mining is intended to often previously unknown extract patterns and trends. This capability is important for detecting and preventing acts of terrorism. The challenge is to develop good data mining tools for this purpose.

As we have stated in previous chapters, there are data mining tools that extract patterns. But the question is, are these patterns useful? We still need human analysts to analyze the patterns and determine which ones are useful and which ones are spurious. Data mining tools could give out false positives and false negatives. This could be quite dangerous, especially for counter-terrorism, business intelligence, financial applications, and medical applications; giving out false negatives and false positives could cause disastrous effects if the advice is followed by an organization or by an analyst. Therefore, we need to develop tools that extract only useful patterns and trends.

While Chapter 19 provided an overview of data mining for real-time threats and nonreal-time threats, in this chapter we will discuss the use of mining databases on the Web for counter-terrorism. Again, we have stated that it is likely that much of the data will eventually be on the Web, whether on the Internet or on private intranets. Therefore, we need to develop techniques that mine not only databases, but also databases on the Web.

We will focus on mining various aspects of Web databases. Essentially, we will discuss the technologies we spoke about in Chapters 5 and 11 to see how they can be applied for counter-terrorism. One major concern for us is data sharing for data mining. For data mining, we need to have complete and accurate data. This means that organizations should be willing to share data. We will also discuss distributed data mining and federated data mining for counter-terrorism.

Note that all of the technologies will be analyzed for counter-terrorism. That is, while these technologies themselves were discussed in Chapter 11, their applications to counter-terrorism will be the main focus here. As we have stated, we are not counter-terrorism experts. All of the information on counter-terrorism has been provided from newspaper articles and documentaries. Our goal is to raise awareness of what data mining and Web data mining could do for counter-terrorism.

WEB DATABASE MINING

In this section, we will discuss Web database mining applications for counter-terrorism.

Data Sharing and Data Mining

One of the main goals of a database management system is to enable users to share the data. Data sharing is key to database management. One of the functions of the database management system is to ensure that the integrity of the data is maintained so that user has access to complete and accurate data. Various access control rules may be enforced to ensure that the user accesses only the data to which he is authorized.

One of the organizational challenges in maintaining databases is to determine which data to share with others. If the database is centralized, then it may be partitioned, i.e., different partitions managed by different managers for different purposes. For example, one partition could be used for travel data, another partition could be used to manage data pertaining to airplanes. If the data is distributed, then each database in the distributed environment may be managed by a different manager. If the databases are heterogeneous, then different agencies may be managing the different databases. We will revisit distributed databases as well as heterogeneous and federated databases in a later section.

As we have stated, with data mining we need to ensure that the data is accurate and complete. Otherwise, we may not be able to find useful patterns. Note that especially for counter-terrorism applications, the key is to make links and associations. For example, if there is a sniper shooting in Alabama and another in Maryland, we want the data mining tool to automatically make the links between the two states. For the data mining tool to make the links, both states have to share databases. We are not saying that by just sharing databases the data mining tools will make the links. However, without sharing, the analyst in Maryland will not know that similar shootings have occurred in Alabama unless he reviews every shooting occurring every minute throughout the world. In a way, the ideal solution is for the mining tool to reason with incomplete information about the data in another organization. We discussed link analysis and reasoning under incompleteness in Chapter 19. This is one of the biggest challenges in data mining for counter-terrorism. Another alternative is to have a brokering or managing organization to ensure that the various agencies collaborate and share information. This managing organization could be the Department of Homeland Security.

Let us consider another example. Suppose various states are maintaining data about individuals enrolled in flight schools. The databases in Minnesota will have to be shared with the databases in other states to get the full picture. Then one could make associations between the data in different databases and make predictions.

One solution to the data sharing problem is to have a centralized database managed by a central database management system. We have heard of all the problems with having central databases. Some of the issues are discussed in our previous book [THUR97]. Both for technical and political reasons, it may be impossible to manage a very large central database. Furthermore, data may be managed by state officials especially to make quick decisions. If they have to get permission from a central administrator, it may not be expedient. However, in some other cases we may need to have central databases. The state and federal chief information officers have to determine which databases to centralize and which ones to distribute.

Whether we have centralized databases or distributed databases, we need policies and procedures to determine which data to share under what conditions. Under emergency situations, we may need to share all of the data. The question is, when do we decide there is an emergency situation? Perhaps data mining could be used to determine that there are missing pieces and that more information is needed. Consider the sniper example. Suppose the data mining tool is applied to all of the data gathered in the Washington, D.C. area. This tool may not come up with any useful patterns. It can then pose a query about similar shootings. Based on the answers received, it could perhaps make the links. If the tool does not make the links, then humans have to work together and grant permission to the tool to access the databases in other states. Therefore, technologists, policy makers, law enforcement officials, possibly lawyers, and government officials have to work together to share data so that the data mining tools can make the links.

We have often heard it said that the attacks of September 11, 2001, could have been prevented if all the data had been available. Some have argued that even if the data had been there, it would have been very difficult to make the connection between flight training, ethnic origin, one-way airline tickets, and other unusual patterns. We are not saying that link analysis

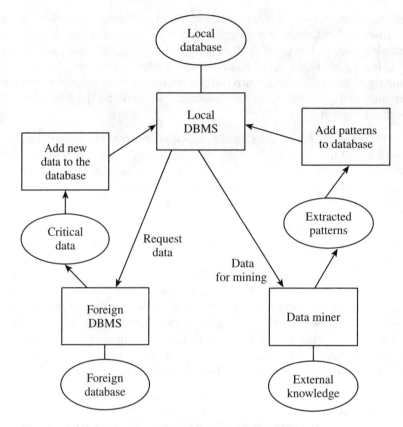

Exhibit 1.   Data Sharing and Data Mining

would have found the answers. But perhaps link analysis may have made people aware that something unusual was happening. In any case, we cannot make any judgments because much of the information may be classified. Nevertheless, we should invest in technologies such as database management and data sharing so that it would be less difficult to make links and associations.

Another challenge is for data to be current. That is, as new data is generated, it has to be taken into consideration for analysis. The same is true as new patterns are detected. Exhibit 1 illustrates some of the ideas that we have discussed in this section.

Web Database Functions, Data Mining, and Counter-Terrorism

In this section, we will examine some Web database functions and data mining to see how they can be applied for counter-terrorism. Consider query processing. One of the options is to integrate a query processor with the data mining tool. Essentially, we have an intelligent query processor, which poses queries if it finds that there is insufficient data to mine and extract patterns.

Consider, for example, information about flight schools. The query processor may not be able to figure out what is going on based solely on information in Minnesota. It will ask questions such as, "can you give me information about other fight schools?" Then the query processor will compare the data in various databases, looking for certain patterns, such as individuals who are learning to fly but are not interested in take-offs and landings. Now, some people may legitimately want experienced pilots to handle those tasks for them; they may just want to fly the airplane for the thrill of it. So how does the data mining tool differentiate between those who have ulterior motives and those who just want to experience the excitement of flying an airplane? Perhaps the query processor may ask some questions about the individuals. What are their hobbies? What are their travel patterns? Why are they making frequent trips to another country? What are the other characteristics that may seem unusual? Essentially, an intelligent query processor has to reason with the information it has, decide what it wants, and ask these questions. We will address this topic again when we discuss question answering in Chapter 21.

Let us consider transaction management. A data miner has to examine the various transactions and, in this case, Web transactions, to determine any suspicious behavior. For example, the data miner may analyze the transaction logs and determine what kinds of financial transactions have taken place. It may also analyze the transactions in real-time. As we have stated in the previous chapter, real-time data mining is a challenge. We will revisit this in Chapter 22.

There have been some recent discussions about a possible plan to analyze purchase transactions to determine suspicious behavior. There are, of course, privacy considerations. However, as we have stressed, unless we have the complete picture, we cannot expect the data mining tool to find useful results. The challenge is to carry out privacy-sensitive and privacy-enhanced data mining. We will revisit this point in another chapter.

Other database functions include metadata management and storage management. Because metadata is an important aspect, we will discuss it in a later section. Storage management is also key for data mining. For example, how do we structure and organize the database? Again, our application here is counter-terrorism. We need to analyze such things as frequently posed queries and then develop appropriate indices.

In this section, we have examined database functions and data mining and analyzed their applications for counter-terrorism. Effective database management and data mining are key to finding patterns and trends. Find-

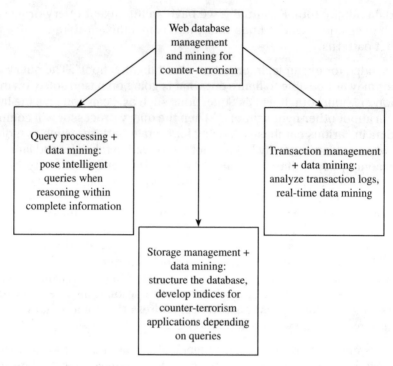

Exhibit 2. Web Database Management, Mining, and Counter-Terrorism

ing patterns and trends is important for counter-terrorism. Therefore, this is an area that needs a lot of attention. We need to start using the tools to determine their inadequacies. We need to start or redirect some of the research programs so that we can develop longer-term solutions to the problem. Essentially, we need a multipronged approach. We need to focus on near-term solutions as to what we can do today, what we can do next year, and what we can do in five years. Note that various Web mining tools have emerged, and we have listed them in Part II. We have heard the claim that some of these tools can be used for counter-terrorism. We need to carry out a very objective analysis of the tools to decide whether this is indeed the case. If these tools can be used today, can they solve all our problems? What other problems need attention? There are many challenging opportunities for those working in data management and data mining.

Exhibit 2 illustrates some of the essential points we have discussed in this section. It should be noted that much of our discussions and examples focus on noninformation-related terrorism. We are doing this to illustrate the key points. Many of our arguments also apply for other attacks such as intrusion detection, bio-terrorism, and critical infrastructure attacks. We will use examples from these attacks as needed in future sections and chapters.

SEMISTRUCTURED DATABASE MINING

The previous section focused on general Web database management, mining, and counter-terrorism. In this section, we will examine semistructured data mining from a counter-terrorism viewpoint. The main issue here is that much of the data on the Web will be unstructured or semistructured, such as video, audio, and text. For example, there are many newspaper articles that have to be analyzed for counter-terrorism applications. Many of the news clips are in the form of text, audio, and video. Therefore, one needs to mine the documents to extract patterns and trends.

Essentially, what we have discussed in the previous section applies here. But mining semistructured and unstructured data is as important as mining structured data. For example, many of the government databases appear to be structured. But these databases now have to be integrated with newspaper articles, video clips, and audio clips. Then the integrated databases have to be mined to extract patterns.

We illustrate the point with an example. Suppose a hospital has information in structured databases about patients, symptoms, and diagnoses. Then there is some news in the form of text and video about a smallpox breakout. The hospital has to link the breaking news with the structured databases it maintains on patients to rapidly determine if any of its patients may have contracted smallpox. Note that one could contract smallpox through terror attacks or normal means. But the disease is deadly and therefore appropriate actions have to be taken.

We will revisit mining text, images, audio, and video data when we discuss information retrieval, Web mining, and counter-terrorism in Chapter 21. Closely related to this topic is mining XML databases. As we have stated, XML is becoming the standard document representation language on the Web. Special extensions to XML have been proposed for various applications including medical, financial, and various command-and-control applications. These XML documents have to be mined to obtain patterns and links. For example, information about flight training and travel patterns may be in the form of XML documents. These documents have to be mined and links have to be analyzed. Exhibit 3 illustrates the key points we have discussed in this section.

METADATA MINING

As we have discussed in Part II, metadata has two roles when it comes to mining. One is that the metadata can be used to give guidance to the data miner. The other is that metadata itself could be mined to extract useful patterns and trends. We examine both for counter-terrorism.

Consider, for example, certain integrity constraints, such as "John and James never travel together," or "John has never traveled outside of the

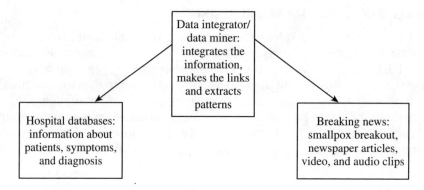

Exhibit 3. Mining Semistructured Databases

United States." This metadata information can be used to guide the mining processes. For example, from the metadata we know that John has not traveled outside of the United States. Then we may not request the information "what countries has John visited?" Another example is the following metadata: database A has information about flight training and database B has information about smallpox vaccines. Then the data miner does not query database A to get information about smallpox vaccines.

In many ways, mining the metadata is like mining the data. That is, essentially we mine the information about the data to give us some patterns and trends in addition to mining the data itself. Consider, for example, the metadata that has information "database A contains information about those vaccinated with smallpox vaccine between September 20 and September 30, 2002." Using this information, the data miner could infer that perhaps a smallpox outbreak has occurred. Then it can do some further mining on the data itself as to where and when the outbreak occurred.

We have given a brief discussion of metadata mining for counter-terrorism. This is mainly because metadata mining is still not a mature area, and it is only recently that we are having discussions about applying data mining for counter-terrorism. We need to do a lot of investigation to identify the issues and challenges. Exhibit 4 illustrates our discussion on metadata mining.

WAREHOUSE MINING

In this section, we will examine data warehousing and mining technologies to see how they can be applied for counter-terrorism. As we have stated in Chapters 5 and 11, warehousing is a key technology to integrate diverse and disparate data sources for decision making. That is, rather than integrating the heterogeneous data sources as we may not need all of the data, we bring essential data into the warehouse. Once the data is

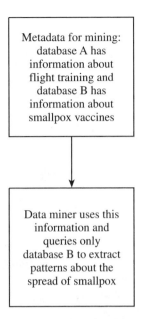

Exhibit 4.   Metadata Mining

brought into the warehouse, we can make associations and links. This is especially useful for counter-terrorism applications, and we will illustrate with examples.

Consider data sources that have information about travel patterns, flight training records, previous police records, ethnic origins, and religious beliefs of various individuals. There may be some data that may not be relevant for counter-terrorism applications. An example is the fact that the flight training school has two toilets. This is fairly obvious, as one could expect one toilet for men and one for women. One may not want to bring this information into the warehouse. Once the relevant information is brought into the warehouse, then one can make correlations and links such as those who have enrolled in flight training schools have traveled often to Germany. One could also build another warehouse with information about smallpox vaccines, biological data, hospital information, and other related medical information. One could analyze the information in both warehouses and come to the conclusion that those who have enrolled in flight training schools have traveled often to Germany and have also purchased many books on the spread of smallpox.

Essentially, warehousing technology is critical to assimilate diverse information and make correlations and links. That is, data management, data warehousing, and data mining are all important technologies for counter-terrorism. Furthermore, many of these systems have to operate on

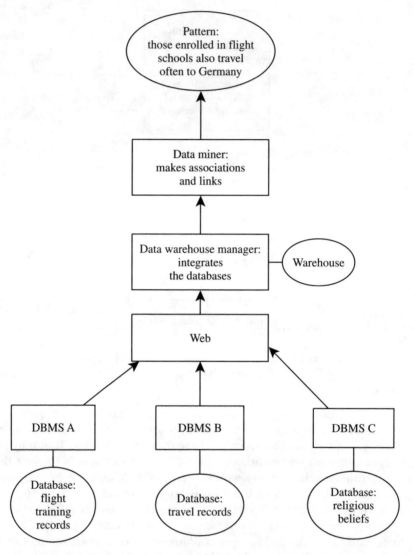

Exhibit 5.   Warehousing for Counter-Terrorism

the Web. Therefore, we need to consider Web database management, Web data warehousing, and Web mining for counter-terrorism. Exhibit 5 illustrates our discussion about data warehousing.

DISTRIBUTED AND HETEROGENEOUS DATABASE MINING

We briefly discussed mining distributed databases in an earlier section. One of the decisions that an agency has to make is whether to make its

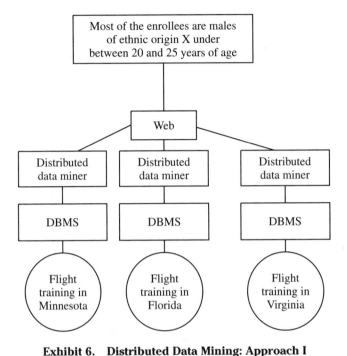

Exhibit 6.   Distributed Data Mining: Approach I

database centralized or distributed. We have discussed the pros and cons of each approach in our previous book [THUR97], as well as in this chapter. In this section, we assume that the databases are distributed and discuss mining for counter-terrorism.

As we have mentioned in [THUR97], one may distribute the database due to the fact that it is cumbersome to maintain a single database. For example, consider a law enforcement agency such as the FBI. The FBI may maintain a very large distributed database, perhaps one component in each state to make it more manageable. These distributed databases have to be tightly integrated so that the information is available to anyone, any time, and at any place. Because it is one agency, we can assume that there is 100 percent data sharing, although there may be some special rules enforced in each state. If data is shared and there is no special rule, then we can use distributed data mining to extract patterns and trends. This is illustrated in Exhibits 6 and 7. We assume that each state maintains a database about flight training records and travel patterns of people in its state, and the distributed data miner can extract patterns and trends. Note that while Exhibit 6 illustrates a truly distributed data mining approach, Exhibit 7 illustrates an approach where we integrate the data first and then carry out mining.

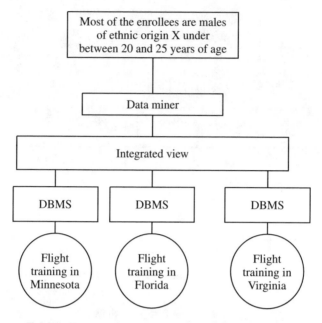

Exhibit 7.   Distributed Data Mining: Approach II

Next, let us consider heterogeneous databases. Different agencies have different databases, often heterogeneous in nature. These databases have to be integrated and mined to extract information. We discussed many of the challenges in integrating heterogeneous databases in [THUR97]. Mining heterogeneous databases was discussed in [THUR98]. We briefly discussed some of the challenges in Chapters 5 and 11. We illustrate heterogeneous database mining for counter-terrorism in Exhibit 8. Here we assume that the databases are first integrated and mined. Note that the other approach is to mine the individual databases and then integrate the results, as illustrated in Exhibit 9. Mining legacy databases is also a challenge. For example, data that is in a legacy database may be 20 years old but may be still quite relevant. Typical examples are immigration and law enforcement databases. These databases may have valuable information. The questions are, do we migrate the databases and then mine or do we mine the data in the legacy databases? Some of these issues were discussed in [THUR98]. The same issues apply for counter-terrorism.

One other technology of much interest for inter-agency data sharing and mining is federated data mining. We introduced this term in Chapter 11. Various organizations have to share data and form federations. They may negotiate which data to share with one another and export to the federation. They may make trade-offs. Federated data mining for counter-terrorism is illustrated in Exhibits 10 and 11. In the first approach, we

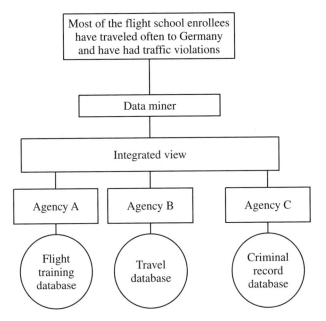

Exhibit 8.   Data Mining on Heterogeneous Data Sources: Approach I

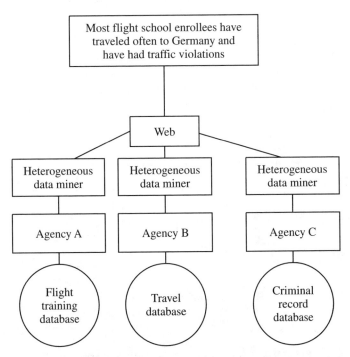

Exhibit 9.   Data Mining on Heterogeneous Data Sources: Approach II

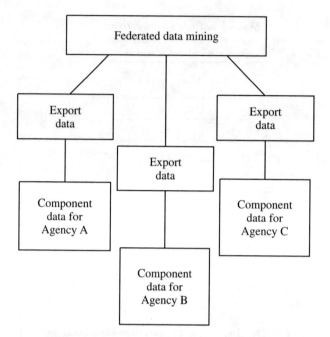

Exhibit 10.   Federated Data Mining: Approach I

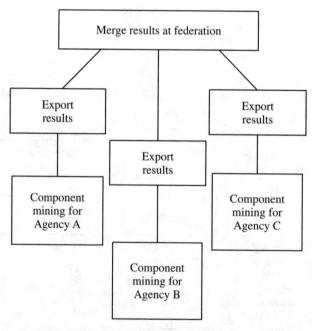

Exhibit 11.   Federated Data Mining: Approach II

export the data and then mine, and in the second approach we mine the data and then export the results. Note that we have briefly discussed the issues and challenges; much research is still needed. In addition, we need policy makers, technologists, and government officials to work together to make federated data mining a success. Ultimately, we believe that this is where the answer lies. It will be very difficult to share all of the data, especially in view of the issues of privacy, civil liberties, and the sensitive nature of the data. Therefore, agencies will have to negotiate and make trade-offs. One can perhaps think of the Department of Homeland Security as functioning at the federation level. Federated data mining could be carried out at the federation level while component data mining, such as data mining at the CIA and the FBI, could be carried out at the component level. Note that these are just our ideas and not the policies of the United States government.

OTHER ASPECTS

In this section, we discuss the push/pull architecture we discussed in Chapter 11. One of the challenges is what and when to push and pull. Consider, for example, information about sniper attacks. When an attack occurs in one state, should the data management system push information to data management systems in other states? On the other hand, when a sniper attack occurs in one state, should it pull information from other states? Both are useful models, and perhaps we need to do a combination of the two approaches. Similarly, for the spread of smallpox, should hospitals notify other hospitals immediately and push the information, or should a hospital pull the information as needed?

The answers to these questions depend on the urgency of the matter. In the case of smallpox, one could argue that because the spread could be deadly, we may want to push the information. Even in the case of the sniper attacks, we may want to push the information to prevent further attacks. Perhaps in the case of flight training data, we may want to pull the information if it is deemed that there are no real-time constraints.

The question is, what does mining have to do with the push/pull models? In Chapter 11, we discussed how mining may be integrated into the architecture. For example, one may want to mine first and then decide what to push or pull. That is, data mining may detect patterns and trends and, if urgent, could send out alerts that it is time to push or pull the data. Exhibit 12 illustrates data mining and push/pull architectures for counter-terrorism.

SUMMARY

This chapter has provided an overview of Web database mining for counter-terrorism. We started with a discussion of data sharing and data

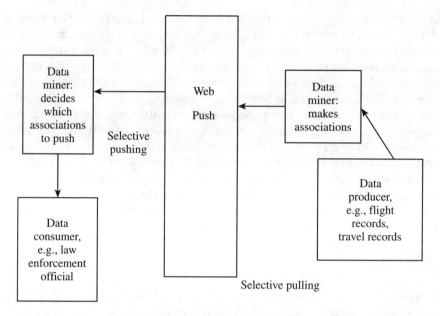

Exhibit 12.   Push/Pull Architectures

mining and then showed how the functions of a Web database miner could help handle attacks. Then we discussed semistructured data mining, meta-data mining, and data warehousing aspects as well as distributed and heterogeneous database mining, with a focus on counter-terrorism.

While Chapter 19 focused on Web data mining for counter-terrorism in general, this chapter has focused on database mining aspects. The next few chapters will examine information retrieval and data mining as well as information management and data mining for counter-terrorism. As we have mentioned, our goals are to raise awareness of the potential uses of data mining for counter-terrorism and to examine the technologies that we have discussed so far to determine how they could be applied to prevent and detect attacks.

Chapter 21
Information Retrieval and Web Mining for Counter-Terrorism

INTRODUCTION

Chapter 6 discussed information retrieval. Essentially, we provided an overview of text, image, video, and multimedia information retrieval. In Chapter 12, we examined information retrieval systems and discussed the impact of Web mining. Chapter 12 also provided an overview of search engines and Web mining. We then provided an overview of text, image, audio, video, and multimedia data mining. In this chapter, we will discuss the applications of information retrieval and Web mining for counter-terrorism.

As we have stated in earlier chapters, there is a lot of data on the Web that is unstructured. That is, much of the data on the Web is not in relational databases. The Web has newspaper articles, images, speeches, and video clips. These different data types have to be mined to extract patterns and trends. Furthermore, the search engines are incorporating mining capabilities. Searching and mining on the Web or otherwise is becoming very important for counter-terrorism applications. For example, there are many newspaper articles reporting on various associations, attacks, biographical information, events, and other activities. There are also images on the Web of presidents, terrorists, and government officials as well as video files of various people. This data has to be mined so that attacks can be detected and prevented. Search engines are also very useful. For example, if a sniper attack occurs in Maryland, the search engine should also search databases in other states to determine if similar shootings have occurred.

This chapter will explore information retrieval and Web mining for counter-terrorism. As we have stressed throughout this book, we are not claiming that multimedia data mining and intelligent search engines will solve the counter-terrorism problem. Our goal is to explore the use of these technologies and raise awareness of the potential applications of data mining for counter-terrorism.

EXPLOITING AND USING INTELLIGENT SEARCH ENGINES

In Chapter 12, we discussed incorporating data mining into search engines. Search engines are an essential part of searching and retrieving information on the Web. Note that many of the agencies have internal Webs or intranets; these intranets also need some form of search engines.

We will illustrate the use of search engines with examples. Suppose a patient arrives in a hospital in Kansas with smallpox-like symptoms. The medical staff has to take some immediate actions. First of all, the staff has to know the exact symptoms of smallpox. Because smallpox is a rare disease, some of the staff may not be experienced. The Web and various medical library resources will be useful. Next, the staff must alert other hospitals. They have to notify everyone with whom the patient has come into contact. The Web facilitates such alerts. They have to search the Web or other sources to see if there is information about similar occurrences elsewhere, and take various actions based on this information.

A data mining system incorporated with a search engine could perform all of these tasks automatically. We are not saying that there are such data mining tools in existence today. But such tools will have to be developed. We will revisit this topic again when we discuss semantic Web mining for counter-terrorism.

Another example is the recent sniper attacks. Suppose there are sniper shootings in Maryland and similar shootings have occurred in Alabama. Then the search engine should search the Web to determine that similar shootings have occurred in both Mayland and in Alabama. The ultimate goal of data mining is to carry out intelligent searching without the human in the loop. That is, as soon as the shooting occurs in Maryland, the tool should automatically search the Web to see if there are similar occurrences. Currently, many of the data mining tools need human assistance and prompting to ask the right questions.

A third example is managing flight training records. If someone suspicious in Minnesota expresses an interest in learning to fly but not in take-offs or landings, the data mining tool should search the Web to see if there are similar occurrences. Here, the Web could be the Internet or the intranets maintained by flight schools that are linked.

Searching is used not just to detect potential attacks, but also used for handling first and emergency responses. For example, suppose there is an attack on a building. Then the system should search to find out about similar attacks that have occurred and what emergency response measures were taken. While there may have been prior discussions on emergency responses during emergency preparedness, the actual situation may be quite different from what would have been anticipated. Therefore, any information on what actions to take would be useful. Similarly, hospitals should be prepared for bio-terrorism attacks. However, when the actual attacks occur, there may be some unexpected situations. Searching the Web and getting information about actions to take based on lessons learned would be most helpful.

Today, search engines have become an integral part of our lives. If we want to find information about current affairs, spread of diseases, world news, and information about public figures, we turn immediately to the Web, whereas ten years ago we would very likely go to the library. However, that has changed quite a bit now as much of the information is now available on the Web. We need to exploit these search engines and integrate them with the data mining tools so that an analyst can get the right information at the right time. We also need filters for irrelevant information so that the analyst is not burdened with too much information. The task of the analyst is very difficult, especially in life-or-death situations. We need to develop effective search and analysis tools to detect and prevent terrorist attacks.

We have briefly discussed how the technologies described in Chapter 12 can be applied for counter-terrorism. Exhibit 1 illustrates some of our discussion on search engines for counter-terrorism. It should be noted that the Web and search engines could also be exploited by the terrorist. That

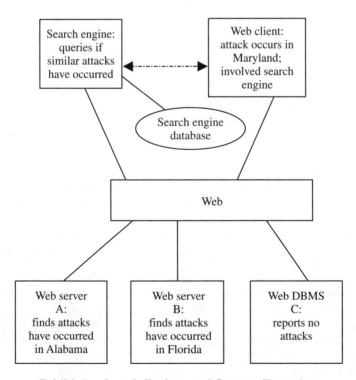

Exhibit 1. Search Engines and Counter-Terrorism

is, the terrorist could carry out searches about buildings, hospitals, and people to plot their terror attacks. There are conflicts here. The more technology we develop, the better it will be to combat terrorism; however, the very technology we develop may go into the wrong hands. This is why there are discussions about whether to publish critical research in areas such as microbiology and bacteriology. We do not want the information to get into the wrong hands. But at the same time, we need the information to combat terrorism. We can expect much debate about making technical information public. We need policymakers, lawyers, and technologists to work together.

APPLYING MULTIMEDIA DATA MINING

In this section, we discuss how multimedia data mining could be applied for counter-terrorism. In particular, we will discuss text, image, audio, and video mining. Note that these technologies were discussed in Chapter 12. Therefore, we will not elaborate on these technologies. We will focus on how they may be applied for counter-terrorism.

Text Mining

Text is everywhere, in the form of newspapers, books, news briefs, reports, transcripts, etc. Text is not just in English but can be in any of the hundreds of languages in the world. As we have stated, we need the complete picture to carry out data mining. Therefore, we need to have all the text data in front of us to carry out useful mining. For example, one part of text may be in English and another in French. We may need both French and English text for mining. The question is, do we translate French into English and carry out mining? Or do we mine the data in French and then integrate with the results from mining the English text? This is called multilingual data mining.

Another aspect of text mining is mining e-mail messages. Many e-mail messages are in text form. There is a lot of hidden information that could possibly be extracted from e-mail and chat room communication. We need to effectively mine this information. However, this raises privacy concerns as e-mail messages are often considered private. In any case, certain countries have made it legal for corporations to analyze employees' e-mail messages. This is not the last we will hear about this topic.

Preventing children from accessing inappropriate material on the Internet, such as pornographic material, is also a concern. While much of this information is in the form of images and video, there is also text in pornography. Recently, the National Academy of Sciences convened a panel headed by former Attorney General, the Honorable Richard Thornburgh. I gave some presentations to this panel in July 2000 on how data mining could be used to detect pornographic content and eventually this technol-

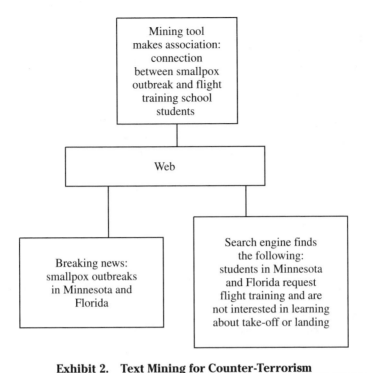

Exhibit 2. Text Mining for Counter-Terrorism

ogy could perhaps be used to protect children from accessing such information on the Internet.

Exhibits 2 through 5 illustrate text mining that we have discussed. In Exhibit 2, we show the various pieces of text that may be relevant in making the connection. Exhibits 3 through 5 illustrate three approaches for multilingual text mining. As we have stated in Chapter 12, one option for text mining is to extract keywords and then mine the keywords. Another option is to mine the text directly. As we have mentioned, the details of text mining were given in Chapter 12. Our goal here is to examine text mining and see how it can be applied to counter-terrorism. Essentially, it is about reading a piece of news and making the link between this piece and another that may have been reported months ago. For example, consider a smallpox outbreak in 2004. One could read the details and also find that a similar outbreak occurred in 1914. Then the two cases can be analyzed and causes can be determined.

Image Mining

In this section, we will examine how image mining may be applied for counter-terrorism. There is an increasing amount of images on the Web of people, buildings, maps, and fingerprints. Law enforcement agencies are

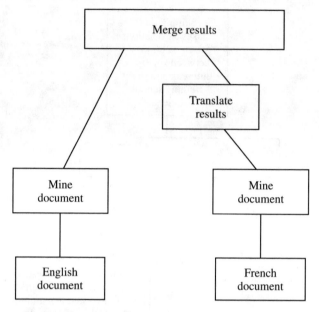

Exhibit 3.   Multilingual Data Mining: Approach I

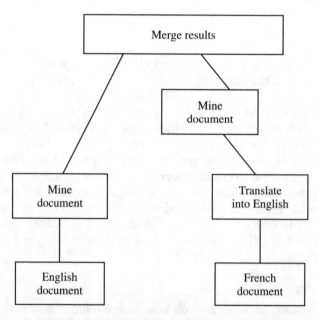

Exhibit 4.   Multilingual Data Mining: Approach II

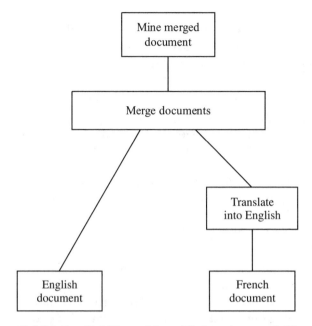

Exhibit 5. Multilingual Data Mining: Approach III

examining fingerprint images to catch criminals. For example, the Immigration and Naturalization Service (INS) has fingerprints of all immigrants. Suppose fingerprints are taken at a crime scene and these prints are then matched with what the INS has on file. Law enforcement agencies may find exact or approximate matches and, as a result, get the names of the criminals. The challenge here is to match the images rapidly.

Facial recognition techniques are being developed for recognizing faces and features. These techniques are being investigated for possible utilization at airports and other security checkpoints. For example, these techniques may be quite useful at INS checkpoints and borders. While some of this image analysis is not exactly image mining, one could incorporate image mining so that unusual patterns can be detected.

A good example of image mining is detecting unusual patterns from aerial images. This was discussed in Chapter 12 and is especially useful for counter-terrorism activities. For example, one could analyze images over certain regions to determine whether any suspicious activities such as nuclear tests are being conducted. One could also detect new construction in image analysis. For example, if one detects the construction of a building in the middle of a desert, this could be analyzed further for suspicious behavior.

Image analysis is also important for protecting children from pornography on the Internet. There are lots of images on the Internet that are inappropriate for children. One needs to carry out image mining and analysis to detect such images. Filters have to be developed to discard these images before displaying the content to children.

Another area related to images and image mining is steganography. The idea is to hide sensitive information in the images. This information is not seen by those watching the images. One uses a combination of encryption techniques to decode and extract the sensitive information from the images. As an example, a terrorist leader could post videos and images on various Web sites. These images and videos may contain information about potential terrorist plans. Only those who belong to the terrorist ring will be able to decode and extract the sensitive information. The challenge for counter-terrorism specialists is to be able to develop techniques to break the code.

We have provided a brief overview of how image mining and image analysis could help toward counter-terrorism. The challenge is rapid searching of images as well as analysis for unusual patterns and anomalies. Exhibit 6 illustrates some of our discussion on image mining for counter-terrorism.

Video Mining

While there is some work being done on text mining and to a lesser extent on image mining, video mining is still in its infancy. One option is to extract and mine metadata and text from video. One could also extract images from video and mine the image data. As we have mentioned in Chapter 12, the challenge is to mine video data directly.

The question is, how does mining video data help counter-terrorism? One is that certain terrorists may release videos frequently of their activities. While the video data released by terrorists may not contain much information about hidden patterns and trends, it will still be useful to analyze and perhaps mine the video data to see what patterns can be detected. For example, who is seen with whom in the video? Are there people in the video who may be well known (i.e., notorious) and worth investigating? There could also be hidden information in the video. The challenge for counter-terrorism specialists is to decode and extract the hidden information. This area is called steganography and was discussed under image mining.

One could also mine video clips of presidential visits, films, documentaries, and other similar video data to extract often previously unknown information. For example, President X may be seen frequently with Jane Doe in video clips, a fact that may not have been obvious at a casual glance. That is, some analysis of the video clips is needed to make such observa-

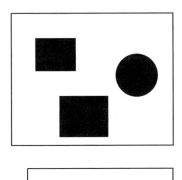

Images

Image miner

Filtered images
to protect children
from violent material

Exhibit 6. Image Mining for Preventing Violence

tions. Then one needs to determine the reasons for such an association. If Jane Doe is under suspicion for drug abuse, then one may also need to investigate President X.

Video mining is also needed to detect pornographic and X-rated video data on the Internet so that it is not accessed by children. We have heard of cases where children have watched violence and sex on the Internet and have gone on to commit crimes such as school shootings. This is also a form of terrorism.

Essentially, like text and image mining, video mining is also of much use for counter-terrorism applications. In Chapter 12, we examined video mining technology. In this section, we showed how this technology may be used for counter-terrorism. We need to proceed with developing the technology further. Exhibit 7 illustrates video mining for counter-terrorism.

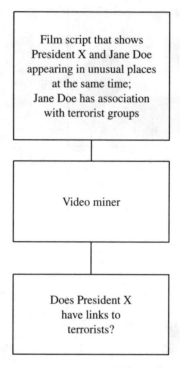

Exhibit 7. Video Mining for Counter-Terrorism

Audio Mining

Previous sections discussed text, image, and video mining for counter-terrorism. In this section, we will examine audio mining. Chapter 12 discussed audio mining technology. It also has applications in counter-terrorism. For example, there are many tape recordings of speeches from terrorists. There are also telephone conversations as well as general speech communication between people. Certain patterns may be extracted from audio data. A recent article in *IEEE Computer* magazine discussed audio mining [IEEE02]. The challenge is to incorporate intelligence into sound detection, speech and voice recognition, and audio processing techniques.

Audio mining is even less developed than video mining. However, recently there has been some work on recognizing conversations in different languages, understanding and analyzing code words in conversations, and analyzing speeches by terrorists, presidents, and others. There are also phone calls that come from terrorists demanding ransoms, requests to release prisoners, etc. Such threatening calls also need to be analyzed.

At present, it is difficult to distinguish between audio mining and audio retrieval. That is, as we have mentioned in Chapter 12, it is difficult to state

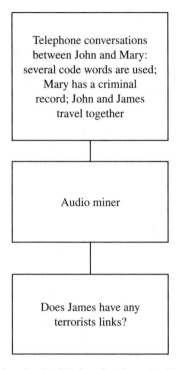

Exhibit 8.   Audio Mining for Counter-Terrorism

that this is where audio retrieval ends and audio mining begins. As we have stated, we should not be too concerned about the distinctions. We have to strive to develop better audio retrieval and intelligent audio retrieval techniques, which not only carry out searching, but also extract hidden patterns and trends. Exhibit 8 illustrates audio mining for counter-terrorism.

Multimedia Data Mining

The previous sections have discussed mining individual data types. We are now seeing more data of mixed or multimedia data types. For example, many Web pages have text, video, images, and audio for a news story. We will need techniques for mining multimedia data types. Chapter 12 discussed the technologies involved. In this section, we will briefly examine the applications to counter-terrorism.

Consider the information that was provided to us on the Web as well as on television about the September 11, 2001, attacks. We saw in one screen text data, images, videos of buildings collapsing, people talking all at the same time. While mining individual data types is still required, we need the ability to mine the combination of data types. For example, we may first mine the text, then mine the images, and finally integrate the two. Alterna-

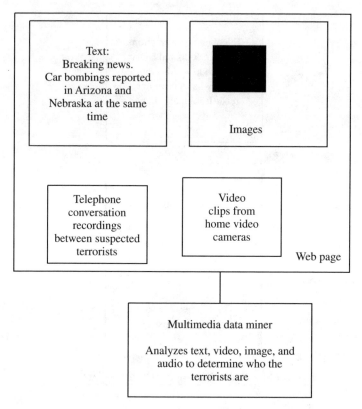

Exhibit 9. Multimedia Data Mining for Counter-Terrorism

tively, we may want to extract text from images and mine the text data and the text extracted for images.

Consider the case of the sniper shootings. We have text data, images of the crime scene, videos of neighboring scenarios, moving vehicles, reports by newscasters, etc. We need to mine the collection of data to get the full picture.

Essentially, we need to master the techniques for mining individual data types before we can successfully mine multimedia data. Nevertheless, we need to start research also on multimedia data mining. Exhibit 9 illustrates multimedia data mining for counter-terrorism.

OTHER ASPECTS

In Chapter 12, we also discussed mining XML documents as well as integrating mining into question answering systems. The previous chapter discussed mining XML documents for counter-terrorism. In this section, we will briefly examine the applications of mining question answering systems.

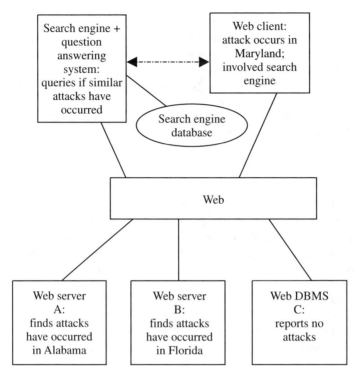

Exhibit 10.   Question Answering and Counter-Terrorism

Earlier in this chapter, we discussed the importance of question answering systems for counter-terrorism. For example, if a sniper attack occurs in Maryland, the system should search the Web and ask questions such as "have similar attacks occurred elsewhere?" The system should also guide the analyst in posing appropriate questions to get the answer that he or she needs. The analyst is typically flooded with information in the form of text, images, video, and audio data, and the goal is to make the job of the analyst easier. Intelligent question answering systems should incorporate some form of data mining capability so that the system could help the analyst by finding the right information at the right time.

Exhibit 10 illustrates question answering for counter-terrorism. While question answering systems research began in the late 1960s, these early systems were essentially yes/no systems. Today, we are beginning to see more sophisticated systems. There is still much research to be done. Essentially, we need search engine capability plus data mining plus question answering capability to be able to ask the right questions so that the analyst can have the right answers at the right time.

SUMMARY

This chapter has examined the technologies discussed in Chapters 5 and 12 and discussed their applications for counter-terrorism. We started with intelligent search engines and then discussed mining multimedia data. Essentially, we discussed the applications of mining text, images, audio, and video for counter-terrorism. Then we briefly discussed the applications of question answering systems to counter-terrorism. Essentially, in all of the examples we have discussed, the idea is to mine and gather business intelligence, analyze the information, and take actions.

While Chapter 20 focused on mining the Web databases for counter-terrorism, in this chapter we discussed information retrieval and mining for counter-terrorism. The next chapter will discuss information management and mining for counter-terrorism. This will be followed by a discussion of semantic Web mining as well as Web usage mining for counter-terrorism. As we have stated, our goal is to raise awareness of the potential uses of data mining for counter-terrorism. As we have stated, while some of our examples mildly reflect the real world (e.g., the September 11, 2001, attacks and the Maryland sniper attacks), most of them are hypothetical. We use these examples mainly to illustrate the key points. Our goal is to raise awareness of the potential power of data mining and Web mining for counter-terrorism.

Chapter 22
Information Management and Web Mining for Counter-Terrorism

INTRODUCTION

Chapter 7 discussed information management. Essentially, we provided an overview of collaboration, knowledge management, sensor information management, and other technologies. In Chapter 13, we discussed information management and Web mining. In particular, we examined information management systems and discussed the impact of Web mining. In this chapter, we will discuss the applications of information management and Web mining for counter-terrorism.

As we have stated in earlier chapters, our goal is to raise awareness of the use of information management and Web mining for counter-terrorism. We are not stating that information management will solve all our problems. Nevertheless, it should be considered in our endeavor to develop solutions in counter-terrorism. Data and information sharing are key goals and, therefore, information management technologies such as collaboration and knowledge management are useful tools for this purpose.

COLLABORATIVE DATA MINING

With collaborative data mining, different analysts from the same agency or from different agencies collaboratively mine the data. As mentioned in Chapter 13, the data could be in multiple data sources or it could be in shared databases. Exhibit 1 illustrates the idea of analysts from different agencies collaborating with each other to discover patterns across various data sources. In this approach, collaborative computing, data mining, and heterogeneous database integration technologies have to work together.

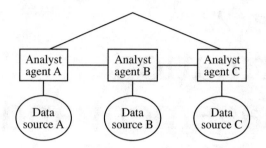

Exhibit 1.   Collaboration among Mining Agents

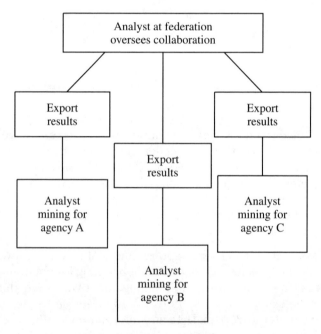

Exhibit 2.   Collaborative Data Mining: Approach II

Another scenario for collaborative data mining is illustrated in Exhibit 2. Here we illustrate a federated environment where analysts are autonomous but cooperate with one another. At the federation level, which in the real world could possibly be at the Department of Homeland Security level, one could ensure that analysts from different agencies work well together but at the same time maintain their autonomy.

KNOWLEDGE MANAGEMENT AND WEB MINING

Chapter 7 discussed knowledge management in some detail. Knowledge management is essentially about corporations using the resources effectively to run their day-to-day business, including information sharing and collaboration. In Chapter 13, we discussed knowledge management and Web mining. One needs to mine the knowledge to gather business intelligence, especially about internal resources. In this chapter, we will discuss knowledge management for counter-terrorism.

After the attacks of September 11, 2001, I remember reading about knowledge management and the need for effective strategies for organizations to be made aware of the possible threats. For example, by mining the knowledge of an organization, we can perhaps determine various insider threats. Who are likely to betray the organization and even commit espionage? For example, we could mine information about employees' travel patterns, phone conversations, e-mail, work habits, computer usage, Web usage, etc., to determine whether a threat exists to the company or to the nation. Of course, this means that employees' privacy and civil liberties could be violated. Here again, there are trade-offs.

Recently, I was on a panel where the audience mentioned that information is constantly being gathered about us, whether we like it or not. For example, if someone dies suddenly, there is enough information to find out who his relatives are and whom to inform. This may be true. But mining all the information that has been collected will be much more powerful than humans making the correlations.

Mining the knowledge can also give military organizations information about what defensive and offensive strategies to use. We could mine knowledge that a military or intelligence organization could be gathering, and the mined knowledge could be used to fight wars, develop strategies, and combat terrorism.

From this brief discussion, it can be seen somewhat that mining the knowledge that the corporation gathers about individuals and resources could be used to manage the human resources, gather business intelligence, manage customers, define military strategies, detect insider threats, and carry out many more activities to combat terrorism and malicious attacks. Exhibit 3 illustrates knowledge management for counter-terrorism.

TRAINING AND WEB MINING

We discussed training and Web mining in Chapter 13. There are many ways Web mining can contribute to training. For example, we need to mine the data on the Web to develop training exercises for military personnel. We can also use this information to determine what resources are needed at which commands. That is, by effectively mining the data on the Web or otherwise, we can get lot of hidden information about what is likely to happen and prepare ourselves for the event. Let us suppose that through data

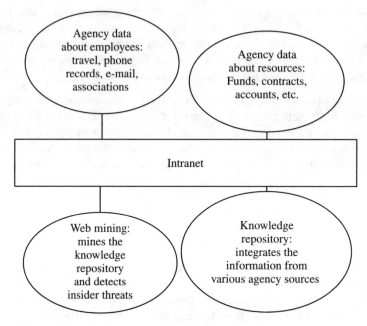

Exhibit 3. Knowledge Management for Counter-Terrorism

mining we get information that certain buildings are going to be attacked in a certain way. We can then prepare troops and firefighters how to best respond to such terrorist acts. As we have mentioned, training can also be used for Web mining.

We illustrate training and Web mining for counter-terrorism in Exhibit 4. Web mining tools can be used to train analysts, design training manuals, develop military training exercises, and plan strategies. Note that we have briefly discussed the applications of training and Web mining for counter-terrorism. We feel that this is still a largely unexplored area and more research is needed on this topic.

AGENTS AND WEB MINING

Agents are essentially processes executing on the Web. Agents may carry out Web mining. On the other hand, Web mining may be used to help the agents complete certain tasks such as locating resources and information to process queries, etc. The agents that carry out Web mining could also carry out various counter-terrorism tasks. These include agents for intelligent searching, agents for making correlations, agents for carrying out insider threat analysis, agents for intrusion detection, and agents for preventing and detecting biological substances, among others.

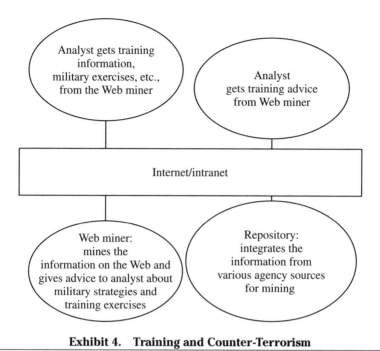

Exhibit 4.   Training and Counter-Terrorism

Exhibit 5 illustrates various types of agents that perform counter-terrorism tasks. These agents may collaborate with each other producing results and solutions. Agents may also act on behalf of analysts and other law enforcement officials in combating terrorism.

WIRELESS INFORMATION MANAGEMENT AND WEB MINING

In Chapter 13, we discussed Web mining for wireless computing. We also briefly illustrated how it could help prevent and detect terrorist attacks. For example, suppose someone wants to travel to a certain place in six months. With data mining, we could extract information not only about the climate, but also about potential political problems, terrorist attacks, and advise the traveler about the best options. Another example is a traveler needing immediate help with a medical situation caused perhaps by a bio-chemical attack. With intelligent search techniques, we could get the information he needs. But when we add effective Web mining capabilities to the information retrieval systems, we can go further, advising the traveler about where to go for the help he needs if no such help is available in the place that he is visiting.

Web mining can also help with tracking the wireless user. This user may be a terrorist. Therefore, if we want to track the whereabouts of a user, we can mine information about a wireless phone conversation. Wireless

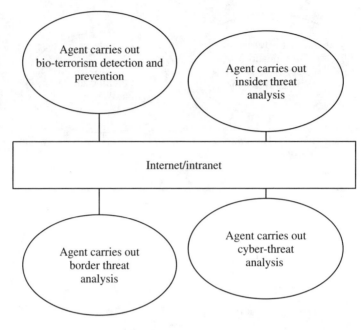

Exhibit 5.   Agents and Counter-Terrorism

phone conversations can also be mined in general so that we can detect terrorist movements and plans. Essentially, there are many applications for Web mining in wireless computing and these applications could help counter-terrorism. Exhibit 6 illustrates our discussion.

SENSOR INFORMATION MANAGEMENT AND WEB MINING

Chapter 13 also discussed sensor Web mining and illustrated some applications for counter-terrorism. Streams that emanate from the sensors are data, and the stream data will have to be mined to extract useful information. Sensor data could be information about tracking certain individuals or information from sensors tracking the temperature in a manufacturing plant. We need to mine the data to determine potential problems. If we see that an individual is making frequent trips to shops that sell chemicals and firearms, then law enforcement officials may want to take a closer look at that individual's movements and habits. That is, with appropriate mining of the data emanating from these sensors, we could make connections, links, and associations.

Another example is mining the information emanating from video cameras installed in shopping malls, airports, and other public places. This video data may also be in the form of streams and will have to be mined to detect suspicious behavior.

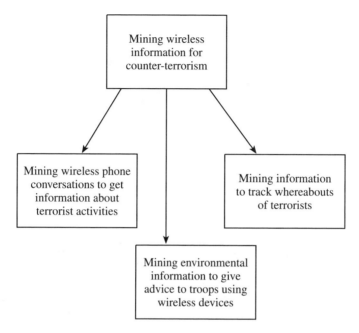

Exhibit 6. Wireless Information Management and Counter-Terrorism

One of the emerging technologies is biological sensors. The idea is to develop sensors that can detect terrorists carrying biological and chemical agents. The spread of biological agents will also have to be detected. The information gathered has to be mined, possibly in real-time, to find out whether similar attacks have occurred and what emergency response measures to take. Exhibit 7 illustrates sensor data mining for counter-terrorism.

QUALITY OF SERVICE AND WEB MINING

We discussed quality of service and Web mining in Chapter 13. Essentially, this has to do with real-time data mining. Some have argued that it may not be possible to develop models in real-time and, therefore, it may not be possible to carry out real-time data mining. The point is, for some applications we have no choice but to develop techniques that will prevent and detect attacks in real-time and, therefore, we need to examine this whole area.

There are various applications for real-time data mining in counter-terrorism. These include detection and prevention of intrusions and biological and other terrorist attacks. For example, consider the case where a terrorist carries a bomb onto an airplane. Techniques are needed to detect this in real-time. Information has to be gathered at various security checkpoints before boarding. This information has to be mined in real-time so that attacks are prevented. Exhibit 8 illustrates this.

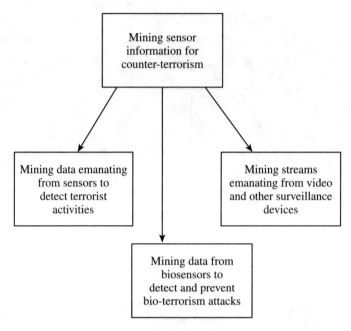

Exhibit 7. Sensor Data Mining and Counter-Terrorism

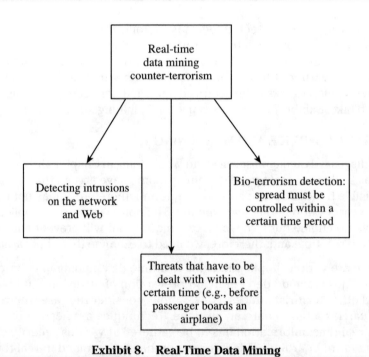

Exhibit 8. Real-Time Data Mining

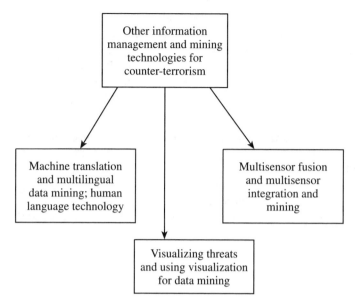

Exhibit 9.   Other Mining Technologies and Counter-Terrorism

As mentioned in Chapter 13, quality of service implies that we have to make trade-offs. In some cases, partial but timely answers may be better than complete answers obtained too late. Also, we need the capability to rapidly sift through the data to determine what needs real-time analysis and what can be analyzed later. There are many research challenges in real-time data mining.

SOME OTHER ASPECTS

There are several other information technologies that have applications in counter-terrorism. These include visualization, machine translation, human language technology, including natural language processing and speech technology. We discussed some of them in Chapter 20.

Human language technology and mining various languages are important because terrorists come from different nations and speak different languages. Understanding the speech of the terrorists is also important. Visualization of the mined information is useful in determining where clusters of terrorists and terrorist activities are coming from. Exhibit 9 illustrates some of these other aspects.

SUMMARY

This chapter has examined the technologies discussed in Chapter 13 and analyzed their applications for counter-terrorism. In particular, we examined collaboration, knowledge management, training, agents, wireless computing, sensor computing, and quality of service. Note that there are many more information management technologies and some of them were discussed in previous chapters. These include information retrieval and multimedia information management. A discussion of all of the information management technologies is not possible in this book. We have selected the technologies that we think are important.

While our discussions have been brief, our main goal is to raise awareness of the applications of information management for counter-terrorism. Information management also includes decision support, visualization, natural language processing, machine translation, and many other technologies. Many of these technologies have applications in counter-terrorism. We need a more in-depth analysis to be carried out together with counter-terrorism experts.

Chapter 23
Semantic Web Mining for Counter-Terrorism

INTRODUCTION

As mentioned in Chapter 14, there have been developments in both the semantic Web and Web mining. The challenge now is to carry out semantic Web mining (see [NGDM02]). The question is, what does it mean to mine the semantic Web? Note that the semantic Web is about machine-understandable Web pages, making the Web more intelligent and able to perform useful services for the user. This means that the information in the Web pages may have to be mined so that the machine can understand the Web pages. Essentially, we need to carry out machine learning on the Web pages and other information on the Web.

Another challenge is to also mine the RDF and XML documents and develop semantic Web services. One can also mine the ontologies and other databases on the Web so that the Web is made more intelligent. While we briefly discussed the semantic Web in Chapter 8, and semantic Web mining in Chapter 14, in this chapter we will explore the applications of semantic Web mining for counter-terrorism.

SEMANTIC WEB MINING FOR COUNTER-TERRORISM

Chapter 8 discussed the semantic Web and provided an example concept of operation for the semantic Web. Chapter 14 discussed semantic Web mining and provided an example concept of operation for semantic Web mining. In this section, we discuss semantic Web mining for counter-terrorism. Semantic Web mining is essentially mining Web pages so that the machine can understand the information better. It also means mining the data sources to develop a better semantic Web. For example, Web pages may have newspaper articles and video releases on terrorists and plans. This information has to be mined so that the machine can understand the Web pages and advise the analyst about potential attacks.

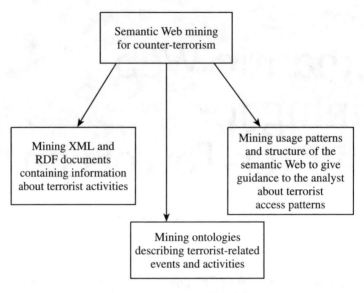

Exhibit 1.   Semantic Web Mining

Semantic Web mining is essentially about mining XML and RDF documents as well as mining ontologies and metadata. It also includes mining the data sources on the Web and mining the data relating to the information management technologies. The semantic Web is essentially an evolution of the Web. We will not end with the semantic Web. It will evolve as far as we can see. In the same way, semantic Web mining will evolve from Web mining. The ultimate goal is to make the Web easier for humans to use. In addition, we want to mine the large quantities of information on the Web so that humans can better perform their tasks. In the case of counter-terrorism operations, the analysts and counter-terrorism experts will have to use the guidance given by the semantic Web about terrorist and security threats to make decisions. Exhibit 1 provides a high-level view of the semantic Web and Web mining for counter-terrorism.

Exhibit 2 illustrates a concept of operation of semantic Web mining for counter-terrorism. As we have mentioned in Chapter 8, the brokering service provides the matching between subscribers and publishers. With semantic Web mining, the brokering services use Web mining to determine the best publishers for the subscribers and also give advice both to the publishers and subscribers. That is, it is not just a matching service. It mines the information and data sources to find not only the best match but also provide advice for future services and enhancements.

In Chapter 8, we discussed ontologies for the semantic Web. In Chapter 14, we discussed the relationship between ontologies and Web mining. The question now is, how can ontologies and ontology mining help counter-ter-

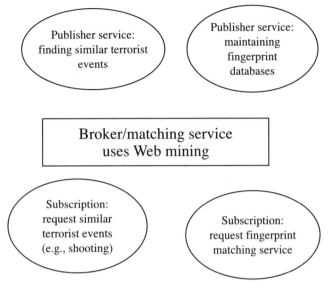

Exhibit 2. Concept of Operation for Semantic Web Mining

rorism? Ontologies are key to specifying information about terrorists, threats, and counter-measures. This is a vocabulary that analysts can use in developing solutions to the threats. If there is no common understanding, it will be difficult to understand each other. Furthermore, semantic heterogeneity could lead to disasters. Once ontologies about terrorists and attacks are developed, then we can mine the ontologies to extract information for the analyst.

In Chapter 8, we discussed semantic interoperability. Here, RDF and XML documents have to interoperate. Extensive research has been carried out on semantic heterogeneity in heterogeneous and federated databases. Many of the concepts are also applicable to the semantic Web. Note that this is essentially what we discussed in Chapter 14. Interoperability between databases, ontologies, and XML/RDF documents are important because the analyst needs the big picture to carry out mining. That is, with incomplete data it will be difficult to mine and get the information for preventing and detecting attacks. Exhibits 3 and 4 illustrate interoperability for counter-terrorism.

In Chapter 8, we provided an overview of Web services. This is one of the rapidly growing areas in Web technology. The idea is essentially to provide a number of Web services, including publishing, subscription, directory, and many others. Web users make use of the services by calling appropriate service routines. In Chapter 14, we discussed mining and Web services. Data mining can be used to broker the information. That is, the

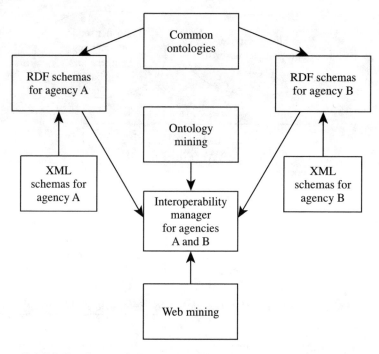

Exhibit 3.   Semantic Interoperability for Counter-Terrorism I

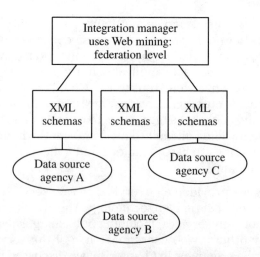

Exhibit 4.   Semantic Interoperability for Counter-Terrorism II

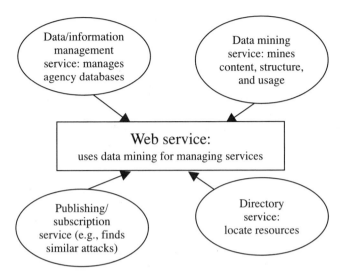

Exhibit 5. Web Services and Web Mining

broker service could use data mining to match publishers with subscribers. This is an area that is still largely unexplored. While we have the various pieces such as Web services and Web mining, we need to integrate the two to provide better quality services to the users. Exhibit 5 illustrates semantic Web mining and Web services for counter-terrorism.

BUILDING THE SEMANTIC WEB AND WEB MINING FOR COUNTER-TERRORISM

As we have stated in Chapters 8 and 14, we have many technologies in place for the semantic Web, including XML, RDF, XML and RDF schemas, ontologies, interoperability, Web mining, agents, etc. Now the challenge is in building the semantic Web. That is, we need to put everything together to build the semantic Web. As we have stated, one viewpoint states that we are now ready to build the semantic Web, while another viewpoint states that the semantic Web is still a few years away [INFO02]. We believe that the semantic Web will continue to evolve. Note that the technologies will also continue to evolve. Therefore, we propose an incremental evolution. We have to ensure that the new technologies are introduced without disrupting any of the existing Web access and support. That is, we need seamless integration of the old and new technologies. XML, RDF, and data, information, and knowledge management technologies will be inserted as the Web evolves. This is the biggest challenge. That is, not only do we have to develop new technologies and enhance the existing technologies, but we also have to insert them so that we can develop the semantic Web. There are also different communities with different needs. In the case of counter-

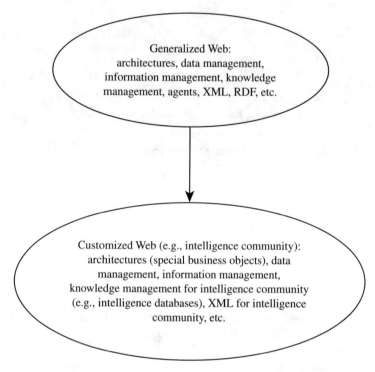

Exhibit 6.   Building the Semantic Web for Community I

terrorism applications, the intelligence community will have its own needs while the law enforcement community will have different needs. Each community will have its own ontologies and RDF schemas. That is, the Web has to be customized. This means we cannot have a single general-purpose Web to support all classes of users. We need specialized Webs. That is, we need to build all the technologies and then customize them to suit the needs of different classes of users.

We are already on the right path. As we have mentioned in earlier chapters, different domain groups, such as E-commerce, wireless, and multimedia, are developing customized XML specifications. It has been pointed out to us that the geographic information systems community is developing its own markup language (e.g., GML, Geographic Markup Language), the medical community is developing its own XML specifications, and various Department of Defense and intelligence communities are developing their own markup languages and intranets. That is, XML is getting customized. We can expect other technologies to be customized as well. Exhibits 6 and 7 illustrate some general trends toward building the Web. Note that while Exhibit 6 customizes the semantic Web for the intelligence community, Exhibit 7 customizes the semantic Web for the law enforcement commu-

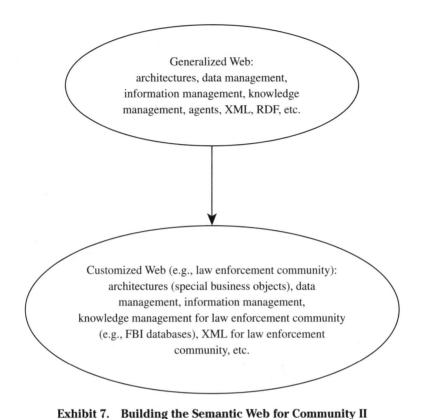

Exhibit 7. Building the Semantic Web for Community II

nity. Eventually, these two semantic Webs will have to interoperate. Inter-operation of the semantic Webs is a major research challenge.

There is also the challenge of using Web mining with the semantic Web. We have shown the need for semantic Web mining in Chapter 14. Various groups are working on semantic Web mining, such as the group in Karlsruhe, Germany (see [NGDM02]). That is, while Web mining could be used to help build the semantic Web, the semantic Web can also help with Web mining. For example, the semantic Web is supposed to develop ontologies and knowledge. These ontologies can be used to support Web mining. On the other hand, we can expect to see the use of Web mining for building the semantic Web. An example for counter-terrorism is a law enforcement analyst logged on to the semantic Web using Web mining to get all the information he needs to carry out his activities. The Web gives him advice, guides him in his analysis, helps with question answering, con-tinually evaluates the current situation and events, and informs the analyst as needed. The semantic Web built for the military community can help with strategies for carrying out military and real-time operations.

While there is still much to do in customizing the semantic Web in addition to building it, we are moving in the right direction. We need to start experimenting with the semantic Web for various counter-terrorism applications and deploy them as they are being developed. We also need to develop technologies for the interoperation of different semantic Webs across agencies.

SUMMARY

This chapter has provided a broad overview of semantic Web mining for counter-terrorism. We examined the semantic Web concepts discussed in Chapters 8 and 14 for counter-terrorism applications, and then described some preliminary ideas on building the semantic Web and using semantic Web mining techniques for such applications. Essentially, we have to customize the semantic Web for special communities such as law enforcement and intelligence. Many of these agencies have their own intranets. We need to build the semantic Web capabilities both for intranets and for the Internet. Semantic Web mining should be an integrated capability built into the semantic Web. We also examined the use of Web services and Web mining for counter-terrorism.

The last four chapters essentially examined data management, information retrieval, information management, and semantic Web technologies with respect to Web mining, and analyzed their applications for counter-terrorism. Essentially, we have focused on Web content mining for counter-terrorism applications. The next chapter will discuss Web usage and Web structure mining for counter-terrorism. In Chapter 25, we will discuss the important topic of privacy and civil liberties. Until now, we have stressed the importance of data gathering. We have also stressed the need for business intelligence analysis for combatting terrorism. But we cannot ignore privacy and civil liberties. Then, in Chapter 26 we will revisit the discussions in Chapter 18 on security threats, and examine how the solutions we have proposed in Chapters 18 through 24 could be used. In Chapter 27, we will discuss business intelligence analysis for counter-terrorism in more detail.

Chapter 24
Web Usage and Structure Mining for Counter-Terrorism

INTRODUCTION

The preceding chapters discussed the use of Web content mining for counter-terrorism. Note that Web content mining is essentially mining the data on the Web. That is, Web content mining is about data mining carried out on the Web. Much of the discussions in Chapters 20 through 23 are applicable for data mining even if the data mining is not carried out on the Web. In Chapter 20, we discussed Web database management and mining for counter-terrorism. Chapter 21 addressed information retrieval and Web mining for counter-terrorism. Chapter 22 discussed various information management technologies and mining for counter-terrorism. Chapter 23 discussed semantic Web mining for counter-terrorism.

In this chapter, we will examine the other two aspects of Web mining for counter-terrorism: Web usage mining and Web structure mining for counter-terrorism. Note that some details of these applications were given in Chapter 15. We examine the techniques discussed in Chapter 15 to see how they can be applied for counter-terrorism.

WEB USAGE MINING FOR COUNTER-TERRORISM

Web usage mining is about analyzing the usage of Web pages. For example, Web traffic analysis, clickstream analysis, giving advice to Web users about browsing patterns, etc., are also part of Web usage mining. Note that we also need to mine the links to determine where a user is on the Web before giving advice. That is, there is a close relationship between Web usage mining and Web structure mining.

In this section, we will examine Web usage mining to see how it can be applied for counter-terrorism. One aspect is that we need to analyze Web traffic patterns. This is the case from Web pages that may be of interest to the terrorist. These may include Web pages of various agencies, technologies, and products. We have heard it over and over again that technologies that are available to us are also available to the terrorist. Therefore, we should always be one step ahead in developing, using, and understanding the technologies. With Web pages of interest, such as government Web pages, we need to find out whether the people who access them are terrorists or legitimate users. Terrorists may also hack into internal systems and intranets to get highly sensitive information about various agency plans and strategies. With Web usage mining, Web traffic, Web logs, and other information have to be mined and unusual patterns have to be extracted. For example, sometimes there may be extensive Web traffic between 5 and 6 A.M. for no apparent reason. Such traffic needs to be analyzed to determine whether it is coming from legitimate users or from suspicious or unauthorized users.

Other aspects of Web usage mining are to help the analyst in browsing Web pages and advising him where to go next. As mentioned, some form of Web structure analysis is also involved. For example, consider the recent sniper case in the Washington, D.C., area. When an analyst is analyzing various pages on the FBI's (Federal Bureau of Investigation) intranet, the system should determine that the analyst has to search for similar shootings in other parts of the country and advise the agent about other Web pages to search.

Web usage mining is also needed to gather business intelligence. As we have mentioned, business intelligence is about getting intelligence for an organization to carry out its business. Often we relate business intelligence to commercial businesses and customer relationship management. Business intelligence also has applications in defense and intelligence. For example, a military organization may gather business intelligence by analyzing the Web pages on its intranets as well as on the public networks. With the information gathered, it could gain some intelligence about its competitor. Law enforcement and intelligence agencies can also carry out similar analysis to improve their operations. We will revisit business intelligence in Chapter 27 when we draw parallels between E-commerce and counter-terrorism.

Web usage mining is also helpful to find out the plans of adversaries. That is, we can mine the Web activities of terrorists to get information about their plans. In this way, terrorists are monitored not only on the street, but also on the Web. We need to follow up on who they visit, who they are exchanging e-mail with, how many times they visit a Web page, and many other details to develop profiles of terrorists. Note that this involves not just Web usage mining, but also Web content mining.

Note that it is difficult to determine the type of Web mining used, whether Web content mining, Web structure mining, or Web usage mining. There are differences, of course. However, to carry out an activity we need to combine all types of mining. Exhibit 1 illustrates the use of Web usage mining for counter-terrorism.

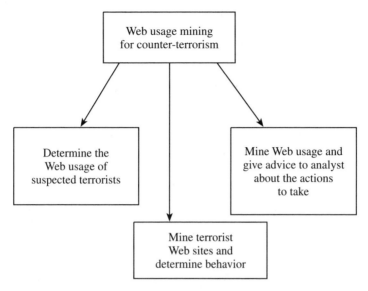

Exhibit 1. Web Usage Mining

We also need to ask the question, what types of results can we expect as a result of Web usage mining? Consider, for example, Web traffic analysis. What outcomes can we expect? We could form clusters, for example, that between 2 and 5 A.M. certain Web pages are being accessed by individuals from France, and between 5 and 8 A.M. access is coming from India. Once the clusters are formed, one can mine and make associations within the clusters. For example, it appears that John always accesses a Web page after James accesses it, and Jane accesses the same Web page a half an hour later. This usually happens on weekdays and not on weekends. The weekend patterns are quite different. Access from France and India occurs in the evenings and not during the daytime. Also, Web users from France and India have similar access patterns. So the question is, is there a connection between the two? Is there a connection between John, James, and Jane? Note that all these examples are hypothetical. We are using them to illustrate the concepts. Exhibit 2 illustrates the outcomes of Web usage mining.

WEB STRUCTURE MINING FOR COUNTER-TERRORISM

Web structure mining is essentially about mining the links and extracting patterns. That is, graph structures that form the nodes and links on the Web are mined and certain patterns are extracted. We discussed some concepts on Web structure mining in Chapter 15. In this section, we discuss the applications of Web structure mining for counter-terrorism.

The connection between Web structure mining and counter-terrorism is more difficult to establish. For example, for Web content mining, we were

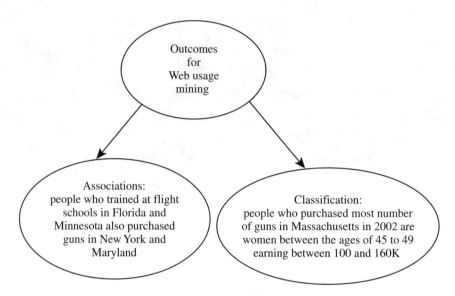

Exhibit 2.   Outcomes for Web Usage Mining for Counter-Terrorism

able to show many applications in counter-terrorism. In fact, Chapters 19 through Chapter 23 were devoted to this topic. With Web usage mining, the relationship was less obvious. But we were still able to establish some applications of Web usage mining. For example, one could monitor the Web traffic patterns to determine whether there is unusual behavior. With Web structure mining, it is more difficult to show the connection. Nevertheless, we will discuss some applications.

With Web structure mining, we could get some statistics about the links. For example, for a Web page we could get the number of links pointing to that page. Now suppose the Web page has some information about terrorist activities. By finding out the number of links, we can determine the interest in that Web page. Once we carry out Web structure mining, then perhaps we could mine the content to figure out which Web pages are pointing to that particular Web page. That is, Web content mining may be used in conjunction with Web structure mining.

Another question is, what types of outcomes can we expect from Web structure mining? As stated in Chapter 15, we could establish clusters of patterns as well as develop associations between Web pages. For example, there could be two Web pages that are not connected but have identical links associated with them. Then the challenge is to find the associations between the Web pages. Essentially, there could be two Web pages discussing information about two suspect individuals and these Web pages could have identical links. The question is, what are the relationships between the two individuals?

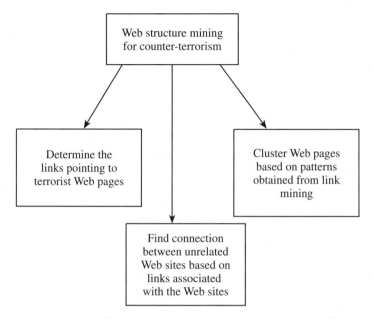

Exhibit 3.   Web Structure Mining for Counter-Terrorism

As mentioned by various counter-terrorism experts, the challenge is to connect the dots. There are many complex links. What kind of link analysis can we do? How can we connect the dots to establish the relationship? The nodes in this case are Web pages and links connections between Web pages. In general, the nodes contain information and data, and the links represent relationships between the data in the nodes. How can we then find a link between two unrelated nodes? This would then give us some connection between the information and data contained in the nodes. One node could be a Web page about sniper attacks in Maryland and the other node could be a Web page about sniper attacks in Alabama. These two nodes may be unconnected. The challenge is to establish the connection that the sniper who attacked in Maryland and in Alabama is one and the same.

Exhibit 3 illustrates Web structure mining for counter-terrorism. We have used the sniper case to illustrate the points. There is still much to do in developing and applying the technology for counter-terrorism. Furthermore, we also need to determine the relationship between Web content mining, Web usage mining, and Web structure mining.

SUMMARY

This chapter has discussed Web usage mining and Web structure mining, and showed how they could be applied for counter-terrorism. With Web usage mining, we could analyze Web traffic as well as carry out clickstream analysis. We discussed several Web products for Web usage mining. Web structure mining is essentially mining Web links and finding out the structure of the Web. For example, with Web structure mining we could find out the number of Web pages pointing to a particular Web page. After we carry out Web structure mining, then we could apply Web usage mining as well as Web content mining.

The discussion in this chapter is rather preliminary. While we have some concrete ideas on Web content mining for counter-terrorism, the ideas on Web usage mining are less concrete and the ideas on Web structure mining are even more vague. We need to continue with research on Web mining in general and Web usage and structure mining in particular. At the same time, we need to develop examples and scenarios for terrorist activities to see how Web usage mining and Web structure mining could be applied.

The last six chapters have focused on Web mining and data mining for counter-terrorism. As we have stressed, Web mining for us is much broader than just data mining; it encompasses data mining. This is because the data on the Web is both structured and unstructured, Therefore, we need to mine relational databases as well as multimedia databases on the Web. In addition, we need to mine Web usage and Web structure. We need to carry out business intelligence analysis to develop strategies. As we have stated, our discussion of counter-terrorism is obtained from various newspapers and documentaries. We are not counter-terrorism experts. Our goal is to raise awareness of the potential applications of Web and data mining. Counter-terrorism experts need to work with data miners to develop concrete solutions.

The last six chapters have also stressed the need for having good and complete data for mining. That is, we have stated that we need all kinds of information about terrorists. This means that information may be collected about innocent people, a process that may violate the privacy and civil liberties of these individuals. While we are focusing on Web mining for counter-terrorism, we also need to examine privacy issues. Privacy will be the subject of Chapter 25. Then in Chapter 26, we will revisit the discussion in Chapter 18 to see how all the potential solutions proposed in Chapters 19 through 24 and the privacy discussion in Chapter 25 could help with developing solutions to various terrorist threats.

Chapter 25
National Security, Privacy, Civil Liberties, and Web Mining

INTRODUCTION

Up to this point, our discussions have focused on the positive role of Web mining. Web technologies and data mining can be used to improve efficiency, quality of data, marketing and sales, and much more. Furthermore, even in the case of information security problems, data mining tools could be used to detect abnormal behavior and intrusions in the system. Data mining also has many applications in detecting fraudulent behavior and insider threats. While all of these applications of the Web and data mining can benefit humans, there is also a dangerous side to these technologies, because they could pose serious threats to the privacy of individuals. This is the topic addressed in this chapter. Our discussion is very much influenced by the threats to privacy due to data mining. This is because data mining tools are available on the Web and even naïve users can apply these tools to extract information from the data stored on the Web and, consequently, violate the privacy of individuals. Furthermore, as we have stressed in this book, to carry out effective data mining and extract useful information for counter-terrorism, we need to gather all kinds of information about individuals. This information could be a serious threat to the individuals' privacy and civil liberties.

Privacy is getting more attention partly because of counter-terrorism and national security. We started giving talks on privacy issues relating to data mining back in 1996 [THUR96a] and wrote about data mining and privacy in one of our earlier books [THUR98]. While this work received some attention, the topic did not get the widespread attention it is receiving today. Recently, we have heard a lot about national security versus privacy in newspapers and television talk shows. This is mainly due to the fact that people are now realizing that to handle terrorism, the government may need to collect information about individuals. This is causing a major concern with civil liberties organizations.

Our main focus in this book has been on Web and data mining for counter-terrorism and national security. In the previous chapters, we discussed how data mining can help counter-terrorism activities. As we have just stated, this also means that we have to gather all kinds of information about people, events, activities, and entities. This means that there is a threat to privacy. That is, national security initiatives bring about some new threats to privacy. This chapter addresses some of the privacy challenges.

One of the challenges to securing databases is the inference problem. Inference is the process of users posing queries and deducing unauthorized information from the legitimate responses that they receive. This problem has been discussed quite a lot over the past two decades. However, data mining makes this problem worse. Users now have sophisticated tools that they can use to get data and deduce patterns that could be sensitive. Without these data mining tools, users would have to be fairly sophisticated in their reasoning to be able to deduce information from posing queries to the databases. That is, data mining tools make the inference problem quite dangerous. We are beginning to realize that the work we have carried out to handle the inference problem could now be used to handle the privacy problem. That is, the inference problem can be rephrased as the privacy problem. We will address the inference problem in this chapter.

As we have stated, data mining approaches such as Web mining seriously compromise the privacy of the individuals. One can have all kinds of information about various individuals in a short space of time through browsing the Web. We now have much data in the form of digital libraries and databases on the Web. Even without mining, privacy of individuals may be compromised. Data mining and Web mining make the privacy problem even more serious. Therefore, protecting the privacy of individuals is becoming a major concern.

We are discussing privacy last not because it is any less important than the other topics we have addressed. Our reason is to show the contrast between national security and privacy. That is, while data mining may be an important technology for national security, it may also be a threat to privacy. As we have mentioned, the challenge is to provide solutions to enhance national security and at the same time ensure privacy. Research on privacy-sensitive data mining is being conducted at various laboratories (e.g., Agrawal at IBM Almaden, Gehrke at Cornell University, and Clifton at Purdue University; for example, see [AGRA02]). While there is some progress, we still have a long way to go.

BACKGROUND OF THE INFERENCE PROBLEM

Inference is the process of posing queries and deducing unauthorized information from the legitimate responses received. For example, the names and salaries of individuals may be unclassified separately, but while taken together they are classified. Therefore, one could retrieve names and employee numbers, and then later retrieve that information to make the associations between names and salaries.

In the early 1970s, much of the work on the inference problem was on statistical databases. Organizations such as the Census Bureau were interested in this problem. However, in the mid-1970s and through the 1980s, the Department of Defense started an active research program on multilevel secure databases, and research on the inference problem (for example, see [AFSB83]) was conducted as part of this effort. The pioneers included Morgenstern [MORG87], Thuraisingham [THUR87], and Hinke [HINK88].

We have conducted extensive research on this subject and worked on various aspects. In particular, it was shown that the general inference problem was unsolvable by Thuraisingham [THUR90a], and approaches were developed to handle various types of inference. These approaches included those based on security constraints as well as those based on conceptual structures (for example, see [THUR91a] and [THUR95]). These approaches handled the inference problem during database design, query, and update operations (see the scenario in Exhibit 1). Furthermore, logic-based approaches were also developed to handle the inference problem (for example, see [THUR91b]).

Much of the earlier research on the inference problem did not take data mining into consideration. With data mining, users now have tools to make

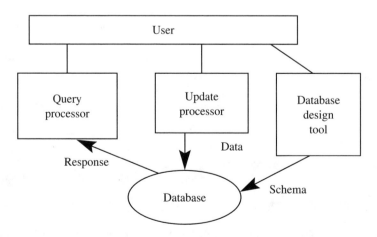

Exhibit 1. Addressing Inference during Query, Update, and Database Design

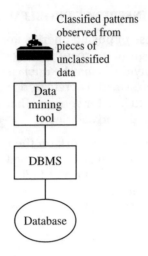

Classified patterns
observed from
pieces of
unclassified
data

Data
mining
tool

DBMS

Database

Exhibit 2.   Inference Problem

deductions and patterns, which could be sensitive. Therefore, in the next section we address inference problem and data mining. We also add some information on data warehousing and inference.

MINING, WAREHOUSING, AND INFERENCE

First let us give a motivating example where data mining tools are applied to cause security problems. Consider a user who has the ability to apply data mining tools. This user can pose various queries and infer sensitive hypotheses. That is, the inference problem occurs via data mining. This is illustrated in Exhibit 2. There are various ways to handle this problem. Given a database and a particular data-mining tool, one can apply the tool to determine if sensitive information can be deduced from the unclassified information legitimately obtained. If so, then there is an inference problem. There are some issues with this approach. One is that we are applying only one tool. In reality, the user may have several tools available to him. Furthermore, it is impossible to cover all the ways that the inference problem could occur. Some of the security implications are discussed in [CLIF96].

Another solution is to build an inference controller that can detect the motives of the user and prevent the inference problem from occurring. Such an inference controller lies between the data mining tool and the data source or database, possibly managed by a database management system. This is illustrated in Exhibit 3. Discussions of security issues for data warehousing and mining are also given in [THUR96a].

Clifton [CLIF99a] has also conducted some theoretical studies on handling the inference problems that arise through data mining. Clifton's

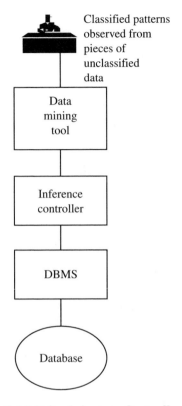

Classified patterns observed from pieces of unclassified data

Exhibit 3. Inference Controller

approach states that if it is possible to cause doubts in the mind of the adversary that his data mining tool is a good one, then he will not have confidence in the results. For example, if the classifier is not a good one for data mining through classification, then there cannot be sufficient confidence in the rules produced. Therefore, there will not be sufficient confidence in the data mining results. What are the challenges in making this happen? That is, how can we ensure that an adversary will not have enough confidence in the results? One of the ways is to give only samples of the data to an adversary so that one cannot build a good classifier from these samples (Exhibit 4 illustrates this scenario). The question then is, what should the sample be? Clifton has used classification theory to determine the limits of what can be given. This work is still preliminary. There have been some concerns also about this approach, as one could give multiple samples to different groups, and the groups can work together in building a good classifier. But the answer to this is that one needs to keep track of what information is being given out. At the keynote address I gave on data mining and security at the Pacific Asia Data Mining Conference in Melbourne, Australia, in April 1998, it was suggested that the only way to

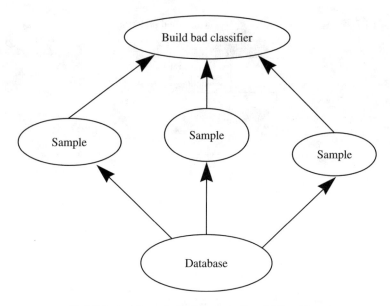

Exhibit 4. Samples without a Good Classifier

handle the inference problem is not to give out any samples. But this could mean denial of service. That is, data could be withheld when it is definitely safe to do so.

Next, let us focus on data warehousing and inference. We have addressed some security issues for warehouses in [THUR96a]. First of all, security policies of the different data sources that form a warehouse have to be integrated in a single policy for the warehouse. This is not a straightforward task, because one has to maintain security rules during the transformations. For example, one cannot give access to an entity in the warehouse, while the same person cannot have access to that entity in the data source. Next, the warehouse security policy has to be enforced. In addition, the warehouse has to be audited. Finally, the inference problem also becomes an issue here. For example, the warehouse may store average salaries. A user can access average salaries and then deduce the individual salaries in the data sources, which may be sensitive (see the scenario in Exhibit 5). To date, little work has been reported on security and the inference problem for data warehousing. This is an area that needs much research.

INDUCTIVE LOGIC PROGRAMMING AND INFERENCE

In the previous section, we discussed data mining and the inference problem. In our research, we have used deductive logic programming extensively to handle the inference problem. We have specified what we

Give access to average salary

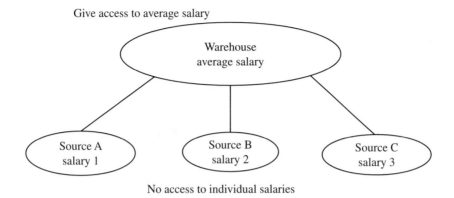

No access to individual salaries

Exhibit 5. Warehousing and Inference

have called security constraints (for example, see [THUR95]) and then augmented the database system with an inference engine, which makes deductions to determine if the constraints are violated. That is, the inference engine, by using the constraints, determines if the new information deduced causes security problems. If this is the case, the data is not released.

The question is, can this approach be used to control inferences using inductive logic programming techniques? Note that with inductive logic programming, one can infer rules from the data. From the various parent–children and grandparent–grandchildren relationships, we can infer that the parent of a parent is a grandparent. Exhibit 6 is a possible architecture for such an inference controller based on inductive logic programming. This inference controller is based on inductive logic programming. It queries the database, gets the responses, and induces the rules. Some of these rules may be sensitive or lead to giving out sensitive information. Whether the rule is sensitive or can lead to security problems is specified in the form of constraints. If a rule is sensitive, then the inference controller will inform the security officer that the data has potential security problems and may have to be reclassified.

In other words, the inference controller that we have mentioned here does not operate on run time. As we have mentioned, it is very difficult to handle all types of data mining tools and prevent users from getting unauthorized information to queries. What the inference controller does is give advice to the security officer regarding potential problems with the data and safety of the data. Some of the issues on inductive inference, which is essentially the technique used in inductive logic programming, to handle the inference problem in secure databases is given in [THUR90b].*

---

* For a discussion of logic programming, see [LLOY87].

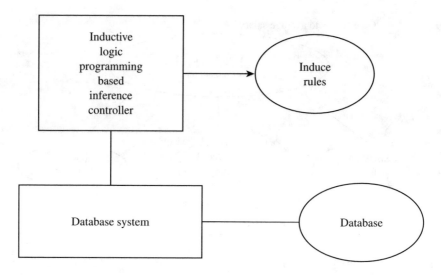

Exhibit 6.   Inference Controller Based on Inductive Logic Programming

PRIVACY ISSUES

At the IFIP (International Federation for Information Processing) working conference on database security in 1997, the group began discussions on privacy issues and the role of Web, data mining, and data warehousing (for example, see [IFIP97]). This discussion continued at the IFIP meeting in 1998 where it was felt that the IFIP group should monitor the developments made by the Security Working Group of the World Wide Web consortium. The discussions included those based on technical, social, and political aspects (see Exhibit 7). However, it was only at the IFIP Conference in July 2002 that there was tremendous interest in privacy. In this section, we will examine all aspects.

First of all, with the World Wide Web, there is now an abundance of information about individuals that we can obtain within seconds. This informa-

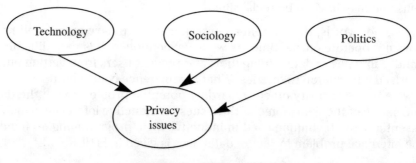

Exhibit 7.   Privacy Issues

tion could be obtained through mining or just from information retrieval. Therefore, we need to enforce controls on databases and data mining tools. This is a very difficult problem, especially with respect to data mining, as we have seen in the previous section. In summary, we need to develop techniques to prevent users from mining and extracting information from the data, whether it is on the Web or on servers. This goes against all that we have said about mining in the previous chapters. That is, we have portrayed mining as something that is critical for users to have so they can get the right information at the right time. Furthermore, they can also extract previously unknown patterns. This is all true. However, we do not want the information to be used in an incorrect manner. For example, based on information about a person, an insurance company could deny insurance or a loan agency could deny loans. In many cases, these denials may not be legitimate. Therefore, information providers have to be very careful about what they release. Also, data mining researchers have to ensure that security aspects are addressed.

Next, let us examine the social aspects. In most cultures, privacy is important. However, there are certain cultures where it is impossible to ensure privacy. These could be related to political or technological issues or the fact that people have been brought up believing that privacy is not critical. There are places where people divulge their salaries without thinking twice about it, but in many countries, salaries are very private and sensitive. It is not easy to change cultures overnight, and in many cases you do not want to change them, as preserving cultures is very important. So what overall effect does this have on data mining and privacy issues? We do not have an answer to this yet because we are only beginning to look into it.

Next, let us examine the political and legal aspects, including policies and procedures. What sort of security controls should we enforce for the Web? Should these security polices be mandated or should they be discretionary? What are the consequences of violating the security policies? Who should administer these policies? Who should manage and implement them? How is data mining on the Web impacted? Can one control how data is mined on the Web? Once we have made technological advances on security and data mining, can we enforce security controls on data mining tools? How is information transferred between countries? Again, we have no answers to these questions. We have, however, begun discussions. Note that some of the issues we have discussed are related to privacy and data mining, and others are related to privacy in general.

We have raised some interesting questions on privacy issues and data mining as well as privacy in general. As mentioned earlier, data mining is a threat to privacy. The challenge is to protect privacy and at the same time retain all the benefits of data mining. At the 1998 Knowledge Discovery in Database Conference, there was an interesting panel on privacy issues for

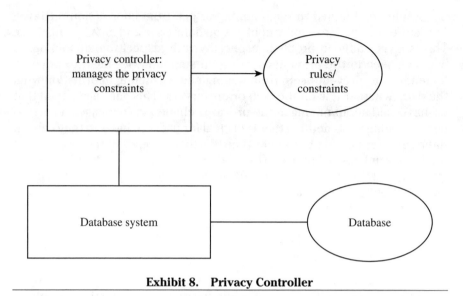

Exhibit 8. Privacy Controller

Web mining. It appears that data mining and security communities are interested in security and privacy issues. Much of the focus at that panel was on legal issues [KDD98].

INFERENCE PROBLEM AND PRIVACY

In an earlier section, we discussed the inference problem. In general, when we think of the inference problem, we have secrecy in mind. However, many of the concepts also apply for privacy. For example, in a previous work, we discussed security constraints ([THUR95]). For example, the locations and missions of naval ships as a group are classified, but individually they are unclassified. Similarly, we can define privacy constraints such as names and salaries or names and health care records taken together are private and individually they are public.

When inference is considered a privacy problem, then we can use the inference controller approach to address privacy. For example, we can develop privacy controllers, as illustrated in Exhibit 8. Furthermore, we can also have different degrees of privacy. For example, names and ages together could be less private than names and salaries together. Names and health care records together could be most private. We can then assign some probability or fuzzy value associated with the privacy of an attribute or a collection of attributes.

Much work has been carried out on the inference problem in the past. We need to revisit this research and see whether it is applicable for the privacy problem.

PRIVACY-ENHANCED DATA MINING

Recently, there is much discussion about privacy-enhanced or sensitive data mining. Various researchers, such as Agrawal at IBM Almaden Research Center, Gherke at Cornell University, and Clifton at Purdue University, are investigating approaches for privacy-enhanced data mining. The idea is to continue with mining and at the same time ensure privacy as much as possible.

We give some details on the approach we are proposing. Note that we mine the data to extract patterns and trends. The privacy constraints determine which patterns are private and to what extent. For example, suppose we could extract names and health care records. If we have a privacy constraint that states that names and health care records are private, then this information is not released to the general public. If the information is semi-private, then it is released to those who have a need to know. Essentially, the inference controller approach we have discussed is one solution to achieving some level of privacy. It could be regarded as a type of privacy-sensitive data mining. In our research, we have found many challenges to the inference controller approach we have proposed (see [THUR95]). These challenges will have to be addressed when handling privacy constraints.

Note that not all approaches to privacy-enhanced data mining are the same. Researchers are taking different approaches to such data mining. Some have argued that privacy-enhanced data mining may be time consuming and may not be scalable. However, we need to investigate this area more before we can come up with viable solutions.

CIVIL LIBERTIES VS. NATIONAL SECURITY

Civil liberties are about protecting the privacy, human, and civil rights of the individual. There are various civil liberties organizations and laws protecting the rights of individuals (see, for example, www.aclu.org or [ACLU]).

There has been much debate recently among counter-terrorism experts, civil liberties organizations, and human rights lawyers about the privacy of individuals. That is, gathering information about people, mining information about people, conducting surveillance activities, and examining personal communications such as e-mail and phone conversations are all threats to privacy and civil liberties. However, what are the alternatives if we are to combat terrorism effectively? Today, we do not have any effective solutions. Do we wait until privacy violations occur and then prosecute, or do we wait until national security disasters occur and then gather information? What is more important? Protecting nations from terrorist attacks or protecting the privacy of individuals? This is one of the major challenges faced by technologists, sociologists, and lawyers. That is, how can we have

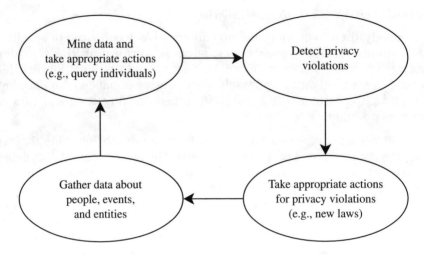

Exhibit 9.   Civil Liberties vs. National Security

privacy and at the same time ensure the safety of nations? What should we be sacrificing?

I have served on panels on national security, database technologies, and privacy as well given various keynote addresses. I have heard audiences say that if they can be guaranteed security, then they would not mind sacrificing privacy. However, they would not want to sacrifice privacy for a false sense of security. On the other hand, I have heard people say that some security is better than nothing. Therefore, even if one cannot guarantee national security, if some security is provided, then sacrificing privacy is not an issue. I have also heard from human rights lawyers about privacy violations by government under the pretext of national security. Some others are very nervous that all the information gathered about individuals may get into the wrong hands one day after and things could be disastrous. Yet others say that on no account will they sacrifice privacy.

While we have no solutions today, we will certainly hear more about it in coming years. The question is, if we assume that there will be no misuse of information, then should we sacrifice privacy for security? Is it reasonable to make such an assumption? On the other hand, should national security be of utmost importance? Should we prosecute on a case-by-case basis those who have violated individual privacy (as illustrated in Exhibit 9)? Do we have adequate laws? We have no answers, just questions. However, I have been raising awareness since my first keynote address on this topic in 1996 at the IFIP Database Security Conference. It is only now that we are hearing more about this. We still have much to do here.

SUMMARY

This chapter is devoted to the important area of privacy related to Web and data mining. While there have been efforts on applying data mining for handling security problems such as intrusion detection (for example, see [CLIF99b]), in this chapter we have focused on the negative effects of data mining. In particular, we discussed the inference problem that can result due to mining as well as ways of compromising privacy, especially due to Web data access.

First, we gave an overview of the inference problem that results from mining and then discussed approaches to handling this problem. Warehousing and inference issues were also discussed. Then we provided an overview of privacy issues. We ended this chapter with a discussion of civil liberties vs. national security.

While little work has been reported on privacy issues for Web and mining, we are moving in the right direction. There is increased awareness of the problems, and groups such as the IFIP Working Group in Database Security are making this a priority. As research initiatives are started in this area, we can expect some progress to be made. Note that there are also social and political aspects to consider. However, we first need the technology before we can enforce various policies and procedures. In addition, the number of Web security conferences is also increasing, including workshops on privacy (see [ACM02]). However, as the Web becomes more sophisticated, there is also the potential for more and more threats. Therefore we have to be ever-vigilant and continue to investigate, design, and implement various privacy measures for the Web.

Chapter 26
Revisiting Security Threats with Respect to Web Mining

INTRODUCTION

Much of Part III has focused on Web mining and data mining for counter-terrorism. In Chapter 18, we discussed various security threats and counter-measures. Chapters 19 through 24 focused on applying Web mining and data mining technologies for counter-terrorism. Essentially, we examined the technologies discussed in Part II and how they may be applied to detect and possibly prevent terrorist attacks. In this chapter, we revisit the threats discussed in Chapter 18, and summarize the counter-measures based on Web and data mining for the various threats. We also briefly summarize our discussions on privacy given in Chapter 25.

Note that while there may be some repetition of what we have discussed in previous chapters, in this chapter we take another stab at discussing counter-measures. That is, while the previous chapters examine a particular data mining technology for counter-terrorism such as collaborative data mining, multimedia data mining, knowledge management and data mining, in this chapter we examine how the solutions proposed in the previous chapters could be used to handle various threats, including natural disasters; malicious threats; noninformation- and information-related threats; biological, chemical, and nuclear threats; attacks on critical infrastructures; and nonreal-time and real-time threats.

NATURAL DISASTERS, HUMAN ERROR, AND MALICIOUS ATTACKS

As we have stated in Chapter 18, threats may be due to natural disasters, human error, or malicious attacks. Data mining could be used to both detect and prevent these situations. For example, we may analyze geographical, weather, and geological data to detect hurricanes and earthquakes. Various data quality tools could be used to detect human error. These data quality tools may have data mining capabilities. Also, data mining may be of help for first responders and continued monitoring of situations.

Malicious attacks may include bombings, airplane hijackings, sniper shootings, computer and network intrusions, and other activities. Certain malicious attacks, such as using an airplane to bomb a building, must be handled in real-time using real-time data mining techniques. Nonreal-time attacks include various plans carried out by terrorists for future attacks. We need to gather information about terrorists and activities and then make links and associations.

The data mining outcomes and techniques to handle various threats include associations where links between terrorists and activities are made, clustering where terrorist groups may be placed in clusters based on trends and observations, and anomaly detection where, for example, image data is analyzed and unusual patterns, such as buildings in the middle of the desert, are detected. Web mining and data mining research shows much promise for handling natural disasters and malicious attacks. We need training examples for counter-terrorism, which are not easy to find. Some of them may be classified. In this case, we need to conduct modeling and simulation activities to get training examples so that we can get some use out of the data mining techniques.

NONINFORMATION-RELATED TERRORISM

In Chapter 18, we discussed noninformation-related terrorism, terrorist attacks not dealing with computers. It is difficult to say that something is not information-related because many of the activities are now coordinated through computers. Even the terrorists use e-mail messaging and telecommunications equipment.

Noninformation-related terrorist activities include hijacking airplanes, bombing buildings, sniper shootings, insider threats, and transportation and border security violations. Data mining techniques may be used to prevent and detect these threats. As we have mentioned in the previous chapters, we need to gather data about terrorists and mine the data. Certain attacks may have to be dealt with in real-time. That is, we need real-time data mining. Image mining and fingerprinting techniques are needed, for example, to detect immigration violations at borders and entry points. Such techniques are also needed to detect connections between terrorists in various places. Surveillance analysis techniques and sensor/stream data mining techniques are needed, for example, for handling transportation security threats. Text mining of newspaper articles and other public and private databases containing text data is needed to make connections and associations between various phrases. Data mining techniques are also useful to detect insider threats. We can mine the e-mail messages and phone conversations of employees and detect suspicious behavior. This, of course, may violate the privacy and civil liberties of the individual. As we have stressed, ensuring national security and privacy are conflicting goals.

In Chapter 24, we discussed some aspects. We need more research in areas such as privacy-enhanced data mining.

INFORMATION-RELATED TERRORISM

As mentioned in Chapter 18, by information-related terrorism, we essentially mean cyber-terrorism. Cyber-security is the area that deals with cyber-terrorism. We listed various cyber-attacks, including access control violations, unauthorized intrusions, jamming the networks, and denials of service. We are hearing that cyber-attacks will cause corporations billions of dollars. For example, one could masquerade as a legitimate user and swindle a bank of billions of dollars.

Data mining and Web mining may be used to detect and possibly prevent cyber-attacks. For example, anomaly detection techniques could be used to detect unusual patterns and behaviors. Link analysis may be used to trace viruses to the perpetrators. Classification may be used to group various cyber-attacks and then use the profiles to detect an attack when it occurs. Prediction may be used to determine potential future attacks based on information about terrorists learned through e-mail and phone conversations. For some threats, nonreal-time data mining may suffice and for certain other threats such as network intrusions, we may need real-time data mining.

As we have mentioned, it is difficult to say that an attack is information- or noninformation-related. That is, we often need to use some form of information in electronic media for detecting and preventing attacks. Our grouping is mainly for convenience.

BIOLOGICAL, CHEMICAL, AND NUCLEAR ATTACKS

As we have mentioned in Chapter 18, we are at risk for biological, chemical, and nuclear attacks. Such attacks have the potential of killing millions of people. Entire countries may be wiped out by biological or nuclear attacks. Therefore, it is essential that we develop appropriate biological, chemical, and nuclear defense mechanisms. Data mining needs to be investigated for this purpose.

We need to model the spread of diseases to develop mechanisms such as biological sensors to detect that certain individuals are carrying viruses. Once the virus is spread, we need real-time data mining techniques to determine the cause of the problem and the actions to be taken. For example, do we mass vaccinate or ring vaccinate? If it is the latter, then we need to find out who has come in contact with the infected individuals. Nonreal-time data mining techniques are needed for long-term analyses. Who are likely to contract smallpox? Now that we know that countries X, Y, and Z have developed the smallpox virus, who is likely to maliciously spread the disease, and what should we do about it? Who else has the smallpox virus? We can also gather a lot of historical information on the Web to find out how various groups have dealt with the disease. Then we mine the information to see what we can do about it now.

Data mining and Web mining for biological, chemical, and nuclear attacks offer some hope. However, we are just beginning to explore the technology. Before we develop various data mining techniques, we need to understand the nature of the attacks and the spread of biological agents to determine how existing techniques could be applied and what types of new techniques are needed. We need not only data miners and counter-terrorism experts, we also need biologists, engineers, chemists, and mathematicians to work together to solve these problems. We also need the support of social scientists and psychologists because they may understand cultures and behaviors.

ATTACKS ON CRITICAL INFRASTRUCTURES

As mentioned in Chapter 18, attacks on critical infrastructures could cripple a nation and its economy. Infrastructure involves telecommunications, electric power, natural gas, reservoirs and water supplies, food supplies, crops, and other assets that are valuable to a nation.

Various data mining techniques may be used to detect and prevent infrastructure attacks. Some of these attacks may have to be dealt with in real-time. That is, we do not have the luxury of waiting even a few hours before we can determine what has happened and why it has happened. We need real-time data mining techniques. These techniques will be discussed in the next section.

We also need to gather information about terrorist actions and mine the information so that future attacks can be prevented. For example, if someone goes to a store and purchases large quantities of pesticides, then there might be something suspicious about this person's behavior. He could be checked to determine if he has a legitimate need for these chemicals. If not, then what are his intentions?

Attacks on telecommunications may be considered as a form of intrusion. These attacks may have to be handled in real-time. Also, we may need to gather a lot of information about telecommunications, electric power, and other infrastructures for a period of time to see if there is a pattern that is developing. For example, telecommunications may be jammed for half an hour every other week. This may seem innocent, but in reality it may be an attack, which could cause billions of dollars to corporations.

The data mining techniques include those for detecting anomalies. What is wrong with the infrastructure? How should it function in a normal environment? What are the faults? Are they malicious? How can they be handled? How can errors and attacks be controlled? How can we limit the damage? What prevention measures should we take? With effective Web mining and data mining, we may be able to come up with answers to the questions we have posed.

NONREAL-TIME THREATS VS. REAL-TIME THREATS

In Chapter 18, we examined nonreal-time as well as real-time threats. In this section, we will see how Web mining and data mining could handle such threats. However, after having discussed various Web and data mining technologies in Chapters 19 through 24, we are now in a better position to analyze various solutions.

With nonreal-time threats, we need to gather data over a period of time and build warehouses to analyze the data with data mining tools. Data to be gathered includes information about terrorists, terrorist events, and all details about the events. Information about various attacks is also gathered in Web databases and databases on the intranets. Analysts have to mine these databases. They may have to carry out collaborative data mining. Data may not be structured. Various multimedia databases as well as knowledge repositories have to be mined. We have also discussed various data mining techniques for handling nonreal-time threats. For example, we can make associations between those enrolled in flight training schools and those purchasing firearms. We can also group the terrorist population based on various patterns and trends observed. For example, people coming from region A are likely to be suicide bombers, while people coming from region B are likely to be snipers.

In the case of real-time threats, we need to analyze them in real-time. That is, we need to build models in real-time as well as analyze data in real-time. We may have to develop tools to rapidly sift through and mine only relevant data. Quality of service is an important factor. That is, when we mine in real-time, we may be more interested in getting quick results, even if they are vague. That is, we need to make trade-offs for real-time data mining. Various biological and chemical threats are real-time threats. The spread of smallpox, for example, has to be detected in real-time and appropriate actions need to be taken. Essentially, while we can use data warehouses and various mining techniques for analyzing historical data for nonreal-time threats, we need to meet timing constraints to handle real-time threats. Real-time data mining may also include mining sensor and stream data. Such data may be emanating from surveillance cameras and has to be mined before an attack takes place.

REVISITING PRIVACY

Chapter 25 addressed privacy concerns. As we have stated, while data mining has many applications in counter-terrorism, it is also a threat to privacy. We have stressed the need to have good data to carry out mining. This means that we may need to gather data about various individuals, some of whom may not be considered suspicious. We may need to gather as much information as possible, and then mine to see who is suspicious. This causes serious threats to privacy.

The question is, what do we do? That is, do we sacrifice privacy for the sake of national security or do we ensure privacy at the expense of national security? We discussed various alternatives in Chapter 25. We need to develop techniques for privacy-sensitive data mining. We also believe that technology alone will not be sufficient. We need technologists, counter-terrorism specialists, government officials, lawyers, policy makers, and social scientists to work together. For example, we may need to conduct surveys to see what the general population feels about privacy and national security. Are they willing to sacrifice privacy for national security and, if so, to what extent? Then we need the experts to work together to come up with viable solutions.

SUMMARY

This chapter has examined the various threats discussed in Chapter 18 and described how Web mining and data mining may be applied to handle these threats. Essentially, we examined the discussions in Chapters 19 through 25 and summarized the applications of Web mining and data mining. We examined natural disasters, malicious attacks, noninformation- and information-related terrorism, attacks on critical infrastructures, and non-real-time and real-time threats. We analyzed various data mining outcomes and techniques such as clustering, link analysis, and anomaly detection for counter-terrorism. While there is some duplication in what we have discussed here and in previous chapters, essentially this chapter brings together the various data mining technologies such as multimedia data mining, collaborative data mining, and Web database mining and discusses their applications for counter-terrorism. Note that in the previous chapters we examined essentially one technology at a time and showed how it may be applied for counter-terrorism.

The last several chapters in Part III have focused on applying Web data mining for counter-terrorism applications. We also discussed the privacy concerns. We need to develop data sharing and data mining techniques that can preserve privacy as much as possible. While this chapter is the logical closure to Part III, we have added one more chapter (i.e., Chapter 27) to discuss parallels between E-commerce and counter-terrorism and to show the need for business intelligence. Chapter 27 essentially lays the foundation for building systems to combat terrorism.

Chapter 27
E-Commerce, Business Intelligence, and Counter-Terrorism

INTRODUCTION

Part I discussed supporting technologies for Web mining, Part II discussed concepts in Web mining, and Part III discussed applications of Web and data mining for counter-terrorism. In particular, we examined each technology discussed in Parts I and II and its potential applications in counter-terrorism. In this chapter, we will draw parallels between E-commerce and counter-terrorism as they are both applications of the Web. Note that our assumption is that much of the data will eventually be on the Web either through intranets and private networks or public networks and the Internet.

In Chapter 2, we discussed E-commerce. As we have stated, E-commerce is the killer application for the Web. Chapter 2 described models, architectures, and functions for E-commerce. In this chapter, we will examine the models, architectures, and functions discussed in Chapter 2 to see how they can be applied for counter-terrorism. In particular, we will see how organizations can collaborate on the Web, and how architectures such as the federated architectures can be used for counter-terrorism applications. We will also examine business intelligence, which is important for E-commerce, and see how it can be applied for counter-terrorism applications.

Essentially, this chapter attempts to put together various technologies for counter-terrorism applications. That is, we examine the building blocks upon which such applications can be built. We use our experience with E-commerce applications to discuss some ideas. While the previous chapters focused on Web data mining for counter-terrorism, in this chapter we provide the environment needed to carry out Web data mining. It should be noted that it is only recently that we have been discussing information technologies for counter-terrorism. Therefore, we need to develop enterprise architectures and portals for counter-terrorism. The discussion in this chapter is just the first step. We have a very long way to go. That is, we are proposing an integrated architecture for carrying out various counter-terrorism functions. The components will include business objects, data managers, and middleware infrastructures.

Note also that we have been reading a lot of news in *The Washington Post* and *The New York Times* about information awareness from Admiral Poindexter, who heads the Information Awareness Office of the Defense Advanced Research Projects Agency. One of the issues discussed is recording all of the purchases and transactions carried out by everyone in the United States, and analyzing and perhaps mining this information to extract suspicious behavior. While there have been many discussions of privacy aspects related to such an endeavor, as we have stated, to extract patterns and trends, we need complete data. Therefore, we may need to gather information about purchase patterns but perhaps one way is to protect the identity of the individuals initially. Should anything suspicious show up, then the government can request the identity of the individuals. This means that we have to record all transactions, whether E-commerce or otherwise. We also discuss this aspect in this chapter.

MODELS FOR COUNTER-TERRORISM

In this section, we will discuss some models for counter-terrorism. One could also think of these models as models for operation or concepts of operation. Essentially, we have examined the E-commerce models discussed in Chapter 2 to see how they can be adapted for counter-terrorism. Note that the models for E-commerce do not map directly into models for counter-terrorism. Nevertheless, we can learn some lessons from E-commerce. Again, our thesis is that much of the data will either be based on the Internet or on intranets and private or classified networks. Therefore, analysts will have to collaborate with one another within or across agencies.

Exhibit 1 illustrates a scenario where two agencies want to collaborate to handle terrorist problems. These could be intelligence or law enforcement agencies. The collaboration cuts through some sort of federation, possibly managed by the Department of Homeland Security. Note that we have repeatedly discussed the federated architecture as a model for counter-terrorism applications. Furthermore, we are also proposing a tight federation between agencies. This does not mean that we are endorsing the federated architecture or a tight federation. It means that, in our opinion, it may be better for organizations to collaborate through some sort of federation because they will still have information that is private. Furthermore, we believe that a tight federation may be preferred, as it is better for

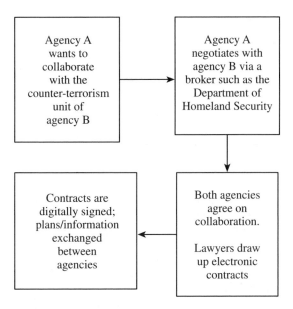

Exhibit 1.   Collaboration through Federations

someone at the top or some sort of broker to negotiate between the different organizations.

Exhibit 2 gives another example where an agency wants to obtain missing information needed for mining from another part of the same agency or from a different agency. Here again, the information may be retrieved through some sort of a federation or a broker. Even if the two organizations are part of the same agency, a federation may be necessary, as even within organizations there may be information that is private to a particular business.

In both cases, we can draw parallels with E-commerce. In the case of E-commerce, organizations collaborate with each other to carry out a business or a transaction. Forming a federation may not be necessary, as organizations often may not want a third party to monitor their transactions, although we cannot rule out federations for E-commerce. In the case of counter-terrorism, we feel that forming federations may be a better choice, as one really needs the right information at the right time to mine and extract patterns, and information sharing may not be part of the organization's culture. In this case, we may need a federated administrator to negotiate and enable collaboration.

ARCHITECTURES FOR COUNTER-TERRORISM

In Chapter 2, we discussed various types of architectures for E-commerce. All of these architectures can be used to build systems for counter-

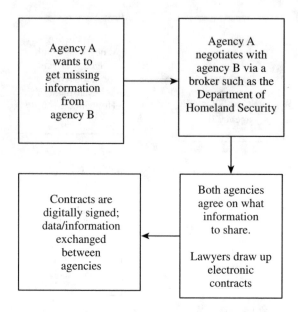

Exhibit 2.   Information Sharing through Federation

terrorism. For example, we could use a client/server architecture, where the analyst is a client and requests information from an agency's servers. In the case of managing distributed data within an agency, we could use the distributed architecture discussed in Chapter 2. The idea here is that data is distributed for various reasons; for example, data pertaining to individuals in Boston should be in databases located in Boston and data pertaining to individuals in New York should be in databases located in New York. We could also form federations between agencies, and the federated architecture discussed in Chapter 2 could be used for this purpose. Finally, we could build business objects for counter-terrorism in the same way business objects have been built for E-commerce and numerous other applications. These business objects could include objects for monitoring, tracking, first-response management, situation monitoring, making correlations, and other activities relating to detecting and preventing terrorist attacks.

We could also utilize the push/pull models discussed in Chapter 5. For example, the consumer could be the analyst and the producer could be the person responsible for gathering, packaging, and delivering data to the analyst. In one scenario, the analyst could be continually pulling information from the producer. In another scenario, the producer pushes information to the analyst. The ideal situation is for the analyst to get the right information at the right time from the producer. We need to carry out some sort of data mining to determine what information to deliver to the analyst.

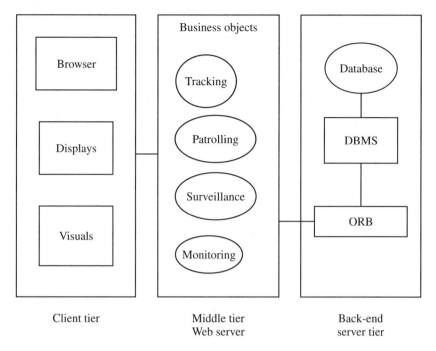

Exhibit 3. Client/Server Architectures for Counter-Terrorism

The roles could also change. For example, the analyst could be the producer of the reports and the person receiving the reports could be the consumer. For example, the analyst could determine what information to send
to the report reader. The report reader could be a person who briefs the
head of the agency. In other words, the roles of the producer and consumer
could vary. The challenge is to produce the right information and deliver it
to the consumer. The consumer has to take the appropriate action with the
information.

Rather than duplicating all types of architectures discussed in Chapter
2, we will illustrate with examples of just two. In the first architecture, we
show how clients communicate with servers via business objects. In the
second architecture, we illustrate federations between different agencies.
These architectures are shown in Exhibits 3 and 4.

Note that there are various aspects to the architectures discussed in
Chapters 2 and 5. One can think perhaps of building systems for counter-
terrorism activities from components. That is, one needs the infrastructure
containing appropriating middleware, services such as data management,
data mining, and applications such as tracking and surveillance. This is
illustrated in Exhibit 5.

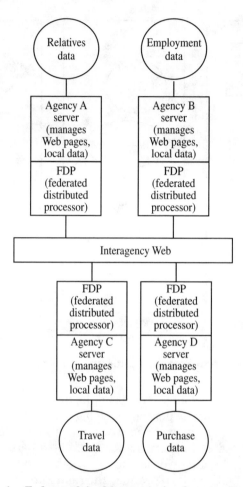

Exhibit 4.   Federated Architectures for Counter-Terrorism

FUNCTIONS FOR COUNTER-TERRORISM

Here again, we draw parallels between E-commerce and counter-terrorism. We can think of three aspects to discussing E-commerce functions for counter-terrorism, as illustrated in Exhibit 6:

1. Client/server functions: Counter-terrorism server functions are typically the information management functions such as database management and data mining. The modules of the server may include modules for managing the data and Web pages, mining terrorist information, security enforcement, as well as transaction management. Client functions may include presentation management and user interface as well as caching data and hosting browsers. There could also be a middle tier, which may implement the business

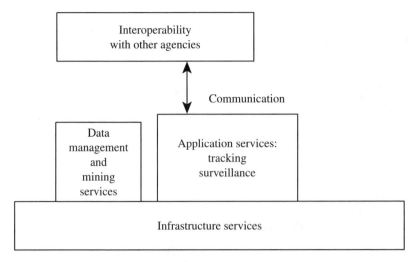

Exhibit 5. Counter-Terrorism Functions

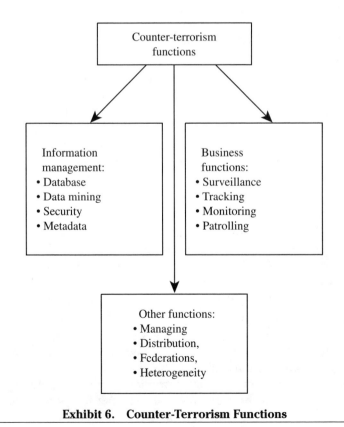

Exhibit 6. Counter-Terrorism Functions

objects to carry out the business functions such as surveillance and tracking.

2. Business functions: Essentially, the functions that are carried out in various transactions.
3. Distribution functions.

Additional issues for counter-terrorism include the legal, ethical, and political considerations. The server functions are impacted by the information management technologies for the Web and Web mining, discussed in Part I. In addition to data management and business functions, the counter-terrorism functions also include those for managing distribution, heterogeneity, and federations. As we have stated, managing federations may be especially important.

REVISITING BUSINESS INTELLIGENCE

Business intelligence is about corporations or organizations gathering information about their clients, competitors, and products so that they can improve their business. Business intelligence is also important for E-commerce. For example, an organization may gather information about their customers' Web access patterns to carry out targeted marketing. It could develop customer profiles, or it can get information about its competitors' strategies and use this information to improve its business.

As we have stated, there are parallels we can draw between E-commerce and counter-terrorism. An agency may gather information about other agencies, adversaries, and terrorists from the Web or otherwise. An agency can monitor Web access patterns and e-mail patterns of various individuals. This information can be mined so that some useful information is extracted. The extracted information may be used to improve the business of the agency. This could mean detecting and preventing counter-terrorism, developing military strategies, and learning about an adversary's capabilities.

Exhibit 7 illustrates business intelligence for counter-terrorism. One can mine the business intelligence to make associations and links, form clusters, and detect anomalies. As we make progress on business intelligence for E-commerce, we can perhaps use the techniques for gathering business intelligence for counter-terrorism.

As we have stated earlier in this chapter, we have been hearing much about information awareness. One of the issues discussed is the recording of all the purchases and transactions carried out in the United States and then analyzing and perhaps mining this information; but to extract patterns and trends, as we have stated, we need complete data, which may violate privacy. Therefore, we may need to gather information about purchase patterns in a way that initially protects the identity of individuals. In

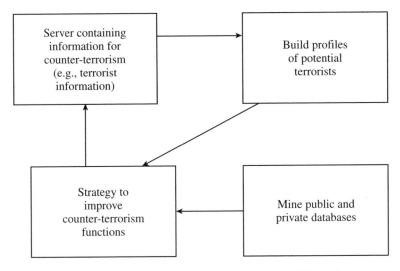

Exhibit 7. Business Intelligence for Counter-Terrorism

the event where something suspicious shows up while mining, the government would request the identity of the individual under suspicion. This means that we have to record all transactions, whether E-commerce or otherwise. That is, there has to be a direct communication between the E-commerce and merchants' servers and government databases. It can be done in either of two ways. One is for the data miners in the federal agencies to retrieve all of the data from the merchants' servers as needed. But this may not be desirable to the merchants, who may prefer to send the information to federal database servers. That is, they many not want to give business-sensitive information to federal agencies. Exhibits 8 and 9 illustrate both approaches. This is part of the intelligence gathering that federal agencies need to carry out. That is, the information they get from the merchants is a form of business intelligence, and the agencies need to use this business intelligence to mine and extract patterns about suspicious behavior.

As we have stated, there are serious privacy considerations in recording all purchases made by individuals. We must pay attention to privacy. That is, while it is very important to gather as much information as possible to carry out mining, we need to come up with effective ways to carry out privacy-sensitive data sharing and data mining. Some initial directions were given in Chapter 25.

SUMMARY

In this chapter, we started with a discussion of models for counter-terrorism, and then discussed architectures and functions for counter-terrorism. We also revisited business intelligence. Essentially, this chapter has

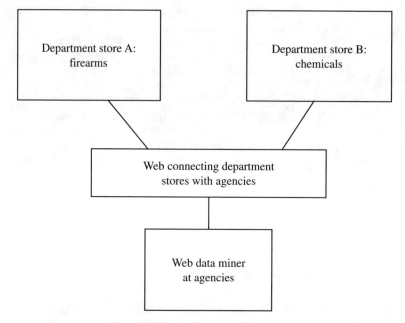

Exhibit 8.   Agency Miner Mines Department Store Databases

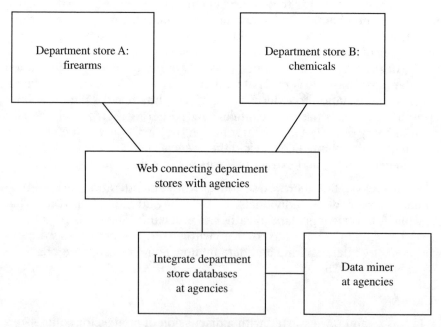

Exhibit 9.   Department Store Sales Databases Integrated at Agencies

briefly examined the parallels between E-commerce and counter-terrorism. While they are very different applications for the Web, Web mining and information management, there are some similarities. They are about organizations negotiating contracts, forming federations, and carrying out business on the Web.

It should, however, be noted that counter-terrorism deals with both information on and outside of the Web. However, our assumption is that much of the data and information will be either on the Internet and public networks or on intranets and private, possibly classified networks.

As we have stated in a previous chapter, just ten years ago people would go to the local library for information. However, during the past few years this has not been the case; people can get much of the information they need on the Web. In fact, much of the background information we needed to write this book has been from the Web. The Web has also enabled us to be less dependent on television because we can get much of our daily news from the Web.

As we have stressed in this book, the Web will continue to evolve and Web technologies will mature. Web mining will play a major role in extracting useful information from vast resources on the Web. We will see developments in Web content mining, Web structure mining, and Web usage mining. E-commerce will continue to be the killer application for the Web. While E-commerce is not enjoying the fame it received before the dot.com bust, it is still going to be a major force in the way business is conducted. Recently, we have seen much focus the application of data mining for counter-terrorism. As E-commerce technologies are developed, we will also begin to see the applications of these technologies for counter-terrorism. Data sharing, collaboration, and negotiating will become essential both for E-commerce and counter-terrorism. While data sharing will be a threat to privacy, we have no choice but to collaborate and share information if we are to mine and get useful results. We believe that Web and data mining will be important for counter-terrorism. Therefore, getting the data organized and ready for mining will be critical.

This brings us to the close of Part III. As we have stressed, our discussion of counter-terrorism is entirely based on articles we have read. We are not counter-terrorism experts. However, to successfully apply data mining techniques to detect and prevent terrorist attacks, data miners have to work with counter-terrorism experts. Only then can we make breakthroughs so that this world becomes a safer place to live.

CONCLUSION TO PART III

This brings us to the end of Part III, all about Web and data mining for counter-terrorism. Chapter 18 provided an overview of the various threats. Chapter 19 briefly reviewed data mining for counter-terrorism. Chapters 20 through 24 examined the technologies discussed in Part II and showed how they may be applied for counter-terrorism. For example, Chapter 20 discussed Web database mining for counter-terrorism. Chapter 21 discussed information retrieval and Web mining for counter-terrorism. Chapter 22 discussed information management and Web mining for counter-terrorism. Chapter 23 discussed semantic Web mining for counter-terrorism. Then, in Chapter 24, we discussed Web usage mining and Web structure mining for counter-terrorism. Chapter 25 discussed the important aspect of privacy.

As we have stated, to carry out good Web and data mining we need good data. If we are to mine for counter-terrorism, we may need to gather information not only about terrorists, but also about several other individuals. This violates privacy. Therefore, in Chapter 25, we examined various privacy issues and gave some guidance as to what we can do such as carry out privacy-enhanced data mining. In Chapter 26, we revisited the threats discussed in Chapter 18 and essentially examined the various Web and data mining technologies discussed in Chapters 19 through 24, and summarized the discussions on Web and data mining to handle the various threats. Finally, in Chapter 27, we discussed the parallels between E-commerce and counter-terrorism and described the use of business intelligence for counter-terrorism.

As we have stressed in this book, technologies such as data mining and data management can only do so much. We need counter-terrorism experts to work with data miners and information technologists to develop solutions. This means that domain specialists have to work with technologists. Our nation and much of the world is moving in the right direction to combat terrorism. Our work is just beginning. In many situations, we have the technologies but we need to know how to effectively use them. In some other cases, we need better technologies. We have a lot to do to develop promising solutions to combat terrorism.

Chapter 28
Summary and Directions

INTRODUCTION

We have discussed various Web data management and information management technologies, as well as how data and information on the Web can be mined. Then we discussed the applications of Web mining and data mining technologies for counter-terrorism. Throughout the book we have discussed business intelligence and its application to counter-terrorism. Essentially, by using business intelligence, an organization can get information about its competitors and adversaries. This information can be used to combat terrorism. This chapter summarizes the contents of the book and provides an overview of the challenges and directions for Web mining and their applications for counter-terrorism. We also provide some suggestions about where to go from here.

SUMMARY OF THE BOOK

Exhibit 1 recaps what we have described throughout this book. Chapter 1 provided an introduction to Web data mining and counter-terrorism. We also discussed the three parts of the book: Part I described supporting technologies for Web data mining, Part II described Web data mining concepts, and Part III, described Web data mining for counter-terrorism. We summarize each chapter in this section.

Chapter 2 gave a broad overview of the Web, E-commerce, and business intelligence. We started with a discussion of the evolution of the Web and then discussed the E-commerce process, which was followed by a discussion of the models, architectures, functions, and information technologies for E-commerce.

Chapter 3 provided an introduction to data mining. We first discussed various technologies for data mining, and then we provided an overview of the concepts in data mining. These concepts include the outcomes of mining, the techniques employed, and the approaches used. The directions and trends, such as mining heterogeneous data sources, mining multimedia data, mining Web data, metadata aspects, and privacy issues, were addressed next. Finally, we discussed the relationship to Web data mining.

413

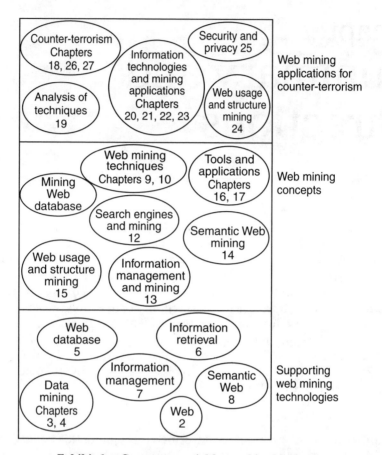

Exhibit 1. Components Addressed in this Book

In Chapter 4, we discussed some of the core data mining technologies. These include data warehousing, machine learning, statistical reasoning, visualization, and decision support. We also discussed architectures for data mining. These core data mining technologies are the supporting technologies for data mining. Furthermore, data mining is a supporting technology for Web data mining.

Chapter 5 discussed various aspects of Web database management. We first provided an overview of Web database management functions. This was followed by discussions of metadata and semistructured databases. Next we discussed distributed, heterogeneous, and legacy databases on the Web. We also provided an overview of data warehousing on the Web as well as architectural aspects. We ended the chapter with a discussion of the relationship of Web database management to Web data mining.

In Chapter 6, we discussed information retrieval systems. We first discussed text, image, video, and audio retrieval systems. Then we addressed multimedia data management. This was followed by a discussion of question answering systems. Next, we provided a brief introduction to markup languages that have close relationships to information retrieval. Finally, we discussed their relationships to Web mining.

Chapter 7 described a number of information management technologies for the Web. The technologies discussed include collaboration, knowledge management, training, agents, and sensor information management. We also discussed the relationship between these technologies and Web mining.

Chapter 8 was devoted to a discussion of the semantic Web. We first provided an overview of the semantic Web and showed how it differs from the Web. Then we discussed some technologies related to the semantic Web, i.e., RDF and ontologies. Next we provided an overview of agents and the DARPA Agent Markup Language program. Finally, we discussed some issues on treating the semantic Web as a database, and examined how various database concepts could be reused to address the semantic Web. Finally, we discussed interoperability issues and provided our view of the Web vs. the semantic Web. We ended the chapter with a discussion of the relationship between the semantic Web and data mining.

Chapter 9 discussed the emerging topic of Web data mining. First, we provided a taxonomy for Web mining, and then discussed Web content mining, Web usage mining, and Web structure mining. Finally, we discussed major applications in E-commerce.

Chapter 10 took various data mining prerequisites and examined their impact on Web data. We started with a discussion of the need for data mining and gave several examples. Next, an overview of data mining techniques was provided. Many of these techniques may be also applied for Web data mining. Finally, we discussed the similarities and differences between data mining and Web data mining.

Chapter 11 discussed various aspects of mining Web databases. Essentially, we examined the concepts in Chapter 5 and discussed the impact of data mining. First, we discussed issues on mining the databases such as integrating data mining into Web query optimization. Then we addressed mining semistructured databases. Metadata mining was discussed next. This was followed by a broad overview of mining distributed and heterogeneous databases. We also discussed approaches to federated data mining. Finally, we discussed architectural aspects of Web data mining.

In Chapter 12, we mainly addressed information retrieval and Web mining. We started with a discussion of search engines and Web mining, and showed the need for incorporating Web mining into search engines so that they can perform intelligent searches. Next, we discussed multimedia data mining, including text mining, image mining, and video mining. Finally, we provided an overview of incorporating Web mining into question answering systems as well as mining XML documents.

Chapter 13 examined the various information management technologies discussed in Chapter 7 and the impact of Web mining. For example, we examined and discussed the relationship between Web mining and collaborative data management, knowledge management, training, agents, wireless information management, sensor information management, and quality of service aspects. Many of the ideas on the Web mining technologies are still quite immature. Nevertheless, we have presented some direction for Web mining.

Chapter 14 provided a broad overview of semantic Web mining. We examined the semantic Web concepts discussed in Chapter 8 and described the impact of Web mining. We started with a discussion of semantic Web mining concepts and concepts of operation. Then we discussed mining XML and RDF documents as well as the semantic interoperability of these documents. We also discussed the use of agents in semantic Web mining, and described the notion of incorporating mining into the semantic Web when the semantic is considered to be a heterogeneous database manager. Finally, we discussed the evolution of the semantic Web, and also examined the use of Web mining in E-commerce.

Chapter 15 provided an overview of Web usage and structure mining. We started with a discussion of various outcomes and techniques for Web usage mining. Then we discussed various types of analysis. Next, we discussed customer relationship management and business intelligence, and mentioned a number of products listed on the kdnuggets Web page (www.kdnuggets.com). As we have mentioned, customer relationship management and business intelligence are key applications to Web mining. In fact, many of these tools may also be applied for counter-terrorism, although we need more investigation. We also addressed Web structure mining in this chapter.

Chapter 16 started with a discussion of prototypes, products, and standards for Web data mining. We first started with a discussion of data mining prototypes and products and then discussed Web mining products. This was followed by a discussion of standards for Web mining. As mentioned earlier, we are not endorsing any of the products. Furthermore, due to the rapid developments in the field, the information about these products may soon be outdated. Therefore, we urge the reader to take advantage of the various commercial and research material available on these products.

Chapter 17 discussed a variety of applications for Web data mining. First, we provided an overview of data mining for E-commerce as well as business intelligence and customer relationship management. Closely related to business intelligence and customer relationship management are marketing, sales, enterprise resource management, and supply chain management. We discussed these applications next. Then we provided an overview of data mining for training, telecommunications, manufacturing, and financial applications. Next, we discussed data mining for physical, social, and engineering sciences. This was followed by a discussion of data mining for medicine and biotechnology. Finally, we touched on counter-terrorism.

Chapter 18 provided a fairly broad overview of various aspects of threats and counter-terrorism measures. First, we discussed natural disasters and human error. Then we divided the threats into various groups including noninformation- and information-related terrorism and biological, chemical, and nuclear threats. We also discussed critical infrastructure threats. Next, we discussed counter-terrorism measures for all types of threats. For example, we need to gather information about terrorists and terrorist groups, mine the information, and extract patterns. In the case of bio-terrorism, for example, we need to prevent terrorist attacks with biological sensors. Finally, we discussed the conflicts between national security and privacy.

Chapter 19 provided a rather broad overview of data mining for counter-terrorism. As we have stated, we have used the terms *data mining* and *Web mining* interchangeably. Again, we can expect much of the data to be on the Web and, therefore, mining the data sources and databases on the Web to detect and prevent terrorist attacks may become a necessity. These databases could be public or private databases. First, we discussed data mining for nonreal-time threats. The idea is to gather data, build profiles of terrorists, learn from examples, and then detect and prevent attacks. The challenge is to find real-world examples because in many cases a particular attack has not happened before. Next, we discussed real-time data mining. The challenge is to build models in real-time. Finally, we discussed data mining outcomes and techniques for counter-terrorism. We focused on link analysis in detail.

Chapter 20 provided an overview of Web database mining for counter-terrorism. We started with a discussion of data sharing and data mining, and then showed how the functions of a Web database miner could help handle attacks. Then we discussed semistructured data mining, metadata mining, data warehousing aspects, and distributed and heterogeneous database mining with a focus on counter-terrorism.

Chapter 21 examined the technologies discussed in Chapters 6 and 12 and discussed their applications for counter-terrorism. We started with intelligent search engines and then discussed mining multimedia data. Essentially, we discussed the applications of mining text, images, audio, and video for counter-terrorism. Then we briefly discussed the applications of question answering systems for counter-terrorism.

Chapter 22 examined the technologies discussed in Chapters 7 and 13 and analyzed their applications for counter-terrorism. In particular, we examined collaboration, knowledge management, training, agents, wireless computing, sensor computing, and quality of service, and showed how these technologies together with Web mining may be used for counter-terrorism.

Chapter 23 provided a broad overview of semantic Web mining for counter-terrorism. We examined the semantic Web concepts discussed in Chapters 8 and 14 for counter-terrorism applications, and then described some preliminary ideas on building the semantic Web and using semantic Web mining techniques for such applications. Essentially, we have to customize the semantic Web for special communities such as law enforcement and intelligence. Many of these agencies have their own intranets. We need to build semantic Web capabilities both for intranets and for the Internet. Semantic Web mining should be an integrated capability built into the semantic Web. We also examined the use of Web services and mining for counter-terrorism.

Chapter 24 discussed Web usage mining and Web structure mining and showed how they may be applied for counter-terrorism. With Web usage mining, one could analyze Web traffic as well as carry out clickstream analysis. Web structure mining is essentially mining the Web links to determine the structure of the Web. For example, with Web structure mining, we could find out the number of Web pages with links pointing to a particular Web page. After we carry out Web structure mining, then we could apply Web usage mining as well as Web content mining.

Chapter 25 was devoted to the important area of privacy related to Web mining and data mining. While there have been efforts to apply data mining for handling security problems such as intrusion detection, in Chapter 25 we focused on the negative effects of data mining. In particular, we discussed the inference problem that can result due to mining, as well as ways of compromising privacy, especially due to Web data access.

Chapter 26 examined the various threats discussed in Chapter 18 and described how Web mining and data mining may be applied. Essentially, we examined the discussions in Chapters 19 through 24 and summarized the applications of Web mining and data mining for counter-terrorism. We examined natural disasters, malicious attacks, noninformation-related terrorism, information-related terrorism, attacks on critical infrastructures, and nonreal-time and real-time threats. We analyzed various data mining outcomes and techniques such as clustering, link analysis, and anomaly detection for counter-terrorism for the various threats.

Finally, in Chapter 27 we started with a discussion of models for counter-terrorism and then discussed architectures and functions for counter-terrorism. We also revisited business intelligence. Essentially, this chapter briefly examined the parallels between E-commerce, business intelligence, and counter-terrorism. While E-commerce and counter-terrorism are very different applications of Web mining, there are similarities between them. Both use business intelligence to improve their strategies. We also discussed technologies for building systems for counter-terrorism. These systems may have infrastructures as well as data managers. Data mining services may also be part of these systems.

We end this book with three appendixes. Appendix A provides an overview of data management systems and the relationship between the books we have written on this topic. Appendix B provides an overview of database systems. Information security is discussed in Appendix C.

CHALLENGES AND DIRECTIONS FOR WEB DATA MINING

This section discusses future directions in Web data mining. In the area of Web database mining, one of the major challenges is scalability. That is, how do you efficiently mine large quantities of data on the Web? Other challenges include getting good quality data for mining, mining multimedia data, and mining usage patterns and structure on the Web. Essentially, we need to determine how to mine all the data out there and extract useful information. We also need to improve mining for applications such as E-commerce. We need the mining tools to work with the Web. Mining for E-commerce will be one of the major directions in information technology. We need to adapt the techniques to help with counter-terrorism activities.

Other directions for Web mining include integration with information retrieval, databases, and information management technologies. We first need to develop tools for database management, information retrieval, and information management on the Web. The data mining tools have to work with these information retrieval, Web database management, and information management tools. For example, we need data mining tools to mine knowledge repositories. We also need better tools for knowledge management.

Exhibit 2 illustrates some of the directions for Web data/information mining. In addition to all of the areas discussed here, we believe that it is time to focus on the foundational aspects. Is there some sort of theory upon which we can develop mining systems? How can we develop good link analysis tools? We need extensive research in this area. Finally, we cannot forget about privacy. We need to develop privacy-sensitive data mining tools.

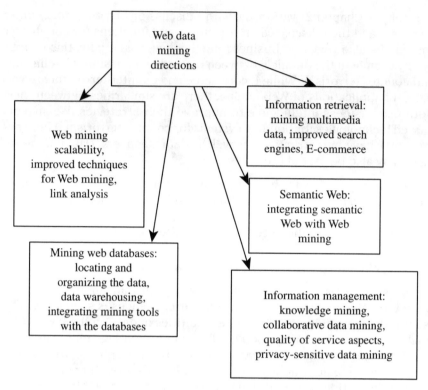

Exhibit 2.   Web Data Mining Directions

CHALLENGES AND DIRECTIONS FOR WEB DATA MINING FOR COUNTER-TERRORISM

Each of the Web data mining technologies discussed in this book and its future developments will have a significant impact on counter-terrorism. As we are seeing, one of the major concerns of our nation today is to detect and prevent terrorist attacks. This is also becoming the goal of many nations in the world. We need to examine the various data mining and Web mining technologies to see how they can be adapted for counter-terrorism. We also need to develop special Web mining techniques for counter-terrorism. As we have stressed in this book, we expect much of the data to be on the Web, either the Internet or private intranets. Analysts will have to collaborate via the Web within or between agencies. Also, the founding of the Department of Homeland Security may perhaps have an impact on how data mining will be carried out. We briefly examine this aspect in the next section.

In addition to improving data mining and Web mining techniques and adapting them for counter-terrorism, we also need to focus on federated

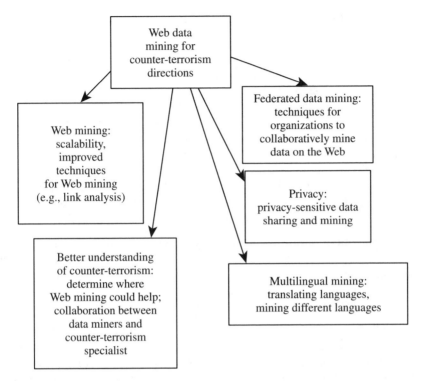

Exhibit 3.   Web Mining for Counter-Terrorism Directions

data mining. We can expect agencies to collaboratively work together. They will have to share and mine the data collaboratively. We can expect to see an increased interest in federated data mining. In this book, we have discussed only the high-level ideas. We need to explore the details.

Some other areas of interest include multilingual data mining. Terrorism is not confined to one country and it respects no borders. It is everywhere, carried out by people from different countries speaking different languages. We need to understand their languages without any ambiguity. We need technologies to understand the various languages and to mine the text in different languages. We also need translators and language experts to work with technologists for multilingual data management and mining.

As we have stressed in this book, we cannot forget about privacy. National security measures will mean violating privacy and civil liberties. We cannot abandon our quest for eliminating terrorism. However, we also have to be sensitive to the privacy of individuals. This will be a major challenge. We need to develop techniques for privacy-sensitive data sharing and data mining. Exhibit 3 illustrates the directions for Web data mining for counter-terrorism.

IMPACT OF THE DEPARTMENT OF HOMELAND SECURITY

As we complete this book, the Department of Homeland Security was recently formed in the United States. The goal of this agency is to prevent and detect terrorist attacks on the United States and its interests. We have tried as much as possible to keep away from politics in this book. Our main goal is to discuss Web data mining technologies and explore their use for counter-terrorism. However, we cannot discuss counter-terrorism without at least mentioning the Department of Homeland Security. In this section, we will express our ideas on how this newly formed department could make use of data mining and Web data mining to prevent and detect terrorism. As we have stated throughout this book, the ideas and conclusions expressed are those of the author and do not reflect the policies or procedures of the United States government or any other organization.

The Department of Homeland Security is a very young department as we write this section. Therefore, we have no information on the details of this department except that its goal is to combat terrorism. Therefore, information management technologies in general and Web data mining in particular could be critical technologies for the functioning of this department.

First of all, to carry out useful Web and data mining, we need to have good data. This means we need to gather all kinds of data about various individual and events and have the data ready for mining. Various agencies gather different types of data. These agencies have to share data to form the big picture. The shared data then has to be mined. One can envisage the Department of Homeland Security to perhaps oversee the sharing of relevant data and ensure that appropriate mining is carried out. That is, we see this department performing the functions of a federated database administrator. It could also carry out federated data mining. Note that we have discussed federated data management and mining in various chapters of this book.

As we have read in the newspapers, various agencies such as the Immigration and Naturalization Service will be brought under this newly formed department. In Chapter 18, we discussed the threats that could occur at our borders. We also discussed how data mining could be used to detect and prevent potential terrorist attacks that could be carried out, for example, by illegal immigrants or those smuggling drugs and firearms into this country. Therefore, in addition to overseeing data sharing and data mining across agencies, the Department of Homeland Security could also develop its own tools and techniques to mine the data that is available to the various offices that constitute this department.

Essentially, we need excellent communication between officials functioning at all levels and between several agencies. This could mean having chief information officers at the various departments and officers who carry out the information management functions within and across organizations. We also need chief technology officers who ensure that appropriate technologies are brought into the departments and eventually systems for counter-terrorism are built. Note that in Chapter 27, we discussed the preliminaries of putting together systems consisting of various services such as a data management service and data mining service. We need to explore the use of object technologies and component technologies on developing such systems. At this point, we cannot say that there will be just one system for counter-terrorism. We may need multiple systems. But the key is for these various systems to interoperate with each other.

While there have been various discussions on the pros and cons of forming the Department of Homeland Security, from a technology point of view, we believe that effective data sharing and data mining are critical to combat terrorism. Therefore, if it means that it can be best accomplished through this newly formed department, then we need such a department. Our goal is to gather, organize, and mine the data to get useful results. Business intelligence analysis technologies have to be used effectively to identify threats and develop strategies and counter-measures. However, we cannot forget about privacy. By forming the Department of Homeland Security, we hope that while we strive to develop technologies to combat terrorism, we do not forget about the privacy and civil liberties of individuals.

WHERE DO WE GO FROM HERE?

We have provided a broad overview of Web data mining and their applications in counter-terrorism. We have stressed gathering business intelligence and analysis. The intelligence to develop strategies is essential to combat terrorism. We have also given many references should the reader need in-depth coverage of a particular topic, especially in Web mining. However, all the reading is not going to give the reader a better appreciation for what Web mining is all about. It is certainly useful to have a good knowledge in Web mining technologies and to be able to speak intelligently about it. However, if we want to know what the details are, then we need hands-on experience with the tools. As in the case of many technologies, data mining and Web mining get better with practice; we urge the reader to work with practical applications in using the tools and possibly developing the tools. We also urge the reader to keep up with the literature about the tools. The Web page at www.kdnuggets.com provides a good overview of the current tools.

We have also discussed applying Web mining and data mining for counter-terrorism. As we have stated, we are not counter-terrorism experts. Our information on counter-terrorism has been obtained from the Web as well as from various newspapers. We have given some idea on where data mining and Web mining could be applied. In particular, techniques such as clustering, link analysis, market basket analysis, and anomaly detection can be used to detect and possibly prevent terrorist activities. The key is to make the associations between various events and activities. We have given various examples to illustrate how Web mining could be used to make the links and associations. It is very important that we have a good idea about what is out there. That is, how effective are the existing tools? We need to carry out a subjective evaluation of the existing tools and then identify areas that need research and development. Data mining specialists have to work with vendors and counter-terrorism specialists to develop new tools. As we have stressed, we also need to work with sociologists and psychologists to understand the cultures that produce terrorists. Finally, we need to involve law makers to determine privacy laws as well as to put together a plan for privacy-sensitive data mining.

The world is facing many challenges. There have been recent devastating terrorist activities. While terrorism has existed for a long time, it is only with the September 11, 2001, attacks that many of us are aware of the extent to which these attacks can cause devastation. Terrorist attacks can claim thousands of lives and cripple an economy. Therefore, we have to strive to develop technologies to make this world a safer place to live. Data management, information retrieval, information management, data mining, and Web mining are all important technologies for counter-terrorism.

We must note that technology alone cannot not solve our problems. We need to develop a culture of collaboratively working together. The human aspect is also very important. For example, we need technologists to work closely with sociologists and psychologists. In addition, the technologists also have to work with counter-terrorism experts. We need to take advantage of commercial business intelligence analysis tools and products as much as possible and create means for military intelligence analysis. While we continue to develop technologies for national security, we cannot forget about privacy. We need to develop techniques for privacy-sensitive data sharing and data mining. We need policy makers, law makers, and technologists to work together to ensure the security of our nation without sacrificing the privacy of individuals. This will be our major challenge.

As we have stressed throughout this book, we have made two major assumptions. One is that we have assumed that the Web is not just based on the Internet. The Web could also be based on public networks, private intranets, and unclassified networks. That is, many organizations have their own internal Web. We also assumed that much of the data will eventually be on the Web in one form or another. This means that Web data mining encompasses data mining. This is why we chose to discuss Web data mining technologies instead of just data mining technologies. We have discussed Web content mining, which is essentially data mining on the Web, Web usage mining, and Web structure mining. Furthermore, the Web has both structured and unstructured data, and therefore it is much more complex to mine, for example, the Web data than mining relational databases.

We started talking about data mining and privacy as early as 1996 at the IFIP Database Security Conference. At that time, we did not expect that there would be a strong need for data mining and data sharing. It is only after the September 11, 2001, attacks that many of us are aware of the urgent need to develop technologies for national security. This also means that only after September 11th have many of us become aware of the impact on privacy as well. Our main motivation to write this book was to make readers aware of the potential uses of data and Web mining for counter-terrorism. It is our duty to ensure that David Bernard and the thousands of others who died as a result of the terrorist attacks on September 11th and millions of others who have died around the world due to terrorism have not died in vain.

Part IV
Appendixes

Appendix A
Data Management Systems: Developments and Trends

In this appendix, we provide an overview of the developments and trends in data management as discussed in our previous book [THUR97]. Because data plays a major role in Web data management, a good understanding of data management is essential for Web data management.

Recent developments in information systems technologies have resulted in computerizing many applications in various business areas. Data has become a critical resource in many organizations, and therefore efficient access to data, sharing the data, extracting information from the data, and making use of the information have become urgent needs. As a result, there have been several efforts on integrating the various data sources scattered across several sites. These data sources may be databases managed by database management systems or they could simply be files. To provide interoperability between multiple data sources and systems, various tools are being developed. These tools enable users of one system to access other systems in an efficient and transparent manner.

We define data management systems as systems that manage the data, extract meaningful information from the data, and make use of the information extracted. Therefore, data management systems include database systems, data warehouses, and data mining systems. Data could be structured, such as that found in relational databases, or it could be unstructured such as text, voice, imagery, and video. There have been numerous discussions in the past to distinguish between data, information, and knowledge.* We do not attempt to clarify these terms. For our purposes, data could be just

---

* More recently, the area of knowledge management is receiving much attention. We addressed knowledge management in Chapter 13. More details are given in [MORE98].

bits and bytes or it could convey some meaningful information to the user. We will, however, distinguish between database systems and database management systems. A database management system is that component which manages the database containing persistent data. A database system consists of both the database and the database management system.

A key component to the evolution and interoperation of data management systems is the interoperability of heterogeneous database systems. Efforts on interoperability between database systems have been reported since the late 1970s. However, it is only recently that we are seeing commercial developments in heterogeneous database systems. Major database system vendors are now providing interoperability between their products and other systems. Furthermore, many of the database system vendors are migrating toward the client/server architecture which facilitates distributed data management capabilities. In addition to efforts on interoperability between different database systems and client/server environments, work is also directed toward handling autonomous and federated environments.

DEVELOPMENTS IN DATABASE SYSTEMS

Exhibit 1 provides an overview of developments in database systems technology. While the early work in the 1960s focused on developing products based on the network and hierarchical data models, much of the developments in database systems took place after the seminal paper by Codd describing the relational model ([CODD70]; see also [DATE90]). Research and development work on relational database systems was carried out during the early 1970s, and several prototypes were developed throughout the 1970s. Notable efforts include IBM's System R and the University of California–Berkeley's Ingres. During the 1980s, many relational database system products were being marketed (notable among these products are those of Oracle, Sybase, Informix, Ingres, IBM, Digital Equipment, and Hewlett Packard). During the 1990s, products from other vendors have emerged (e.g., Microsoft). In fact, numerous relational database system products have been marketed to date. However, Codd has stated that many of the systems that are being marketed as relational systems are not really relational (see, for example, the discussion in [DATE90]). He then discussed various criteria that a system must satisfy to qualify as a relational database system. While the early work focused on issues such as data modeling, normalization theory, query processing and optimization strategies, query languages, and access strategies and indexes, the focus later shifted toward supporting a multiuser environment. In particular, concurrency control and recovery techniques were developed. Support for transaction processing was also provided.

Research on relational database systems as well as on transaction management was followed by research on distributed database systems

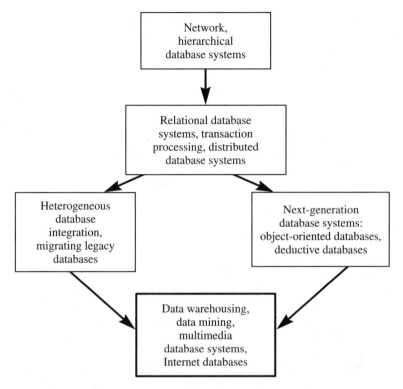

Exhibit 1.   Developments in Database Systems Technology

around the mid-1970s. Several distributed database system prototype development efforts also began around the late 1970s. Notable among these efforts include IBM's System R*, DDTS (Distributed Database Testbed System) by Honeywell, SDD-I and Multibase by Computer Corporation of America, and Mermaid by System Development Corporation. Furthermore, many of these systems function in a heterogeneous environment. During the early 1990s, several database system vendors provided data distribution capabilities for their systems. Most of the distributed relational database system products are based on client/server architectures. The idea is to have the client of vendor A communicate with the server database system of vendor B. In other words, the client/server computing paradigm facilitates a heterogeneous computing environment. Interoperability between relational and nonrelational commercial database systems is also possible. The database systems community is also involved in standardization efforts. Notable among these efforts are the ANSI/SPARC three-level schema architecture;* the IRDS (Information Resource Dictionary

*ANSI/SPARC is the American National Standards Institute/Systems Planning and Requirements Committee.

System) standard for data dictionary systems; the relational query language, SQL (Structured Query Language); and the RDA (Remote Database Access) Protocol.

Another significant development in database technology is the advent of object-oriented database management systems. Active work in developing such systems began in the mid-1980s, and they are now commercially available (notable among them include the products of Object Design, Ontos, Gemstone Systems, and Versant Object Technology). It was felt that new-generation applications such as multimedia, office information systems, CAD/CAM,* process control, and software engineering have different requirements. Such applications utilize complex data structures. Tighter integration between the programming language and the data model is also desired. Object-oriented database systems satisfy most of the requirements of these new-generation applications [CATT91].

According to the Lagunita report published as a result of a National Science Foundation (NSF) workshop in 1990 (see [NSF90] and [SIGM90]), relational database systems, transaction processing, and distributed (relational) database systems are stated as mature technologies. Furthermore, vendors are marketing object-oriented database systems and demonstrating the interoperability between different database systems. The report goes on to state that as applications are becoming increasingly complex, more sophisticated database systems are needed. Furthermore, because many organizations now use different types of database systems, the systems need to be integrated. Although work has begun to address these issues, and commercial products are available, several issues still need to be resolved. Therefore, database systems researchers in the early 1990s faced challenges in two areas: next-generation database systems and heterogeneous database systems.

Next-generation database systems include object-oriented, functional, high-performance, real-time, scientific, temporal, and intelligent (sometimes called logic or deductive) database systems, database systems that handle incomplete and uncertain information, and special parallel architectures to enhance the performance of database system functions.** Ideally, a database system should provide the support for high performance transaction processing, model complex applications, represent new kinds of data, and make intelligent deductions. While significant progress had been made during the late 1980s and early 1990s, there is much to be done before such a database system can be developed.

Heterogeneous database systems have been receiving considerable attention during the past decade [ACM90]. The major issues include handling different data models, different query processing strategies, different

* CAD/CAM is computer aided design/computer aided manufacturing.
** For a discussion of the next-generation database systems, see [SIGM90].

transaction processing algorithms, and different query languages. Should a uniform view be provided to the entire system, or should the users of the individual systems maintain their own views? These are questions that have yet to be answered satisfactorily. It is also envisaged that a complete solution to heterogeneous database management systems is a generation away. While research should be directed toward finding such a solution, work should also be carried out to handle limited forms of heterogeneity to satisfy the customer needs. Another type of database system that has received some attention lately is a federated database system. Note that some have used the terms *heterogeneous database system* and *federated database system* interchangeably. While heterogeneous database systems can be part of a federation, a federation can also include homogeneous database systems.

The explosion of users on the Internet and the Web as well as developments in interface technologies has resulted in even more challenges for data management researchers. A second workshop was sponsored by NSF in 1995, and several emerging technologies have been identified as important in the 21st century [NSF95]. These include digital libraries, managing very large databases, data administration issues, multimedia databases, data warehousing, data mining, data management for collaborative computing environments, security, and privacy. Another significant development in the 1990s is the development of object-relational systems. Such systems combine the advantages of object-oriented and relational database systems. Also, many corporations are now focusing on integrating their data management products with Internet technologies. Finally, for many organizations there is an increasing need to migrate legacy databases and applications to newer architectures and systems such as client/server architectures and relational database systems. We believe there is no end to data management systems. As new technologies are developed, there are new opportunities for data management research and development.

A comprehensive view of all data management technologies is illustrated in Exhibit 2. As shown, traditional technologies include database design, transaction processing, and benchmarking. Then there are database systems based on data models such as relational and object-oriented. Database systems may depend on features they provide such as security and real-time. These database systems may be relational or object-oriented. There are also database systems based on multiple sites or processors such as distributed and heterogeneous database systems, parallel systems, and systems being migrated. Finally, there are the emerging technologies such as data warehousing and mining, collaboration, and the Internet. Any comprehensive text on data management systems should address all of these technologies. We have selected some of the relevant

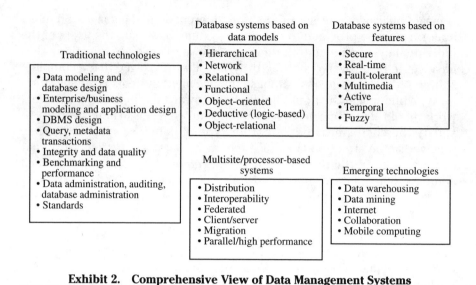

Exhibit 2. Comprehensive View of Data Management Systems

technologies and put them in a framework. This framework is described later in this appendix.*

STATUS, VISION, AND ISSUES

Significant progress has been made on data management systems. However, many of the technologies are still stand-alone, as illustrated in Exhibit 3. For example, multimedia systems are yet to be successfully integrated with warehousing and mining technologies. The ultimate goal is to integrate multiple technologies so that accurate data, as well as information, is produced at the right time and distributed to the user in a timely manner. Our vision for data and information management is illustrated in Exhibit 4.

The work discussed in [THUR97] addressed many of the challenges necessary to accomplish this vision. In particular, integration of heterogeneous databases, as well as the use of distributed object technology for interoperability, was discussed. While much progress has been made on the system aspects of interoperability, semantic issues still remain a challenge. Different databases have different representations. Furthermore, the same data entity may be interpreted differently at different sites. Addressing these semantic differences and extracting useful information from the heterogeneous, and possibly multimedia, data sources are major challenges. This book has attempted to address some of the challenges through the use of data mining.

---

* In our previous book, *Data Management Systems Evolution and Interoperation,* we selected certain topics in data management and explained the various concepts.

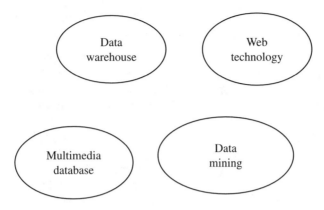

Exhibit 3.   Stand-Alone Systems

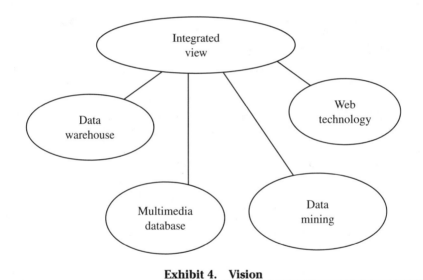

Exhibit 4.   Vision

DATA MANAGEMENT SYSTEMS FRAMEWORK

For the successful development of evolvable interoperable data management systems, heterogeneous database systems integration is a major component. However, there are other technologies that have to be successfully integrated with each other to develop techniques for efficient access and sharing of data as well as for the extraction of information from the data. To facilitate the development of data management systems to meet the requirements of various applications in fields such as medical, financial, manufacturing, and military, we have proposed a framework, which can be regarded as a reference model for data management systems.

APPENDIX A: DATA MANAGEMENT SYSTEMS

Various components from this framework have to be integrated to develop data management systems to support the various applications.

Exhibit 5 illustrates our framework, which can be regarded as a model for data management systems.* This framework consists of three layers. One can think of the component technologies, which we will also refer to as components, belonging to a particular layer that is more or less built upon the technologies provided by the lower layer. Layer 1 is the Database Technology and Distribution layer. This layer consists of database systems and distributed database systems technologies. Layer 2 is the Interoperability and Migration layer. This layer consists of technologies such as heterogeneous database integration, client/server databases, and multimedia database systems to handle heterogeneous data types, and migrating legacy databases.** Layer 3 is the Information Extraction and Sharing layer. This layer essentially consists of technologies for some of the newer services supported by data management systems, including data warehousing, data mining [THUR98], Internet databases, and database support for collaborative applications.***,**** Data management systems may utilize lower-level technologies such as networking, distributed processing, and mass storage. We have grouped these technologies into a layer called the Supporting Technologies layer. This supporting layer does not belong to the data management systems framework. This supporting layer also consists of some higher-level technologies such as distributed object management and agents.***** Also shown in Exhibit 5 is the Application Technologies layer. Systems such as collaborative computing systems and knowledge-based systems which belong to the Application Technologies layer, may utilize data management systems. Note that the Application Technologies layer is also outside of the data management systems framework.

The technologies that constitute the data management systems framework can be regarded as some of the core technologies in data manage-

---

* Note that the three-layer model is subjective and is not a standard model. This model has helped us in organizing our views on data management.
** We have placed multimedia database systems in Layer 2, as we consider it a special type of a heterogeneous database system. A multimedia database system handles heterogeneous data types, such as text, audio, and video.
*** Note that one could also argue whether database support for collaborative applications should be discussed here. This is because collaborative computing is not part of the data management framework. However, such applications do need database support, and our focus has been on this support.
**** Although Internet database management is an integration of various technologies, we have placed it in Layer 3 because it still deals with information extraction. Note that the data management framework consists of technologies for managing data as well as for extracting information from the data. However, what one does with the information, such as collaborative computing, sophisticated human–computer interaction, natural language processing, and knowledge-based processing, does not belong to this framework. These tasks belong to the Application layer.
***** Note that technologies such as distributed object management enable interoperation and migration.

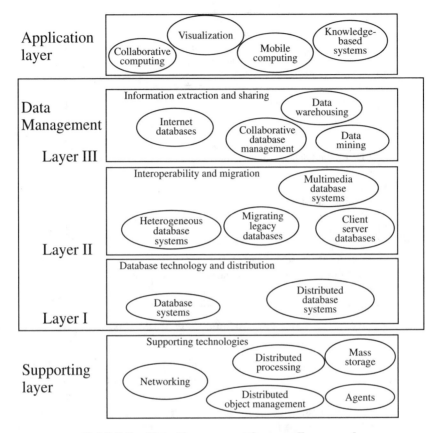

Exhibit 5. Data Management Systems Framework

ment. However, features such as security, integrity, real-time processing, fault tolerance, and high-performance computing are needed for many applications utilizing data management technologies. Applications utilizing data management technologies may be medical, financial, or military. We illustrate this in Exhibit 6, where a three-dimensional view relating data management technologies with features and applications is given. For example, one could develop a secure distributed database management system for medical applications or a fault-tolerant multimedia database management system for financial applications.*

Integrating the components belonging to the various layers is important to developing efficient data management systems. In addition, data management technologies have to be integrated with the application technolo-

---

* In some cases, one could also consider multimedia data processing and reengineering, which is an essential part of system migration, to be at the same level as features such as security and integrity. They could also be regarded as emerging technologies.

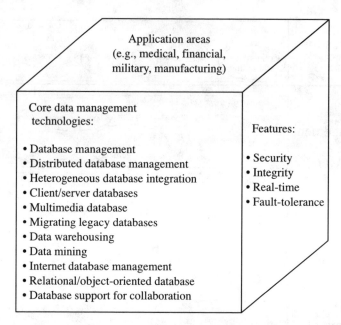

Application areas
(e.g., medical, financial,
military, manufacturing)

Core data management
technologies:

- Database management
- Distributed database management
- Heterogeneous database integration
- Client/server databases
- Multimedia database
- Migrating legacy databases
- Data warehousing
- Data mining
- Internet database management
- Relational/object-oriented database
- Database support for collaboration

Features:

- Security
- Integrity
- Real-time
- Fault-tolerance

Exhibit 6.   A Three-Dimensional View of Data Management

gies to develop successful information systems. However, at present there is limited integration between these various components. Our previous book, *Data Management Systems Evolution and Interoperation,* focused mainly on the concepts, developments, and trends belonging to each of the components shown in the framework. Furthermore, our current book on Web data management, which we also refer to as Internet data management, focuses on the Internet database component of Layer 3 of the framework shown in Exhibit 5.

BUILDING INFORMATION SYSTEMS FROM THE FRAMEWORK

Exhibit 5 illustrates a framework for data management systems. As shown, the technologies for data management include database systems, distributed database systems, heterogeneous database systems, Internet databases, multimedia database systems, migrating legacy databases, data warehousing, data mining, and database support for collaboration. Furthermore, data management systems take advantage of supporting technologies such as distributed processing and agents. Similarly, application technologies such as collaborative computing, visualization, expert systems, and mobile computing take advantage of data management systems.*

* Note that databases could also support expert systems, as in the case of collaborative applications.

438

```
┌─────────────────────────┐
│                         │
│      Collaboration,     │
│      visualization      │
│                         │
└─────────────────────────┘

   ┌─────────────────────────┐
   │   Multimedia database,  │
   │   distributed database  │
   │        systems          │
   └─────────────────────────┘

 ┌─────────────────────────┐
 │      Mass storage,      │
 │       distributed       │
 │       processing        │
 └─────────────────────────┘
```

**Exhibit 7.   Framework for Multimedia Data Management
for Collaboration**

Many of us have heard the term *information systems* on numerous occasions. These systems have sometimes been used interchangeably with data management systems. In our terminology, information systems are much broader than data management systems, but they do include data management systems. In fact, a framework for information systems will include not only the data management system layers, but also the supporting technologies layer as well as the application technologies layer. That is, information systems encompass all kinds of computing systems. They can be regarded as the finished product that can be used for various applications. That is, while hardware is at the lowest end of the spectrum, applications are at the highest end.

We can combine the technologies of Exhibit 5 to put together information systems. For example, at the application technology level, one may need collaboration and visualization technologies so that analysts can collaboratively carry out some tasks. At the data management level, one may need both multimedia and distributed database technologies. At the supporting level, one may need mass storage as well as some distributed processing capability. This special framework is illustrated in Exhibit 7. Another example is a special framework for interoperability. One may need some visualization technology to display the integrated information from the heterogeneous databases. At the data management level, we have heterogeneous database systems technology. At the supporting technology level, one may use distributed object management technology to encapsulate the heterogeneous databases. This special framework is illustrated in Exhibit 8.

439

APPENDIX A: DATA MANAGEMENT SYSTEMS

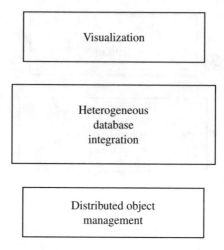

Exhibit 8.   Framework for Heterogeneous Database Interoperability

Finally, let us illustrate the concepts that we have described by using a specific example. Suppose a group of physicians wants a system where they can collaborate and make decisions about various patients. This could be a medical video-teleconferencing application. That is, at the highest level, the application is a medical application and, more specifically, a medical video-teleconferencing application. At the application technology level, one needs a variety of technologies including collaboration and teleconferencing. These application technologies will make use of data management technologies such as distributed database systems and multimedia database systems. That is, one may need to support multimedia data such as audio and video. The data management technologies in turn draw upon lower-level technologies such as distributed processing and networking. We illustrate this in Exhibit 9.

In summary, information systems include data management systems as well as application layer systems such as collaborative computing systems and supporting layer systems such as distributed object management systems.

While application technologies make use of data management technologies, and data management technologies make use of supporting technologies, the ultimate user of the information system is the application itself. Today, numerous applications make use of information systems. These applications are from multiple domains such as medical, financial, manufacturing, telecommunications, and defense. Specific applications include signal processing, E-commerce, patient monitoring, and situation assessment. Exhibit 10 illustrates the relationship between the application and the information system.

440

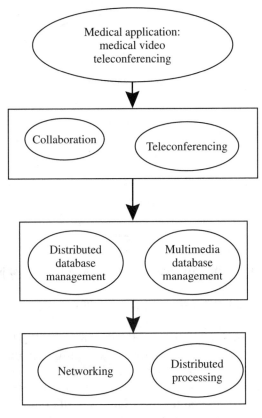

Exhibit 9.   Specific Example

RELATIONSHIP BETWEEN THE TEXTS

We have published several books on data management and mining ([THUR97], [THUR98], [THUR00], [THUR01], and [THUR02]). All of these books have evolved from the framework that we illustrated in this appendix and address different parts of the framework. The connection between these texts is illustrated in Exhibit 11.

SUMMARY

In this appendix, we have provided an overview of data management. We first discussed the developments in data management and then provided a vision. Then we illustrated a framework for data management. This framework consists of three layers: the database systems layer, the interoperability layer, and the information extraction layer. Web data management belongs to Layer 3. Finally, we showed how information systems could be built from the technologies of the framework.

APPENDIX A: DATA MANAGEMENT SYSTEMS

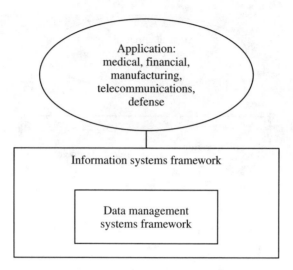

Exhibit 10. Application–Framework Relationship

Let us repeat what we mentioned in Chapter 1, now that we have described the data management framework we introduced in [THUR97]. The chapters in this book not only discuss multimedia data management and mining concepts, they also show how multimedia data management and mining could be applied to the various applications such as E-commerce. Many of the technologies discussed in the framework of Exhibit 5 have been useful in the discussion of multimedia data management and mining, including database systems, distributed database systems, data warehousing, and data mining. In addition, some other features for data management such as metadata and security also play a role in various chapters of this book. For example, metadata for multimedia databases was the subject of Chapter 4. Security and privacy issues were discussed both with respect to the Web and with respect to multimedia data management and mining in Chapter 10.

We believe that data management is essential to many information technologies, including data mining, multimedia information processing, interoperability, collaboration, and knowledge management. This appendix stresses data management. The remaining appendixes focus on various other key technologies for Web mining including database systems, the Web, and E-commerce.

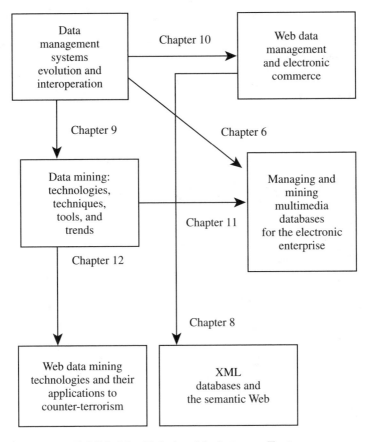

Exhibit 11. Relationship between Texts

References

[ACM90] Special issue on heterogeneous database systems, *ACM Computing Surveys,* September 1990.

[CATT91] Cattell, R., *Object Data Management Systems,* Addison-Wesley, Reading, MA, 1991.

[CODD70] Codd, E.F., A relational model of data for large shared data banks, *Communications of the ACM,* 13, 6, June 1970.

[DATE90] Date, C.J., *An Introduction to Database Management Systems,* Addison-Wesley, Reading, MA, 1990 (6th ed. published in 1995 by Addison-Wesley).

[MORE98] Morey, D., Knowledge management architecture, in *Handbook of Data Management,* Thuraisingham, B., Ed., Auerbach Publications, New York, 1998.

[NSF90] Proceedings of the Database Systems Workshop, report published by the National Science Foundation, 1990.

[NSF95] Proceedings of the Database Systems Workshop, report published by the National Science Foundation, 1995.

[SIGM90] Next-generation database systems, *ACM SIGMOD Record,* December 1990.

[THUR97] Thuraisingham, B., *Data Management Systems Evolution and Interoperation,* CRC Press, Boca Raton, FL, 1997.

APPENDIX A: DATA MANAGEMENT SYSTEMS

[THUR98] Thuraisingham, B., *Data Mining: Technologies, Techniques, Tools, and Trends,* CRC Press, Boca Raton, FL, 1998.

[THUR00] Thuraisingham, B., *Web Data Management and Electronic Commerce,* CRC Press, Boca Raton, FL, 2000.

[THUR01] Thuraisingham, B., *Managing and Mining Multimedia Databases for the Electronic Enterprise,* CRC Press, Boca Raton, FL, 2001.

[THUR02] Thuraisingham, B., *XML, Databases, and the Semantic Web,* CRC Press, Boca Raton, FL, 2002.

Appendix B
Database Systems and Related Technologies

Database systems play a key role in Web data management. Having good data is key to effective Web data management, and therefore, we give considerable attention to database systems in this book. It should be noted that we are taking a data-oriented perspective to the Web.

Database systems technology has advanced a great deal during the past four decades from the legacy systems based on network and hierarchical models to relational and object-oriented database systems based on client/server architectures. This appendix provides an overview of the important developments in database systems relevant to the contents of this book. Much of the discussion in the book builds on the information presented in this appendix.

As stated in Appendix A, we consider a database system to include both the database management system (DBMS) and the database (see also the discussion in [DATE90]). The DBMS component of the database system manages the database. The database contains persistent data. That is, the data is permanent even if the applications go away.

RELATIONAL AND ENTITY-RELATIONSHIP DATA MODELS

It is widely accepted among the data modeling community that the purpose of a data model is to capture the universe that it is representing as accurately, completely, and naturally as possible [TSIC82]. Various data models have been proposed, and we have provided an overview in our previous book [THUR97]. In this section, we discuss the essential points of the relational data model, as it is the most widely used today. In addition, we also discuss the entity-relationship data model, as some of the ideas have been used in object models, and furthermore, entity-relationship models are being used extensively in database design. There do exist many other models such as logic-based models, hypersemantic models, and functional models. Discussion of all of these models is beyond the scope of this book.

445

Exhibit 1. **Relational Database**

EMP

SS#	Ename	Salary	D#
1	John	20K	10
2	Paul	30K	20
3	Mary	40K	20

DEPT

D#	Dname	Mgr
10	Math	Smith
20	Physics	Jones

We do provide an overview of an object model later in this appendix, as object technology is essential for the Web and some of the ideas in XML have been influenced by object models.

Relational Data Model

With the relational model [CODD70], the database is viewed as a collection of relations. Each relation has attributes and rows. For example, Exhibit 1 illustrates a database with two relations, EMP and DEPT. EMP has four attributes: SS#, Ename, Salary, and D#. DEPT has three attributes: D#, Dname, and Mgr. EMP has three rows, also called tuples, and DEPT has two rows. Each row is uniquely identified by its primary key. For example, SS# could be the primary key for EMP and D# for DEPT. Another key feature of the relational model is that each element in the relation is an atomic value such as an integer or a string. That is, complex values such as lists are not supported.

Various operations are performed on relations. The SELECT operation selects a subset of rows satisfying certain conditions. For example, in the relation EMP, one may select tuples where the salary is more than $20K. The PROJECT operation projects the relation onto some attributes. For example, in the relation EMP one may project onto the attributes Ename and Salary. The JOIN operation joins two relations over some common attributes. A detailed discussion of these operations is given in [DATE90] and [ULLM88].

Various languages to manipulate the relations have been proposed. Notable among these languages is the ANSI standard, SQL (Structured Query Language). This language is used to access and manipulate data in relational databases [SQL3]. There is wide acceptance of this standard among database management system vendors and users. It supports schema definition, retrieval, data manipulation, schema manipulation, transaction management, integrity, and security. Other languages include the relational calculus first proposed in the Ingres project at the University of California–Berkeley [DATE90]. Another important concept in relational databases is the notion of a view. A view is essentially a virtual relation and is formed from the relations in the database. For further details, we refer to [DATE90].

Exhibit 2. Entity-Relationship Representation

Entity-Relationship Data Model

One of the major drawbacks of the relational data model is its lack of support for capturing the semantics of an application. This resulted in the development of semantic data models. The entity-relationship (ER) data model developed by Chen [CHEN76] can be regarded as the earliest semantic data model. In this model, the world is viewed as a collection of entities and relationships between entities. Exhibit 2 illustrates two entities, EMP and DEPT. The relationship between them is WORKS.

Relationships can be either one–one, many–one, or many–many. If it is assumed that each employee works in one department and each department has one employee, then WORKS is a one–one relationship. If it is assumed that an employee works in one department and each department can have many employees, then WORKS is a many–one relationship. If it is assumed that an employee works in many departments, and each department has many employees, then WORKS is a many–many relationship.

Several extensions to the entity-relationship model have been proposed. One is the entity-relationship-attribute model where attributes are associated with entities as well as relationships, and another has introduced the notion of categories into the model (see, for example, the discussions in [ELMA85] and [YANG88]). It should be noted that ER models are used mainly to design databases. That is, most database CASE (computer aided software engineering) tools are based on the ER model, where the application is represented using such a model, and subsequently the database (possibly relational) is generated. Current database management systems are not based on the ER model. That is, unlike the relational model, ER models did not take off in the development of database management systems.

ARCHITECTURAL ISSUES

This section describes various types of architectures for a database system. First, we illustrate a very high-level centralized architecture for a database system. Then we describe a functional architecture for a database system. In particular, the functions of the DBMS component of the database system are illustrated in this architecture. Then we discuss the ANSI/SPARC's three-schema architecture, which has been more or less accepted by the database community [DATE90]. Finally, we describe extensible architectures.

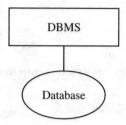

Exhibit 3.   Centralized Architecture

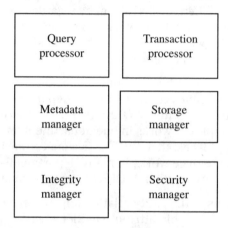

Exhibit 4.   Functional Architecture for a DBMS

Exhibit 3 is an example of a centralized architecture. Here, the DBMS is a monolithic entity and manages a database, which is centralized. Functional architecture illustrates the functional modules of a DBMS. The major modules of a DBMS include the query processor, transaction manager, metadata manager, storage manager, integrity manager, and security manager. The functional architecture of the DBMS component of the centralized database system architecture (of Exhibit 3) is illustrated in Exhibit 4.

Schema describes the data in the database. It has also been referred to as the data dictionary or contents of the metadatabase. Three-schema architecture was proposed for a centralized database system in the 1960s. This is illustrated in Exhibit 5. The levels are the external schema, which provides an external view; the conceptual schema, which provides a conceptual view; and the internal schema, which provides an internal view. Mappings between the different schemas must be provided to transform one representation into another. For example, at the external level, one could use ER representation. At the logical or conceptual level, one could

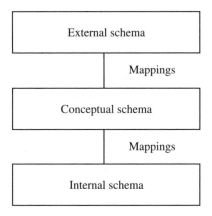

Exhibit 5. Three-Schema Architecture

use relational representation. At the physical level, one could use a representation based on B-Trees.*

There is also another aspect to architectures: extensible database architectures. For example, for many applications, a DBMS may have to be extended with a layer to support objects or to process rules or to handle multimedia data types or even to do mining. Such an extensible architecture is illustrated in Exhibit 6.

DATABASE DESIGN

Designing a database is a complex process. Much of the work has been done on designing relational databases. There are three steps, which are illustrated in Exhibit 7. The first step is to capture the entities of the application and the relationships between the entities. One could use the entity-relationship model for this purpose. More recently, object-oriented data models, which are part of object-oriented design and analysis methodologies, are becoming popular to represent the application.

The second step is to generate the relations from the representations. For example, from the entity-relationship diagram of Exhibit 2, one could generate the relations EMP, DEPT, and WORKS. The relation WORKS will capture the relationship between employees and departments.

The third step is to design good relations. This is the normalization process. Various normal forms have been defined in the literature (for example, see [MAIE83] and [DATE90]). For many applications, relations in

---

* Note that a B-Tree is a representation scheme used to physically represent the data. However, it is at a higher level than the bits and bytes levels. For a discussion on physical structures and models, see [DATE90].

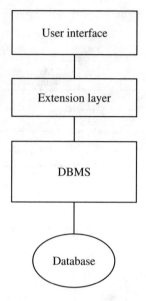

Exhibit 6.   Extensible DBMS

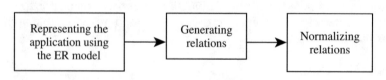

Exhibit 7.   Database Design Process

third normal form would suffice. With this normal form, redundancies, complex values, and other situations that could cause potential anomalies are eliminated.

DATABASE ADMINISTRATION

A database has a database administrator (DBA). It is the responsibility of the DBA to define the various schemas and mappings. In addition, the functions of the administrator include auditing the database as well as implementing appropriate backup and recovery procedures.

The DBA could also be responsible for maintaining the security of the system. In some cases, the system security officer (SSO) maintains security. The administrator should determine the granularity of the data for auditing. For example, in some cases there is tuple (or row)-level auditing while in other cases there is table (or relation)-level auditing. It is also the administrator's responsibility to analyze the audit data.

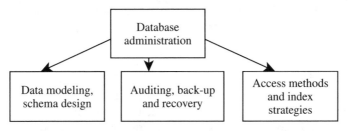

Exhibit 8. Some Database Administration Issues

Note that there is a difference between database administration and data administration. Database administration assumes there is an installed database system. The DBA manages this system. Data administration functions include conducting data analysis, determining how a corporation handles its data, and enforcing appropriate policies and procedures for managing the data of a corporation. Data administration functions are carried out by the data administrator. For a discussion of data administration, we refer to [DMH94], [DMH95], [DMH96], [DMH98], [DOD94], and [DOD95]. Exhibit 8 illustrates various database administration issues.

DATABASE MANAGEMENT SYSTEM FUNCTIONS

The functional architecture of a DBMS was illustrated in Exhibit 4. The functions of a DBMS carry out its operations. A DBMS essentially manages a database, and it provides support to the user by enabling him to query and update the database. Therefore, the basic functions of a DBMS are query processing and update processing. In some applications such as banking, queries and updates are issued as part of transactions. Therefore, transaction management is also another function of a DBMS. To carry out these functions, information about the database has to be maintained. This information is called metadata. The function that is associated with managing the metadata is metadata management. Special techniques are needed to manage the data stores that actually store the data. The function that is associated with managing these techniques is storage management. To ensure that these functions are carried out properly and that the user gets accurate data, there are some additional functions, including security management, integrity management, and fault management (i.e., fault tolerance).

These are some of the essential functions of a DBMS. However, more recently there is emphasis on extracting information from the data. Therefore, other functions of a DBMS may include providing support for data mining, data warehousing, and collaboration.

This section focuses only on the essential functions of a DBMS: query processing, transaction management, metadata management, storage management, maintaining integrity, security control, and fault tolerance. Note that we do not have a special section for update processing, as we can handle it as part of transaction management.

Query Processing

Query operation is the most commonly used function in a DBMS. It should be possible for users to query the database and obtain answers to their queries. There are several aspects to query processing. First of all, a good query language is needed. Languages such as SQL are popular for relational databases. Such languages are being extended for other types of databases. The second aspect is techniques for query processing. Numerous algorithms have been proposed for query processing in general and for the JOIN operation in particular (see also [KIM85]). Also, different strategies are possible to execute a particular query. The costs for the various strategies are computed, and the one with the least cost is usually selected for processing. This process is called query optimization. Cost is generally determined by the disk access. The goal is to minimize disk access in processing a query.

As stated earlier, users pose a query using a language. The constructs of the language have to be transformed into the constructs understood by the database system. This process is called query transformation. Query transformation is carried out in stages based on the various schemas. For example, a query based on the external schema is transformed into a query on the conceptual schema. This is then transformed into a query on the physical schema. In general, rules used in the transformation process include the factoring of common subexpressions and pushing selections and projections down in the query tree as much as possible. If selections and projections are performed before the joins, then the cost of the joins can be reduced by a considerable amount.

Exhibit 9 illustrates the modules in query processing. The user interface manager accepts queries, parses the queries, and then gives them to the query transformer. The query transformer and query optimizer communicate with each other to produce an execution strategy. The database is accessed through the storage manager. The response manager gives responses to the user.

Transaction Management

A transaction is a program unit that must be executed in its entirety or not executed at all. If transactions are executed serially, then there is a performance bottleneck. Therefore, transactions are executed concurrently. Appropriate techniques must ensure that the database is consistent when multiple transactions update the database. That is, transactions must satisfy the ACID (atomicity, consistency, isolation, and durability) properties.

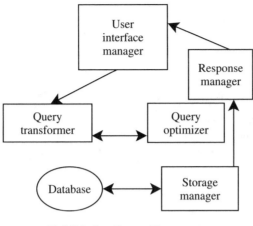

Exhibit 9. Query Processor

Major aspects of transaction management are serializability, concurrency control, and recovery. These are discussed briefly in this section. For a detailed discussion of transaction management, see [DATE90] and [ULLM88]. A good theoretical treatment of this topic is given in [BERN87].

- *Serializability:* A schedule is a sequence of operations performed by multiple transactions. Two schedules are equivalent if their outcomes are the same. A serial schedule is a schedule where no two transactions execute concurrently. An objective in transaction management is to ensure that any schedule is equivalent to a serial schedule. Such a schedule is called a serializable schedule. Various conditions for testing the serializability of a schedule have been formulated for a DBMS.
- *Concurrency control:* Concurrency control techniques ensure that the database is in a consistent state when multiple transactions update the database. Three popular concurrency control techniques that ensure the serializability of schedules are locking, time-stamping, and validation.
- *Recovery:* If a transaction aborts due to some failure, then the database must be brought to a consistent state. This is transaction recovery. One solution to handling transaction failure is to maintain log files. The transaction's actions are recorded in the log file. So, if a transaction aborts, then the database is brought back to a consistent state by undoing the actions of the transaction. The information for the undo operation is found in the log file. Another solution is to record the actions of a transaction, but not make any changes to the database. Only if a transaction commits should the database be updated. There are some issues, however. For example, the log files

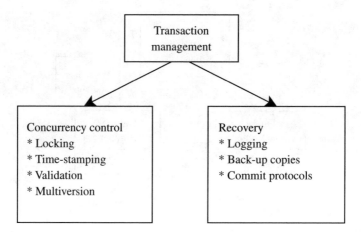

Exhibit 10. Some Aspects of Transaction Management

have to be kept in stable storage. Various modifications to these techniques have been proposed to handle different situations.

When transactions are executed at multiple data sources, then a protocol called two-phase commit is used to ensure that the multiple data sources are consistent. Exhibit 10 illustrates the various aspects of transaction management.

Storage Management

The storage manager is responsible for accessing the database. To improve the efficiency of query and update algorithms, appropriate access methods and index strategies have to be enforced. That is, in generating strategies for executing query and update requests, the access methods and index strategies that are used need to be taken into consideration. The access methods used to access the database will depend on the indexing methods. Therefore, creating and maintaining appropriate index files is a major issue in database management systems. By using an appropriate indexing mechanism, the query processing algorithms may not have to search the entire database. Instead, the data to be retrieved could be accessed directly. Consequently, the retrieval algorithms are more efficient. Exhibit 11 illustrates an example of an indexing strategy where the database is indexed by projects.

Much research has been carried out on developing appropriate access methods and index strategies for relational database systems. Some examples of index strategies are B-Trees and hashing [DATE90]. Current research is focusing on developing such mechanisms for object-oriented database systems with support for multimedia data.

454

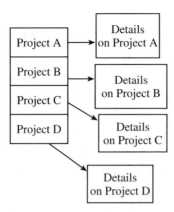

Exhibit 11.   An Example Index on Projects

Metadata Management

Metadata describes the data in the database. For example, in the case of the relational database illustrated in Exhibit 1, metadata would include the following information: the database has two relations, EMP and DEPT; EMP has four attributes, DEPT has three attributes, etc. One of the main issues is developing a data model for metadata. In our example, one could use a relational model to model the metadata also. The metadata relation REL shown in Exhibit 12 consists of information about relations and attributes.

In addition to information about the data in the database, metadata also includes information on access methods, index strategies, security constraints, and integrity constraints. One could also include policies and procedures as part of the metadata. In other words, there is no standard definition for metadata. There are, however, efforts to standardize metadata [META96]. Metadata becomes a major issue with some of the recent developments in data management such as digital libraries. Some of the issues are discussed in Part II of this book.

Exhibit 12.   Metadata Relation

Relation REL

Relation	Attribute
EMP	SS#
EMP	Ename
EMP	Salary
EMP	D#
EMP	D#
EMP	Dname
EMP	Mgr

Once the metadata is defined, it has to be managed. What are the techniques for querying and updating the metadata? Because all of the other DBMS components need to access the metadata for processing, what are the interfaces between the metadata manager and the other components? Metadata management is fairly well understood for relational database systems. The current challenge is in managing the metadata for more complex systems such as digital libraries and Internet database systems.

Database Integrity

Concurrency control and recovery techniques maintain the integrity of the database. In addition, there is a need to enforce integrity constraints. There are two types of integrity constraints enforced in database systems. These are application-independent integrity constraints and application-specific integrity constraints. Integrity mechanisms also include techniques for determining the quality of the data. For example, what is the accuracy of the data and that of the source? What are the mechanisms for maintaining the quality of the data? How accurate is the data on output? In [AFSB83], the authors discussed only the enforcement of application-independent and application-specific integrity constraints. The focus was on the relational data model. For a discussion of integrity based on data quality, see [MIT]. Note that data quality is very important for mining and warehousing. If the data that is mined is not good, then one cannot rely on the results.

Application-independent integrity constraints include the primary key constraint, the entity integrity rule, the referential integrity constraint, and the various functional dependencies involved in the normalization process (see the discussion in [DATE90]).

Application-specific integrity constraints are those constraints that are specific to an application. Examples include "an employee's salary cannot decrease" and "no manager can manage more than two departments." Various techniques have been proposed to enforce application-specific integrity constraints. For example, when the database is updated, these constraints are checked and the data is validated. Aspects of database integrity are illustrated in Exhibit 13.

Database Security

In this section, the focus is on discretionary security because this is the area that we are interested in with respect to warehousing and mining.* The major issues in security are authentication, identification, and enforcing appropriate access controls. For example, what are the mechanisms for identifying and authenticating the user? Will simple password mechanisms

---

* Note that multilevel security issues for database systems were addressed in [AFSB83].

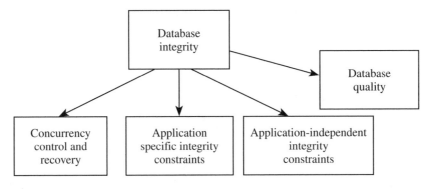

Exhibit 13.   Some Aspects of Database Integrity

Exhibit 14.   Access Control Rules

- Members of Group A can access all information in employee database except salary values.
- John, who is a member of Group A, has access to salary values.
- Name and salary values taken together can only be accessed by members of Group B.

---

suffice? With respect to access control rules, languages such as SQL have incorporated GRANT and REVOKE statements to grant and revoke access to users. For many applications, simple GRANT and REVOKE statements are not sufficient. There may be more complex authorizations based on database content. Negative authorizations may also be needed. Access to data based on the roles of the user is also being investigated.

Numerous papers have been published on discretionary security in databases. These can be found in various security-related journals and conference proceedings (for example, see [IFIP]). Some aspects of database security are illustrated in Exhibit 14.

Fault Tolerance

The previous two sections discussed database integrity and security. A closely related feature is fault tolerance. It is almost impossible to guarantee that the database will function as planned. In reality, various faults could occur. These could be hardware faults or software faults. As mentioned earlier, one of the major issues in transaction management is to ensure that the database is brought back to a consistent state in the presence of faults. The solutions proposed include maintaining appropriate log files to record the actions of a transaction in case its actions have to be retraced.

Another approach to handling faults is checkpointing. Various checkpoints are placed during the course of database processing. At each check-

Exhibit 15.	Some Aspects of Fault Tolerance

```
Checkpoint A

Start Processing

*

*

Acceptance Test

If OK, then go to Checkpoint B

Else Roll Back to Checkpoint A

Checkpoint B

Start Processing

*

*
```

point, it is ensured that the database is in a consistent state. Therefore, if a fault occurs during processing, then the database must be brought back to the last checkpoint. This way, it can be guaranteed that the database is consistent. Closely associated with checkpointing are acceptance tests. After various processing steps, the acceptance tests are checked. If the techniques pass the tests, then they can proceed further. Some aspects of fault tolerance are illustrated in Exhibit 15.

DISTRIBUTED DATABASES

Although many definitions of a distributed database system have been given, there is no standard definition. Our discussion of distributed database system concepts and issues has been influenced by the discussion in [CERI84]. A distributed database system includes a distributed database management system (DDBMS), a distributed database, and a network for interconnection. The DDBMS manages the distributed database. A distributed database is data that is distributed across multiple databases. Our choice architecture for a distributed database system is a multidatabase architecture, which is tightly coupled. This architecture is illustrated in Exhibit 16. We have chosen such an architecture in order to explain the concepts for both homogeneous and heterogeneous systems based on this approach. In this architecture, the nodes are connected via a communication subsystem and local applications are handled by the local DBMS. In addition, each node is also involved in at least one global application, so there is no centralized control in this architecture. The DBMSs are connected through a component called the distributed processor (DP). In a

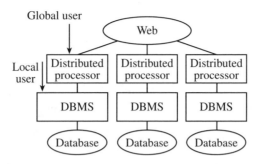

Exhibit 16.   An Architecture for a DDBMS

homogeneous environment, the local DBMSs are homogeneous, while in a heterogeneous environment the local DBMSs may be heterogeneous.

Distributed database system functions include distributed query processing, distributed transaction management, distributed metadata management, and enforcing security and integrity across the multiple nodes [BELL92]. The DP is a critical component of the DDBMS. It is this module that connects the different local DBMSs. That is, each local DBMS is augmented by a DP. The modules of the DP are illustrated in Exhibit 17. The components are the distributed metadata manager (DMM), the distributed query processor (DQP), the distributed transaction manager (DTM), the distributed security manager (DSM), and the distributed integrity manager (DIM). DMM manages the global metadata. The global metadata includes information on the schemas that describe the relations in the distributed database, the way the relations are fragmented, the locations of the fragments, and the constraints enforced. DQP is responsible for distributed query processing; DTM is responsible for distributed transaction management; DSM is responsible for enforcing global security constraints; and DIM is responsible for maintaining integrity at the global level. Note that the modules of the DP communicate with their peers at the remote nodes.

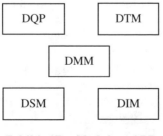

Exhibit 17.   Modules of DP

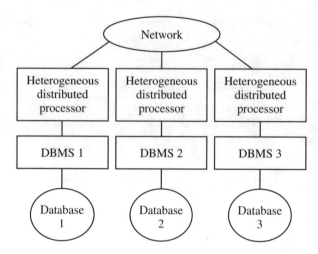

Exhibit 18.   Interoperability of Heterogeneous Database Systems

For example, the DQP at node 1 communicates with the DQP at node 2 for handling distributed queries.

HETEROGENEOUS DATABASE INTEGRATION

Exhibit 18 illustrates an example of interoperability between heterogeneous database systems. The goal is to provide transparent access, both for users and applications, for querying and executing transactions (for example, see [ACM90], [IEEE91], and [WIED92]). Note that in a heterogeneous environment, the local DBMSs may be heterogeneous. Furthermore, the modules of the DP have both local DBMS specific processing as well as local DBMS-independent processing. We call such a DP a heterogeneous distributed processor (HDP). Some of these issues are discussed in more detail in [THUR97].

There are several technical issues that need to be resolved for the successful interoperation between these diverse database systems. Note that heterogeneity could exist with respect to different data models, schemas, query processing techniques, query languages, transaction management techniques, semantics, integrity, and security. There are two approaches to interoperability. One is the federated database management approach where a collection of cooperating, autonomous, and possibly heterogeneous component database systems, each belonging to one or more federations, communicates with each other. The other is the client/server approach where the goal is for multiple clients to communicate with multiple servers in a transparent manner.

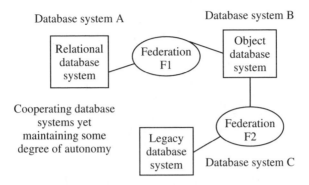

Exhibit 19.   Federated Database Management

FEDERATED DATABASES

As stated by Sheth and Larson [SHET90], a federated database system is a collection of cooperating but autonomous database systems belonging to a federation. That is, the goal is for the database management systems that belong to a federation to cooperate with one another and yet maintain some degree of autonomy. Note that to be consistent with the terminology, we distinguish between a federated database management system and a federated database system. A federated database system includes both a federated database management system, the local DBMSs, and the databases. The federated database management system is the component that manages the different databases in a federated environment.

Exhibits 19 and 20 illustrate a federated database system. Database systems A and B belong to federation F1, while database systems B and C belong to federation F2. We can use the architecture illustrated in Exhibit 18 for a federated database system. In addition to handling heterogeneity, the HDP also has to handle the federated environment (see Exhibit 20). That is, techniques have to be adapted to handle cooperation and autonomy. We have called such an HDP an FDP (federated distributed processor). An architecture for a federated database system is illustrated in Exhibit 20.

Exhibit 21 illustrates an example of an autonomous environment. There is communication between components A and B and between B and C. Due to autonomy, it is assumed that components A and C do not wish to communicate with each other. Component A may get requests from its own user or from component B. In this case, it has to decide which request to honor first. Also, there is a possibility for component C to get information from component A through component B. In such a situation, component A may have to negotiate with component B before it gives a reply to component B. The developments to deal with autonomy are still in the research stages.

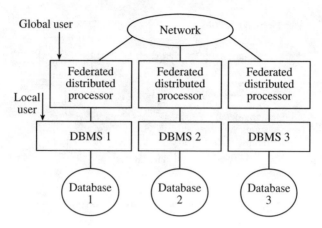

Exhibit 20.   Architecture for a Federated Database System

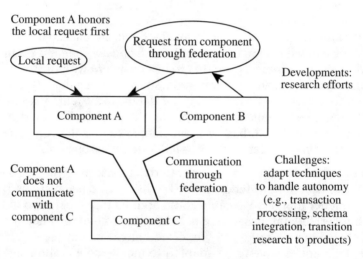

Exhibit 21.   Autonomy

The challenge is to handle transactions in an autonomous environment. Transitioning the research into commercial products is also a challenge.

CLIENT/SERVER DATABASES

Earlier sections described interoperability between heterogeneous database systems and focused on the federated database systems approach. In this approach, different database systems cooperatively interoperate with each other. This section describes another aspect of interoperability which is based on the client/server paradigm. Major database system vendors have migrated to the client/server architecture. With

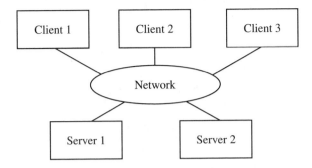

Exhibit 22.   Client/Server Architecture-Based Interoperability

this approach, multiple clients access the various database servers through some network. A high level view of client/server communication is illustrated in Exhibit 22. The ultimate goal is for multivendor clients to communicate with multivendor servers in a transparent manner. A specific example of client/server communication is illustrated in Exhibit 23.

One of the major challenges in client/server technology is to determine the modules of the distributed database system that need to be placed at the client and server sides. Exhibit 24 shows an approach where all the modules of the distributed processor of Exhibit 17 are placed at the client side, while the modules of the local DBMS are placed at the server side. Note that with this approach the client does a lot of processing; this is called the "fat client" approach. There are other options also. For example,

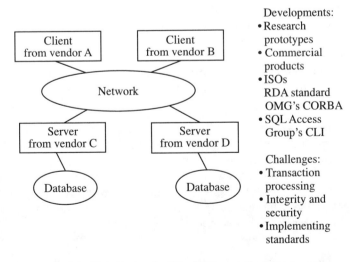

Exhibit 23.   Example Client/Server Architecture

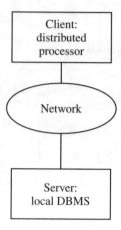

Exhibit 24. An Approach to Place the Modules

some of the modules of the distributed processor could be part of the server, in which case the client would be "thinner."

In order to facilitate the communication between multiple clients and servers, various standards are being proposed. One example is the International Standards Organization's (ISO) Remote Database Access (RDA) standard. This standard provides a generic interface for communication between a client and a server. Microsoft's open database connectivity (ODBC) is also becoming increasingly popular for clients to communicate with the servers. OMG's CORBA provides specifications for client/server communication based on object technology (see [OMG95]). Here, one possibility is to encapsulate the database servers as objects and the clients to issue appropriate requests and access the servers through an object request broker. Other standards include IBM's DRDA (distributed relational database access) and the SQL Access Group's call level interface (CLI).* While much of the development has been in query processing, the challenges are in transaction processing, semantic heterogeneity, integrity, and security.

In our previous book [THUR97], we described various aspects of client/server interoperability: in particular, technical issues for client/server interoperability; architectural approaches; three of the standards proposed for communication between clients and servers such as RDA, ODBC, and CORBA; and metadata aspects. Some good references are [ORFA94] and [ORFA96]. We will revisit distributed object management systems such as CORBA in the appendix on object management.

---

* It is now part of the Open Group. Note that the products and standards have evolved over the years and are continually changing. The reader is encouraged to keep up with the developments. Much of the information can be obtained on the Web.

MIGRATING LEGACY DATABASES AND APPLICATIONS

Many database systems developed some 20 to 30 years ago are becoming obsolete. These systems use older hardware and software. Over the next few decades, many of today's information systems and applications will also become obsolete. Due to resource and, in certain cases, budgetary constraints, new developments of next-generation systems may not be possible in many areas (for example, see [BENS95]). Therefore, current systems need to become easier, faster, and less costly to upgrade and less difficult to support. Legacy database system and application migration is a complex problem, and many of the efforts underway are still not mature. While a good book has been published on this subject [BROD95], there is no uniform approach for migration. Because migrating legacy databases and applications is becoming a necessity for most organizations, both government and commercial, one could expect a considerable amount of resources to be expended in this area in the near future. The research issues are also not well understood.

Migrating legacy applications and databases also has an impact on heterogeneous database integration. Typically, a heterogeneous database environment may include legacy databases as well as some of the next-generation databases. In many cases, an organization may want to migrate the legacy database system to a client/server architecture and still want the migrated system to be part of the heterogeneous environment. This means that the functions of the heterogeneous database system may be impacted due to this migration process.

Two candidate approaches have been proposed for migrating legacy systems. One is to do all of the migration at once. The other is incremental migration. That is, as the legacy system is migrated, the new parts have to interoperate with the old parts. Various issues and challenges to migration are discussed in [THUR97]. Exhibit 25 illustrates an incremental approach to migrating legacy databases through the use of object request brokers.

DATA WAREHOUSING

Data warehousing is one of the key data management technologies to support data mining and data analysis. Several organizations are building their own warehouses. Commercial database system vendors are marketing warehousing products. In addition, some companies are specializing only in developing data warehouses. What is a data warehouse? The idea behind it is that it is often cumbersome to access data from the heterogeneous databases. Several processing modules need to cooperate with each other to process a query in a heterogeneous environment. Therefore, a data warehouse will bring together the essential data from the heterogeneous databases. This way the users need to query only the warehouse.

APPENDIX B: DATABASE SYSTEMS AND RELATED TECHNOLOGIES

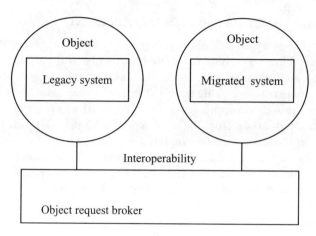

Exhibit 25. Migrating Legacy Databases

Author: not
n ref list

As stated by Inmon [INMO93], data warehouses are subject-oriented. Their design depends to a great extent on the application utilizing them. They integrate diverse and possibly heterogeneous data sources. They are persistent. That is, data warehouses are very much like a database. They vary with time. This is because as the data sources from which the warehouse is built are updated, the changes have to be reflected in the warehouse. Essentially, data warehouses provide assistance to decision support functions of an enterprise or an organization. For example, while the data sources may have the raw data, the data warehouse may have correlated data, summary reports, and aggregate functions applied to the raw data.

Exhibit 26 illustrates a data warehouse. The data sources are managed by database systems A, B, and C. The information in these databases is merged and put into a warehouse. There are various ways to merge the information. One is to simply replicate the databases. This does not have any advantages over accessing the heterogeneous databases. The second case is to replicate the information, but to remove any inconsistencies and redundancies. This has some advantages, as it is important to provide a consistent picture of the databases. The third approach is to select a subset of the information from the databases and place it in the warehouse. There are several issues here. How are the subsets selected? Are they selected at random or is some method used to select the data? For example, one could take every other row in a relation (assuming it is a relational database) and store these rows in the warehouse. The fourth approach, which is a slight variation of the third approach, is to determine the types of queries that users would pose, then analyze the data, and store only the

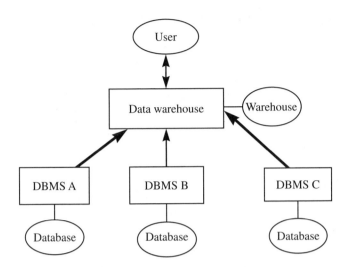

Exhibit 26. Data Warehouse Example

data that is required by the user. This is called online analytical processing (OLAP) as opposed to online transaction processing (OLTP).

With a data warehouse, data may often be viewed differently by different applications. That is, the data is multidimensional. For example, the payroll department may want data to be in a certain format, while the project department may want data to be in a different format. The warehouse must provide support for such multidimensional data.

In integrating the data sources to form the warehouse, a challenge is to analyze the application and select appropriate data to be placed in the warehouse. At times, some computations may have to be performed so that only summaries and averages are stored in the data warehouse. Note that it is not always the case that the warehouse has all the information for a query. In this case, the warehouse may have to get the data from the heterogeneous data sources to complete the execution of the query. Another question is, what happens to the warehouse when the individual databases are updated? How are the updates propagated to the warehouse? How can security be maintained? These are some of the issues that are being investigated.

OBJECT TECHNOLOGY

Object technology, also referred to as OT or OOT (object-oriented technology), encompasses different technologies. These include object-oriented programming languages, object database management systems, object-oriented design and analysis, distributed object management, and

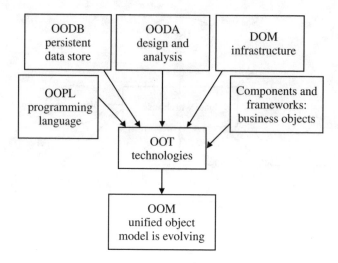

Exhibit 27. Object Technologies

components and frameworks. The underlying theme for all these types of object technologies is the object model. That is, the object model is the very essence of object technology. Any object system is based on some object model, whether it is a programming language or a database system. The interesting aspect of an object model is that everything in the real world can be modeled as an object.

An overview of the various object technologies is illustrated in Exhibit 27. For a more detailed discussion of object technology, see [THUR00].

Object Data Model

Since the birth of object technology sometime during the 1970s, numerous object models have been proposed. In fact, some recent object models trace back to the Simula language in the 1960s. Initially, these models were to support programming languages such as Smalltalk. Later, these models were enhanced to support database systems as well as other complex systems. This section provides an overview of the essential feature of object models. Note that many of the features presented here are common for object models developed for different types of systems such as programming languages, database systems, modeling and analysis, and distributed object management systems.

While there are no standard object models, the Unified Modeling Language (UML) proposed by the prominent object technologies pioneers (Rumbaugh, Booch, and Jacobson) has gained increasing popularity and has almost become the standard object model in recent years. Our discussion of the object model has been influenced by much of our work in object

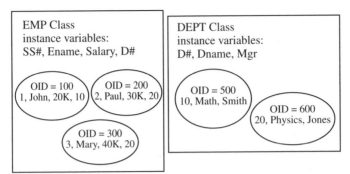

Increase - Salary (OID, Value)
Read - Salary (OID, amount)
Amount : = Amount + Value
Write - Salary (OID, Amount)

Exhibit 28. Objects and Classes

database systems as well as the one proposed by Won Kim et al. [BANE87]. We call it an object-oriented data model.*

The key points in an object-oriented model are encapsulation, inheritance, and polymorphism. With an object-oriented data model, the database is viewed as a collection of objects [BANE87]. Each object has a unique identifier called the object-ID. Objects with similar properties are grouped into a class. For example, employee objects are grouped into EMP class while department objects are grouped into DEPT class, as shown in Exhibit 28. A class has instance variables describing the properties. Instance variables of EMP are SS#, Ename, Salary, and D#, while the instance variables of DEPT are D#, Dname, and Mgr. The objects in a class are its instances. As illustrated in the figure, EMP has three instances, and DEPT has two instances.

A key concept in object-oriented data modeling is encapsulation. That is, an object has well-defined interfaces. The state of an object can only be accessed through interface procedures called methods. For example, EMP may have a method called Increase-Salary. The code for Increase-Salary is illustrated in Exhibit 28. A message, "Increase-Salary(1, 10K)," may be sent to the object with an object ID of 1. The object's current salary is read and updated by $10K.

---

* Two types of object models have been proposed for databases. One is the object-oriented data model proposed for object-oriented databases and the other is the object-relational data model proposed for object-relational databases. We discuss the object-oriented data model in this section. Object-relational models are discussed in the section on object database management.

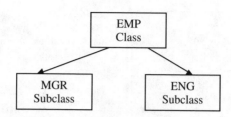

Exhibit 29.   Class–Subclass Hierarchy

A second key concept in an object model is inheritance where a subclass inherits properties from its parent class. This feature is illustrated in Exhibit 29, where the EMP class has MGR (manager) and ENG (engineer) as its subclasses. Other key concepts in an object model include polymorphism and aggregation.* These features are discussed in [BANE87]. Further information can also be obtained in [THUR97]. Note that a second type of inheritance is when the instances of a class inherit the properties of the class.

A third concept is polymorphism. This is the situation where one can pass different types of arguments for the same function. For example, to calculate the area, one can pass a sphere or a cylinder object. Operators can be overloaded also. That is, the add operation can be used to add two integers or real numbers.

Another concept is the aggregate hierarchy, also called the composite object or the IS-PART-OF hierarchy. In this case, an object has component objects. For example, a book object has component section objects. A section object has component paragraph objects. Aggregate hierarchy is illustrated in Exhibit 30.

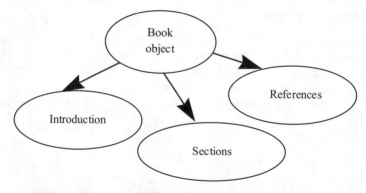

Exhibit 30.   Aggregate Object

* Inheritance is also known as the IS-A hierarchy. Aggregation is also known as the IS-PART-OF hierarchy.

Objects also have relationships between them. For example, an employee object has an association with the department object, which is the department he is working in. Also, the instance variables of an object could take integers, lists, arrays, or even other objects as values. All of these concepts are discussed in [CATT91]. Object Data Management Group is also proposing standards for object data models [ODMG93].

Other Object Technologies

Programming Languages. Object-oriented programming languages (OOPL) essentially go back to Simula in the 1960s. However, it really became popular with the advent of Smalltalk by Xerox Palo Alto Research Center in the late 1970s. Smalltalk is a pure object-oriented programming language where everything is considered an object. Implementations of Smalltalk were being developed throughout the 1980s. Around the mid-1980s, languages such as LISP and C were being made object-oriented by extending them to support objects. One such popular extension is the C++ language. In the early to mid-1990s, much of the programming was carried out in C++. Around the 1990s, Sun Microsystems wanted to develop a language for its embedded computing and appliance business that would not have all of the problems associated with C++ (such as pointers). The resulting language, first named Oak, was eventually called Java. Java became immensely popular because of the Internet.

Database Systems. We have discussed three types of object database systems [THUR00]. One is the object-oriented database system, which makes object-oriented programming languages persistent. The second is the extended-relational system, which extends relational database systems with object layers. The third is the object-relational system where objects are nested within relations.

The previous sections addressed object-oriented programming languages and object-oriented database management. Around the same time (i.e., in the 1980s), there was a lot of interest in using object technology to design and analyze applications. Prior to that, various analysis techniques such as structured analysis and Jackson diagrams were used to analyze the application. At the same time, entity-relationship models were very popular to represent the entities of the application and the relationships between them.

Design and Analysis. With the advent of OOT, interest increased on using objects to model and analyze applications. Various design and analysis methodologies were being proposed. Notable among them were the method of Booch, usecases by Jacobson, and OMT (object modeling technique) by Rumbaugh et al. There was so much debate about this subject that, at the 1993 OOPSLA (Object-Oriented Programming Systems, Languages, and Applications) Conference there was an extremely contentious debate on this subject. Surprisingly, within the next two years it was announced that the three groups were merging and were producing a unified methodology. This unified methodology is called UML (Unified Modeling Language) [FOWL97]. UML has essential features from the three approaches and is now more or less a standard for object modeling and analysis.

Distributed Object Management. Distributed object management (DOM) technology is being used increasingly to interconnect heterogeneous databases, systems, and applications. With this approach, the various systems and applications are encapsulated as objects, and the objects communicate with each other through exchanging messages. An example of a DOM system that is being used as middleware to connect heterogeneous database systems is a system based on OMG's CORBA. CORBA is a specification that enables heterogeneous applications, systems, and databases to interoperate with each other. As stated in [OMG95], there are three major components to CORBA: (1) the object model; (2) the object request broker (ORB), through which clients and servers communicate with each other; and (3) the Interface Definition Language (IDL), which specifies the interfaces for client/server communication.

Components and Frameworks. These are some of the latest object technologies that have really taken off since the mid-1990s. When talking to various people and reading different texts, I have found that the terms *components* and *frameworks* have no standard definitions. There was an excellent survey of the field in the *Communications of the ACM* magazine in October 1997 by Fayad and Schmidt [ACM97]. In a sense, a framework can be considered a skeleton with classes and interconnections. One then instantiates this skeleton for various applications. Frameworks are being developed for different application domains, including financial and medical systems. Components on the other hand are classes, objects, and relationships between them that can be reused. Components can be built for different applications. There are components for financial, medical, and telecommunication applications. These components are also called business objects.

SUMMARY

This appendix has discussed various aspects of database systems and provided a lot of background information to understand the various chapters in this book. We began with a discussion of various data models. We chose relational and entity-relationship models because they are more relevant to what we have addressed in this book. Then we provided an overview of various types of architectures for database systems. These included functional and schema architectures. Next, we discussed database design aspects and database administration issues. This appendix also provided an overview of the various functions of database systems, including query processing, transaction management, storage management, metadata management, security, integrity, and fault tolerance.* Finally, we briefly discussed distributed databases and interoperability. This was followed by a discussion of data warehousing, data mining, and object technology.

Many of the chapters in this book discuss various data management and data mining system aspects related to multimedia information processing. These include query processing, storage management, metadata management, security, distribution, and interoperability.

References

[ACM90] Special issue on federated databases, *ACM Computing Surveys,* 1990.

[ACM91] Special issue on next-generation database systems, *Communications of the ACM,* October 1991.

[ACM97] Special issue on components, *Communications of the ACM,* October 1997.

[BANE87] Banerjee, J. et al., A data model for object-oriented applications, *ACM Transactions on Office Information Systems,* Vol. 5, 1987.

[BELL92] Bell, D. and Grimson, J., *Distributed Database Systems,* Addison-Wesley, Reading, MA, 1992.

[BENS95] Bensley, E. et al., Evolvable systems initiative for real-time command and control systems, Proceedings of the 1st IEEE Complex Systems Conference, Orlando, FL, November 1995.

[BERN87] Bernstein, P. et al., *Concurrency Control and Recovery in Database Systems,* Addison-Wesley, Reading, MA, 1987.

[BROD84] Brodie, M. et al., *On Conceptual Modeling: Perspectives from Artificial Intelligence, Databases, and Programming Languages,* Springer-Verlag, New York, 1984.

[BROD86] Brodie, M. and Mylopoulos, J., *On Knowledge Base Management Systems,* Springer-Verlag, New York, 1986.

[BROD88] Brodie, M. et al., *Readings in Artificial Intelligence and Databases,* Morgan Kaufmann, San Francisco, 1988.

[BROD95] Brodie, M. and Stonebraker, M., *Migrating Legacy Databases,* Morgan Kaufmann, San Francisco, 1995.

[CATT91] Cattel, R., *Object Data Management Systems,* Addison-Wesley, Reading, MA, 1991.

[CERI84] Ceri, S. and Pelagatti, G., *Distributed Databases, Principles and Systems,* McGraw-Hill, New York, 1984.

[CHEN76] Chen, P., The entity relationship model: Toward a unified view of data, *ACM Transactions on Database Systems,* Vol. 1, 1976.

[CHOR94] Chorafas, D., *Intelligent Multimedia Databases,* Prentice-Hall, Englewood Cliffs, NJ, 1994.

[CODD70] Codd, E.F., A relational model of data for large shared data banks, *Communications of the ACM,* Vol. 13, 1970.

[DAS92] Das, S., *Deductive Databases and Logic Programming,* Addison-Wesley, Reading, MA, 1992.

* Various texts and articles have been published on database systems. Examples include [BROD84], [BROD86], [BROD88], [CERI84], [CHOR94], [DAS92], [DATE90], [FROS86], [KORT86], [LLOY87], [PRAB97], [THUR97], [THUR98], [THUR00], and [ULLM88].

APPENDIX B: DATABASE SYSTEMS AND RELATED TECHNOLOGIES

[DATE90] Date, C.J., *An Introduction to Database Management Systems,* Addison-Wesley, Reading, MA, 1990 (6th ed. published in 1995 by Addison-Wesley).

[DMH94] *Data Management Handbook,* von Halle, B. and Kull, D., Eds., Auerbach Publications, New York, 1994.

[DMH95] *Data Management Handbook Supplement,* von Halle, B. and Kull, D., Eds., Auerbach Publications, New York, 1995.

[DMH96] *Data Management Handbook Supplement,* Thuraisingham, B., Ed., Auerbach Publications, New York, 1996.

[DMH98] *Data Management Handbook Supplement,* Thuraisingham, B., Ed., Auerbach Publications, New York, 1998.

[DOD94] Proceedings of the 1994 DoD Database Colloquium, San Diego, August 1994.

[DOD95] Proceedings of the 1994 DoD Database Colloquium, San Diego, August 1995.

[ELMA85] Elmasri, R., The entity category relationship model, *Data and Knowledge Engineering Journal,* Vol. 1, 1985.

[FOWL97] Fowler, M. et al., *UML Distilled: Applying the Standard Object Modeling Language,* Addison-Wesley, Reading, MA, 1997.

[FROS86] Frost, R., *On Knowledge Base Management Systems,* Collins Publishers, London, U.K., 1986.

[IEEE91] Special issue in heterogeneous database systems, *IEEE Computer,* 1991.

[IFIP] Proceedings of the IFIP Conference Series in Database Security, North Holland.

[KIM85] Kim, W. et al., *Query Processing in Database Systems,* Springer-Verlag, New York, 1985.

[KORT86] Korth, H. and Silberschatz, A., *Database System Concepts,* McGraw-Hill, New York, 1986.

[LLOY87] Lloyd, J., *Logic Programming,* Springer-Verlag, Heidelberg, 1987.

[LOOM95] Loomis, M., *Object Databases,* Addison-Wesley, Reading, MA, 1995.

[MAIE83] Maier, D., *Theory of Relational Databases,* Computer Science Press, Rockville, MD, 1983.

[META96] Proceedings of the 1st IEEE Metadata Conference, Silver Spring, MD, April 1996.

[MIT] MIT technical reports on data quality.

[ODMG93] Object Database Standard: ODMB 93, Object Database Management Group, Morgan Kaufmann, San Francisco, 1993.

[OMG95] *Common Object Request Broker Architecture and Specification,* OMG Publications, John Wiley, New York, 1995.

[OOPS94] OOPSLA 94 Workshop on CORBA, Portland, OR, 1994.

[ORFA94] Orfali, R. et al., *The Essential Client/Server Survival Guide,* John Wiley, New York, 1994.

[ORFA96] Orfali, R. et al., *The Essential Distributed Objects Survival Guide,* John Wiley, New York, 1996.

[PRAB97] Prabhakaran, B., *Multimedia Database Systems,* Kluwer Publications, Norwood, MA, 1997.

[SHET90] Sheth, A. and Larson, J., Federated database systems, *ACM Computing Surveys,* September 1990.

[SQL3] SQL3, American National Standards Institute, draft, 1992.

[THUR97] Thuraisingham, B., *Data Management Systems Evolution and Interoperation,* CRC Press, Boca Raton, FL, 1997.

[THUR98] Thuraisingham, B., *Data Mining: Technologies, Techniques, Tools, and Trends,* CRC Press, Boca Raton, FL, December 1998.

[THUR00] Thuraisingham, B., *Web Information Management and Electronic Commerce,* CRC Press, Boca Raton, FL, June 2000.

[THUR01] Thuraisingham, B., *Managing and Mining Multimedia Databases,* CRC Press, Boca Raton, FL, June 2001.

[TSIC82] Tsichritzis, D. and Lochovsky, F., *Data Models,* Prentice-Hall, Englewood Cliffs, NJ, 1982.

[ULLM88] Ullman, J. D., *Principles of Database and Knowledge Base Management Systems,* Vols. I and II, Computer Science Press, Rockville, MD, 1988.

[WIED92] Wiederhold, G., Mediators in the architecture of future information systems, *IEEE Computer,* March 1992.

[YANG88] Yang, D. and Torey, T., A practical approach to transforming extended ER diagrams into the relational model, *Information Sciences Journal,* 1988.

Appendix C
Data and Information Security

The number of computerized databases has been increasing rapidly over the past three decades. The advent of the Internet, as well as networking capabilities, has made access to data and information much easier. For example, users can now access large quantities of information in a short span of time. As more and more tools and technologies are being developed to access and use the data, there is also an urgent need to protect the data. Many government and industrial organizations have sensitive and classified data that has to be protected. Various other organizations such as academic institutions also have sensitive data about their students and employees. As a result, techniques for protecting the data stored in database management systems (DBMS) have become an urgent need.

Over the past three decades, various developments have been made on securing the databases. Much of the early work was on statistical database security. Then in the 1970s, as research in relational databases began, attention was directed toward access control issues. In particular, work on discretionary access control models began. While some work on mandatory security started in the late 1970s, it was not until the Air Force summer study (in 1982) that many of the efforts in multilevel secure database management systems were initiated [AFSB83]. This resulted in the development of various secure database system prototypes and products. In the 1990s, with the advent of new technologies such as digital libraries, the World Wide Web, and collaborative computing systems, there was much interest in security not only with the government organizations but also with the commercial industry.

This appendix provides an overview of the various developments in information security with special emphasis on database security. Because much of this book is on Web data management, we give some consideration to secure database systems. For a detailed discussion of the information in this appendix, we refer to [FERA00].

ACCESS CONTROL AND OTHER SECURITY CONCEPTS

Access control models include those for discretionary security and mandatory security. In this section, we discuss both aspects of access control and also consider other issues.

In discretionary access control models, users or groups of users are granted access to data objects. These data objects could be files, relations, objects, or even data items. Access control policies include rules such as "user U has read access to relation R1 and write access to relation R2." Access control could also include restrictions, where user U does not have read access to relation R.

In mandatory access control, subjects that act on behalf of users are granted access to objects based on some policy. A well-known policy is the Bell and LaPadula policy [BELL75], where subjects are granted clearance levels and objects have sensitivity levels. The set of security levels form a partially ordered lattice where Unclassified < Confidential < Secret < Top Secret. The policy has two properties: (1) a subject has read access to an object if its clearance level dominates that of the object, and (2) a subject has write access to an object if its level is dominated by that of the object.

Other types of access control include role-based access control. Here, access is granted to users based on their roles and the functions they perform. For example, personnel managers have access to salary data, project mangers have access to project data, etc. The idea is generally to give access on a need-to-know basis.

While the early access control policies were formulated for operating systems, these policies have been extended to include other systems such as database systems, networks, and distributed systems. For example, a policy for networks includes policies for not only reading and writing but also for sending and receiving messages.

Other security policies include administration policies. These policies include those for ownership of data as well as how to manage and distribute the data. Database administrators as well as system security officers are involved in formulating the administration policies.

Security policies also include policies for identification and authentication. Each user or subject acting on behalf of a user has to be identified and authenticated, possibly using some password mechanisms. Identification and authentication becomes more complex for distributed systems. For example, how can a user be authenticated at a global level?

The steps to developing secure systems include developing a security policy, developing a model of the system, designing the system, and verifying and validating the system. The methods used for verification depend on the level of assurance that is expected. Testing and risk analysis is also

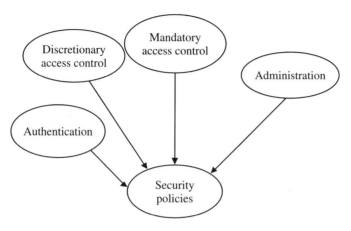

Exhibit 1.   Secure Policies

part of the process. These activities will eliminate or assess the risks involved. Exhibit 1 illustrates various types of security policies.

SECURE SYSTEMS

In the previous section, we discussed various policies for building secure systems. In this section, we elaborate on various types of secure systems.

Much of the research in the 1960s and 1970s was on securing operating systems. Early security policies such as the Bell and LaPadula policy were formulated for operating systems. Subsequently, secure operating systems such as Honeywell's SCOMP and MULTICS were developed (see IEEE83]). Other policies such as those based on noninterference also emerged in the early 1980s.

While early research on secure database systems was reported in the 1970s it was not until the early 1980s that active research began in this area. Much of the focus was on multilevel secure database systems. The security policy for operating systems was modified slightly. For example, the write policy for secure database systems was modified to state that a subject has write access to an object if the subject's level is that of the object. Because database systems enforced relationships between data and had semantics, there were additional security concerns. For example, data could be classified based on content, context, and time. The problem of posing multiple queries and inferring sensitive information from legitimate responses became a concern, known as the inference problem. Also, research was carried out not only on securing relational systems but also object systems.

Research on computer networks began in the late 1970s. Over time, the networking protocols were extended to incorporate security features. The

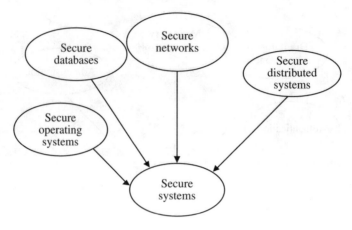

Exhibit 2. Secure Systems

result was secure network protocols. The policies include those for reading, writing, and sending and receiving messages. Research on encryption and cryptography has received much prominence due to networks and the Internet. Security for stand-alone systems was extended to include distributed systems, including distributed databases and distributed operating systems. Much of the research on distributed systems now focuses on securing the Internet, known as Web security, as well as securing systems such as distributed object management systems.

As new systems emerge, such as data warehouses, collaborative computing systems, multimedia systems, and agent systems, security for such systems has to be investigated. With the advent of the Internet and the World Wide Web, security is being given serious consideration by not only the government organizations but also commercial organizations. With E-commerce, it is important to protect the company's intellectual property. Exhibit 2 illustrates various types of secure systems.

SECURE DATABASE SYSTEMS

Work on discretionary security for databases began in the 1970s, when security aspects were investigated for System R at IBM's Almaden Research Center. Essentially, the security properties specified the read and write access that a user may have to relations, attributes, and data elements. In the 1980s and 1990s, security issues were investigated for object systems. Here, the security properties specified the access that users had to objects, instance variables, and classes. In addition to read and write, method execution access was also specified.

Since the early 1980s, much of the focus has been on multilevel secure database management systems. These systems essentially enforce the mandatory policy discussed previously in this appendix with the modification described as well. Since the 1980s, various designs, prototypes, and commercial products of multilevel database systems have been developed. Ferrari and Thuraisingham give a detailed survey of some of the developments [FERA00]. Efforts such as SeaView by SRI International and Lock Data Views by Honeywell extended relational models with security properties. One challenge was to design a model where a user sees different values at different security levels. For example, at the unclassified level an employee's salary may be $20K and at the secret level it may be $50K. In the standard relational model, such ambiguous values cannot be represented due to integrity properties.

Note that several other significant developments have been made on multilevel security for other types of database systems. These include security for object database systems [THUR89]. In this effort, security properties specify read, write, and method-execution policies. Much work was also carried out on secure concurrency control and recovery. The idea is to enforce security properties and still maintain consistency without having covert channels. Research was also carried out on multilevel security for distributed, heterogeneous, and federated database systems. Another area that received much attention was the inference problem. For details on the inference problem, we refer to [THUR93]; for secure concurrency control, we refer to the numerous algorithms by Bertino and Jajodia (for example, see [BERT97]). For information on secure distributed and heterogeneous databases as well as secure federated databases, we refer to [THUR91] and [THUR94].

As database systems become more sophisticated, securing these system will become more and more difficult. Some of the current work focuses on securing data warehouses, multimedia databases, and Web databases (for example, see [IFIP], [IFIP97], and [IFIP98]). Exhibit 3 illustrates various types of secure database systems.

EMERGING TRENDS

In the mid-1990s, research in secure systems expanded to include emerging systems such as collaborative computing, multimedia computing, and data warehouses. Data mining resulted in new security concerns. Because users now have access to various data-mining tools, it could exacerbate the inference problem. This is because the data-mining tool may make correlations and associations that may be sensitive. On the other hand, data mining could also help with security problems such as intrusion detection and auditing.

The advent of the Web resulted in extensive investigations of security for digital libraries and E-commerce. In addition to developing sophisticated encryption techniques, security research also focused on securing

APPENDIX C: DATA AND INFORMATION SECURITY

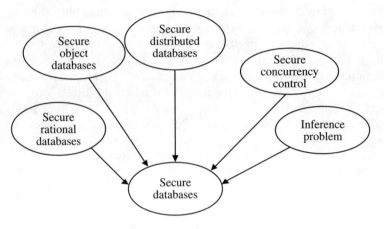

Exhibit 3.   Secure Database Systems

Web clients as well as servers. Programming languages such as Java were designed with security in mind. Much research was also carried out on securing agents.

Secure distributed system research focused on security for distributed object management systems. Organizations such as OMG started working groups to investigate security properties. As a result, we now have secure distributed object management systems commercially available. Exhibit 4 illustrates various emerging secure systems and concepts. More details are given in [FERA00].

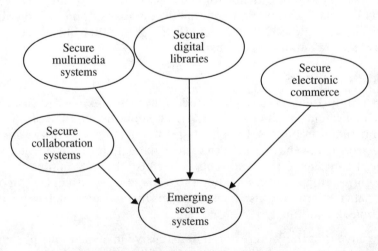

Exhibit 4.   Emerging Secure Systems

IMPACT OF THE WEB

The advent of the Web has greatly impacted security. Security is now part of mainstream computing. Government and commercial organizations are concerned about security. For example, in a financial transaction, millions of dollars could be lost if security is not maintained. With the Web, all sorts of information is available about individuals, and therefore privacy may be compromised.

Various security solutions are being proposed to secure the Web. In addition to encryption, focus is on securing clients and servers. That is, end-to-end security has to be maintained. Web security also has an impact on E-commerce. That is, it is critical that security is maintained when one carries out transactions on the Web. Information such as credit card numbers and social security numbers have to be protected.

All of the security issues discussed in the previous sections have to be considered for the Web. For example, appropriate security policies have to be formulated. This is a challenge, as no one person owns the Web. The various secure systems, including secure operating systems, secure database systems, secure networks, and secure distributed systems, may be integrated in a Web environment. Therefore, this integrated system has to be secure. Problems such as the inference problem may be exacerbated due to the various data-mining tools. The various agents on the Web have to be secure. In certain cases, trade-offs need to be made between security and other features. That is, quality of service is an important consideration. In addition to technological solutions, legal aspects also have to be examined. That is, lawyers and engineers have to work together. Research on securing the Web is just beginning. Exhibit 5 illustrates aspects of Web security.

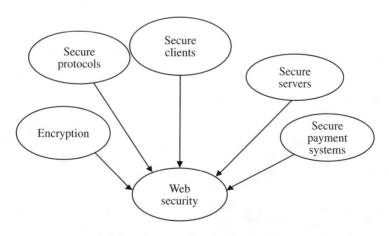

Exhibit 5.   Aspects of Web Security

APPENDIX C: DATA AND INFORMATION SECURITY

SUMMARY

This appendix has provided a brief overview of the developments in secure systems. We first discussed basic concepts in access control as well as discretionary and mandatory policies. Then, we provided an overview of secure systems. In particular, secure operating systems, secure databases, secure networks, and secure distributed systems were discussed. Next, we provided some details on secure databases. Finally, we discussed some research trends and the impact of the Web.

Directions in secure database systems will be driven by the developments on the Web. Database systems are no longer stand-alone systems. They are being integrated into various applications such as multimedia, E-commerce, mobile computing systems, digital libraries, and collaboration systems. Therefore, security issues for all these new-generation systems will be very important. Furthermore, there are many developments on various object technologies such as distributed object systems and components and frameworks. Security for such systems is being investigated. Eventually, the security policies of the various subsystems and components have to be integrated to form policies for entire systems. There will be many challenges in formulating policies for such systems. New technologies such as data mining will help security concerns such as intrusion detection and auditing. However, these technologies can also violate the privacy of individuals. This is because adversaries can now use the mining tools to extract unauthorized information about various individuals. Finally, migrating legacy databases and applications will continually be a challenge. Security issues for such operations cannot be overlooked.

Essentially, this appendix is a summary of a more-detailed paper on secure database systems by Ferrari and Thuraisingham, which can be found in [FERA00].

References

[AFSB83] Air Force summer study board report on multilevel secure database systems, Department of Defense document, 1983.

[BELL75] Bell, D. and LaPadula, L., Secure computer systems: Unified exposition and multics interpretation, technical report no. ESD-TR-75–306, Hanscom Air Force Base, Bedford, MA, 1975.

[BERT97] Bertino, E. and Jajodia, S., Secure concurrency control, *IEEE Transactions on Knowledge and Data Engineering,* 1997.

[FERA00] Ferrari, E. and Thuraisingham, B., Database security: Survey, in *Advanced Database Technology and Design,* Piattini, M. and Diaz, O., Eds., Artech House, London, U.K., 2000.

[IEEE83] Special issue on computer security, *IEEE Computer,* 1983.

[IFIP] Proceedings of the IFIP Conference Series in Database Security, North Holland.

[IFIP97] Proceedings of the IFIP 1997 Conference Series in Database Security, Panel on data warehousing and data mining security, North Holland.

[IFIP98] Proceedings of the IFIP 1998 Conference Series in Database Security, Panel on data mining and web security, North Holland.

[THUR89] Thuraisingham, B., Security for object-oriented database systems, Proceedings of the ACM OOPSLA Conference, 1989.

[THUR91] Thuraisingham, B., Security for distributed database systems, *Computers and Security,* 1991.

[THUR93] Thuraisingham, B. et al., Design and implementation of a database inference controller, *Data and Knowledge Engineering Journal,* North Holland, Vol. 8, December 1993.

[THUR94] Thuraisingham, B., Security for federated database systems, *Computers and Security,* Elsevier Science, Oxford, U.K., 1994.

Appendix D
References

[ACLU] American Civil Liberties Union, http://www.aclu.org.

[ACM90a] Special issue on federated databases, *ACM Computing Surveys,* 1990.

[ACM90b] Special issue on heterogeneous database systems, *ACM Computing Surveys,* September 1990.

[ACM91a] Special issue on computer-supported cooperative work, *Communications of the ACM,* December 1991.

[ACM91b] Special issue on next-generation database systems, *Communications of the ACM,* October 1991.

[ACM94] Proceedings of the ACM Multimedia Database System Workshop, October 1994.

[ACM95] Special issue on digital libraries, *Communications of the ACM,* May 1995.

[ACM96] Special issue on data mining, *Communications of the ACM,* November 1996.

[ACM97] Special issue on components, *Communications of the ACM,* October 1997.

[ACM99] *Communications of the ACM,* May 1999.

[ACM01] ACM SIGMOD Record, September 2001.

[ACM02] ACM Computer Security Conference Workshop on Privacy, Washington, D.C., November 2002.

[ADRI96] Adriaans, P. and Zantinge, D., *Data Mining,* Addison-Wesley, Reading, MA, 1996.

[AFCE] AFCEA Federal Data Mining Symposium, 1997–2000.

[AFCE97] Proceedings of the AFCEA Data Mining Symposium, Washington, D.C., December 1997.

[AFSB83] Air Force summer study board report on multilevel secure database systems, Department of Defense document, 1983.

[AGRA02] Agrawal, R, Privacy sensitive data mining, White House presentation on data mining for counter-terrorism, Washington, D.C., February 2002.

[AGRA93] Agrawal, A. et al., Database mining: A performance perspective, *IEEE Transactions on Knowledge and Data Engineering,* 5, December 1993.

[AIPA95] Proceedings of the Symposium on Advanced Information Processing and Analysis, Tysons Corner, MD, March 1995.

[AIPA96] Proceedings of the Symposium on Advanced Information Processing and Analysis, Tysons Corner, MD, March 1996.

[BANE87] Banerjee, J. et al., A data model for object-oriented applications, *ACM Transactions on Office Information Systems,* Vol. 5, 1987.

[BEA] http://www.beasys.com.

[BELL75] Bell, D. and LaPadula, L., Secure computer systems: Unified exposition and multics interpretation, technical report no. ESD-TR-75–306, Hanscom Air Force Base, Bedford, MA, 1975.

[BELL92] Bell, D. and Grimson, J., *Distributed Database Systems,* Addison-Wesley, Reading, MA, 1992.

[BENS95] Bensley, E. et al., Evolvable systems initiative for real-time command and control systems, Proceedings of the 1st IEEE Complex Systems Conference, Orlando, FL, November 1995.

[BERN87] Bernstein, P. et al., *Concurrency Control and Recovery in Database Systems,* Addison-Wesley, Reading, MA, 1987.

APPENDIX D: REFERENCES

[BERR97] Berry, M. and Linoff, G., *Data Mining Techniques for Marketing, Sales, and Customer Support,* John Wiley, New York, 1997.

[BERT97] Bertino, E. and Jajodia, S., Secure concurrency control, *IEEE Transactions on Knowledge and Data Engineering,* 1997.

[BOLZ01] Bolz, F. et al., *The Counterterrorism Handbook: Tactics, Procedures, and Techniques,* CRC Press, Boca Raton, FL 2001.

[BROD84] Brodie, M. et al., *On Conceptual Modeling: Perspectives from Artificial Intelligence, Databases, and Programming Languages,* Springer-Verlag, New York, 1984.

[BROD86] Brodie, M. and Mylopoulos, J., *On Knowledge Base Management Systems,* Springer-Verlag, New York, 1986.

[BROD88] Brodie, M. et al., *Readings in Artificial Intelligence and Databases,* Morgan Kaufmann, San Francisco, 1988.

[BROD95] Brodie, M. and Stonebraker, M., *Migrating Legacy Databases,* Morgan Kaufmann, San Francisco, 1995.

[CARB98] Carbone, P., *Data Mining, Handbook of Data Management,* Thuraisingham, B., Ed., Auerbach Publications, New York, 1998.

[CATT91] Cattel, R., *Object Data Management Systems,* Addison-Wesley, Reading, MA, 1991.

[CERI84] Ceri, S. and Pelagatti, G., *Distributed Databases, Principles and Systems,* McGraw-Hill, New York, 1984.

[CHEN76] Chen, P., The entity relationship model: Toward a unified view of data, *ACM Transactions on Database Systems,* Vol. 1, 1976.

[CHES94] Cheswick, W. and Bellovin, S., Firewalls and Internet security: Repelling the wily hacker, Addison-Wesley, Reading, MA, 1994.

[CHOR94] Chorafas, D., *Intelligent Multimedia Databases,* Prentice Hall, Englewood Cliffs, NJ, 1994.

[CLIF96] Clifton, C., Text mining, private communication, Bedford, MA, January 1996.

[CLIF97] Clifton C., Privacy issues for data mining, private communication, Bedford, MA, April 1998.

[CLIF98] Clifton, C., Image mining, private communication, Bedford, MA, July 1998.

[CLIF99a] Clifton C., Data mining and security, Proceedings of the IFIP Conference on Database Security, Seattle, July 1999.

[CLIF99b] Clifton, C., Data mining for intrusion detection, IFIP 1999 Database Security Conference Panel, July 1999.

[CLIF01] Clifton, C. and Thuraisingham, B., Standards and data mining, *Computer Standards and Interface Journal,* North Holland, 2001.

[CODD70] Codd, E.F., A relational model of data for large shared data banks, *Communications of the ACM,* Vol. 13, 1970.

[COOL98] Cooley, R., Taxonomy for web mining, private communication, Bedford, MA, August 1998.

[CORR99] Corradi, A., Montanari, R., and Stefanelli, C., Security issues in mobile agent technology, Proceedings of IEEE FTDCS, Cape Town, South Africa, December 1999.

[CRIS] Cross industry standard process for data mining, http://www.crisp-dm.org.

[DAML] http://www.daml.org.

[DARPA98] Workshop on knowledge discovery in databases, Defense Advanced Research Projects Agency, Pittsburgh, June 1998.

[DAS92] Das, S., *Deductive Databases and Logic Programming,* Addison-Wesley, Reading, MA, 1992.

[DATE90] Date, C.J., *An Introduction to Database Management Systems,* Addison-Wesley, Reading, MA, 1990 (6th ed. published in 1995 by Addison-Wesley).

[DAVE97] Davenport, T., *Working Knowledge: How Organizations Manage What They Know,* Harvard Business School Press, 1997.

[DE98] IEEE Data Engineering Conference, Orlando, FL, February 1998.

[DECI] Decision Support Journal, Elsevier/North Holland Publications.

[DEGR86] DeGroot, T., *Probability and Statistics,* Addison-Wesley, Reading, MA, 1986.

[DEUT99] Deutch, A. et al., XML-QL: A query language for XML, http://w3c1.inria.fr.

[DIGI95] Proceedings of the Advances in Digital Libraries Conference, McLean, VA, May 1995.

[DIPI99] DiPippo, L., Hodys, E., and Thuraisingham, B., Towards a real-time agent architecture: A white paper, Proceedings of IEEE WORDS, Monterey, CA, 1999.

[DMH94] *Data Management Handbook,* von Halle, B. and Kull, D., Eds., Auerbach Publications, New York, 1994.

[DMH95] *Data Management Handbook Supplement,* von Halle, B. and Kull, D., Eds., Auerbach Publications, New York, 1995.

[DMH96] *Data Management Handbook Supplement,* Thuraisingham, B., Ed., Auerbach Publications, New York, 1996.

[DMH98] *Data Management Handbook Supplement,* Thuraisingham, B., Ed., Auerbach Publications, New York, 1998.

[DOD94] Proceedings of the 1994 DoD Database Colloquium, San Diego, August 1994.

[DOD95] Proceedings of the 1995 DoD Database Colloquium, San Diego, August 1995.

[ELLI99] Ellison, H., *Handbook of Chemical and Biological Warfare Agents,* CRC Press, Boca Raton, FL, 1999.

[ELMA85] Elmasri, R., The entity category relationship model, *Data and Knowledge Engineering Journal,* Vol. 1, 1985.

[FAYY96] Fayyad, U. et al., *Advanced in Knowledge Discovery and Data Mining,* MIT Press, Cambridge, MA, 1996.

[FELD95] Feldman, R. and Dagan, I., Knowledge discovery in textual databases (KDT), Proceedings of the 1995 Knowledge Discovery in Databases Conference, Montreal, Canada, August 1995.

[FERA00] Ferarri, E. and Thuraisingham, B., Database security: Survey, in *Advanced Database Technology and Design,* Piattini, M. and Diaz, O., Eds., Artech House, London, U.K., 2000.

[FIRE] Building Internet firewalls tutorial, http://www.greatcircle.com.

[FOWL97] Fowler, M. et al., *UML Distilled: Applying the Standard Object Modeling Language,* Addison-Wesley, Reading, MA, 1997.

[FROS86] Frost, R., *On Knowledge Base Management Systems,* Collins Publishers, London, U.K., 1986.

[GHOS98] Ghosh, A., *E-Commerce Security, Weak Links And Strong Defenses,* John Wiley, New York, 1998.

[GRIN95] Grinstein, G. and Thuraisingham, B., Data mining and visualization: A position paper, Proceedings of the Workshop on Databases in Visualization, Atlanta, October 1995.

[GRAY96] Gray, J. et al., Data Cube: A Relational Aggregation Operator Generalizing Grou-By, Cross-Tab, and Sub-Total, in Proceedings of the International Conference on Data Engineering, New Orleans, LA, 1996.

[GRUP98] Grupe, F. and Owrang, M., Database Mining Tools, *Data Management Handbook Supplement,* B. Thuraisingham, Ed., Auerbach Publications, NY, 1998.

[GUO] Guo, Y., Kensington Data Mining, http://ruby.doc.ic.ac.uk.

[GUPT02] Gupta, A. et al., Collaborative commerce and knowledge management, *Knowledge Management Journal,* January 2002.

[HAN98] Han, J., Data mining, keynote address, Second Pacific Asia Conference on Data Mining, Melbourne, Australia, April 1998.

[HAN01] Han, J. and Kamber, M., *Data Mining Concepts and Techniques,* Morgan Kaufmann, San Francisco, 2001.

[HARV96] Harvard Business School articles on knowledge management, Harvard University, 1996.

[HINK88] Hinke, T., Inference and aggregation detection in database management systems, Proceedings of the 1988 Conference on Security and Privacy, Oakland, CA, April 1988.

[HTML] http://www.cwru.edu.

[ICDE] IEEE International Conference on Data Engineering, 1998–2002.

APPENDIX D: REFERENCES

[ICDM] IEEE International Conference on Data Mining, 1999–2002.

[ICTA97] Panel on Web Mining, International Conference on Tools for Artificial Intelligence, Newport Beach, CA, November 1997.

[IEEE83] Special issue on computer security, *IEEE Computer,* 1983.

[IEEE89] IEEE Computer Society tutorial on parallel database systems, 1989.

[IEEE91] Special issue on heterogeneous database systems, *IEEE Computer,* 1991.

[IEEE95] IEEE Multimedia Database Systems Workshop, Blue Mountain Lake, NY, August 1995.

[IEEE98] IEEE Data Engineering Bulletin, March 1998.

[IEEE99] Special issue on collaborative computing, *IEEE Computer,* September 1999.

[IEEE00] Special issue on E-business, *IEEE Computer,* October 2000.

[IEEE02] Special issue on audio mining, *IEEE Computer,* October 2002.

[IFIP] Proceedings of the International Federation for Information Processing Conference Series in Database Security, North Holland.

[IFIP97] Proceedings of the International Federation for Information Processing 1997 Conference Series in Database Security, Panel on data warehousing and data mining security, North Holland.

[IFIP98] Proceedings of the International Federation for Information Processing 1998 Conference Series in Database Security, Panel on data mining and web security, North Holland.

[ILP97] Summer school on inductive logic programming, Prague, Czech Republic, September 1998.

[IMIE92] Imielinski, T. et al., Distributed databases for mobile computing, Proceedings of the Very Large Database Conference, Vancouver, British Columbia, August 1992.

[INFO1] *Information Week,* December 2001.

[INMO93] Inmon, W., Building the Data Warehouse, John Wiley & Sons, NY, 1993.

[INFO02] Semantic web, *Information Week,* October 2002.

[JAVA] Java programming language, http://www.javasoft.com.

[JDBC] Java database connectivity, http://java.sun.com.

[JONE99] Jones, S., Collaborative computing workspace, *Linux Journal,* 1999.

[JUNG98] Junglee Corporation, Virtual database technology, XML, and the Evolution of the Web, *IEEE Data Engineering Bulletin,* June 1998.

[KDD] Proceedings of the Knowledge Discovery in Databases Conference, 1998–2001.

[KDD95] Proceedings of the Knowledge Discovery in Databases Conference, Montreal, Canada, August 1995.

[KDD96] Proceedings of the Knowledge Discovery in Databases Conference, Portland, OR, August 1996.

[KDD97] Proceedings of the Knowledge Discovery in Databases Conference, Newport Beach, CA, August 1997.

[KDD98] Panel presentations, Knowledge Discovery in Database Conference, New York, 1998.

[KDD99] Tutorial presentation, Knowledge Discovery in Database Conference, San Diego, CA, 1999.

[KDDN] http://www.kdnuggets.com.

[KIM85] Kim, W. et al., *Query Processing in Database Systems,* Springer-Verlag, New York, 1985.

[KORT86] Korth, H. and Silberschatz, A., *Database System Concepts,* McGraw-Hill, New York, 1986.

[LEE99] Berners-Lee, T., Weaving the Web, HarperCollins, San Francisco, 1999.

[LEE01] Berners-Lee, T. et al., The semantic Web, *Scientific American,* May 2001.

[LIN97] Lin, T.Y., Ed., *Rough Sets and Data Mining,* Kluwer Publishers, Norwood, MA, 1997.

[LLOY87] Lloyd, J., *Logic Programming,* Springer-Verlag, Heidelberg, 1987.

[LOOM95] Loomis, M., *Object Databases,* Addison-Wesley, Reading, MA, 1995.

[MAIE83] Maier, D., *Theory of Relational Databases,* Computer Science Press, Rockville, MD, 1983.

[MDDS94] Proceedings of the Massive Digital Data Systems Initiative Workshop, CMS Report, 1994.

[MERL97] Merlino, A. et al., Broadcast news navigation using story segments, Proceedings of the 1997 ACM Multimedia Conference, Seattle, November 1998.

[META96] Proceedings of the 1st IEEE Metadata Conference, Silver Spring, MD, April 1996.

[MICR] http://www.microsoft.com.

[MIT] MIT technical reports on data quality.

[MITC97] Mitchell, T., *Machine Learning*, McGraw-Hill, New York, 1997.

[MORE98a] Morey, D., Web mining, private communication, Bedford, MA, June 1998.

[MORE98b] Morey, D., Knowledge management architecture, in *Handbook of Data Management*, Thuraisingham, B., Ed., Auerbach Publications, New York, 1998.

[MORE01] *Knowledge Management*, Morey, D., Maybury, M., and Thuraisingham, B., Eds., MIT Press, Cambridge, MA, 2001.

[MORG87] Morgenstern, M., Security and inference in multilevel database and knowledge base systems, Proceedings of the 1987 ACM SIGMOD Conference, San Francisco, June 1987.

[NETG] http://www.netgen.com.

[NG97] Ng, R., Image mining, private communication, Vancouver, British Columbia, 1997.

[NGDM02] NSF Next-Generation Data Mining Workshop, Baltimore, MD, November 2002.

[NSF90] Proceedings of the Database Systems Workshop, report published by the National Science Foundation, 1990.

[NSF95] Proceedings of the Database Systems Workshop, report published by the National Science Foundation, 1995.

[ODBC] Open database connectivity, http://www.microsoft.com.

[ODI] http://www.odi.com.

[ODMG93] Object Database Standard: ODMB 93, Object Database Management Group, Morgan Kaufmann, San Francisco, 1993.

[OLE] Object Linking and Embedding, www.roth.net/conference/perl/1999/ole.ppt.

[OMG] www.omg.org.

[OMG95] *Common Object Request Broker Architecture and Specification*, OMG Publications, John Wiley, New York, 1995.

[ONTO] http://www-db.stanford.edu.

[OOPS94] OOPSLA 94 Workshop on CORBA, Portland, OR, 1994.

[ORAC1] http://www.oracle.com.

[ORAC2] http://www.oracle.com.

[ORFA94] Orfali, R. et al., *The Essential Client/Server Survival Guide,* John Wiley, New York, 1994.

[ORFA96] Orfali, R. et al., *The Essential Distributed Objects Survival Guide,* John Wiley, New York, 1996.

[PAKD] Proceedings of the Knowledge Discovery in Databases Conference, 1997–2002.

[PAKD97] Proceedings of the Pacific Asia Data Mining Conference, Singapore, February 1997.

[PAKD98] Proceedings of the Pacific Asia Data Miming Conference, Melbourne, Australia, April 1998.

[PAKDD] Pacific Asia Data Mining Conference, 1997–2002.

[PMML] PMML 1.0 — Predictive Model Markup Language, Data Mining Group, http://www.dmg.org.

[PRAB97] Prabhakaran, B., *Multimedia Database Systems,* Kluwer Publications, Norwood, MA, 1997.

[QUIN93] Quinlan, R., *C4.5: Programs for Machine Learning,* Morgan Kaufmann, San Francisco, 1993.

[RDF] http://www.w3.org.

[ROSE99] Rosenthal, A., XML presentation, MITRE Corp., 1999.

[SGML] http://www.uic.edu.

[SHET90] Sheth, A. and Larson, J., Federated database systems, *ACM Computing Surveys,* September 1990.

[SHRI02] Shrivastava, J., Web mining, Proceedings of the Next-Generation Data Mining Workshop, Baltimore, November 2002.

APPENDIX D: REFERENCES

[SIGM] Proceedings of the ACM SIGMOD Conference, 1997–2001.

[SIGM90] Next-generation database systems, *ACM SIGMOD Record,* December 1990.

[SIGM96] Proceedings of the ACM SIGMOD Conference Workshop on Data Mining, 1996.

[SIGM98] Proceedings of the ACM SIGMOD Conference, Seattle, June 1998.

[SIGM01] Proceedings of the ACM SIGMOD Conference, Santa Barbara, CA, May 2001.

[SIMO95] Simoudis, E. et al., Recon Data Mining System, Technical Report, Lockheed Martin Corporation, 1995.

[SQL3] SQL3, American National Standards Institute, draft, 1992.

[THUR87] Thuraisingham, B., Multilevel security for relational database systems augmented by an inference engine, *Computers and Security,* Vol. 6, 1987.

[THUR89] Thuraisingham, B., Security for object-oriented database systems, Proceedings of the ACM OOPSLA Conference, 1989.

[THUR90a] Thuraisingham, B., Recursion theoretic properties of the inference problem, MITRE report, June 1990.

[THUR90b] Thuraisingham, B., Novel approaches to handle the inference problem, Proceedings of the 1990 RADC Workshop in Database Security, Castile, New York, June 1990.

[THUR91a] Thuraisingham, B., Security for distributed database systems, *Computers and Security,* 1994.

[THUR91b] Thuraisingham, B., On the use of conceptual structures to handle the inference problem, Proceedings of the 1991 IFIP Database Security Conference, Shepherdstown, WV, November 1991.

[THUR91c] Thuraisingham, B., Nonmonotonic types of multilevel logic for multilevel secure data and knowledge base management system, Proceedings of the IEEE Computer Security Foundations Workshop, Franconia, NH, June 1991.

[THUR93a] Thuraisingham, B. et al., Design and implementation of a database inference controller, *Data and Knowledge Engineering Journal,* North Holland, Vol. 8, December 1993.

[THUR93b] Thuraisingham, B., Object database management for PACS applications, *MITRE Information Systems Journal,* 1993.

[THUR94] Thuraisingham, B., Security for federated database systems, *Computers and Security,* Elsevier Science, Oxford, U.K., 1994.

[THUR95] Thuraisingham, B. and Ford, W., Security constraint processing in a distributed database management system, *IEEE Transactions on Knowledge and Data Engineering,* 1995.

[THUR96a] Thuraisingham, B., Data warehousing, data mining and security, keynote address, IFIP Database Security Conference, Como, Italy, July 1996.

[THUR96b] Thuraisingham, B., *Internet Database Management, Database Management,* Auerbach Publications, New York, 1996.

[THUR96c] Thuraisingham, B., Interactive data mining, Proceedings of Compugraphics Conference, Paris, France, December 1996.

[THUR97] Thuraisingham, B., *Data Management Systems Evolution and Interoperation,* CRC Press, Boca Raton, FL, 1997.

[THUR98] Thuraisingham, B., *Data Mining: Technologies, Techniques, Tools, and Trends,* CRC Press, Boca Raton, FL, 1998.

[THUR99] Thuraisingham, B. and Clifton, C., Managing and mining multimedia databases, keynote address, SAS Data Mining Conference, Cary, NC, September 1999.

[THUR00] Thuraisingham, B., *Web Data Management and Electronic Commerce,* CRC Press, Boca Raton, FL, 2000.

[THUR01] Thuraisingham, B., *Managing and Mining Multimedia Databases for the Electronic Enterprise,* CRC Press, Boca Raton, FL, 2001.

[THUR02] Thuraisingham, B., *XML, Databases, and the Semantic Web,* CRC Press, Boca Raton, FL, 2002.

[TKDE93] *IEEE Transactions on Knowledge and Data Engineering,* December 1993.

[TKDE96] *IEEE Transactions on Knowledge and Data Engineering,* December 1996.

[TSIC82] Tsichritzis, D. and Lochovsky, F., *Data Models,* Prentice-Hall, Englewood Cliffs, NJ, 1982.

[TSUR98] Tsur, D. et al., Queryflocks: A generalization of association rule mining, Proceedings of the 1998 ACM SIGMOD Conference, Seattle, WA, June 1998.

[TURB97] Turban, E. and Aronson, J., *Decision Support Systems and Intelligent Systems,* Prentice Hall, Englewood Cliffs, NJ, 1997.

[ULLM88] Ullman, J. D., *Principles of Database and Knowledge Base Management Systems,* Vols. I and II, Computer Science Press, Rockville, MD 1988.

[VIS97] Proceedings of the 1995 Workshop on Visualization and Databases, Grinstein, G., Ed., Phoenix, October 1997.

[VLDB] Proceedings of the Very Large Database Conference Series, 1998–2002.

[VLDB98] Proceedings of the Very Large Database Conference, New York, August 1998.

[W3C] http://www.w3c.org.

[WDM99] Workshop on Web Data Mining, San Diego, CA, August 1999.

[WIDO98] Widom, J., Lore DBMS, Stanford Database Workshop, Palo Alto, CA, 1998.

[WIED92] Wiederhold, G., Mediators in the architecture of future information systems, *IEEE Computer,* March 1992.

[WML] http://www.oasis-open.org.

[WOEL86] Woelk, D. et al., An object-oriented approach to multimedia databases, Proceedings of the ACM SIGMOD Conference, Washington, D.C., June 1986.

[WORK1] Semantic Web Workshop, Stanford University, Palo Alto, CA, July 2001.

[WORK2] NSG-EU Semantic Web Workshop, Sophia Antipolis, France, October 2001.

[WSDL] http://www.w3.org.

[WWW] Proceedings of the World Wide Web Conference Series, 1998–2002.

[XCC] http://www.itpapers.com.

[XKM] http://www.dmreview.com.

[XML1] http://www.W3C.org.

[XML2] http://www.xml.org.

[XMLQL] http://www.w3.org.

[XMLSQL] http://www.xml.com.

[YANG88] Yang, D. and Torey, T., A practical approach to transforming extended ER diagrams into the relational model, *Information Sciences Journal,* 1988.

About the Author

Bhavani Thuraisingham, Ph.D., recipient of IEEE Computer Society's prestigious 1997 Technical Achievement Award for "outstanding and innovative contributions to secure distributed data management," and the recipient of IEEE's 2003 Fellow Award for "pioneering research in secure systems including database systems, distributed systems, and the Web" is the director of the Data and Applications Security (DAS) program at the National Science Foundation (NSF). Previously, she was the director of the Information and Data Management (IDM) program at NSF. She is on IPA (Interagency Personnel Action) to NSF from the MITRE Corporation since October 2001. In this position, she is responsible for funding research in information and data management technologies as well as in data and applications security. She is also developing strategies for the advancement of these technologies in the United States, and collaborates with other major research funding organizations both in the United States and abroad to provide technical directions. Previously, she set directions in bioinformatics and geoinformatics as part of a team at NSF. She is currently part of a team at NSF setting directions for cyber-security. She is also the leader of the Information Management focus area for NSF's Information Technology Research Program. She is part of the NSF team involved with various unclassified interagency activities in data management and data mining and the application of these technologies to counter-terrorism.

Prior to her current position at NSF, she worked for the MITRE Corporation since January 1989. Between May 1999 and September 2001, she was a chief scientist in data management at the MITRE Corporation's Information Technology Directorate in Bedford, Massachusetts. In this position, she provided technology directions in data, information, and knowledge management for the Information Technology Directorate of MITRE's Air Force Center. In addition, she was also an expert consultant in computer software to MITRE's work for the Internal Revenue Service. In this position, she evaluated the commercial research conducted at various Fortune 500 corporations in information technology, including the financial, telecommunications, and data processing industries. Her recent research focused on data mining as it relates to multimedia databases and database security, distributed object management with emphasis on real-time data management, and Web data management applications in electronic commerce. She also served as adjunct professor of computer science at Boston University for two years and taught a course in advance data management and data mining. As part of her IPA agreement with NSF, she works one day a week at MITRE conducting research in secure data management.

Between June 1995 and May 1999, she was the department head in data and information management in MITRE's Information Technology Division in the Intelligence Center. In this position, she was responsible for the management of about 30 technical staff in four key areas: distributed databases, multimedia data management, data mining and knowledge management, and distributed objects and quality of service. Prior to that, she held various technical positions including lead, principal, and senior principal engineer, and was head of MITRE's research in Evolvable Interoperable Information Systems as well as Data Management, and co-director of MITRE's Database Specialty Group. Between 1993 and 1999, she managed 15 research projects under the Massive Digital Data Systems effort for the intelligence community, and was also a team member of the AWACS modernization research project for the Air Force. Before that, she led team efforts on the designs and prototypes of various secure database systems, including secure distributed database systems, secure object systems, and the inference problem for government sponsors, including the Air Force, Army, Navy, and the National Security Agency between 1989 and 1993.

Prior to joining MITRE in January 1989, Dr. Thuraisingham worked in the computer industry. She was first a Senior Programmer/Analyst with Control Data Corporation for over two years, working on the design and development of the CDCNET product. Later, she was a Principal Research Scientist with Honeywell for over three years conducting research, development, and technology transfer activities. She was also an adjunct professor of computer science and a member of the graduate faculty at the University of Minnesota between 1984 and 1988. Prior to starting her industrial experience and after completing her Ph.D., she was a visiting faculty member, first in the Department of Computer Science at the New Mexico Institute of Technology, and then at the Department of Mathematics at the University of Minnesota between 1980 and 1983. Dr. Thuraisingham received her Ph.D. degree in the United Kingdom at the age of 24. In addition to being an IEEE Fellow, she is a distinguished lecturer for IEEE, member of the ACM, the British Computer Society, and AFCEA. She has a certification in Java programming and has also completed a Management Development Program. She is the recipient of the 2001 National Woman of Color Technology Research Leadership Award and was named one of Silicon India's top seven technology innovators in the United States of South Asian origin in 2002.

Dr. Thuraisingham has published over 400 technical papers and reports, including over 50 journal articles, and is the inventor of three U.S. patents for MITRE on database inference control. She has also served on the editorial boards of various journals, including *IEEE Transactions on Knowledge and Data Engineering,* the *Journal of Computer Security,* and *Computer Standards and Interfaces Journal,* currently serves on the technical advisory board for IASTED, and has served on the conferences and tutorials board for IEEE. She gives tutorials in data management, data security, and data mining, and has taught courses at both the MITRE Institute and the AFCEA Educational Foundation for several years. She has chaired or co-chaired several conferences and workshops, including IFIP's 1992 Database Security Conference, ACM's 1993 Object Security Workshop, ACM's 1994 Objects in Healthcare Information Systems Workshop, IEEE's 1995 Multimedia Database Systems Workshop, IEEE's 1996 Metadata Conference, AFCEA's 1997 Federal Data Mining Symposium, IEEE's 1998 COMPSAC Conference, IEEE's 1999 WORDS Workshop, IFIP's 2000 Database Security Conference, IEEE's 2001 ISADS Conference, and IEEE's 2002 COMPSAC Web Security Workshop. She is a member of OMG's real-time special interest group, founded the C4I special interest group, has been a member of various industry and government standards groups, and has served on panels in data management, data mining, and security. She has edited several books as well as special journal issues and was the consulting editor of the *Data Management Handbook* series by CRC's Auerbach Publications for 1996 and 1997. She is the author of the books *Data Management Systems Evolution and Interoperation; Data Mining: Technologies, Techniques, Tools, and Trends; Web Data Management and Electronic Commerce; Managing and Mining Multimedia Databases;* and *XML, Databases and the Semantic Web* for CRC Press.

Dr. Thuraisingham has given invited presentations at conferences, including keynote addresses at the IFIP Database Security Conference (1996), the ACM Symposium on Applied Computing (1997), the Second Pacific Asia Data Mining Conference (1998), SAS Institute's Data Mining Technology Conference (1999), the IEEE Artificial Neural Networks Conference '99, the IEEE ICTAI Conference '99, the IFIP Integrity and Control Conference '01, the IEEE WORDS Workshop '02, the IASTED Applied Informatics '02, the IEEE ICTAI Conference '02, the IEEE Multimedia Software Engineering '02, and the IASTED Applied Informatics Conference '03. She has also delivered the featured addresses at AFCEA's Federal Database Colloquium from 1994 through 2001. She has been a featured speaker at several object world conferences by Software Comdex as well as the client/server world and data warehousing conferences by DCI, and also recently gave a featured talk on Federated Databases for Bioinformatics at the 4th Annual Bioinformatics Conference in Boston. Her presentations are worldwide and she also gives seminars and lectures at various universities around the world, including the Universities of Oxford and Cambridge in England, as well as at Stanford University and the Massachusetts Institute of Technol-

ABOUT THE AUTHOR

ogy, and participates in panels at the National Academy of Sciences and the Air Force Scientific Advisory Board. She is an expert Information Technology consultant to the Department of Health and Human Services States bio-terrorism efforts, and gives several presentations on data mining for counter-terrorism, including recent keynote addresses at the White House in Washington, D.C., and at the United Nations in New York.

Index

Internet
   databases, 436
   developments around, 17
   material inappropriate for children
     found on, 346
Intranets
   data on private, 314, 327
   mining of information on corporate, 280
Intrusion detection, 48, 172, 283, 481
Intrusions, malicious, 298
Investigation agency, 151
IRDS, *see* Information Resource Dictionary
   System
ISO, *see* International Standards
   Organization
ITtoolbox, 248

J

Java
   applets, 18, 109, 111, 307
   database connectivity (JDBC), 270
   programming
     environment, 68
     language, 18
   programs, embedding of SQL calls into,
     72
   Virtual Machine, 264, 307
JDBC, *see* Java database connectivity
JD Edwards, 280
Jet Propulsion Laboratory (JPL), 257, 258
JPL, *see* Jet Propulsion Laboratory

K

Kana Communications, 248
kdnuggets Web site, 279, 280
Killer application, Web, 18, 21, 132, 240
Knowledge
   discovery process, 269
   learning from prior, 54
   management, 5, 31, 33, 57, 103, 360
     agents for, 236
     collaborative, 109
     components, 107
     cycle, 108
     definition of, 106
     important aspects of, 107
     team spirit and, 107
     technologies, 108
     tools, 265
     Web data mining and, 221, 222
   real-world, 156
   repositories, mining of, 222

Knowledge/data/information/pattern
   discovery, 35
   extraction, 35
KnowledgeSync 2000, 248

L

Law enforcement, 316, 373
Legacy databases, 40, 60, 78, 81, 129, 338
   extract schemas from, 190
   migrating, 465, 466
   mining of, 189
Linear discriminate analysis techniques, 52
Linear regression techniques, 52
Link analysis, 322
Locator agents, 235, 236
Lockheed Martin, 36
LogMetrix, 248
Lumio ReCognition, 262
Lycos, 195

M

Machine
   learning, 43, 53, 57, 65, 87, 163
     data mining and, 54
     technique, 164
   translation, 119
Malicious attacks, threats due to, 395
Malicious intrusions, 298
Market basket analysis, 279
Marketing organization, 152
MarketMiner, 248
MarketSwitch, 249
Markup languages, 89, 99, 217
Massive Digital Data Systems Project, 258
Mass storage technology, 71
MDP, *see* Multimedia distributed processor
Medical applications, danger of false
     positives and negatives for, 327
Medicine, data mining in, 285
Megaputer WebAnalyst, 262
Message-oriented middleware (MOM), 84
Metadata
   extraction, 86, 204
   foundation for processing, 124
   global, 459
   management, 4, 44, 60, 95, 169, 455
   mining, 47, 179, 333, 335
   repositories, 75
   role of in mining, 180
Microsoft
   ActiveX, 308
   Distributed OLE/COM, 80